The Self-Reflexive Art of Don DeLillo

The Self-Reflexive Art of Don DeLillo

Graley Herren

BLOOMSBURY ACADEMIC
NEW YORK · LONDON · OXFORD · NEW DELHI · SYDNEY

BLOOMSBURY ACADEMIC
Bloomsbury Publishing Inc
1385 Broadway, New York, NY 10018, USA
50 Bedford Square, London, WC1B 3DP, UK

BLOOMSBURY, BLOOMSBURY ACADEMIC and the Diana logo are trademarks of
Bloomsbury Publishing Plc

First published in the United States of America 2019

Cover design by Eleanor Rose
Cover image: Rene Magritte, (1898–1967); *La reproduction interdite*, 1937.
Rotterdam, Museum Boijmans van Beuningen © 2018. Photothèque R. Magritte /
Adagp Iamges, Paris / SCALA, Florence.

Library of Congress Cataloging-in-Publication Data
Names: Herren, Graley, author.
Title: The self-reflexive art of Don DeLillo / Graley Herren.
Description: New York, NY: Bloomsbury Academic, 2019. |
Includes bibliographical references and index.
Identifiers: LCCN 2019007930 (print) | LCCN 2019012376 (ebook) | ISBN 9781501345067
(ePub) | ISBN 9781501345074 (ePDF) | ISBN 9781501345050(hardback :alk. paper) |
Subjects: LCSH: DeLillo, Don–Criticism and interpretation. |
Self-consciousness (Awareness) in literature.
Classification: LCC PS3554.E4425 (ebook) | LCC PS3554.E4425 Z68 2019
(print) | DDC 813/.54–dc23 LC record available at
https://lccn.loc.gov/2019007930

ISBN: HB: 978-1-5013-4505-0
ePDF: 978-1-5013-4507-4
eBook: 978-1-5013-4506-7

Typeset by Deanta Global Publishing Services, Chennai, India
Printed and bound in the United States of America

To find out more about our authors and books visit www.bloomsbury.com
and sign up for our newsletters.

In memory of my father
Charles Herren
(1940–2017)

CONTENTS

Preface viii
Acknowledgments xiv
List of Abbreviations xvii

1　How to make metafiction: A genealogy for
　 Don DeLillo's self-reflexive art 1

2　American Narcissus: Lacanian reflections
　 in *Americana* 21

3　*Libranth*: Nicholas Branch's Joycean labyrinth 41

4　"The Martiniad": Nick Shay as embedded author
　 in *Underworld* 59

5　The artistic gestation of Klara Sax 81

6　Performing self-dialogue in "The DeLillo variations" 113

7　Art stalkers 139

8　Literary triangulation: DeLillo-O'Hara-Oates 165

9　A miniature star: Remains and returns in the
　 metafiction of *Zero K* 189

10　A portrait of the ARTIS: Jeff Lockhart as embedded
　　 author in *Zero K* 211

Coda 233

Notes 237
Bibliography 248
Index 259

PREFACE

The Self-Reflexive Art of Don DeLillo examines the writer's career-long meditation on the creation and reception of art. For half a century DeLillo has been writing about artists who create mirror realities through their art, and more recently he has turned his attention to spectators who use art as projection screens for their personal obsessions. He frequently draws self-reflexive attention to the creative process by embedding an artist-figure within his own work: a character subtly implicated as the creator of the very narrative we are reading or watching. The present study is the first to identify and systematically analyze this signature metafictional motif.

My book grows out of and extends the significant body of scholarship devoted to DeLillo's work. Any examination of DeLillo owes a huge debt to Tom LeClair. His first interview with the author is a treasure trove of revelations, and it remains to this day the best DeLillo interview ever done. LeClair's critical monograph *In the Loop: Don DeLillo and the Systems Novel* (University of Illinois Press, 1987) pointed the way through the intricate looping systems which characterize so many of DeLillo's early works. However, my study focuses chiefly on works published after LeClair's groundbreaking book. My understanding and appreciation of middle and late DeLillo has been immeasurably enriched by numerous critics; some who deserve special mention are John Duvall, Tim Engles, Linda Kauffman, Jesse Kavadlo, Randy Laist, and John McClure.

Three books stand above all the others as shaping influences on *The Self-Reflexive Art of Don DeLillo*: Mark Osteen's *American Magic and Dread: Don DeLillo's Dialogue with Culture* (University of Pennsylvania Press, 2000), David Cowart's *Don DeLillo: The Physics of Language* (University of Georgia Press, 2002), and Peter Boxall's *Don DeLillo: The Possibility of Fiction* (Routledge, 2006). Each of these books has something different to recommend it. Osteen exceeded by leaps and bounds all the previous scholarship on DeLillo. His brilliant readings of individual novels through 2000 hold up as well today as when they were first published. Osteen remains one of the great trailblazers of DeLillo studies. Cowart's book is theoretically astute while still remaining highly readable and lucid. His 2002 book locates DeLillo firmly within the contexts of postmodern literature and poststructuralist thought. Cowart is a master prose stylist who avoids the impenetrable jargon and resists the ideological pieties which too often bog down lesser critics of DeLillo. Boxall is the critic with whom I feel the greatest affinity. His 2006 book joins those of Osteen and Cowart on the top rung of DeLillo studies to date. He and I both come to DeLillo from a background in Samuel Beckett, and this deeply informs our shared perspectives. Boxall's utterly compelling reading of *Ratner's Star* as a dream inside a dream (inside another dream) is one of the early inspirations behind my argument about the embedded authors and narratives inside so many DeLillo works. My book builds upon the instructive examples of Osteen, Cowart, and Boxall, extending their surveys to include several DeLillo works published in the years since their monographs appeared.

For all my critical debts, *The Self-Reflexive Art of Don DeLillo* is quite distinct from previous scholarship. Osteen, Cowart, and Boxall cover DeLillo's entire canon up to the point of their respective publications. A book's thesis must necessarily be quite broad in order to account for all of DeLillo's diverse works. I have chosen instead to focus my study much more tightly, tracing a series of related themes on artistic creators and spectators and the self-reflexive nets enmeshing them. These themes are already prominent in DeLillo's first novel *Americana*, but they emerge as absolutely central in his middle and late work. Because my book does not aim to be exhaustive, I can be more selective in my primary sources, following DeLillo's self-reflexivity where it leads and bypassing texts less relevant to my thesis. The reader will notice, for instance, that one of DeLillo's most famous novels, *White Noise*, attracts very little attention in my study. On the other hand, *Underworld* and *Zero K* are so rich and diverse in their self-reflexivity, and so fundamental to my arguments, that they deserve two chapters apiece.

Even with an emphasis upon art, the present study does not provide an all-encompassing catalogue of every artist featured in DeLillo's work. His self-reflexive meditations are most provocative when he contemplates artists in media other than his own. He confided to LeClair,

> I try to examine psychological states by looking at people in rooms, objects in rooms. It's a way of saying we can know something important about a character by the way he sees himself in relation to objects. People in rooms have always seemed important to me. I don't know why or ask myself why, but sometimes I feel I'm *painting* a character in a room, and the most important thing I can do is set him up in relation to objects, shadows, angles. (14, emphasis in original)

This painterly approach is borne out time and again in his work, and it guides my decision to emphasize visual artists in *The Self-Reflexive Art of Don DeLillo*. DeLillo sees most clearly in the mirror of art when his glimpses are discreet and indirect. His portraits of artists in media other than writing benefit from his sophisticated self-reflexive strategies of misprision, occlusion, deflection, projection, and triangulation.

My criteria for selection deserves a few more words since it results in what might seem some odd omissions. For instance, readers might be surprised to discover that a character like Bill Gray, the fictional novelist from *Mao II*, is of only limited interest in my book. Gray is a reclusive writer in the mold of J. D. Salinger, and he makes some profound observations about the hidden nature of his craft. For instance, he asserts, "When a writer doesn't show his face, he becomes a local symptom of God's famous reluctance to appear" (*M* 36). Later he adds, "The writer who won't show his face is encroaching on holy turf. He's playing God's own trick" (*M* 37). These are worthwhile observations with respect to my central arguments. Bill Gray might even gesture in the direction of my "embedded author" theme; it is possible, for instance, to interpret Gray as the narrative agency behind the prison scenes involving Jean-Claude Julien, the poet being held hostage. Then again, who could be surprised by a novelist inventing a fictional scene in which he vicariously imagines his way into someone else's experience and perspective? That's what authors do, obviously. And there's the rub: Gray as Creator is too obvious. The reclusive writer may hide from the *world*, but I am far more interested in those author-figures who hide from the *reader*. My emphasis in *The Self-Reflexive Art of Don DeLillo* is on his secret artists, those who do not announce their authorial status but instead observe the standard of stealth articulated by Stephen Dedalus in James Joyce's *A Portrait of the Artist as a Young Man*: "The artist, like the God of the creation, remains within or behind or beyond or above his handiwork, invisible, refined out of existence, indifferent, paring his fingernails" (189). I focus on hidden creators residing "within or behind or beyond or above" their creations. By the light of day they may work as historians, waste management executives, sculptors, or compliance and ethics officer, but behind the scenes they operate as covert double agents composing parts of the very narratives that we read.

* * *

The Self-Reflexive Art of Don DeLillo consists of ten chapters. Chapter 1 introduces the foundational principles of DeLillo's self-reflexive art and places his work within the broader context of metafiction, or more specifically historiographic metafiction. I outline the importance of mirrors, labyrinths, and games as manifestations of DeLillo's self-reflexive impulse, and I trace his descent in a metafictional genealogy including James Joyce, William Gaddis, Jorge Luis Borges, and Vladimir Nabokov. Chapter 2, "American Narcissus: Lacanian Reflections on *Americana*," expands upon DeLillo's crucial self-reflexive trope of the mirror. I apply key concepts from the theories of Jacques Lacan—particularly his mirror stage of ego development, his revisions to the Freudian Oedipus Complex, his location of lack and absence as the engine of desire, and his notions of the gaze seminal to psychoanalytic film theory—to illuminate the narcissistic art of David Bell, the protagonist and narrator of *Americana* (1971). David returns compulsively to various reenactments of a primal erotic confrontation with his mother. But DeLillo's treatment of the incest taboo owes less to Freud's Oedipus than Lacan's Narcissus, as David Bell remains fixated on fantasies, dreams, and misrecognized reflections of self.

Having established a self-reflexive framework in *Americana*, Chapter 3 leaps forward into a major novel from DeLillo's middle period. "*Libranth*: Nicholas Branch's Joycean Labyrinth" examines *Libra* (1988) as a metafictional labyrinth. I argue that CIA historian Nicholas Branch not only is a character in the novel but also functions as the embedded author of the narrative. James Joyce used this autological approach in *A Portrait of the Artist as a Young Man*, and *Libra* replicates this metafictional structure, borrowing a number of themes and motifs from Stephen Dedalus and the mythical artificer Daedalus along the way. Although Dedalus succeeds in using his winged art to escape his imprisonment, Branch ultimately fails. The artifice he creates becomes his metafictional prison.

Chapters 4 and 5 take parallax views of DeLillo's masterpiece *Underworld* (1997). In "'The Martiniad': Nick Shay as Embedded Author in *Underworld*," I examine a special sequence of chapters focusing on Cotter Martin and his father Manx. I argue that protagonist Nick Shay is actually the creator of those chapters about the Martins. *Underworld* offers the most brilliant example of DeLillo's signature motif of the embedded author. Nick ostensibly creates "The Martiniad" to provide the missing link in the provenance of his prized Bobby Thomson homerun ball. But he also uses the father-son relationship of the Martins to work through his unresolved issues of abandonment and loss with his own father. In the next chapter, "The Artistic Gestation of Klara Sax," I shift attention to DeLillo's most fully realized portrait of an artist. DeLillo depicts the evolving work of Klara Sax in terms of the gestational process of childbirth. Emphasizing the themes of conception, gestation, delivery, metamorphosis, death, and rebirth, Chapter 5 charts the sexual liberation and artistic transformation of Klara from a timid Bronx housewife and amateur painter to the boldly audacious creator of *Long Tall Sally*, a massive assemblage of brightly painted decommissioned B-52 bombers in the Arizona desert. In a novel often dominated by subterranean forces aligned with dissolution and death, Klara Sax emerges as the triumphant representative of life and art in *Underworld*.

One of the distinguishing features of *The Self-Reflexive Art of Don DeLillo* is my emphasis upon late DeLillo, that is, on his work published after the epic *Underworld*. The second half of my book is devoted entirely to this period of his career. Chapter 6, "Performing Self-Dialogue in 'The DeLillo Variations,'" offers the first critical study of DeLillo's creative non-fiction piece "Counterpoint: Three Films, a Book, and an Old Photograph" (2004), where he identifies surprising affinities between composer Glenn Gould, novelist Thomas Bernhard, and jazz innovator Thelonious Monk. This chapter also examines DeLillo's treatments of time, mortality, and memory in the work of performance artist Lauren Hartke in *The Body Artist* (2001). Finally, Chapter 6 highlights DeLillo's self-reflexive exploration of another medium in the play *Love-Lies-Bleeding* (2005), where I argue that the entire action is imagined by artist Alex Macklin *in extremis*. Performance becomes an increasingly important dimension in late DeLillo, and these three pieces enact distinct self-dialogues in three different genres. Chapter 7 is simply titled "Art Stalkers." This chapter focuses on DeLillo's most compulsive spectators who appropriate certain artworks to fuel their pathologies. He offers harrowing variations on the theme of "art stalkers"—men who become obsessed with and begin pursuit of women they meet at museums, galleries, or theaters. Such characters are featured in several late works, including the novels *Falling Man* (2007) and *Point Omega* (2010) and the short stories "Baader-Meinhof" (2002) and "The Starveling" (2011). DeLillo blurs the borders between art and reality to terrifying effect, depicting spectators who merge so completely with fetishized artworks that they attempt to extend these works violently into the world. In Chapter 8, "Literary Triangulation: DeLillo-O'Hara-Oates," I consider DeLillo's innovative variation on his "art stalker" theme in the short story "Midnight in Dostoevsky" (2009). The narrator Robby and his college friend Todd are developing artists who follow an old man around town and invent the details of his life. The story is animated by deeply repressed sexual tension which DeLillo reveals indirectly through literary triangulation: a form of deflection and sublimation where one character works through his feelings toward another by redirecting them through a third figure. DeLillo reiterates this process intertextually through an extended series of references to Frank O'Hara's poetry and Francisco de Zurbarán's paintings. Chapter 8 also posits a critical triangulation with Joyce Carol Oates's story "Three Girls," using her overt treatment of homoerotic desire to shed light into the darkened corners of "Midnight in Dostoevsky."

The final two chapters both focus on DeLillo's remarkable novel *Zero K* (2016). Chapter 9, "A Miniature Star: Remains and Returns in the Metafiction of *Zero K*," frames *Zero K* as an exercise in literary cryonics, metempsychosis, and anagram. The novel focuses remorselessly on death, both individual and planetary, yet it does so by reanimating several characters, tropes, and themes from previous DeLillo works, particularly *Ratner's Star*. As I argue in the final chapter, "A Portrait of the ARTIS: Jeff Lockhart as Embedded Author in *Zero K*," the novel also represents the apotheosis of DeLillo's signature metafictional strategy of the embedded author. At the heart of *Zero K* lies a Beckettian internal monologue from the perspective of the frozen character Artis Martineau. Evidence points to this solipsistic text as actually authored by protagonist and narrator Jeff Lockhart. DeLillo ultimately indulges Jeff's solipsism only to counter it with fiction that affirms the numinous mysteries of life and death. When working on an active living author, one never knows what directions the subject's future writing might take. But even if DeLillo were never to publish another book, story, or play, *Zero K* would serve admirably as a fitting culmination of his self-reflexive art.

I close with a brief self-reflexive exercise of my own, a transcription of a curious dream. As I read back over that Coda, the effect is largely comic: my absurd Irish ramble with Don DeLillo. The dream's lingering effect for me is more mysterious, however, and dappled with reflected light from the works I've been studying for years. Perhaps déjà vu is a symptom of overexposure to DeLillo. Or maybe like Nicholas Branch in *Libra* I have immersed myself so completely in the fantasies of "men in small rooms" that I have become one of them. It is difficult to gaze deeply into DeLillo's metafictional mirrors without eventually seeing one's own reflection.

ACKNOWLEDGMENTS

This book would not have been possible without the timely help of many people. Xavier University has been my academic home for over twenty years, and I have always received generous support from students, colleagues, and administrators for my teaching and research. I have taught DeLillo works in multiple courses, but I was particularly privileged in spring 2017 to teach an honors section of Literature and the Moral Imagination devoted entirely to Don DeLillo's fiction. Thanks to those students for their fresh insights at just the right moment in the life of this book. I also discussed portions of my work with Xavier colleagues and thank Norman Finkelstein, Tyrone Williams, Tim White, and Niamh O'Leary for their feedback. I am indebted to my previous department chair Alison Russell and my college deans Janice Walker and David Mengel for their support, both in terms of conference travel and a crucial research sabbatical.

Those conferences gave me the opportunity to meet various DeLillo scholars, and I am particularly indebted to Mark Osteen and Jackie Zubeck for their wisdom, collegiality, and encouragement in the early stages of this project. I also benefited enormously from the help of John Duvall. When he accepted my article on "Art Stalkers" for *Modern Fiction Studies*, it felt like my admission ticket into DeLillo studies had been stamped, and it inspired me to keep pursuing the ideas which eventually resulted in this book. Since then I have been extremely lucky to work with several editors who enriched my understanding of DeLillo and sharpened the focus of my arguments and prose. In addition to Jackie Zubeck and John Duvall, my special thanks to Crystal Alberts, Daniel Jernigan, Katie Da Cunha Lewin, Kris Miller, and Kiron Ward.

Portions of this book first appeared as articles or chapters in the following journals and books, and I appreciate permission to reproduce that (heavily revised) work in *The Self-Reflexive Art of Don DeLillo*:

"American Narcissus: Lacanian Reflections on DeLillo's *Americana*." *Orbit: Writing Around Pynchon* 4.2 (2016). Web. http://dx.doi.org/10.16995/orbit.87

"Cosmological Metafictions: Gnosticism in Don DeLillo's *Libra*." *Religion & Literature* 47.2 (2016): 87–116.

"'The Martiniad': Nick Shay as Embedded Author within Don DeLillo's *Underworld*." *Critique: Studies in Contemporary Fiction* 56.4 (2015): 449–65.

"Don DeLillo's Art Stalkers." *Modern Fiction Studies* 61.1 (2015): 138–67.

"DeLillo Variations: A Contrapuntal Reading of 'Counterpoint,' *The Body Artist*, and *Love-Lies-Bleeding*." *Review of Contemporary Fiction* 34.1 (2014): 13–34.

"*Libranth*: Nicholas Branch's Joycean Labyrinth in Don DeLillo's *Libra*." *Don DeLillo: Contemporary Critical Perspectives*. Eds. Katherine Da Cunha Lewin and Kiron Ward. London: Bloomsbury, 2018. 49–63.

"*Love-Lies-Bleeding*: Self-Portrait of the Artist as a Dying Man." *DeLillo after the Millennium*. Ed. Jacqueline A. Zubeck. Lanham, MD: Lexington Books, 2017. 137–55.

Given my emphasis upon art in this book, it was important to include numerous images relevant to an intertextual, multidisciplinary appreciation of DeLillo's work. As anyone who has attempted it knows, the process of acquiring the necessary permissions can be long, winding, frustrating, and expensive. Fortunately, I encountered a number of very helpful people along the way who made inclusion of this material possible. Some who deserve special mention are: Meghan Brown, Megan Cohen, Bryan Costales, Konstanze Ell, Jo Farb Hernandez, Cathy Koutsavlis, Todd Leibowitz, Frances Mulraney, Keelan Pacot, Michelle Press, Piper Severance, Jeremy Winchester, and Nicole Zizzi. My extensive discussion of Frank O'Hara's poem "Meditations in an Emergency" in Chapter 8 comes by permission of Grove/Atlantic, and they wanted me to add that any third-party use of this material, outside of this publication, is prohibited. I would not have been able to afford all of these permissions on my own. Therefore, I am deeply grateful to Associate Dean Rachel Chrastil for securing funds from the college and provost offices. I also appreciate all the helpful assistance from Caitlin Staley in processing the many individual transactions.

You would not be reading *The Self-Reflexive Art of Don DeLillo* were it not for Bloomsbury. My warmest gratitude goes out to Haaris Naqvi for encouraging me to submit my manuscript and for advocating on my behalf with the Bloomsbury editorial board. I am also tremendously thankful to the three anonymous readers who reviewed my manuscript and offered many perceptive suggestions which helped guide my revisions for the final draft. While completing the book I have also benefited from the pleasant and efficient aid of Amy Martin, my excellent editorial assistant at Bloomsbury and a credit to her alma mater Xavier University.

Finally, my deepest debts are closest to home. Nothing would be possible without the foundation of love and support provided by my parents, Charles and Bonnie Herren. My father died during my work on this project, and the book is dedicated to him. It is equally true that none of my work would be possible without the love and support of my wife Cathy and our son Dylan. At one point or another every book by and about Don DeLillo has spent time stacked around me on our kitchen-table-turned-office. Cathy and Dylan patiently indulge my flights of fancy and always give me a safe place to land, for which I'm extremely lucky and forever grateful.

LIST OF ABBREVIATIONS

Primary sources by Don DeLillo

A	*Americana*
AB	"American Blood"
BM	"Baader-Meinhof"
BA	*The Body Artist*
C	*Cosmopolis*
CP	"Counterpoint"
DR	*The Day Room*
EZ	*End Zone*
FM	*Falling Man*
GJS	*Great Jones Street*
IRF	"In the Ruins of the Future"
L	*Libra*
LLB	*Love-Lies-Bleeding*
M	*Mao II*
MD	"Midnight in Dostoevsky"
N	*The Names*
NTD	"Notes Toward a Definitive Meditation"
PWH	"Pafko at the Wall" [Harper's]
PWS	*Pafko at the Wall* [Scribner]
P	*Players*
PO	*Point Omega*

PH   "The Power of History"

RS   *Ratner's Star*

RD   *Running Dog*

S   "The Starveling"

U   *Underworld*

V   *Valparaiso*

WN   *White Noise*

ZK   *Zero K*

1

How to make metafiction

A genealogy for Don DeLillo's self-reflexive art

In his essay on "How to Make a Universe" (1960), John Barth proclaims, "The storytellers' trade is the manufacture of universes" (17). His manifesto seeks to counter prevailing views of the author's relationship with external reality: "You hear it said that the novelist offers you an attitude toward life and the world. Not so, except incidentally or by inference. What he offers you is not a *Weltanschauung* but a *Welt*; not a view of the cosmos, but a cosmos itself" (17). Barth's fabulist faith in the artist's world-making powers is a foundational principle of metafiction. Despite the seeming omnipotence of this claim, Barth also understood that the self-contained cosmos of art could end up functioning as a self-reflexive prison for creator, character, and reader alike. He devised the perfect emblem for this metafictional dilemma in his story "Lost in the Funhouse" (1967). Ambrose is a would-be writer who can never simply experience his life without relentlessly reflecting upon everything in terms of narrative construction. His story about going on family vacation, visiting an amusement park, taking a girl he likes into the Hall of Mirrors, and getting hopelessly lost becomes an allegory of the metafictional project. The character is situated as a mirror between author and reader, and all are ensnared in a maze of reflections. Ambrose explicitly declares his metafictional vocation in the final paragraph: "He wishes he had never entered the funhouse. But he has. Then he wishes he were dead. But he's not. Therefore he will construct funhouses for others and be their secret operator—though he would rather be among the lovers for whom funhouses are designed" (97).

Around the same time Ambrose was getting lost in the funhouse, Don DeLillo was beginning work on what would become his first novel *Americana*. DeLillo is a direct descendent in the metafictional lineage, although his debts to this tradition have been underappreciated. Barth's description above depicts metafiction as a retreat from the real world into an alternate universe of the author's own design. This may not, at first, sound compatible with DeLillo, a conscientious citizen of the real world with deep commitments to interrogating the history, culture, politics, and ideology of the late twentieth and early twenty-first centuries. However, from the start DeLillo's engagement with his times has involved confronting and reflecting back the epidemic spread of unreality, a haunted funhouse where images have become detached and indistinguishable from their real-world referents. Hamlet famously defined the function of art as holding a mirror up to nature.[1] But what are the implications for art when nature itself has become a mirror, when simulacra have proliferated to the point where they displace the real? Art becomes a reflection of a reflection, a mise en abyme of infinite regression, a Hall of Mirrors with no exit. Metafiction identifies and critiques this predicament from the inside by replicating the mirror-maze. Enter the self-reflexive art of Don DeLillo.

* * *

Many critics have commented upon isolated references to mirrors in DeLillo's work, but his devotion is more ardent and persistent than that. Mirrors are as ubiquitous to DeLillo as "men in small rooms" and just as fundamental. Consider the following lists (by no means exhaustive) of instances where DeLillo characters confront their images in mirrors. Here are some examples from early DeLillo:

- *Americana* (1971): "I had almost the same kind of relationship with my mirror that many of my contemporaries had with their analysts. When I began to wonder who I was, I took the simple step of lathering my face and shaving. It all became so clear, so wonderful. I was blue-eyed David Bell" (*A* 11).
- *Great Jones Street* (1973): "Hanes looked weak and sick, a reproduction of my image in the mirror when I first arrived at Great Jones and cut myself shaving" (*GJS* 210).
- *Ratner's Star* (1976): "Finally he stepped in, . . . bolting himself in the stainless steel apartment and noting in the mirror how unlike himself he looked" (*RS* 7).
- *Players* (1977): "He could see himself across the room, angling in and out of view, in the mirror over the dresser. . . . Interesting, his formal apartness. The distance he'd perfected" (*P* 196).

Then in middle DeLillo we find these variations:

- *White Noise* (1985): "In the motel mirror was my full-length wife, white-bodied, full-bosomed, pink-kneed, stub-toed, wearing only peppermint legwarmers, like a sophomore leading cheers at an orgy" (*WN* 256).
- *Libra* (1988): "He winced all the time in front of mirrors when he pasted on his homemade eyebrows and mohair toupee. . . . Moments after he put down the phone, Ferrie was in a small room behind Guy Banister's office, making faces in the mirror as he adjusted the semicircular eyebrows" (*L* 29).
- *Mao II* (1992): "She said, 'In some places where you eat standing up you are forced to look directly into a mirror. This is total control of the person's responses, like a consumer prison. And the mirror is literally inches away so you can hardly put the food in your mouth without hitting into it'" (*M* 88–89).
- *Mao II* (1992): "He looked in the mirror and saw he hadn't shaved in some days. The scrape on his face was no better and no worse. Better if anything and certainly not worse" (*M* 200).
- *Underworld* (1997): "She smoked her last cigarette of the day in the spare room, looking at the wall. She put out the cigarette by grinding it into the bathroom mirror and then she flushed it down the toilet and went to bed" (*U* 714).

The rate of multiplication increases in late DeLillo:

- *Valparaiso* (1999): "*Delfina*: What do you see when you look in the mirror? *Michael*: Somebody somewhere else" (*V* 92).
- *The Body Artist* (2001): "She looked at her face in the bathroom mirror and tried to understand why it looked different from the same face downstairs, in the full-length mirror in the front hall, although it shouldn't be hard to understand at all, she thought, because faces look different all the time and everywhere, based on a hundred daily variables, but then again, she thought, why do I look different?" (*BA* 65).
- *Cosmopolis* (2003): "His bathroom mirror had a readout telling him his temperature and blood pressure at that moment, his height, weight, heart rate, pulse pending medication, whole health history from looking at his face, and I was his human sensor, reading his thoughts, knowing the man in his mind" (*C* 153).
- "The Starveling" (2011): "There was his face in the mirror, gradually becoming asymmetrical, features no longer on the same axis, brows unaligned, jaw crooked, his mouth slightly aslant. / When did this begin to happen? What happens next?" (*S* 190).

- *Zero K* (2016): "When he looks in the mirror he sees a simulated man" (*ZK* 82).
- *Zero K* (2016): "Yesterday after I washed my face I looked in the mirror, seriously and deliberately looked. And I found myself becoming disoriented," he said, "because in a mirror left is right and right is left. But this wasn't the case. What was supposed to be my false right ear was my true right ear." / "That's how it seemed." / "That's how it was" (*ZK* 184).
- *Zero K* (2016): "I watch Emma stand before the full-length mirror. . . . On an impulse I walk into the image and stand next to her. We look for a number of seconds, the pair of us, without comment or self-consciousness or any sign of amusement, and I understand that this is a telling moment. . . . Here we are, all this and more, things that normally escape the inquiring eye, a single searching look, so much to see, each of us looking at both of us, and then we shake it all off and walk down four flights into the pitch of street noise that tells us we're back among others, in unsparing space" (*ZK* 207–08).
- *Zero K* (2016): "Then I looked at my face in the bathroom mirror, double-checking the effectiveness of the close shave I'd given myself twenty minutes earlier. I recalled something Ross had said about his right ear in the mirror being his real right ear instead of the mirror-image left ear. I had to concentrate hard to convince myself that this was not the case" (*ZK* 209).

What is going on here? A couple of characters are egomaniacs in love with their reflections; a few are losers who despise what they see; most are disoriented and unsettled by their images. Some characters stare into the mirror to reassure themselves of their stable, coherent identities; others turn toward the mirror to tighten their loosening grips on reality. Some gaze in the mirror only to find a stranger looking back at them; others seem vaguely to intuit themselves as objects of the reader's gaze on the other side of the looking glass, or as suspects in the author's interrogation room. They all, individually and collectively, draw self-reflexive attention to the mirroring processes at work within their fictional worlds. In her reunion scene with former lover Nick Shay, Klara Sax muses, "Sometimes I think everything I've done since those years, everything around me in fact, I don't know if you feel this way but everything is vaguely—*what*—fictitious" (*U* 73, emphasis in original). Indeed everything she has done and will do and everything around her *is fictitious*, not only because contemporary America has become increasingly unreal, but also because she is an invented character in the fictional cosmos of *Underworld*, an image reflected in DeLillo's Hall of Mirrors.

Linda Hutcheon characterizes all metafiction as essentially narcissistic in her book *Narcissistic Narrative: The Metafictional Paradox*. However, as she is careful to stress, "'Narcissistic'—the figurative adjective chosen here to designate this textual self-awareness—is not intended as derogatory but rather as descriptive and suggestive" (1). She adds, "Nor are the inevitable psychoanalytic connotations to be taken negatively, as many who have not read Freud himself on the subject might tend to do. In fact, it was Freud who conferred on narcissism the status of the 'universal original condition of man,' making it the basis of more than just pathological behaviour" (1). Her salient point is that "*it is the narrative text, and not the author, that is being described as narcissistic*" (1, emphasis added). Hutcheon adds that self-reflexivity has been a prominent feature of the novel since the genre's inception, but contemporary metafiction pursues this impulse to new extremes. She traces "the line of succession from the early self-consciousness of Cervantes and Sterne, to the *Künstlerroman*, to the novel about novels. The 'narcissistic' change is one of degree, not kind" (12–13). There is a distinct line within the modern and postmodern "narcissistic narrative" as well, and for DeLillo it begins with James Joyce.

James Joyce and mirror language

In an extensive 1993 interview for *The Paris Review*, DeLillo cited Joyce's *A Portrait of the Artist as a Young Man* (1916) and *Ulysses* (1922) as formative influences on his artistic sensibilities. He recalled reading Joyce and a few other seminal writers when he was eighteen, during the idyllic summer of 1955 at a lazy job as park attendant in the Bronx:

> And this is where I read Faulkner, *As I Lay Dying* and *Light in August*. . . . And then James Joyce, and it was through Joyce that I learned to see something in language that carried a radiance, something that made me feel the beauty and fervor of words, the sense that a word has a life and a history. And I'd look at a sentence in *Ulysses* or in *Moby-Dick* or in Hemingway—maybe I hadn't gotten to *Ulysses* at that point, it was *Portrait of the Artist*—but certainly Hemingway and the water that was clear and swiftly moving and the way the troops went marching down the road and raised dust that powdered the leaves of the trees. All this in a playground in the Bronx. (88)

Of all the things he might have emphasized about Joyce, it was the writer's reverence for language that made the deepest impression. Consider, for example, the elegant symmetry of language and structure in *A Portrait*. In his 1991 introduction to the Signet Classics edition of the novel,

Hugh Kenner emphasizes the central importance of chiasmus. Joyce frequently writes sentences that use certain words in a certain order in the first half, only to repeat those words in reverse order in the second half: the ABBA pattern known as chiasmus. I say that "Joyce" writes these sentences, but *A Portrait* employs free indirect discourse to mirror Stephen's perspective, preoccupations, and linguistic cadences, so that the frequent appearance of chiasmus is as much a product of Stephen's way of thinking as it is of Joyce's way of writing. Take, for instance, the mirror symmetry of young Stephen's fascination with the lines:

> *Pull out his eyes,*
> *Apologise,*
> *Apologise,*
> *Pull out his eyes.*
> *Apologise,*
> *Pull out his eyes,*
> *Pull out his eyes,*
> *Apologise.* (Joyce 6)

Kenner notes that the title of Joyce's novel was commonly used by painters for their self-portraits, including several by Rembrandt. Kenner then posits an ingenious analogy between the portrait painter's use of mirrors for his art and Joyce's use of mirroring strategies in his novel. He provides the following diagram to illustrate this chiasmic structure:

{	o	‖	o	}
Background	Painter	Mirror	Painter's image	Background
Dublin	Joyce	Silence[2]	Stephen	"Dublin"

Kenner notes the perfect balance and symmetry of this technique: "And the five-part book itself is chiasmic, its second half a mirror of its first" (12). Anyone who has read *Ratner's Star* and studied Tom LeClair's detailed schema of the chapters knows that this is precisely the mirroring technique DeLillo uses in that carefully structured novel.[3] As DeLillo told LeClair in their 1982 interview, "In *Ratner's Star* I tried to weave this secret life of mankind into the action of the book in the form of a history of mathematics, a cult history, the names of the leaders kept secret until the second half of the book, *the mirror image*, when the names appear in reverse order" (11, emphasis added). In his 2016 interview with Carolyn Kellogg he volunteered this: "Let me tell you one thing that comes to mind about 'Ratner's Star.' It's that the words in the title sort of sum up the book it is. You have the second word, star, S-T-A-R, and then you have Ratner's, R-A-T with an S at the end, so that one set of letters in the title mirrors another set of letters. Same four letters are in both words" (Kellogg). This is the same novel where astronomer-turned-mystic Shazar Lazarus Ratner proclaims, "Creation depends on an anagram" (*RS* 223), and logician Edna Lowns asserts, "Language is the mirror of the world" (*RS* 392).

James Augustine Aloysius Joyce (**JAAJ**) may well have regarded chiasmus as his rhetorical birthright. So, too, may Donald Richard DeLillo (**DRD**); or, if you prefer, DonalD RichaRD DeLillo (**DDRRDD**). This manic wordplay may seem a folly to the uninitiated, but DeLillo freely admits his obsession with word-mirrors. He told Kim Echlin in 1997:

> I have a curious audiovisual sense of language. I now hear a rhythm in my head, the beat and cadence of sentences, but I also see the letters as they take shape on the page. I use a little manual typewriter. I see correspondences—visual correspondences—that strike me, letters in a given word, words in a given line. Not long ago I realized something about the first sentence in my first novel, *Americana*, "And then we came to the end of another dull and lurid year." The words 'dull' and 'lurid' could just as easily be two other words, but there is a visual contact between those two words. Lurid is almost dull spelt backwards, except for the "r." I realize retrospectively that I've been doing that all along without really knowing it. (147)

Having made this self-discovery, he kept remarking upon it to other interviewers. In 1999 he put it this way to Maria Moss: "Almost all the letters in 'lurid' are also in 'dull.' One word is almost the other, *a mirror image. I do this all the time*, but it's instinctive" (164, emphasis added). From the beginning—literally from the first sentence—DeLillo's fictional worlds, at the macrocosmic and microcosmic levels, are made out of mirrors.

William Gaddis and *Mise en Abyme*

William Gaddis was another expert manufacturer of metafictional mirrors who powerfully influenced DeLillo. Gaddis's monumental first novel *The Recognitions* (1955) establishes a number of prototypes DeLillo later followed in his own fiction. This notoriously difficult and intensely self-reflexive novel includes dozens of characters, but two are most important with respect to metafictional mirrors: the painter Wyatt Gwyon and the writer Otto Pivner. Wyatt's father is a Calvinist minister, and the family assumes that the son will follow in his father's footsteps. Like Stephen Dedalus, however, from a young age Wyatt hears a different calling toward art. His Aunt May takes charge of his strict religious education, and she berates him when she discovers his hidden drawings. In a passage that clearly echoes the "*non serviam*" section of Father Arnall's sermon in *A*

Portrait (Joyce 103), Aunt May equates Wyatt's artistic pretensions with Lucifer's sinful pride. What is most striking in Gaddis's re-imagination of that sermon is the portrayal of art as inherently blasphemous because it treads upon God's exclusive power to create. Aunt May scolds:

> —Lucifer was the archangel who refused to serve Our Lord. To sin is to falsify something in the Divine Order, and that is what Lucifer did. His name means Bringer of Light but he was not satisfied to bring the light of Our Lord to man, he tried to steal the power of Our Lord and to bring his own light to man. He tried to become original, she pronounced malignantly, shaping that world round the whole structure of damnation, repeating it, crumpling the drawing of the robin in her hand,—original, to steal Our Lord's authority, to command his own destiny, to bear his own light! That is why Satan is the Fallen Angel, for he rebelled when he tried to emulate Our Lord Jesus. And he won his own domain, didn't he. Didn't he! And his own light is the light of the fires of Hell! Is that what you want? Is that what you want? Is that what you want? (Gaddis 34)

Although Aunt May is portrayed as a fanatical zealot (and, judging by the passage above, a closeted Gnostic), she sets up some crucial tensions which animate the rest of *The Recognitions*: conflicts between divine creation and artistic counterfeit, between authentic original and fake reproduction. Gaddis surely does not endorse Aunt May's anathematization of art, but he does share her view of the material world as fallen and corrupt, a distorted mirror inundated with sham demiurges and their false images.

Wyatt defies Aunt May's warnings and tries to support himself as an artist. When that doesn't pan out, he turns first to art restoration and then to art forgery. He is legitimately talented and sincerely committed to art, despite his crimes against originality, and he attempts to preserve some sense of reverence and integrity even as he is surrounded by mediocrities, users, and craven patrons who reduce his work to mere commodity. For all his faults, Wyatt Gwyon constitutes Gaddis's most sympathetic portrait of an artist in *The Recognitions*. He is the positive mise en abyme embedded within the work. The negative mise en abyme is Otto Privner. Gaddis critic Steven Moore describes Otto as "a comic double, a funhouse mirror reflection" of Wyatt (54–55). Although Otto is a writer, he adopts the painter Wyatt as his mentor for a time, only to exploit him as the model for a pathetically derivative play. Otto is a talentless plagiarist who represents all the worst elements of art as petty substitute for originality and authenticity. He is a mirror of a mirror. Even his name is a chiasmic mirror: O>T><T<O.

One of the most telling passages about the function of mirrors in *The Recognitions* is provided by Esme. She is a drug addict stuck in a doomed relationship with Otto, but she also sits as a model for Wyatt's art forgeries. Like the Old Masters invoked by Hugh Kenner, Wyatt utilizes mirrors for his paintings. Esme has a nightmare about these mirrors which she reports to Otto: "—They are evil, she said, thinking of her own dream now. —To be trapped in one, and they are evil. If you knew what they know. There are evil mirrors where he works, and they work with him, because they are mirrors with terrible memories, and they know, they *know*, and they tell him these terrible things and then they trap him" (Gaddis 221, emphasis in original).

Gaddis's sustained and integral incorporation of mise en abyme in *The Recognitions* guided DeLillo toward similar effects in his metafiction. His first novel *Americana* establishes the mirror as his predominant trope. The artist at the center of *Americana* is filmmaker David Bell, who later becomes the chronicler of the narrative we read. David (DaViD) is a narcissist in love with his own image. He also adores the movies. Not surprisingly, when he transitions from film lover to filmmaker, the movie he shoots is a thinly veiled reflection of his own life and personal preoccupations. In an enormously prescient passage which sets the standard for so many mirror experiments in DeLillo's subsequent work, David defines his approach to this film:

What I'm doing is kind of hard to talk about. It's a sort of first-person thing but without me in it in any physical sense, except fleetingly, not exactly in the Hitchcock manner but brief personal appearance nonetheless, *my mirror image* at any rate. Also my voice when I start using sound. It's a reaching back for certain things. But not just that. It's also an attempt to explain, to consolidate. Jesus, I don't know. It'll be part dream, part fiction, part movies. An attempt to explore parts of my consciousness. Not quite autobiographical in the Jonas Mekas sense. I've said part movies. By that I mean certain juxtapositions of movies with reality, certain images that have stayed with me, certain influences too. I mean *you can start with nothing but your own mirror reality and end with an approximation of art.* (A 263, emphasis added)

David's film mirrors his experiences and consciousness, and David's narrative reflects his "mirror reality" film. At the heart of both is a signature shot of David in the mirror (A 241, 347). It is a dizzying mise en abyme effect. David Cowart observes,

Bell's film begins and ends with a shot of Austin Wakely, his surrogate, standing in front of a mirror that reflects the recording camera and its operator, the autobiographical subject of the film. A perfect piece of hermeticism, this shot announces an infinite circularity; it suggests that nothing in the rest of the film will manage to violate the endless circuit of the signifying chain. It suggests, too, the complexity—indeed, the impossibility—of determining the truly authentic subject among its own proliferating masks. (133)

Like *The Recognitions*, *Americana* replicates contemporary conditions in which authenticity and essential identity are permanently contested and perpetually deferred. The "infinite circularity" and "endless circuit of the signifying chain" described by Cowart may constitute a hermetically sealed, self-contained cosmos like that invoked by Barth; but they also constitute a trap like that conjured up in Esme's nightmare, a mirror-maze from which the subject can never escape.

Jorge Luis Borges and mirror labyrinths

The foremost mirror-maker and labyrinth-builder of fabulist fiction is Jorge Luis Borges. DeLillo has spoken about an intriguing mirroring exercise he uses involving Borges. He confided to Adam Begley,

> A writer takes earnest measures to secure his solitude and then finds endless ways to squander it. To break the spell I look at a photograph of Borges, a great picture sent to me by the Irish writer Colm Tóbín. The face of Borges, against a dark background—Borges fierce, blind, his nostrils gaping, his skin stretched taut, his mouth amazingly vivid; his mouth looks painted; he's like a shaman painted for visions, and the whole face has a kind of steely rapture. I've read Borges of course, although not nearly all of it, and I don't know anything about the way he worked—but the photograph shows us a writer who did not waste time at the window or anywhere else. So I've tried to make him my guide out of lethargy and drift, into the otherworld of magic, art and divination. (90)

In this evocative tribute DeLillo comes across like one of his characters confronting a mirror, staring at an image which is not his own but trying to transfigure himself into resembling the face (blindly) looking back at him. Revealing as this motivational ritual may be, the resemblance that matters most can be found in the authors' respective works.

Take, for instance, "Tlön, Uqbar, Orbis Tertius," first published in 1940 but popularized in the English-speaking world through the collection *Labyrinths* (1962). In this story the narrator and his collaborator Bioy Casares conduct a "vast debate over the way one might go about composing a first-person novel whose narrator would omit or distort things and engage in all sorts of contradictions, so that a few of the book's readers—a *very* few—might divine the horrifying or banal truth" (Borges 68, emphasis in original). Without sharing what that truth is, the narrator makes an assertion about the danger of mirrors: "Down at the far end of the hallway, the mirror hovered, shadowing us. We discovered (very late at night such a discovery is inevitable) that there is something monstrous about mirrors. That was when Bioy remembered a saying by one of the heresiarchs of Uqbar: *Mirrors and copulation are abominable, for they multiply the number of mankind*"

(68, emphasis in original). We're only a page into the story and already most readers will be lost in the maze. Who is the narrator—Borges himself? What or where is Uqbar? How can we trust anything we're being told if we begin with writers who are admittedly plotting to mislead their readers? And if mirrors and copulation are monstrous because they generate new entities into being, then isn't the story we are reading equally guilty of the same abomination?

Rather than answering these questions, the narrator guides the reader deeper into the labyrinth, where, to borrow a line used repeatedly in DeLillo's labyrinthine *Libra*, "There is a world inside the world" (*L* 13, 47, 153, 277). Borges invents a fictional place called Uqbar, and he invents writers in Uqbar who themselves conceived the imaginary realm of Tlön. In the absence of any concrete evidence for the existence of either (beyond an alleged fragment from an unverified encyclopedia stamped *Orbis Tertius*), the narrator and his fellow fabulists invent the missing history and literature of this alternate world: "The fact is, the most diligent searches have so far proven futile. In vain have we ransacked the libraries of the two Americas and Europe. Alfonso Reyes, weary of those 'subordinate drudgeries of a detective nature,' has proposed that between us, we undertake to *reconstruct* the many massive volumes that are missing" (Borges 72, emphasis in original). He is describing the mechanics not only of fabulation but also of conspiracy, mirrors reflecting mirrors like those DeLillo manipulates to sinister effect in *Libra*. The narrator observes, "Tlön may well be a labyrinth, but it is a labyrinth forged by men, a labyrinth destined to be deciphered by men" (81). The monstrous mirrors of this labyrinth keep replicating images ad infinitum, gradually displacing reality with fantasy, leading the narrator to conclude that eventually "The world will be Tlön" (81).

DeLillo adapts Borges into what Linda Hutcheon terms "historiographic metafiction." In her influential book *A Poetics of Postmodernism*, Hutcheon identifies "the guiding concern of the entire book" as "the problematizing of history by postmodernism" (xii). This leads to her influential taxonomy of historiographic metafiction, which encapsulates so much of DeLillo's work. *A Poetics of Postmodernism* sets out to counter detractors who denounced postmodernism as decadently ahistorical by defining and privileging the category of historiographic metafiction:

> By this I mean those well-known and popular novels which are both intensely self-reflexive and yet paradoxically also lay claim to historical events and personages. ... In most of the critical work on postmodernism, it is narrative—be it in literature, history, or theory—that has usually been the major focus of attention. Historiographic metafiction incorporates all three of these domains: that is, its theoretical self-awareness of history and fiction as human constructs (historio*graphic* meta*fiction*) is made the grounds for its rethinking and reworking of the forms and contents of the past. (*Poetics* 5, emphasis in original)

Hutcheon also stresses that historiographic metafiction "always works *within* conventions in order to subvert them" (5, emphasis in original).

DeLillo recognizes and indulges the allure of pure invention, of imposing order through fantasy on a world of confusion and chaos. Like Borges in his invention of the Tlön fabulists, DeLillo creates embedded authors who themselves create alternate universes, ones that make sense and possess symmetry and elegance, which provide answers to otherwise intractable questions. As a treatment for the metastasizing mystery of the Kennedy assassination, Nicholas Branch in *Libra* invents evidence, characters, and scenes to plug holes in the porous historical record. Nick Shay in *Underworld* devises an alternate world in the form of a mirror family, the Martins, to explain the backstory of Bobby Thomson's homerun ball, but more importantly to compensate for his father's abandonment with a story about a deadbeat dad who decides to return home. In *Zero K*, Jeff Lockhart imagines an internal monologue for Artis Martineau, sealed away in a cryonic pod, as a creative meditation on consciousness trapped between life and death. DeLillo indulges these embedded author's fantasies, but at the same time he critiques their impulse for fabulist invention. This approach of working within conventions as a means of subverting them is not only quintessential DeLillo, but, according to Hutcheon, also the trademark postmodern approach to historiographic metafiction:

> I will argue throughout this study that postmodernism is a fundamentally contradictory enterprise: its art forms (and its theory) at once use and abuse, install and then destabilize convention in parodic ways, self-consciously pointing both to their own inherent paradoxes and provisionality and, of course, to their critical or ironic re-reading of the art of the past. In implicitly contesting in this way such concepts as aesthetic originality and textual closure, postmodernist art offers a new model for mapping the borderland between art and the world, a model that works from a position within both and yet not totally within either, a model that is profoundly implicated in, yet still capable of criticizing, that which it seeks to describe. (*Poetics* 23)

Along these same lines, DeLillo never loses sight of the dire potential consequences of reinventing reality. In *Americana*, David Bell admits to the reader, though not to his ex-wife Meredith, that when he spoke with her he "told nothing but lies. It was very entertaining. Soon I began to understand the attractions of pathological lying. To construct one's own reality" (*A* 58). David explicitly links his pathological lying to the fabulist literary tradition: "The fabulist in me, lurking just below the water-line, welcomed the challenge of topping each new lie and looked forward to some distant nexus of perfection, the super-union of all lies into one radiant and transcendental fiction" (*A* 58). David may see his lies as harmless and rationalize them as "radiant and transcendental fiction," but the reader is meant to recognize his lies as symptomatic of "Americana": America's addiction to the facile images of entertainment and consumerism, and the American government's calculated web of lies used to perpetuate the Vietnam War.

Some four decades later in *Point Omega* (2010) DeLillo used self-reflexive fiction to critique the Bush administration's propensity for truth-defying, world-making fantasy. DeLillo invents Richard Elster, a cerebral war theorist and an architect of the War on Terror, who is himself an inventor of new realities. Elster recalls,

> There were times when no map existed to match the reality we were trying to create. . . . But we were devising entities beyond the agreed-upon limits of recognition or interpretation. Lying is necessary. The state has to lie. There is no lie in war or in preparation for war that can't be defended. We went beyond this. We tried to create new realities overnight, careful sets of words that resemble advertising slogans in memorability and repeatability. These were words that would yield pictures eventually and then become three-dimensional. (*PO* 28–29)

The creative tools of fiction, so liberating for the artist, become perverse and oppressive in the hands of political rogues who convert them into weapons of mass deception.[4] DeLillo is fundamentally influenced by the fabulists, but he also recognizes the capacity for such strategies to be misappropriated by the state. To be fair, Borges himself was acutely aware of the totalitarian threat posed by inventing alternate realities, as the postscript to "Tlön, Uqbar, Orbis Tertius" makes clear. His opposition to fascism, communism, and the Perón dictatorship in Argentina reinforce his commitments outside the text and suggest implicit critique within the text. Borges recognized how monstrous mirrors could be if used to refashion reality into a diabolical labyrinth. DeLillo's historiographic metafiction is rooted as much in the inventions of Borges and company as in the lies of the Johnson, Nixon, and Bush administrations. The ramifications are bigger than politics; they are existential, metaphysical. As the character Singh puts it in DeLillo's novel *The Names* (1982):

> The world has become self-referring. You know this. This thing has seeped into the texture of the world. The world for thousands of years was our escape was our refuge. Men hid from themselves in the world. We hid from God or death. The world was where we lived, the self was where we went mad and died. But now the world has made a self of its own. Why, how, never do we say the simplest thing without falling into a trap? Where do we go, how do we live, who do we believe? This is my vision, a self-referring world, a world in which there is no escape. (*N* 297)

And this was over thirty years before the proliferation of "fake news" and the normalization of "alternative facts" during the Donald Trump era.

The world has become Tlön.

Vladimir Nabokov and mirror games

Before descending too far down this dark rabbit hole, however, let's not forget what a great pleasure it is to read Don DeLillo. For all its intellectual rigor and moral gravitas, his self-reflexive art can also be quite playful. He delights in word games, structural puzzles, secret codes, and literary hide-and-seek. His predilection for games may seem more pronounced in early novels, but the gaming impulse doesn't go away in his middle and late work—it just goes underground. From *Libra* onward, games with the reader are frequently mediated by hidden orchestrators disguised as something or someone else, hidden in plain sight. These players design and execute bank-shot deflections, no-look-pass projections, and triple-play triangulations. To read DeLillo—and especially to *re-read* DeLillo—is to play self-reflexive games with a master.

DeLillo acknowledged his attraction to games in his first interview with LeClair. He observed, "Most games are carefully structured. They satisfy a sense of order and they even have an element of dignity about them. In *Ratner's Star* someone says, 'Strict rules add dignity to a game.' There are many games in *Ratner's Star*, and the book is full of adults acting like children—which is another reason why people play games, of course" (5). Games are self-contained, rule-governed exercises which indulge the desire for order. This sounds a lot like Barth's opening description of the novel as its own coherent cosmos, and indeed games serve a fundamentally metafictional function in DeLillo's work. He said as much to LeClair in reference to his early novels: "*End Zone* and *Ratner's Star* are *books of games*, books in which *fiction itself is a sort of game*" (5, emphasis added). In *Ratner's Star* Jean Sweet Venable elaborates upon fiction as a game. She is assigned to write a journalistic piece on Field Experiment Number One, but her project gradually morphs into an intricate work of fiction. Her remarks on this work in progress double as self-reflexive commentary upon the book in which she's embedded as a character: "I plan to make strict rules that I plan to follow. *Reading my book will be a game with specific rules that have to be learned.* I'm free to make whatever rules I want as long as there's an inner firmness and cohesion, right?" (*RS* 353, emphasis added). DeLillo divulges the mechanics of his own game design for *Ratner's Star*, and in the process delivers instructions by proxy to his own readers about how to play the game of reading the book we hold in our hands.

DeLillo's second novel *End Zone* (1972) is most visibly devoted to games. It focuses upon a college football team and includes deep analysis of the game's inner logic. The novel is also full of Wittgensteinian language games, as befits a fictional cosmos located at Logos College. Part Two consists entirely of a play-by-play description of the big game between Logos and their archrivals Centrex. The opening of this section includes DeLillo's most direct metafictional address to the reader/spectator in any of his novels. "The spectator, at this point, is certain to wonder whether he must now endure a football game in print—the author's way of adding his own neat quarter-notch to the scarred bluesteel of combat writing" (*EZ* 111). DeLillo then completely lays bare the literary device in a self-reflexive passage comparing the game on the field to the game being played between author and reader: "The exemplary spectator is the person who understands that sport is a benign illusion, the illusion that order is possible. . . . The best course is for the spectator to continue forward, *reading himself into the very middle of that benign illusion*" (*EZ* 111–12, emphasis added). The author exposes his own artifice as creator and conductor of this metafictional game: "And of course it remains the author's permanent duty to unbox the lexicon for all eyes to see—a cryptic ticking mechanism in search of a revolution" (*EZ* 113). DeLillo invites the reader to cross through the looking glass and to enter the "benign illusion" of the novel, where he or she is incorporated into the "cryptic ticking mechanism" of fiction and can face off in a metafictional game with the author.

In *End Zone* even a seemingly trivial pursuit like the game "Bang, You're Dead"—where one sneaks up on an opponent, mimics the sound of gunfire, and announces "Bang, you're dead," at which point the victim feigns falling dead to the ground—is played seriously and examined with self-reflexive scrutiny. Quarterback and narrator Gary Harkness muses, "At first, naturally enough, I thought it was all very silly, even for a bunch of bored and lonely athletes. Then I began to change my mind. Suddenly, beneath its bluntness, the game seemed compellingly intricate. It possessed gradations, dark joys, a resonance echoing from the most perplexing of dreams" (*EZ* 32). Gary becomes a champion at this game. "I died well and for this reason was killed quite often" (*EZ* 33). The backdrop of the Vietnam War looms throughout *End Zone*. These athletes must always be aware of the fate that could have awaited them were they not enrolled in college, a fate that might await them still after graduation. All of their games, from football to the sophisticated virtual war games Gary plays with ROTC Major Staley, are rehearsals for killing and dying. Gary's comment on "Bang, You're Dead" might just as well have been nailed to the boot camp barracks door: "To kill with impunity. To die in the celebration of ancient ways" (*EZ* 33). These players know that ultimately they are only pawns in the game of the masters of war.

This highlights an essential appeal of games to many characters in DeLillo. Games provide an outlet and a framework for the powerless to exert some illusory control, if only limited and temporary. DeLillo commented upon both the attraction and the false promise of games in the LeClair interview: "Games provide a frame in which we can try to be perfect. Within sixty-minute limits or one-hundred-yard limits or the limits of a game board, we can look for perfect moments or perfect structures. In my fiction I think this search sometimes turns out to be a cruel delusion" (6). DeLillo was looking back at his early fiction, but the delusive search for perfect structures continues throughout the metafictional games of his mature work. To varying degrees and for a wide variety of reasons, DeLillo's embedded authors—Nicholas Branch of *Libra*, Nick Shay of *Underworld*, Alex Macklin of *Love-Lies-Bleeding*, and Jeff Lockhart of *Zero K*—all feel they have lost control of their lives. Each attempts to impose order, meaning, symmetry, and resolution by crafting alternative narratives embedded within their respective works. While they may fail to achieve full autonomy and agency through these inventions, they do find some consolation through constructing elaborate games of fiction. DeLillo's embedded authors do not announce what they're up to, and it is often not until readers have finished a work before they realize a game was being played at all. But re-readers are in a better position to understand the rules and play their parts. These metafictional games require at least three players: the acknowledged author Don DeLillo, the unacknowledged embedded author concealed within the text, and the reader who is challenged to follow the breadcrumbs, crack the codes, and solve the riddles.

The blueprints for such metafictional games were patented by Vladimir Nabokov. In a lecture on Fyodor Dostoevsky, Nabokov counseled:

> When dealing with a work of art we must always bear in mind that *art is a divine game*. These two elements—the elements of the divine and that of the game—are equally important. It is divine because this is the element in which man comes nearest to God through becoming a true creator in his own right. And it is a game because it remains art only as long as we are allowed to remember that, after all, it is all make-believe, that the people on the stage, for instance, are not actually murdered— in other words, only as long as our feelings of horror or of disgust do not obscure our realization that *we are, as readers or as spectators, participating in an elaborate and enchanting game*. ("Dostoevsky," emphasis added)

This wonderful evocation of art as a divine and enchanting game pertains perfectly to DeLillo's metafiction. Elsewhere Nabokov compared writing a novel to designing a chess problem and reading a novel to solving that problem. In his autobiography *Speak, Memory* he wrote,

It should be understood that competition in chess problems is not really between White and Black but between the composer and the hypothetical solver (just as in a first-rate work of fiction the real clash is not between the characters but between the author and the world), so that a great part of a problem's value is due to the number of 'tries'—delusive opening moves, false scents, specious lines of play, astutely and lovingly prepared to lead the would-be solver astray. (290)

Nabokov made it clear, however, that the vast majority of readers would never be up to the task of solving complex literary puzzles. When Paul Sufrin quoted the above passage back to him in a 1971 interview, Nabokov amended his pronouncement: "I believe I said 'between the author and the reader,' not 'the world,' which would be a meaningless formula, since the creative artist makes his own world or worlds. He clashes with readerdom because he is his own ideal reader and those other readers are so very often mere lip-moving ghosts and amnesiacs" (*Strong Opinions* 183). Most readers are only interested in playing checkers; but with Nabokov one squares off against a chess master. In his lecture on "Good Readers and Good Writers," Nabokov asserted, "Curiously enough, one cannot *read* a book: one can only re-read it. A good reader, a major reader, an active and creative reader is a re-reader" (*Lectures* 3, emphasis in original). One suspects that *Pale Fire* (1962) is the Nabokov novel DeLillo has re-read the most. DeLillo is a direct descendent of Nabokov in the metafictional family tree, and DeLillo's embedded authors trace their lineage through the covert artificer par excellence, Charles Kinbote.

Nabokov's self-reflexive masterpiece is disguised as academic scholarship with all the requisite components: beginning with an editor's Foreword; followed by *Pale Fire: A Poem in Four Cantos*, the final poem composed by the late John Shade; supplemented with a Commentary section consisting of editorial annotations to the poem; and concluding with an Index. But these dry academic conventions conceal an unparalleled achievement in literary gamesmanship. Mary McCarthy was a reader worthy of Nabokov's inventiveness, and her ecstatic review in *The New Republic* captures the novel's protean spirit as well as anyone ever has. She opens by heralding, "*Pale Fire* is a Jack-in-the-box, a Fabergé gem, a clockwork toy, a chess problem, an infernal machine, a trap to catch reviewers, a cat-and-mouse game, a do-it-yourself kit." She closes with this glowing pronouncement:

This centaur-work of Nabokov's, half-poem, half-prose, this merman of the deep, is a creature of perfect beauty, symmetry, strangeness, originality, and moral truth. Pretending to be a curio, it cannot disguise the fact that it is one of the very great works of art of this century, the modern novel that everyone thought dead and that was only playing possum. (McCarthy)

The book purports to focus on Shade's poem, but that agenda is hijacked by his colleague Charles Kinbote, the neurotic, compulsive, vain, duplicitous, desperate, possibly suicidal, and probably insane commentator of *Pale Fire*, who may also be the exiled king of Zembla. Clues are scattered throughout the poem, commentary, and index—but so are red herrings, dead ends, bald-faced lies, and seemingly contradictory and irreconcilable pieces of quasi-evidence. Generations of Nabokov scholars have debated over whether the entire book, poem and all, is actually meant to be understood as written by Shade, or by Kinbote, or by a more obscure colleague named Botkin.[5] It is likewise difficult to determine if Kinbote is in fact King Charles II, or only fantasizes himself to be the exiled king, or has entirely invented the king and his kingdom of Zembla—the etymology of which we're told means "a land of reflections, or 'resemblers'" (265).

Pale Fire is a game of reflections and resemblers from start to finish. The opening lines of the poem draw self-reflexive attention to the mirror dynamics of art and identity in the book:

> I was the shadow of the waxwing slain
> By the false azure in the windowpane;
> I was the smudge of ashen fluff—and I
> Lived on, flew on, in the reflected sky.
> And from the inside, too, I'd duplicate
> Myself . . . . (33)

John Shade, whose name inscribes him as part-shadow and part-ghost, reflects upon the centrality of reflections in his life and art. The fact that the shadow invoked here is linked to a bird (the Icarus-like "waxwing") which dies from crashing into a window pane establishes the potentially fatal dangers of being enthralled by false reflections and resemblers. This omen echoes the drowned Narcissus as surely as it foreshadows Shade's own murder by a supposed Zemblan assassin. The poem also represents Shade's attempt to process his grief over his daughter Hazel's death by drowning. He seeks multiple sources of solace before having an epiphany that his best consolation can be provided through art. Instead of looking outward for answers, he decides to impose structure and meaning from within, approaching reality like art or game—like art *as* game—a self-contained world following strict, coherent rules:

> But all at once it dawned on me that *this*
> Was the real point, the contrapuntal theme; . . .
> Not flimsy nonsense, but a web of sense.
> Yes! It sufficed that I in life could find
> Some kind of link-and-bobolink, some kind

Of correlated pattern in the game,
Plexed artistry, and something of the same
Pleasure in it as they who played it found. (62–63, emphasis in original)

Shade resolves to resurrect Hazel's shade through the poem *Pale Fire*. In doing so he follows the path later trod by so many DeLillo characters, imposing sense through "Plexed artistry" and finding some comfort, perhaps even pleasure, through the "correlated pattern in the game."

John Shade's games with mirrors in the poem are replicated by the king of Resemblers, Charles Kinbote. When he looks at Shade's poem he imagines seeing reflections of himself and his lost mirror-world of Zembla. Like a number of spectators in late DeLillo, he uses a work of art as a screen on which to project his own experiences, obsessions, anxieties, and desires. As one of Kinbote's colleagues at Wordsmith College observes, the visiting scholar's very name is a kind of anagrammatic mirror: "I was under the impression that you were born in Russia, and that your name was a kind of anagram of Botkin or Botkine" (267). This wordplay brilliantly invokes suicide by way of the "bare bodkin" (i.e., dagger) Hamlet considers turning against himself in the "To be or not to be" soliloquy.[6] But the name also has homicidal implications, as Shade himself notes: "Didn't you tell me, Charles, that *kinbote* means regicide in your language?" Charles replies, "'Yes, a king's destroyer,' I said (longing to explain that *a king who sinks his identity in the mirror of exile* is in a sense just that" (267, emphasis added). Nabokov is playing metafictional games at an extremely advanced level here. As Brian Boyd discovered, Nabokov wrote in his 1962 diary, "I wonder if any reader will notice . . . that the nasty commentator is not an ex-king and not even Dr. Kinbote, but Prof. Vseslav Botkin, a Russian and a madman" (*American* 709n4). As if this dazzling array of mirrors reflecting mirrors were not enough, Nabokov concludes *Pale Fire* by inserting a mise en abyme in his own image. Kinbote vows, "I shall continue to exist. I may assume other disguises, other forms, but I shall try to exist. I may turn up yet, on another campus, as an old, happy, healthy, heterosexual Russian, a writer in exile, sans fame, sans future, sans audience, sans anything but his art" (300–01). Did Nabokov create Kinbote/Botkin, or did he/they create him? At the end of a first reading one is inevitably lost in the Hall of Mirrors. But the attentive reader has been given sufficient clues to start over as a re-reader capable of playing the self-reflexive game of *Pale Fire*.

* * *

"Then we came to the end of another dull and lurid year" (*A* 3). The first sentence of DeLillo's first novel begins with an ending. His career as a novelist began with an ending, too, after he quit his job as a copywriter for the Ogilvy, Benson & Mather advertising agency and devoted his attention to writing what became *Americana*. DeLillo learned his trade in image-making of the consumerist variety, but he abandoned that industry in favor of image-making of a very different kind. Fortunately he benefited from literary mentors to guide him through an apprenticeship in self-reflexive art. Forerunners like Joyce, Gaddis, Borges, and Nabokov provided him with models and equipped him with tools to construct his own mirror-worlds. The artistic credo of David Bell in *Americana* might double as that of his author: "I mean you can start with nothing but your own mirror reality and end with an approximation of art" (*A* 263). DeLillo's subsequent works range across a wide variety of subjects, and his style evolves appreciably from his early to middle to late periods. Nevertheless, his core commitment to the mirroring dynamics of metafiction remains remarkably consistent throughout his career.

Furthermore, like his illustrious predecessors, DeLillo sets high standards for his readers, challenging us to engage in the sophisticated games he designs in his novels, stories, and plays. Asked by Adam Begley about his stance toward his audience, he gave this Nabokovian rejoinder: "When my head is in the typewriter the last thing on my mind is some imaginary reader. I don't have an audience; I have a set of standards" (91). However, he then relented and gave this revealing reply:

> But when I think of my work out in the world, written and published, I like to imagine it's being read by some stranger somewhere who doesn't have anyone around him to talk to about books and writing—*maybe a would-be writer*, maybe a little lonely, who depends on a certain kind of writing to make him feel more comfortable in the world. (Begley 91, emphasis added)

It sounds like DeLillo is writing for the eighteen-year-old kid he used to be, sitting on a park bench in the Bronx, having his mind blown by James Joyce. What is most telling is that he conceives of his ideal reader as a "would-be writer": someone engaged in the same work as DeLillo, perhaps the author's successor, maybe even his double, his secret sharer.

As an avid reader of DeLillo who has become a devout writer about DeLillo, I am tempted to identify with the description above and see my reflection in the author's ideal mirror. But I've read enough Joyce, Gaddis, Borges, Nabokov—and DeLillo—to know what a trap is laid by such mirror identifications. Such fantasies are best confined to dreams (see Coda). Instead, the best I can hope for in the following chapters is to offer one committed re-reader's map through select corridors in Don DeLillo's Hall of Mirrors.

2

American Narcissus

Lacanian reflections in *Americana*

In *Don DeLillo: The Physics of Language* David Cowart puts theory in its place with respect to art. He cautions that "to overdo theoretical readings of a writer like DeLillo can be an exercise in the redundant and the pretentious. Theory always threatens to make merely less immediate the fictive praxis" (10). He adds, "Only through the stimulus of art can criticism achieve insights worth the world's time and attention. This is not to say that theory for the sake of theory is objectionable—only that it occupies a branch of learning and pleasure one finds less interesting than art itself" (11). Having issued this disclaimer in his introduction, however, Cowart goes on to deliver some of the most theoretically astute readings of DeLillo's novels to date. I share Cowart's misgivings about overburdening DeLillo's fictional texts with more theoretical apparatus than they can bear. But like him I also believe that judicious application of theory to DeLillo's art can prove mutually illuminating for both. I frankly doubt that Don DeLillo is well versed in the writings of Jacques Lacan, and I make no claims for direct, intentional influence. Nevertheless, a number of Lacan's key concepts— including his theory of the Mirror Stage, his revisions to Freud's Oedipus Complex, his emphasis on lack as the engine of desire, and his reflections on dreams, fantasies, and the gaze—are particularly useful for taking the full measure of DeLillo's first novel, *Americana*.

The incestuous desires motivating protagonist-narrator David Bell are so blatant as to seem almost a caricature of Freud's Oedipus Complex. In *Technology and Postmodern Subjectivity in Don DeLillo's Novels*, Randy Laist identifies "the sheer cartoonishness with which DeLillo dramatizes David's oedipal desire" (39). The first commentator to emphasize the oedipal dimension of the novel was actually DeLillo himself. In a 1972 essay with the cheeky title "Notes Toward a Definitive Meditation (By Someone Else) on the Novel 'Americana,'" DeLillo declares (in third-person voice) the author's intentions: "The author evidently constructed two planes of incest in 'Americana.' One is based on relations (or near relations) between the protagonist and his mother. The second might be called political incest— the notion that baseless patriotism is a psychotic manifestation of love for mother country" (NTD 327). Locating his reading at the convergence of these two incestuous planes, David Cowart dubs David Bell "The American Oedipus" (132, 144). The label sticks. There is no ignoring the Freudian implications of David's unresolved desires for his mother Ann Bell and for subsequent mother-substitutes, particularly the sculptor Sullivan.

Freudian readings of *Americana* are valid and indeed necessary, but I find that they only take us so far. Peeling past the label of American Oedipus, I offer a Lacan-inflected reconsideration of the novel as a distorted and destabilized treatment of the postmodern subject. Viewed from this vantage, *Americana* appears less a portrait of the American Oedipus and more a reflection from the shimmering pool of the American Narcissus. Lacan's Mirror Stage is invaluable to understanding David Bell's construction of self. The primary narcissism that characterizes infantile ego development remains startlingly active in his adult inter- and intra-personal relationships, and this mirror effect is magnified in his attraction to film. Subsequent developments in Lacanian psychoanalysis—particularly his revisions to the Freudian Oedipus Complex, his location of lack and absence as the engine of desire, and his notions of the gaze so seminal to psychoanalytic film theory—provide a framework and language for articulating David's obsessions. He returns compulsively to a primal eroticized encounter with his mother, reenacting it vicariously on film and in the flesh with Sully. However, unlike Oedipus, David never successfully indulges his taboo incestuous desires. Instead he remains transfixed by fantasies, dreams, and misrecognized reflections from the pool of Narcissus.

The Mirror Stage

Lacan's theories of the Mirror Stage draw upon a number of sources, but one of the most important is Freud's "On Narcissism: An Introduction." Freud complicates pathological views of narcissism by positing that "primary narcissism" is part of normal infantile development. "We say that a human being has originally two sexual objects—himself and the woman who nurses him—and in doing so we are postulating a primary narcissism in everyone, which may in some cases manifest itself in a dominating fashion in his object-choice" (88). According to Freud, primary narcissism sets the terms for sexual development of object-libido (erotic attachment directed outward toward others) and ego-libido (self-love turned inward). In a series of papers from the late 1930s Lacan first extended Freud's theories, in conjunction with work on infantile development by Henri Wallon, to formulate his own theory of the Mirror Stage. Commenting in *Family Complexes in the Formation of the Individual* on the narcissistic structure of the ego, Lacan observes of the Mirror Stage,

> The world appropriate to this phase is thus a narcissistic world. In so describing it we are not simply evoking its libidinal structure by the same term to which Freud and Abraham assigned the purely energetic meaning of investment of libido in the body. We also wish to penetrate its mental structure and give it the full meaning of the Narcissus myth. Whether this meaning is taken to indicate death—a vital insufficiency from which this narcissistic world grows; or the mirror image—the imago of the double is central to it; or the illusion of the image—this world, as we shall see, has no place for others. (31)

Already in this nascent piece Lacan is beginning to assemble the building blocks for his mature theories, founded upon the mirroring dynamics at work in self-development.

Lacan's definitive explanation comes in his 1949 essay "The Mirror Stage as Formative of the Function of the I." Here he famously asserts that mirrors and mothers serve comparable functions in ego formation. Between the ages of six months and eighteen months, the infant becomes aware of its reflected image (either in an actual mirror or in some external surface that effectively functions as a mirror, most notably the mother's face). When an infant looks into either, it sees an image of the self; not the self as it is truly experienced in infancy—a physically uncoordinated and mentally chaotic mess—but rather the self as it wants to be—a stable, coherent, ideal Gestalt. The child identifies with the image staring back from the mirror or from the mother and incorporates it as the bedrock of the ego. "But the important point," as Lacan emphasizes, "is that this form situates the agency of the ego, before its social determination, in a fictional direction" (2). That "social determination" will come later with the acquisition of language and the child's passage from the Imaginary Order into the Symbolic Order. At this primal stage, however, the "I" is a facsimile of an idealized image which Lacan refers to as the "imago" (2). Jung had used the psychological term "imago" before Lacan, but the concept has a much longer lineage, harking back to the Judeo-Christian belief in *Imago Dei*: "So God created man in his own image, in the image of God created he him; male and female created he them" (Gen. 1:27). Lacan invokes the *Imago Dei* but fundamentally reformulates it in terms of self-creation. Humans create themselves in their own images, but those images are fictions, conjuring tricks using mirrors and/or mothers. It is important to note how alienating this version of self-creation is, relying upon identification with an external image and internalizing it as one's ego. This fundamental misrecognition (*méconnaissance*) continues to exert a distorting effect on all subsequent stages of self-development and adult relationships.

David Bell's mirrors and mothers

DeLillo delivers a calculated first impression of David Bell as a thoroughgoing narcissist. David ducks out of a party in the first chapter to spend some time alone with his favorite person—himself: "I decided to go into the bathroom and look at myself in the mirror" (*A* 4). He is certainly vain—"I was an extremely handsome young man" (*A* 11)—but DeLillo is establishing much more than that. The American Narcissus displays a fatal obsession with his own image. David claims to find solace in his self-image. In terms that explicitly invoke psychoanalysis he admits, "I had almost the same kind of relationship with my mirror that many of my contemporaries had with their analysts. When I began to wonder who I was, I took the simple step of lathering my face and shaving. It all became so clear, so wonderful. I was blue-eyed David Bell" (*A* 11). As the novel unfolds, a host of neuroses and unresolved anxieties emerge from behind the blue eyes of David Bell. But he uses his imago like a protection charm, keeping his ghosts at bay with an amulet in the mirror of composure and success.

David is powerfully drawn to images projected on the magnified mirror of cinema's big screen. He describes his youthful epiphany of identification with Burt Lancaster: "When I was a teenager I saw Burt in *From Here to Eternity*. He stood above Deborah Kerr on that Hawaiian beach and for the first time in my life I felt the true power of the image" (*A* 13). He worships Lancaster as "the icon of a new religion" and longs to merge completely with *Imago Burt*: "I knew I must extend myself until the molecules parted and I was spliced into the image" (*A* 13). Psychoanalytic film theorists have long noted the narcissistic appeal of cinematic spectatorship. In "Ideological Effects of the Basic Cinematographic Apparatus," Jean-Louis Baudry explains the spectator's identification with film image in explicitly Lacanian terms:

> The arrangement of the different elements—projector, darkened hall, screen—in addition to reproducing in a striking way the *mise-en-scène* of Plato's cave (prototypical set for all transcendence and the topological model of idealism) reconstructs the situation necessary to the release of the "mirror state" discovered by Lacan. This psychological phase, which occurs between six and eighteen months of age, generates *via* the mirror image of a unified body the constitution or at least the first sketches of the "I" as an imaginary function. . . . But for this imaginary constitution

of the self to be possible, there must be—Lacan strongly emphasizes this point—two complementary conditions: immature powers of mobility and a precocious maturation of visual organization (apparent in the first few days of life). If one considers that these two conditions are repeated during the cinematographic projection—suspension of mobility and the predominance of the visual function—perhaps one could suppose that this is more than a simple analogy. (45)

The pioneering psychoanalytic film theorist Christian Metz departs from Baudry, arguing that the film spectator identifies less with the screen image than with the camera as perceiver. Nevertheless, he agrees with Baudry that Lacan provides the psychological blueprint for understanding these imaginary identifications. In his groundbreaking *The Imaginary Signifier* Metz describes the Lacanian Mirror Stage as "the durable mark of the mirror which alienates man in his own reflection and makes him the double of his double, the subterranean persistence of the exclusive relation to the mother" (4). Applying this stage to cinematic spectatorship, he explains, "All this is undoubtedly reactivated by the play of that *other mirror*, the cinema screen, in this respect a veritable psychical substitute, a prosthesis for our primally dislocated limbs" (4, emphasis in original).

DeLillo is a devoted *cineaste* who regularly credits films and filmmakers as formative influences on his art. He scatters cinematic references throughout *Americana*, particularly to Jean-Luc Godard's *Breathless*, Akira Kurosawa's *Ikiru*, and Ingmar Bergman's mother-haunted *Persona*.[1] David Bell is the first of several filmmakers and cinephiles to populate his fiction.

FIGURE 2.1 *A boy (Jörgen Linström) is drawn to a giant screen image of a woman (dissolving between Liv Ullmann and Bibi Andersson) in the opening sequence of Ingmar Bergman's* Persona *(AB Svensk Filmindustri, 1966).*

It is a testament to DeLillo's deep sensitivity to the psycho-physiological mechanisms of film that he intuits the phenomena of infantile regression and narcissistic identification induced by film spectatorship years before Lacan's own writings were widely available in English and well before the leading purveyors of Lacanian film theory (e.g., Baudry, Metz, Laura Mulvey, Slavoj Žižek) had begun to publish their work. DeLillo's art proves to be a step ahead of the theoretical frameworks most useful for situating it.

As his title *Americana* hints, DeLillo presents the reader not only with a protagonist but with an entire country besotted with images. The very dynamics that bewitch him in a narcissistic trance has the entire culture mesmerized. During his trip into the dark, unreal heart of the American Dream, he diagnoses his obsession with images as symptomatic of a larger cultural epidemic: "The dream made no allowance for the truth beneath the symbols, for the interlinear notes, the presence of something black (and somehow very funny) at the mirror rim of one's awareness" (*A* 130). In hindsight the older David is skeptical of his gullible younger self. Still, he concedes that "as a boy, and even later, quite a bit later, I believed all of it, the institutional messages, the psalms and placards, the pictures, the words. Better living through chemistry. The Sears, Roebuck catalog. Aunt Jemima. All the impulses of all the media were fed into the circuitry of my dreams. One thinks of echoes. *One thinks of an image made in the image and likeness of images*" (*A* 130, emphasis added). DeLillo has probably read as little of Jean Baudrillard as of Jacques Lacan, but here again his instincts prove unerringly prescient. Like Lacan, Baudrillard latched upon the mirror as a guiding metaphor for groundless simulations of reality, first in his critique of Marxism, *The Mirror of Production* (1973), and later in his influential diagnosis of contemporary inundation with images divorced from their referents in *Simulacra and Simulation* (1981).[2] Young David Bell is dazzled by the sacramental simulations of commercial America, the groundless, superficial, idealized screen images peddled by his commercial executive father and epitomized by his celluloid *Imago Dei* Burt Lancaster.

Narrating the novel from a distant island in 1999, David finally sees his congenital disease for what it is and implicitly renounces his American birthright. But the David of 1970, the blue-eyed Burt-replica and Bergman-wannabe who heads west to make an autobiographical film, is still completely in the thrall of images. In one of the novel's key passages, he tries to explain his cinematic intentions as essentially an aesthetic of the imago. He tells Ken Wild,

> What I'm doing is kind of hard to talk about. It's a sort of first-person thing but without me in it in any physical sense, except fleetingly, not exactly in the Hitchcock manner but brief personal appearance nonetheless, my mirror image at any rate. Also my voice when I start using sound. It's a reaching back for certain things. But not just that.

It's also an attempt to explain, to consolidate. Jesus, I don't know. It'll be part dream, part fiction, part movies. An attempt to explore parts of my consciousness. Not quite autobiographical in the Jonas Mekas sense. I've said part movies. By that I mean certain juxtapositions of movies with reality, certain images that have stayed with me, certain influences too. I mean *you can start with nothing but your own mirror reality and end with an approximation of art.* (A 263, emphasis added)

Far from rejecting the allure of images, David aims his camera with redoubled intensity into the pool of the American Narcissus. What he sees reflected back, just as Lacan's theories would predict, are images galvanized by his unsatisfied desires for his mother.

"Even from this long way off," David writes from his island retreat in 1999,

it is painful to write about her. It has taken me this long just to organize my thoughts. And although I think I have come to terms with everything, it will be interesting to see whether I can put it on paper clearly and openly. Or whether I must blow some smoke into this or that passage—some smoke to hide the fire. (A 167)

Ann Bell died of cervical cancer during David's junior year of college. His unresolved feelings for her impinge upon all his subsequent relationships. As Cowart rightly observes,

Almost every woman he sleeps with turns out to be a version of his mother. In his relations with women he enacts an unconscious search for the one woman forbidden him, at once recapitulating and reversing the tragically imperfect Oedipal model: as he was rejected, so will he reject successive candidates in what occasionally amounts to a literal orgy of philandering and promiscuity. (140–41)

The most important of these mother-substitutes, in both the novel and in David's film, is Sullivan: "In Sullivan, at once mother and 'mothercountry,' Bell recognizes the most significant—and psychologically dangerous—of these surrogates" (Cowart 141).

David introduces Sullivan, or "Sully," as "a sculptor, thirty-seven years old, unmarried, a tall woman who seemed by her manner or bearing or mere presence to change a room slightly, to make it self-conscious" (A 8). His attraction to Sully is palpable and polymorphous. As a successful artist, she is already doing the kind of work that TV producer David only dreams of. As an attractive woman who hasn't yet succumbed to his seductions, she stands as a challenge to his insatiable libido. And as a woman nine years his elder, she possesses experience, authority, and gravitas that both attracts

FIGURE 2.2 *Alma (left, played by Bibi Andersson) and Elisabeth (right, played by Liv Ullmann) gaze into a mirror (and at the spectator) in Ingmar Bergman's* Persona *(AB Svensk Filmindustri, 1966).*

and intimidates him. "Whether on purpose or not, Sullivan always made me feel totally inadequate. I was drawn to her, terribly" (*A* 8). The novel's central road trip to Fort Curtis in the American heartland, and the "long messy autobiographical-type film" (*A* 205) he decides to make out there, depends entirely upon Sully's participation. "Only Sullivan, I believed, could save me" (*A* 107). He adopts her as muse and potential savior, but most importantly he casts her in his film's lead as alter-imago of the *Imago Mater*, a mirror image of Ann Bell.

The Oedipus Complex and desire as lack

The central unresolved conflict of David Bell's youth, and the climactic scene of his autobiographical film, involves a fateful encounter with his mother. DeLillo's subversive treatment of the so-called primal scene constitutes one of *Americana*'s finest achievements. In order to appreciate the various ways he invokes and unravels the primal scene, one must first reconsider the Oedipus Complex. Freud regarded this phenomenon as the cornerstone of childhood psychosexual development. The Oedipus Complex was as important to Lacan as it was to Freud, though he conceived of it in markedly different ways. Lacan crucially inserts a fourth member into the family drama, the phallus. The phallus emerges in Lacanian psychology as the primary signifier of the Oedipus Complex and the transitional harbinger leading from the Imaginary Order to the Symbolic Order of language and social systems. The phallus certainly retains associations with the penis; it is a metonym for the paternal function—that which defines, prohibits, and decrees—the Law and Name-of-the-Father. But its significance for Lacan extends beyond anatomy and patriarchy. The phallus is the chief signifier of desire, that which the mother presumably wants and which the child crucially lacks.

Lacan asserts in "The Function and Field of Speech and Language" that "man's desire finds its meaning in the desire of the other, not so much because the other holds the key to the object desired, as because the first object of desire is to be recognized by the other" (58). In *Four Fundamental Concepts of Psycho-Analysis* he expresses it even more cogently: "Man's desire is the desire of the Other" (235). Note that Lacan does not focus on desire *for* the Other but on desire *of* the Other. In a subtle but crucial departure from Freud, Lacan focuses on the child not as desiring subject but as the object of desire. Inferring the phallus as that which the mother desires but lacks, and recognizing the father as the supposed possessor of the phallus, the child longs not merely to possess but to become the phallus. This sets up a jealous rivalry with the father which is the hallmark of the Oedipus Complex. Desire propelled by Lack—this is the driving logic behind all of Lacan's pronouncements on the Oedipus Complex. Through the father's prohibition the child learns that it can never become the phallus and must renounce this doomed pursuit. In exchange he is initiated through language into the Law and Name-of-the-Father, a passage from the Imaginary to the Symbolic Order. This is not a one-way, irreversible trajectory, however. With varying degrees of frequency and intensity, the subject reverts to the idealized narcissistic conditions of the Mirror Stage. As mentioned earlier, one venue for such regressive tendencies is the cinema. But the Imaginary Order and the primal scene of its overthrow can also be revisited through fantasies and dreams. David Bell retraces these regressive circuits in *Americana*, oscillating between Narcissus and Oedipus over and over again.

David's devotion to film and images marks him as a man with a foot still planted in the Imaginary realm. Yet we also have ample opportunity to see him at work in the world of his father. Clinton Bell is a legend in the world of commercial advertising. He has mastered the art of the image for market exploitation. When David was growing up in Old Holly, his father's idea of an entertaining evening at home was to gather the family in the basement and watch old reels from his collection of TV commercials (A 84). David fancies himself an artist and has enjoyed some moderate success as the creator of an unconventional television series called "Soliloquy" (A 24). However, as the reader witnesses his mind-numbing routines around the network offices, consisting of callous flirtations, meaningless affairs, inane meetings, and drunken lunches, we realize that David has essentially gone into the family business and is well on his way to becoming his jaded father's son. The novel's well-known opening line sets the mood of malaise: "Then we came to the end of another dull and lurid year" (A 3).[3] David admits to himself, "I was wasting my life" (A 8). While suffering through rounds of Christmas drinks with Clinton, David silently seethes with unresolved oedipal hostility: "I wished he were dead. It was the first honest thought which had entered my mind all day. My freedom depended on his death" (A 85). Searching for that freedom, David turns his back on the world of his father, the world of shallow commercialism and proto-Baudrillardian simulacra. His journey westward represents more than an escape from daily drudgery. It is a regression in Lacanian terms from the Symbolic register back to the Imaginary on a quest to reunite with his dead mother.

David and his entourage make it to Fort Curtis where they take up residence and begin shooting his "mirror reality" movie. The center of the film and of David's personal obsessions is a pivotal encounter with his mother. This scene is so elusive that David reenacts it in three separate incarnations: (1) his narrative recollection of a mysteriously erotic exchange with his mother when he was sixteen years old; (2) his filmed dramatization of that scene featuring Sully as Ann Bell and adolescent Bud Yost as David; and (3) his carnal tryst in a motel room where he tries to satisfy his incestuous desires vicariously through Sully. All three of these reenactments conjure up maternal fantasies and oedipal anxieties, and all are characterized by obfuscation, deflection, slippage, and misrecognition—the modus operandi of the American Narcissus.

Primal scene, take #1:
Bell pantry, Old Holly, 1958

The Bells hosted a cocktail party for their Old Holly neighbors one September evening in 1958. The banal circumstances of a suburban soirée hardly seem favorable for a life-altering epiphany. And yet, by the end of that evening, David's repressed feelings for his mother were dredged up to the surface in a strange confrontation which he struggled to assimilate ever since. The party itself is nothing special. David drifts aimlessly in and out of conversations. The ambience is akin to Benjamin Braddock's party in *The Graduate*, complete with Old Holly's own Mrs. Robinson, "the Collier woman," who salaciously tells David: "You're a young man now and there's no reason why you shouldn't know this. You've grown almost to your full stature. You have a man's body and a man's appetites. This is what I want to say. Women love to be loved" (A 191).[4] Rather than feed his appetite or hers, however, David ducks out of the party for a while, preferring the voyeuristic company of a neighbor woman ironing clothes visible through an open window. Eventually he returns home as the party is winding down.

After the final guests leave, David wanders into the kitchen. "My mother was in there. The refrigerator door was open. She was wearing just one shoe. The other was on the floor, a black shoe, upright near the wall. She held a tray of ice cubes in her hands and she was spitting on the cubes. She disappeared behind the refrigerator door and I could hear her open the freezer compartment and slide the tray back in" (A 195). David replicates Ann's bizarre act of spitting on ice cubes at the chronologically later but narratively earlier opening party, and Sullivan unknowingly repeats Ann's act of standing in one shoe at that same party. In retrospect it becomes clear that the entire novel is constructed as a hall of mirrors leading to and from this primal scene.

The erotic epicenter of David's flashback lies in the darkest recess of the kitchen. He recalls returning downstairs later in the evening to find his mother alone in the dimly lit pantry. "It was only a matter of time," she intones. "There is nothing but time. Time is the only thing that happens of itself. We should learn to let it take us along. The Collier woman is a fool" (A 196). There's a lot to unpack here. What was only a matter of time? That her husband Clinton would have an affair with Mrs. Collier? Or that the foolish Collier woman would lose interest with Bell *père* and set her sights on Bell *fils*? Perhaps Ann refers to her present encounter with David as inevitable, an evening of reckoning for repressed (and possibly mutual) desire. Certainly Freud and Lacan would agree that the oedipal encounter is inevitable, but this scene takes an unconscious drama and makes it all too literal, not to mention about a dozen years too late. More foreboding still, Ann's pronouncement, "It was only a matter of time," may refer to the cancer that lurked dormant inside her, a mother's intuition that the death-knell for this Bell will soon toll for her. Whatever Ann's oracles in the pantry may mean, it is less her words than her actions that remain emblazoned on David's psyche.

Facing his mother in the dark, David surrenders himself to the moment: "I did not move. I felt close to some overwhelming moment. In the dim light her shadow behind her consumed my own. I knew what was happening and I did not care to argue with the doctors of that knowledge. Let it be" (A 196). The head doctor of that knowledge, Sigmund Freud, would call this the primal scene, an oedipal fantasy turned startlingly real. But David doesn't trouble himself with such definitions or scruples. He does pause, however, to acknowledge the shadow of Thanatos within this Arcadian realm of forbidden Eros: "Inside her was something splintered and bright, something that might have been left by the spiral passage of my own body" (A 196). This thought can only be inserted after the fact by the elder David, who did not know at the time that his mother would eventually die of cervical cancer and so could not yet have blamed himself for planting the seeds of death in her womb. For the moment, he seems more interested in spiraling his way back into his mother.

> She was before me now, looking up, her hands on my shoulders. The sense of tightness I had felt in my room was beginning to yield to a promise of fantastic release. It was going to happen. Whatever would happen. The cage would open, the mad bird soar, and I would cry in epic joy and pain at the freeing of a single moment, the beginning of time. Then I heard my father's bare feet on the stairs. That was all. (A 196–97)

There is no coitus here, but there's certainly interruptus. Tellingly, the father intervenes before the son and mother can act upon their desire.

The oedipal dimensions of this primal scene are so overdetermined as to seem almost a parody of Freud. A Lacanian perspective on the scene, however, casts it in a different light. For all the overtly sexual language of build-up and release in David's description, the encounter between son and mother is a dramatization of the disappointment of desire. "Let it be," announces the receptive son; "Thou shalt not" replies the paternal footsteps on the stairs. Whatever it is that David demands, and whatever it is that Ann needs, neither succeeds in satisfying the other before the father's prohibition. The scene reads like a dramatization of Lacan's oft-cited definition of desire in "The Signification of the Phallus": "Thus desire is neither the appetite for satisfaction, nor the demand for love, but the difference that results from the subtraction of the first from the second, the phenomenon of their splitting" (287). The phallus drives the wedge to precipitate that splitting.

While it remains unclear precisely what happened before Clinton Bell's intervention, the primal scene as narrated demands an even more fundamental question: *Did anything happen at all?* DeLillo includes a strange interlude between the ice-cube spitting scene and the erotic pantry scene. David goes to his bedroom upstairs and falls asleep. "After a long time I passed into a thin dreamless sleep, less a state of mind than a dislocation of senses. Coming up out of it for only seconds at a time, I did not know where I was or whether it was morning or the middle of the night" (A 195). After drifting through this "dislocation of senses" for an indeterminate period of time, he claims to have awoken. However, "it was my body that was awake but not my mind" (A 196). Then he goes downstairs, where we're asked to believe that his mother has been waiting alone, perhaps for hours, in hopes that he would return for an intimate rendezvous. Could this really have happened? David wants to think so, but DeLillo leads the reader to doubt it. The author's subsequent "Notes Toward a Definitive Meditation" is no more definitive on this subject, teasingly referencing the "relations (or near relations) between the protagonist and his mother" (NTD 327).

On balance, the evidence suggests that David dreamed the encounter with his mother. But the substance of his fantasy is no less revealing for being only a dream. In "The Direction of the Treatment and the Principles of Its Power," Lacan defines dreaming as "a narcissistic folding back of the libido and a disinvestment of reality" (260). This language implies regression back to the Mirror Stage. The most salient feature of David's encounter with Ann in the pantry is their direct confrontation, and the fantasy of merger that it conjures for David—a merger that regresses farther back than oedipal sexuality to pre-oedipal identification, spiraling his way back to the Mother Imago. Commenting in the same seminar on the function of fantasy, Lacan asserts that "in its fundamental use the phantasy is that by which the subject sustains himself at the level of his vanishing desire, vanishing in so far as the very satisfaction of demand hides his object from him" (272). Instead of conceiving of dream and fantasy as manifestations of wish-fulfillment, Lacan suggests the opposite: they suspend the moment just before desire vanishes, just before the desired object eludes capture.

Primal scene, take #2: Yost pantry, Fort Curtis, 1970

As a 28-year-old auteur, David attempts to recapture the primal scene by fixing it on celluloid. "The camera dislikes evasiveness," remarks Austin-as-David. "As Mr. Hitchcock says, one must not use flashback to deceive" (A 285). David's climactic pantry scene breaks Hitchcock's rule, deceptively reenacting a scene that never really happened in the first place. However, his intent seems finally to undeceive himself about what transpired that night. Instead he ends up becoming even further ensnared in misrecognition and thwarted desire, compounding his failure from the past with a reconfigured but equally disappointing misalliance in the sequel.

David evicts Glenn and Laura Yost from the kitchen and frantically begins shooting the scene between Sully/Ann and Bud/David in the Yost family pantry. Every impetus behind the film has led to this pivotal sequence—and he completely botches it. David makes mistake after mistake, and he knows it. Rather than pause to collect himself and shoot the film properly, he rushes recklessly forward:

> I felt no power doing it this way. The light was worse than bad and I hadn't made the proper readings. I was going too quickly, I was not framing. I was ending shots too soon. But I had to do it and be done with it and maybe this was the best way, to obliterate the memory by mocking it, no power at all, spilling seed into the uncaptured light. (A 317)

The onanistic imagery of that final line identifies this scene as the cinematic equivalent of masturbation. As Mark Osteen notes in *American Magic and Dread*, "The masturbatory image implies that the light and sounds of the past can neither be captured nor banished: to abolish the echoes is to silence the singer as well" (28).

This climax may fail cinematically, but as psychological exercise it is quite illuminating. With the 16mm film rolling, David collapses back in time to his sixteen-year-old former self, and back farther still into a narcissistic fantasy of union with mother.

> Then I began to shoot the last sequence and I found I could not stop. Through the viewfinder I saw them, motionless, supremely patient, steadfast, her long fingers knuckle to tip visible over his shoulders, and I kept shooting for two or three minutes, lost somewhere, bent back in twenty-five watts of brown light, listening for a sound behind me, and of all the things I wondered that evening the last was how much she knew. (*A* 317–18)

By the end of that sentence, it is impossible to tell whether "that evening" refers to the past in Old Holly or the present in Fort Curtis, and whether "she" refers to Sully or to Ann. For David such distinctions are temporarily suspended. As Randy Laist argues,

> David's movie seems to be a way of striking out the contradiction between past and present by compiling them into a single image. The past is imported into the present; the borderline between past and present, between imago and real presence, is set quivering, vibrates, and phases out into indeterminacy as a result of the magic of the filmic conversion. Flesh-Sully and Imago-Sully . . . flow into the same electric channel. (54)

In David's eyes, Sully seems poised to dissolve with him into the *Imago Mater*.

At least that's the fantasy. In practice, however, the reenactment on film simply repeats the initial failures of the primal scene in a different genre. DeLillo's description of David locking eyes with Sully during this scene draws attention to a dimension of cinema that came to dominate psychoanalytic film theory: the gaze. In Laura Mulvey's landmark essay "Visual Pleasure and Narrative Cinema" (published four years after *Americana*) she demonstrates the ways in which "the unconscious of patriarchal society has structured film form" (57). Mulvey coins the term "the male gaze" to describe the fetishized depiction of women's bodies in traditional narrative cinema, designed to feed the scopophilic appetites of the spectator. Mulvey explicitly credits Lacan's Mirror Stage as a seminal influence on her own theories (60–61). The masturbatory language with which DeLillo describes David's view of Sully as Ann anticipates the voyeurist undercurrents of scopophilia that Mulvey would soon codify into "the male gaze."

It would be a mistake, however, to interpret David's film reenactment purely in terms of visual pleasure. As Mulvey notes, the image of woman on screen is also a subliminal source of anxiety:

But in psychoanalytic terms, the female figure poses a deeper problem. She also connotes something that the look continually circles around but disavows: her lack of a penis, implying a threat of castration and hence unpleasure. . . . Thus the woman as icon, displayed for the gaze and enjoyment of men, the active controllers of the look, always threatens to evoke the anxiety it originally signified. (64)

The elusive phallus, signifier of absence, disappointment, and lack at the heart of desire, drove a wedge into David's reenactment of the primal scene as a sixteen-year-old, and it intervenes to dispel David's fantasy once again in this second reenactment. "I focused again, her hands on his shoulders, a strange, a very strange expression, something like the curiosity that follows a man out of a room, a totally uncharacteristic look in her eyes" (A 317). Far from visual pleasure, David stands transfixed in the Medusa-like gaze of the (M)other.

Another disturbance to David's visual pleasure surely comes from his compromised vantage point. More troubling than anything David sees or fails to see through his viewfinder is the fact that, as a third party viewing this scene between Sullivan and Bud from the outside, David is essentially occupying his *father's* position in the oedipal schema, intruding upon the sham-idyllic mother-son union. Having come so far to escape his father's world and retreat into narcissistic fantasy, he ends up reconfirming his inheritance of the Name-of-the-Father. When the American Narcissus stared again into the reflecting pool, he did not expect to see the image of Clinton Bell scowling back at him. From the perspective of late Lacanian theory, however, the gaze is always a source of more anxiety than pleasure because it is inevitably misdirected and misapprehended. In *The Four Fundamental Concepts of Psycho-Analysis*, Lacan maintains, "From the outset, we see, in the dialectic of the eye and the gaze, that there is no coincidence, but, on the contrary, a lure. When, in love, I solicit a look, what is profoundly unsatisfying and always missing is that—*You never look at me from the place from which I see you.*" He adds, "Conversely, *what I look at is never what I wish to see*" (103; emphasis in original).

Primal scene, take #3:
Motel room, Fort Curtis, 1970

Having failed to satisfactorily merge with the *Imago Mater* in either pantry scene, David determines to act out his incestuous desires vicariously with his surrogate mother Sully. It should come as no surprise by this point that David fails again in his quest, though the extent of his failure has not been fully appreciated by DeLillo's critics. The motel episode begins promisingly enough. Naked in bed and primed for action, David seems on the brink of finally consummating his maternal desires, albeit by proxy. However, having fed on fantasy for so long, David seems to have lost his appetite for any other fare. Assured by Sully "I'll do anything you want me to do," David defers gratification and chastely responds, "First, before anything else, I want you to tell me a story" (A 320). A bedtime story as foreplay? At this point, no perversion of the oedipal drama is off limits. Sully rises to the occasion with a gripping story about the fraternal rivalry between her Irish Catholic father and her "bloody Ulsterman of an uncle" (A 320). The tale culminates with Sully caught in a boat during a storm with her mad Uncle Malcolm. Between the lines of his song (". . . So I lay with my man from the North Country" [A 327]) and his howl at the height of the tempest ("*Damn your eyes, daughter*" [A 330]), Sully pieces together that her "uncle" was secretly her biological father. Appropriately, the prologue to sex between David and the woman cast as his mother is a bedtime story about incest.

The succeeding chapter finally delivers in graphic detail the long-awaited sex scene, punctuated by David's occasional editorial asides of "Abomination" (A 333). Multiple critics have pointed out that David's consummation with Sully proves to be an anticlimactic flop. Cowart concludes that this one-night stand "is remarkable for its sustained negative affect" (141). In *Don DeLillo: The Possibility of Fiction*, Peter Boxall contends that "the novel is saturated with the disappointment, the anti-climax of this moment, the failure of the filmic and the bodily to converge in a new, transfigured homeland" (34). According to Joseph Dewey in *Beyond Grief and Nothing: A Reading of Don DeLillo*, "The encounter turns out to be something less than we (and Bell) expect. The sexual positions are graphically rendered; thus, the scene never touches the transcendent or even the erotic (it is all about biting and licking and holes and fingers) but stays unappealingly fleshy, described in graceless metaphors of military occupation" (22). The first critic of David's shortcomings is Sullivan herself. The morning after, she speaks down to him less as an underwhelmed lover than as a disappointed mother to a naughty son: "David, I truly love you and hate you. I love you because you're a beautiful thing and a good boy. . . . And I hate you because you're sick. Illness to a certain point inspires pity. Beyond that point it becomes hateful" (A 336). Worse than her dwindling love, her emerging hostility, and her threadbare pity, Sully exposes David as an outdated caricature of psychosexual angst: "You're such a lovable cliché, my love, and I do hope you've found the center of your sin, although I must say that nothing we did last night struck me as being so terribly odd" (A 336). Laist sums up David's postcoital condition best as an image-driven protagonist stripped of all his imagos: "All of the ways in which David has tried to master his self-image have themselves been derived from pre-existing images. Rather than being the artist who edits this collage of selfhood into a subjective self-representation, he is arranged from without by Sully as the most pitiful kind of cartoon, the cartoon that cartoonishly denies its own cartoonishness" (59–60).

Critical consensus maintains that David's crime isn't so much in having tawdry sex with Sullivan as in being deluded enough to think intercourse of any kind will cure what ails him. However, the critics leave a fundamental question unasked: *Do David and Sully actually have sex at all?* I don't think they do. In an uncanny mirroring of his primal scene reenactment as a teenager, the motel consummation is the stuff that dreams are made on.

While shooting an earlier scene for his film, David invoked Bergman's *Persona* as one of his guiding cinematic prototypes. He mused, "Maybe you've seen *Persona*. There are two women, a nurse and a patient, very different, who slowly begin to merge, to almost drift through each other's personalities and reappear with something added or subtracted, I'm not sure which, but a great movie, unparalleled, about the nature of diminishing existence" (*A* 277). The description of the nurse Alma and the patient Elisabeth doubles for the merger of Sully and Ann into one another. David's imaginary consummation scene with Sully in the motel room also seems modeled after Bergman's *Persona*. After a drunken night of sexual confession, Alma is awoken by the specter of her patient, the silently seductive Elisabeth, entering her room. The two erotically caress each other and then part. However, the next day when Alma asks Elisabeth if she came to her room the night before, she smiles mysteriously and shakes her head.[5]

FIGURE 2.3 *Elisabeth (Liv Ullmann) enters the bedroom of Alma (Bibi Andersson) in what may or may not be a dream in Ingmar Bergman's* Persona *(AB Svensk Filmindustri, 1966).*

The border between sleeping fantasy and waking reality is similarly blurred in *Americana*. As with the earlier Old Holly scene, David takes a nap during intermission, and all the incestuous desires indulged thereafter amount to little more than a wet dream. Sully's tale about Uncle-Father Malcolm has the typical effect of a good bedtime story—it puts David to sleep. He claims to awake, but this claim is dubious: "I woke in the middle of the night. Sullivan was gone. The wind blew a piece of paper across the bed and I got up and lowered the window. Then I smelled cookies baking" (*A* 331). The baking cookies provide a smoking-gun detail carefully prepared for in an earlier chapter. Visiting his friend Brand before the road trip west, David wandered into Brand's kitchen pantry:

> How long had it been since I had stood in a pantry at midnight, the dark shelves lined with cookie jars, jam and spices? Taste and smell can safecrack memory in the shadow of an instant, and in that pantry, nibbling dry cookies with the compulsive fervor of a penitent seeking the message of his past, I returned to a tight hot room in another town, the idle perfume of a summer. (*A* 115)

The pantry triggers memories for David as vividly as Proust's madeleine: pantry→cookies→mother→primal scene. Later in the motel, DeLillo interjects a calculated chapter break after David allegedly wakes. Perhaps the time it takes to turn the page is just long enough for the reader to wonder, "How the hell is Sully baking cookies in their motel room?" She is not. David is dreaming. In his enchanted mind he is not in a motel with Sully but back in the kitchen with Ann. The vicarious consummation conjures a scene which itself never took place outside the realm of imagination. This is pure narcissistic fantasy—a reflection of a reflection of the idealized mirror-image confrontation with Mother.

Dream logic allows David to enter not just the body of Sully but also her mind:

> I began to think her thoughts or what I imagined to be her thoughts. I became third person in my own mind. (Or her mind.) And in her as deep as I could go, hard and wild as I could strive, I listened to what she was thinking. Little mother's sons. He wants to wake up alone. Michelangelo's David. Wasp of the Wild West. He is home at last. (*A* 333–34)

Just as David fantasized being "spliced into the image" of Burt Lancaster (*A* 13), here he imaginatively splices his way into Sully. But projection screens are impenetrable and only reflect back imagos of the self. The next morning David has to ask, "What took place? What occurred or happened? It seems to have slipped my mind?" (*A* 336) Sully avoids specifics: "It stopped raining and the fantasies came out to play. Your home movie had put you in a state of anguish. I tried to console you. You wanted to be drenched in sin, and so I made it my business to help you along. Old friends have obligations to each other" (A 336). Critics have assumed David had sex with his surrogate mother, and that is certainly what he fantasized doing. But I contend that Sully's contributions to drenching David in sin are discharged not sexually but narratively: through the stormy tale of Uncle Malcolm, matching his confession of incestuous longing for his mother with her confession that she was a byproduct of incest (the *Hamlet* variety) between a wife and her husband's brother. The consolation she offers him isn't sex but language. She tells him a story.

Americana's shift from film to narrative, and ultimately to narrative-about-film, traverses the Lacanian register from specular fantasies of the Imaginary to the socialization and language of the Symbolic. None of these routes leads to absolute truth, stable identity, or crisis resolution, but instead loop back and forth in an endless circuit of signification. David Cowart was the first to detect a Lacanian undercurrent in the novel:

> The subject cannot know itself, and language, the Symbolic Order, discovers only its own play, its own energies, never the bedrock reality it supposedly names, glosses, gives expression to. Hence DeLillo actually echoes Lacan . . . in speaking of "interlinear notes" to the text of appearances, a presence at the edge of mirrors, a "truth beneath the symbols." *Americana* is the record of an attempt to break out of the endlessly circular signifying chain of images replicating and playing off each other to infinity. (136)

The attempt fails. The "truth beneath the symbols"—what Lacan terms "the Real"—remains permanently out of reach. David Bell, like the Lacanian child, longs to be folded into the depths of maternal plenitude. However, like the mythical Narcissus, David can never penetrate past the reflective surfaces that bounce back images of himself.

In Ovid's *Metamorphoses* Narcissus laments, "Alas, this fatal image wins my love, as I behold it. But I cannot press my arms around the form I see, the form that gives me joy. What strange mistake has intervened betwixt us and our love?" (Ovid) For Lacan, Narcissus is the epitome of the postmodern subject whose "strange mistake" begins with the primordial confusion of self and other. There is no avoiding this confusion. Alienating misrecognition stands as a sort of Lacanian original sin from which no one is exempt: it is part and parcel with the sin of being born. All of us are inevitably, irreparably splintered subjects from our earliest experiences this side of the womb. What makes David Bell so interesting in the present context is the compulsiveness and ingenuity with which he attempts to deny this rupture and to restore an

FIGURE 2.4 Narcissus *(1597–1599) by Caravaggio. Oil on canvas. Galleria Nazionale d'Arte Antica, Rome, Italy.*

idealized union, even in the face of repeated failure. In *Family Complexes* Lacan characterizes such fantasies as "nostalgia for wholeness":

> If we had to define the most abstract form in which it is found, we would characterise it as a perfect assimilation of totality to being. In this formula . . . will be recognised the nostalgias of humanity; the metaphysical mirage of universal harmony; the mystical abyss of affective fusion; the social utopia of totalitarian dependency—all derived from the longings for a paradise lost before birth and from the most obscure aspirations for death. (23)

Lacanian theory does not abide such pipe dreams, nor does DeLillo's art. David's utopian aspirations, at once deeply personal and representatively national, are systematically exposed in DeLillo's extraordinary first novel as the insubstantial illusions of the American Narcissus.

3

Libranth

Nicholas Branch's Joycean labyrinth

Libra is a labyrinth. It is modeled in part after the original Labyrinth built by Daedalus, the cunning artificer immortalized by Ovid in the *Metamorphoses*. More specifically, *Libra* follows the labyrinthine blueprint of James Joyce's *A Portrait of the Artist as a Young Man*, where Joyce canonized Daedalus as the patron saint of artists by metamorphosing him into Stephen Dedalus. Don DeLillo is a descendent in this literary line. At the beginning of his first published interview, when Tom LeClair asked why he was so reluctant to speak about himself and his work, DeLillo opened with a quote from Stephen Dedalus in *A Portrait*:

> Silence, exile, cunning, and so on. It's my nature to keep quiet about most things. Even the ideas in my work. When you try to unravel something you've written, you belittle it in a way. It was created as a mystery, in part. . . . If you're able to be straightforward and penetrating about this invention of yours, it's almost as though you're saying it wasn't altogether necessary. The sources weren't deep enough. (LeClair 4)

The present essay aims to unravel some of *Libra*'s mysteries, following Ariadne's thread back to the heart of the labyrinth.

In his piece titled "DeLillo's Dedalian Artists," Mark Osteen argues, "DeLillo's artists repeatedly reenact this pattern of seclusion and emergence, entrapment and escape, and their metamorphoses render them temporarily monstrous, malformed, or moribund before they die or emerge in a new guise. DeLillo's artists embody both the Minotaur and Daedalus, who leaves the labyrinth but loses something priceless in his flight to freedom" (137). Osteen directs his lens at three of DeLillo's artistic characters: rock musician Bucky Wunderlick from *Great Jones Street*, novelist Bill Gray from *Mao II*, and performance artist Lauren Hartke in *The Body Artist*. However, DeLillo has also devised several covert artists who surreptitiously lay claim to the Dedalian legacy. He frequently features characters that function as creative agents in/of their narratives, even though they are not ostensibly artists by trade. Mathematician Billy Twillig (*Ratner's Star*), waste management executive Nick Shay (*Underworld*), unemployed currency analyst Benno Levin (*Cosmopolis*), documentarian Jim Finley (*Point Omega*), and compliance and ethics officer Jeff Lockhart (*Zero K*) have each been interpreted by various critics as metafictional artificers; that is, as the authors, narrators, conceivers, or dreamers of all or parts of the narratives in which they are embedded.[1]

One of DeLillo's most intricately imbricated artificers is Nicholas Branch. Officially he is "a retired senior analyst of the Central Intelligence Agency, hired on contract to write the secret history of the assassination of President Kennedy" (*L* 15). Covertly he is a double agent, an insurgent novelist who has penetrated the citadel of history. In the words of Ovid used as the epigraph for *A Portrait*, "*Et ignotas animum dimittit in artes* [And he turned his mind toward unknown arts]" (3). Branch turns his mind toward unknown arts, and in the process he converts his CIA historical archive into a creative writer's workshop, a "room of theories and dreams" (*L* 14). There he conceives a labyrinthine fiction about the Kennedy assassination. The result is the book *Libra*. DeLillo cunningly frames Nicholas Branch as the artificer of the narrative we read. DeLillo invents arch-fabulator Branch, who invents arch-conspirator Win Everett, who invents a prototype for the shooter eventually cast as Lee Harvey Oswald, who is constantly inventing aliases and imagining doubles. Branch identifies deeply with Oswald and the rogue CIA conspirators. He depicts them as his doppelgangers, his secret sharers. He abandons history for fiction, exercising creative license to project his thoughts, experiences, and condition onto his characters.

Nicholas Branch's chief literary exemplar for this regenerative process is James Joyce. Branch borrows several motifs and narrative strategies from *A Portrait* as his paradigm for *Libra*. Like the mythical Daedalus, Branch is an exile who attempts to invent his way out of imprisonment. Like Stephen Dedalus, Branch constructs a *Künstlerroman* with an eye toward freedom, attempting to use fiction as wings to fly past nets cast to ensnare him. However, unlike them both, Branch ultimately fails. The fiction he constructs as a counternarrative to history does not free him. On the contrary, the book itself becomes a labyrinth, a prison-house of language from which none can escape, including the artificer who created it.

Metafictional self-portraits

Over the years DeLillo has acknowledged to multiple interviewers how reading Joyce had a formative impact on him as an aspiring writer.[2] He references Stephen Dedalus directly in his first novel *Americana*, where protagonist David Bell recalls, "At Leighton Gage College I wanted to be known as Kinch. This is Stephen Dedalus's nickname in *Ulysses*, which I was reading at the time" (*A* 143). In *Libra* Nicholas Branch explicitly invokes Joyce in relation to the Kennedy assassination. Reflecting on the Warren Report, "Branch thinks this is the megaton novel James Joyce would have written if he'd moved to Iowa City and lived to be a hundred" (*L* 181). Expanding his scope to encompass all the data in his Library of Babel, his room of theories about the assassination and dreams about the perpetrators, Branch reflects, "This is the Joycean Book of America, remember—the novel in which nothing is left out" (*L* 182). It may sound as if Branch has *Ulysses* in mind as his touchstone, but he ends up channeling *A Portrait* instead, that seminal chronicle of the dark arts cunningly conceived under conditions of silence and exile. Branch's Joycean Book of America is the Joycean Book of the Labyrinth.

In 1983 DeLillo wrote a *Rolling Stone* article on the assassination. As his title unmistakably indicates, he was already conceptualizing this cataclysm in terms of the labyrinth: he called the piece "American Blood: A Journey through the Labyrinth of Dallas and JFK." In retrospect one can see DeLillo conceiving the themes that would gestate over the next five years into *Libra*. Notice, for instance, how his historical understanding of this American assassination bleeds into the European literature best suited to express it:

> What has become unraveled since that afternoon in Dallas is not the plot, of course, not the dense mass of characters and events, but the sense of a coherent reality most of us shared. We seem from that moment to have entered a world of randomness and ambiguity, a world totally modern in the way it shades into the century's "emptiest" literature, the study of what is uncertain and unresolved in our lives, the literature of estrangement and silence. A European body of work, largely. (AB 22)

Taken in tandem with that telling reference to "Labyrinth" in the title, it seems that DeLillo already has his sights on Daedalus-Joyce-Dedalus as the Orion's Belt pointing him toward *Libra*.

DeLillo ruminates in "American Blood" on the trope of the double: "A double in literature sometimes represents the hero's secret self or primitive self. There is a 'mysterious communication' between them, in Joseph Conrad's phrase. Oswald can't be the hero in the traditional tale, which means he must be the secret self" (AB 22). And who is Oswald's secret sharer? DeLillo concludes, "Oswald was his own double" (AB 22). This argument leads down the path of metafiction, since it involves reading Oswald at both author and character:

> "Lee Harvey Oswald" often seems a secret design worked out by men that will never surface—a procedural diagram, a course in fabricated biography. Who put him together? He is not an actor so much as he is a character, a fictional character. . . . Oswald seems to be scripted out of doctored photos, tourist cards, change-of-address cards, mail-order forms, visa applications, pseudonyms. His life as we've come to know it is a construction of doubles. (AB 24)

Essayist DeLillo introduces an approach that Novelist DeLillo will later expand upon, populating *Libra* with multiple authors who double as characters. The mirrored halls of this labyrinth are constructed and presided over by a primary agent of central intelligence: Nicholas Branch.

I am not the first critic to recognize *Libra*'s echoes of *A Portrait*. Jesse Kavadlo describes DeLillo's novel as "an inverted *Künstlerroman*, not a portrait of the artist as a young man but the portrait of the assassin. Oswald the would-be artist lays down the pen and picks up the sword, or worse, the gun with the telescopic sight" (69). Peter Boxall draws an analogy to *A Portrait* by asserting that "Oswald's search, then, for what Joyce's Dedalus describes as a 'mode of life or art' in which to express himself 'freely' and wholly,' is held within a kind of vice of authorship, a pincer action of authorial control" (135). Furthermore, he argues, "Oswald, like Dedalus, attempts to forge his own consciousness. His recurrent image of himself as a man of action, walking in the night in the 'rain-slick streets,' is one that is driven by the idea that he might be able, through a kind of covert, personal insurrection, to forge himself in the smithy of his own revolutionary soul" (135–36). However, Boxall sees Oswald's plans as thwarted by other author-figures in the conspiracy who try to limit his actions, thwart his agency, and conscript him into their plots. He detects Branch as the authorial agency above and behind all the others:

> Of all the controlling figures in the novel, Nicholas Branch is perhaps the most powerful. Branch can appear to be the novel's uber-narrator, retrospectively choreographing the development both of Oswald's convoluted career, and of the Everett/Parmenter/Mackey plot to implicate Oswald in the assassination. Indeed, his influence can appear so powerful, at times, as to virtually drown out the sound of Oswald's voice, as well as those of Everett, Parmenter, and Mackey. (137)

The term "uber-narrator" perfectly captures Branch's central role in the narrative, one where his presence remains palpable even in other characters' scenes. As Boxall puts it, "The narrative is balanced and tuned in such a way that, even as the cast of assassination characters move and speak, we can sometimes see, stirring behind the fabric of their lives, visible through the taut skin of the bright hot skies, the outline of Branch, at his computer, in his room of theories in 1988" (138). I share this metafictional reading and wish to reinforce, extend, and complicate that approach by studying the intertextual palimpsest on which Branch's outline is traced.

Joyce critics beat DeLillo critics to this sort of exegesis by generations. There is a long tradition of reading Stephen as the uber-narrator of *A Portrait*, though Joyceans call it by different names. In *The Teller in the Tale* Louis D. Rubin, Jr., argues that Stephen "is an 'effaced narrator' only in that he never uses the pronoun 'I' to tell his story; in point of fact he is very much *not* effaced, very much present and active, and highly interested in letting the reader know he is there" (146). John Paul Riquelme riffs off Rubin's title in his book *Teller and Tale in Joyce's Fiction: Oscillating Perspectives*. Riquelme agrees that Stephen is the effaced narrator, but he also recognizes the broader epistemological challenge this poses:

> The term *narrator* names a problem for literary criticism. It points to the mediation of a consciousness, the author's, through language, a mediation that occurs in every narration. When we assert the effacing of the narrator, we do not thereby efface the conundrum at the base of storytelling. Impersonality is simply one among many possible disguises, or personae, in narration. . . . As a persona, it can be neither wholly personal nor wholly impersonal, and never absolutely invisible. (131)

In *Ulysses and the Metamorphosis of Stephen Dedalus*, Margaret McBride reads *Stephen Hero*, *Portrait*, and *Ulysses* as "a series of increasingly self-conscious artifices" in which Stephen is the "arranger" or "Author"—"But (and this point cannot be overstated) that Author is never James Joyce. Rather, within every tale there appears a character who is, quite distinctly, a writer, and this writer-artist may be telling the tale. In essence, the three stories follow an identical paradigm: the text creates the writer who in turn creates the text" (13). McBride understands such metafiction "not as autobiographical but as *autological*, as a sophisticated, self-reflexive system dramatizing its own conception and development" (30, emphasis in original).

My understanding of *Libra* is likewise autological. That is, I am not merely reading "Nicholas Branch" as a stand-in and pseudonym for Don DeLillo. I am arguing that, in McBride's words, "the text creates the writer who in turn creates the text." By the final lines of *A Portrait*—"Dublin 1904 / Trieste 1914" (224)—Stephen has embarked upon the odyssey that will ultimately lead him to write the story of his artistic genesis—*A Portrait of the Artist as a Young Man*—the story the reader just finished reading. Similarly, by the conclusion of *Libra* Nicholas Branch has reached the end of his tether as a historian and has made the fateful decision to reconstruct the story instead as fiction, one which not only delivers a fantastic conspiracy to kill President Kennedy but also doubles as his chronicle of artistic apprenticeship, *Libra*, the story the reader just finished reading. Tim Engles argues that there are two protagonists in the novel: "Not only the central character in a story that is being told [Lee Harvey Oswald], but also the teller of that story, an unnamed figure who sorts through incomplete and conflicting bits of evidence in a narrative effort that becomes its own drama" (254). Engles is right about there being a second protagonist; I would argue, however, that we do know the identity of this "unnamed figure"—and it's not the name on the book's cover. Nicholas Branch is as narratologically distinct from Don DeLillo as Stephen Dedalus is from James Joyce. An autological approach to *Libra* reveals Branch as the internal teller of the tale. *A Portrait* serves as the blueprint for Branch's metafictional *Künstlerroman*.[3]

From the nightmare of history
to the dreams of fiction

Both *A Portrait of the Artist as a Young Man* and *Libra* cross the minefield from history to fiction. "History," Stephen Dedalus famously declares in *Ulysses*, "is a nightmare from which I am trying to awake" (28). It is important to note, however, that Stephen had not always held this disillusioned perspective. As a boy in *A Portrait*, Stephen is enthralled by history and feels destined for historic greatness. His father teaches him to lionize Charles Stewart Parnell as the martyred would-be messiah of Ireland, and his priests train him to worship and emulate the examples of the Virgin Mary and Jesus Christ (remember that his namesake Saint Stephen was the first Christian martyr). The first test of his capacity for heroism comes when he protests his unjust corporal punishment from Father Dolan. Summoning up his courage, he reflects, "He would go up and tell the rector that he had been wrongly punished. A thing like that had been done before by somebody in history, by some great person whose head was in the books of history. . . . History was all about those men and what they did" (46–47). His protest at the end of the first chapter is successful, and he is hailed by classmates as a hero (remember that Joyce's first attempt to tell Stephen's story was titled *Stephen Hero*). By the second chapter, however, Stephen has transformed into a malcontented teen, drifting listlessly into squalor as his father's income dwindles and his status diminishes. Nevertheless, he still privately believes he is bound for glory: "The hour when he too would take his part in the life of that world seemed drawing near and in secret he began to make ready for the great part which he felt awaited him the nature of which he only dimly apprehended" (54).

Though Stephen encounters several setbacks and mortifications over the course of the novel, his faith in his future prominence remains intact. But his relationship to history shifts dramatically. As he heeds the calling of his true artistic vocation, he comes to regard history not as the proving ground for his future success but as a fatal trap he must avoid. He tells Davin in Chapter V, "When the soul of a man is born in this country there are nets flung at it to hold it back from flight. You talk to me of nationality, language, religion. I shall try to fly by those nets" (179). The flight metaphor harkens back to Daedalus, but it also anticipates Walter Benjamin's Angel of History:

> This is how one pictures the angel of history. His face is turned toward the past. Where we perceive a chain of events, he sees one single catastrophe that keeps piling ruin upon ruin and hurls it in front of his feet. The angel would like to stay, awaken the dead, and make whole what has been smashed. But a storm is blowing from Paradise; it has got caught in his wings with such violence that the angel can no longer close them. The storm irresistibly propels him into the future to which his back is turned, while the pile of debris before him grows skyward. This storm is what we call progress. (Benjamin 257–58)

This is the fate that awaits Stephen if he gets caught in the storm of Irish history. So he fits himself with sturdier wings and fixes his sights outward toward cosmopolitan Europe and forward toward a future in art. As an artist he hopes to look back on the past in his own terms, not those prescribed by his history, and finally become free "to forge in the smithy of my soul the uncreated conscience of my race" (224).

In his 1997 essay "The Power of History," DeLillo similarly pits fiction against history. He asserts, "Against the force of history, so powerful, visible and real, the novelist poses the idiosyncratic self. Here it is, sly, mazed, mercurial, scared half-crazy. It is also free and undivided, the only thing that can match the enormous dimensions of social reality" (PH). This rendition of history emphasizes its power in the abusive, coercive sense of the word: history as state-sponsored institution for controlling the individual. He enlists the novelist's irrepressible weirdness and creative liberty as the antidote to history.

> It is almost inevitable that the fiction writer, dealing with this reality, will violate any number of codes and contracts. He will engineer a swerve from the usual arrangements that bind a figure in history to what has been reported, rumored, confirmed or solemnly chanted. It is fiction's role to imagine deeply, to follow obscure urges into unreliable regions of experience—child-memoried, existential and outside time. (PH)

He posits an oppositional relationship between fiction and history comparable to a prisoner's position vis-à-vis the penal system. DeLillo's rhetoric in "The Power of History" is relentlessly incarcerational; history aims to bind and fiction seeks to break free: "The novel is the dream release, the suspension of reality that history needs to escape its own brutal confinements." The idiosyncratic, disobedient novelists he champions "will sooner or later state their adversarial relationship with history" (PH).

Nicholas Branch started out as a loyal Agency man entrusted to write the CIA's secret history of the Kennedy assassination. Like Stephen Dedalus, he gradually transforms himself into a fiction maker. Unlike Stephen (at least young Stephen of *A Portrait*), Branch ultimately discovers that one can be bound as irrevocably in fiction as in history. Nevertheless, he first manages to assemble a compelling counternarrative to the history he was charged to write. In the process he tells the story of his own metamorphosis by proxy through his avatars in *Libra*, historical figures whose trajectories likewise lead them away from history into the dreamscapes of fiction. How does a CIA historian figure out how to construct such a metafictional labyrinth? By following the example of the greatest novel about artistic apprenticeship ever written: *A Portrait of the Artist as a Young Man*.

From a young age, Lee like Stephen believes he is destined for historic greatness. He immerses himself in Marxist literature and becomes convinced that his wretchedness is historically determined by capitalism. He vows to join the struggle against this system of exploitation and thus become swept up in history. From Lee's perspective joining history entails sacrificing individuality. The epigraph to Part One of *Libra* establishes this unequivocally. Lee writes to his brother, "Happiness is not based on oneself, it does not consist of a small home, of taking and getting. Happiness is taking part in the struggle, where there is no borderline between one's own personal world and the world in general" (*L* 1). As in both *A Portrait* and "The Power of History," history is here characterized as a system that completely subsumes the individual. At times Lee embraces this self-sacrifice for a greater good. In military prison at Atsugi he reflects,

> Maybe what has to happen is that the individual must allow himself to be swept along, must find himself in the stream of no-choice, the single direction. This is what makes things inevitable. You use the restrictions and penalties they invent to make yourself stronger. History means to merge. The purpose of history is to climb out of your own skin. He knew what Trotsky had written, that revolution leads us out of the dark night of the isolated self. (*L* 101)

Much later, after his defection and return to America and his growing involvement in the assassination conspiracy, a part of him still clings to the romance of surrendering to history: "Summer was building toward a vision, a history. He felt he was being swept up, swept along, done with being a pitiful individual, done with isolation" (*L* 322).

Lee's desire to lose himself in history is at odds with his counterimpulse to achieve personal notoriety. This individualist aspiration is expressed through dreams, fantasies, films, and fiction. The self-mythology of Stephen Hero is answered in *Libra* by Oswald Hero. As an adolescent Lee dreams, "He lay near sleep, falling into reverie, the powerful world of Oswald-hero, guns flashing in the dark. The reverie of control, perfection of rage, perfection of desire, the fantasy of night, rain-slick streets, the heightened shadows of men in dark coats, like men on movie posters. The dark had a power" (*L* 46). He imagines himself as the hero in a spy-thriller or film noir, and this tendency to invent more interesting alter egos expands and diversifies over the course of the novel. He creates multiple aliases and increasingly views his own actions from a detached perspective. As Lee dips his toe into real espionage by divulging secrets about the U-2 spy plane, he views the scene as if it is being performed by someone else: "He was not connected to anything here and not quite connected to himself. . . . He barely noticed himself talking. That was the interesting part. The more he spoke, the more he felt he was softly split in two" (*L* 89, 90). One could psychoanalyze his dissociative behavior as symptomatic of schizophrenia. But in the world of *Libra* it seems more like a fiction writer's habit of mind, the ability to double the self as other (cf. "American Blood"), to convert first person into third person.

It should come as no surprise then that Lee is drawn to writing fiction. Plotting an exit strategy from the Marines and from America, he fills out an application where he lists his vocational interest as "*To be a short story writer on contemporary American life*" (*L* 134, emphasis in original). He tries his hand at writing in the Soviet Union, producing with great effort a few essays and a longer memoir of his experiences. But as his presumptuously titled "Historic Diary" suggests, Lee still regards himself as a servant of history in these early efforts. It takes the Mephisphophelean David Ferrie to lead Lee (whom he calls Leon) down a different path. One can almost see Branch peeking from behind the arras and whispering in Ferrie's ear as he counsels, "There's something else that's generating this event. A pattern outside experience. Something that *jerks* you out of the spin of history. I think you've had it backwards all this time. You wanted to enter history. Wrong approach, Leon. What you really want is out. Get out. Jump out. Find your place and your name on another level" (*L* 384, emphasis in original).

Lee does not find his new place and name until he lands in jail after the assassination. Incarcerated in a Dallas prison cell, he has a vocational epiphany. His calling is not to sacrifice himself to history or to be a patsy in someone else's plot. No, he must seize control of his own story by deliberately and painstakingly reconstructing the assassination on his own terms: "Lee Harvey Oswald was awake in his cell. It was beginning to occur to him that he'd found his life's work. After the crime comes the reconstruction" (L 434). He plans to use his imprisonment as an opportunity to craft a self-portrait of the assassin. "Time to grow in self-knowledge, to explore the meaning of what he's done. . . . This was the true beginning" (L 438). The metafictional mind-merge with Branch is never stronger than in Lee's prison epiphany. It is impossible to distinguish where author ends and character begins in this description of the reconstruction: "They will give him writing paper and books. He will fill his cell with books about the case. He will have time to educate himself in criminal law, ballistics, acoustics, photography. Whatever pertains to the case he will examine and consume. . . . His life had a single clear subject now, called Lee Harvey Oswald" (L 434–35). Is this the raison d'être for Oswald or Branch? At this point that is a distinction without a difference.

Identical as they may appear, however, there are crucial differences between what Oswald aspires to forge in his smithy and what Branch actually forges in his. Lee is vitalized by his prison epiphany to start afresh:

> The more time he spent in his cell, the stronger he would get. Everybody knew who he was now. This charged him with strength. There was clearly a better time beginning, a time of deep reading in the case, of self-analysis and reconstruction. He no longer saw confinement as a lifetime curse. He'd found the truth about a room. He could easily live in a cell half this size. (L 435)

Branch knows better. He knows this is not Lee's Bethlehem but his Golgotha. He knows Lee will not live to begin "his life's work" but will be killed the next day. He also knows that the chore of reconstruction will eventually be handed over to Branch himself. Fifteen years into that impossible historical task, Branch was thoroughly sapped of all strength and zeal for the job. So he turned instead to fiction, the results of which are *Libra*. There he tells the story of Oswald, the assassination conspirators, and the beleaguered CIA historian sentenced to hard labor in the archival labyrinth. Lee's ecstasy echoes that of Stephen at the end of *A Portrait*, which itself echoes Daedalus's escape from the labyrinth: "Old father, old artificer, stand me now and ever in good stead" (224). Branch reconstructs the story in such a way as to negate such optimism. *A Portrait* concludes with Stephen's flight to freedom through art, and Lee is deluded enough to think a soaring triumph as a writer awaits him, too. He is wrong. *Libra* offers instead a myth of The Fall.[4] Branch borrows *A Portrait*'s palette but turns the canvas upside down to portray a spiraling descent into exile, imprisonment, and death.

FIGURE 3.1 Icarus *(1635–37) by Jacob Peter Gowy. Oil on canvas. Museo del Prado, Madrid, Spain.*

The fall

The Labyrinth represents more than artistic ingenuity and inscrutable complexity. It is a sinister emblem steeped in secrecy, shame, and guilt. King Minos had Daedalus build the Labyrinth to conceal the Minotaur, the unholy byproduct of Queen Pasiphaë's sex with a bull. The god Poseidon was responsible for making Pasiphaë desire the bull, but the consummation was made possible by Daedalus, who put his cunning to perverse use by constructing a device to make intercourse between them possible. This was not Daedalus's first abominable act. Before his notorious exploits in Crete, he was a renowned artist in Athens. He was so envious of a rival artist, his nephew Perdix (sometimes called Talos), he hurled him off the Acropolis. According to Ovid, Athena saved Perdix by turning him into a partridge so he could fly to safety (note the appropriateness of Icarus's eventual death by falling as punishment for Daedalus's earlier crime). Variations on the myth maintain that Daedalus succeeded in murdering Perdix and was banished from Athens. Either way, he was on the run from the law long before he built the Labyrinth and those prison-break wings. Had he not been a fugitive he would never have landed in Crete in the first place.[5] Perhaps the profane Labyrinth could only have been conceived by an artificer as devious as he was inventive. No great stretch of the imagination is needed to link the criminals in *Libra* with Daedalus. They are his rightful heirs as diabolical counterfeiters, killers, and exiles.

The rogue CIA agents who conspire against President Kennedy begin their plots in exile. Win Everett, Larry Parmenter, and T. J. Mackey are veterans of the failed Bay of Pigs invasion. Afterward these anti-Castro diehards were each reprimanded and ostracized by the CIA. These outcasts were once devout worshippers of the Agency. Larry Parmenter's wife, Beryl, recognizes his devotion as religious zealotry: "Central Intelligence. Beryl saw it as the best organized church in the Christian world, a mission to collect and store everything that everyone has ever said and then reduce it to a microdot and call it God" (*L* 260). Even as they devise their plots against the commander-in-chief, the plotters convince themselves that they remain loyal to the secret heart of the Agency. Win Everett foresees the day when his plot will be exposed and he will be held accountable; still, he seeks the approval of his superiors and believes he will ultimately be vindicated:

> They would be pleased by his willingness to cooperate. What's more, they would admire the complexity of his plan, incomplete as it was. It had art and memory. It had a sense of responsibility, or moral force. And it was a picture in the world of their own guilty wishes. He was never more surely an Agency man than in the first breathless days of dreaming up this plot. (*L* 364)

Again, one detects the outline of Branch behind such passages. He knows what it is like to be exiled by the CIA and yet remain, as Cranly puts it to Stephen, "supersaturated with the religion in which you say you disbelieve" (212). Branch also knows what it is like to rebel against that authority: *non serviam*: *I will not serve.*

Branch embraces Daedalus and Icarus as guiding spirits from *A Portrait*, but he also borrows the Christian iconography of The Fall, associated with the revolt of Lucifer's band of rebel angels and with the sin of Adam and Eve. This foundational myth is delivered most vividly by Father Arnall in his Chapter III sermon:

> Adam and Eve, my dear boys, were, as you know, our first parents and you will remember that they were created by God in order that the seats

in heaven left vacant by the fall of Lucifer and his rebellious angels might be filled again. Lucifer, we are told, was a son of the morning, a radiant and might angel; yet he fell: he fell and there fell with him a third part of the host of heaven: he fell and was hurled with his rebellious angels into hell. What his sin was we cannot say. Theologians consider that it was the sin of pride, the sinful thought conceived in an instant: *non serviam: I will not serve.* That instant was his ruin. He offended the majesty of God by the sinful thought of one instant and God cast him out of heaven into hell forever. (103, emphasis in original)

The rebel angels' fall into exile from heaven and imprisonment in hell is replicated by defiant humans' fall into exile from the Garden of Eden and imprisonment in this vale of tears called the world; a legacy inherited by us all, according to Catholic theology, in the form of original sin. Young Stephen trembles at his postlapsarian fate. He poignantly reflects,

The snares of the world were its ways of sin. He would fall. He had not yet fallen but he would fall silently, in an instant. Not to fall was too hard, too hard: and he felt the silent lapse of his soul, as it would be at some instant to come, falling, falling but not yet fallen, still unfallen but about to fall. (142)

Soon after, however, Stephen renounces his inheritance of original sin and instead lays claim to his redemptive artistic birthright from Daedalus, innocently ignoring all the sinister elements also associated with the cunning artificer. The old dispensation guaranteed his fall, but his new faith gives him a beatific vision of ascent:

Now, at the name of the fabulous artificer, he seemed to hear the noise of dim waves and to see a winged form flying above the waves and slowly climbing the air. What did it mean? Was it a quaint device opening a page of some medieval book of prophecies and symbols, a hawklike man flying sunward above the sea, a prophecy of the end he had been born to serve and had been following through the mists of childhood and boyhood, a symbol of the artist forging anew in his workshop out of the sluggish matter of the earth a new soaring impalpable imperishable being? (148)

Fortified by this soaring epiphany, Stephen no longer fears the fall. On the contrary, he comes to identify with Lucifer as a kindred rebel against God's yoke. He intentionally echoes Lucifer's *non serviam* in his declaration of artistic independence to Cranly:

I will not serve that in which I no longer believe whether it calls itself my home, my fatherland or my church: and I will try to express myself in some mode of life or art as freely as I can and as wholly as I can, using for my defence the only arms I allow myself to use, silence—exile and cunning. (218)

This is of course the very passage DeLillo invokes in his first interview with Tom LeClair.

Nicholas Branch appropriates the falling iconography from *A Portrait*, adopting and adapting it throughout *Libra*. Win Everett first introduces the theme. Contemplating how to redeem his catastrophe in Cuba, he uses language that distinctly echoes Lucifer's fallen angels: "Then the long slow fall. I wanted to sanctify the failure, make it everlasting. If we couldn't have success, let's make the most of our failure" (*L* 27). Branch structures the chapters in such a way that several end with falling imagery and then segue directly into falling again at the beginning of the next chapter. These chapters are ostensibly taking place at different times and places and involve different subplots. But Branch's presiding genius as the uber-narrator is subtly insinuated through his arrangement of the materials. For instance, at the end of the "26 April" chapter Win drifts off to sleep: "It was all part of the long fall, the general sense that he was dying" (*L* 79). The next chapter, "In Atsugi," wakes with the same imagery: "The dark plane drifted down, sweeping out an arc of hazy sky to the east of the runway" (*L* 80).

The "dark plane" refers to the U-2 spy plane. Branch bookends "In Atsugi" with the slow descent of an ejected pilot from a U-2 plane, the most evocative description of falling in the novel:

He is coming down to springtime in the Urals and he finds that his privileged vision of the earth is an inducement to truth. He wants to tell the truth. He wants to live another kind of life, outside secrecy and guilt and the pull of grave events. This is what the pilot thinks, rocking softly down to the tawny fields of a landscape so gentle and welcoming it might almost be home. (*L* 116)

In fact, as the novel soon reminds us, ejected U-2 pilot Francis Gary Powers falls into secrecy and guilt, not out of it. His descent lands him in the Soviet Union, in prison, and in history. Defector Lee Oswald is allowed to visit him there and instantly intuits the *non serviam* camaraderie of a fellow fallen angel: "Paid to fly a plane and incidentally to kill himself if the mission failed. Well we don't always follow orders, do we? Some orders require thought, ha ha. He wanted to call to the prisoner through the door, *You were right; good for you; disobey*" (*L* 196, emphasis in original). Branch returns to this imagery at the end of Oswald's life. Drifting into delirium after being shot by Jack Ruby, these are the final thoughts Branch gives him: "It is the white nightmare of noon, high in the sky over Russia.

Me-too and you-too. He is a stranger, in a mask, falling" (*L* 440). Revealingly, Lee's dying fall transitions directly into the final Branch section of the novel. You-too and Me-too.

Libranth

Libra is a highly resonant title. Peter Boxall hears in the title "a balanced tension between liberty and zodiacal predestination" (132). The root of "liberty" is the Latin *liber*, which is indeed a near cognate of "Libra," and for that matter of "Labyrinth," too. But "liber" also lies at the root of the French *livre* and the Spanish *libro*, all of which might be housed in an English "library" (or the Texas School Book Depository). I am referring of course to the word *Book*. Wordsmith Don DeLillo is doubtlessly aware this etymology, as was his metafictional mentor Jorge Luis Borges, that great librarian/labyrinth-builder. In Borges's "The Garden of Forking Paths" the sinologist Stephen Albert solves the riddle of Ts'ui Pen's missing labyrinth by recognizing that it refers to a *libro*: "Ts'ui Pen must at one point have remarked, 'I shall retire to write a book,' and at another point, 'I shall retire to construct a labyrinth.' Everyone pictured two projects; it occurred to no one that book and labyrinth were one and the same" (Borges 124).[6] Likewise, the book and the labyrinth are one and the same in *Libra*.

The binary opposition Boxall hears in the title issues from the novel's central conflict between fiction and history, between the free flux of fiction's continuous becoming and the intransigent bind of history's fixed narrative. As Boxall sees it, Oswald is trying to free himself through fictional self-determination, but he keeps getting ensnared by history:

> Oswald's becoming as pure fiction, as a form of invention without rule, is repeatedly returned to historical and discursive formulae which deny the radical, revolutionary possibility of fiction. Indeed, the very process by which Oswald seeks to slip the leash of those forces that are scripting him is that which forces him deeper and deeper into the role which he has been assigned. (*L* 136)

This reading is consistent with the DeLillo's dualistic opposition between history and fiction in "The Power of History." He once told interviewer Kevin Connolly,

> In a theoretical sense I think fiction can be a refuge and a consolation. In *Libra* the national leader still dies, but for one thing, at least we know how it happens. Beyond that, fiction offers patterns and symmetry that we don't find in the experience of ordinary living. Stories are consoling, fiction is one of the consolation prizes for having lived in the world. (31)

Fiction certainly allows an author to impose pattern and symmetry, which theoretically might provide refuge and consolation. Not always, however, and not successfully in *Libra*. Branch may have turned away from history toward fiction in hopes of achieving Dedalian liberty.[7] But instead he constructs a book which functions as a metafictional prison. He and his characters are inextricably trapped inside the *Libranth*.

There are no emancipatory flights of escape as in *A Portrait*. No one gets out of *Libra* alive. The arch-conspirator Win Everett is the first to recognize the metafictional deathtrap:

> Plots carry their own logic. There is a tendency of plots to move toward death. He believed that the idea of death is woven into the nature of every plot. A narrative plot no less than a conspiracy of armed men. The tighter the plot of a story, the more likely it will come to death. A plot in fiction, he believed, is the way we localize the force of the death outside the book, play it off, contain it. (*L* 221)

Death is etched into the very structure of *Libra*. The Oswald chapters are titled with geographical markers and the conspiracy chapters with temporal markers. Had those chapters been numbered as in other DeLillo novels, there would be eleven chapters in Part One and thirteen in Part Two. A reader who notices this demarcation might wonder why the novel isn't divided evenly into two sections of twelve chapters each. In the chapter before "22 November," Branch slyly hints at the answer: "It's not surprising that Branch thinks of the day and month of the assassination in strictly numerical terms—11/22" (L 377). The following chapter detailing the assassination is the 11th in Part Two and the 22nd overall: 11/22, the date of Kennedy's death. The chapter detailing the assassination of Lee Harvey Oswald is the 24th overall: not only the day in November he died but also his age in years at the time. The novel begins with Lee underground in the New York subway and ends by returning him underground with his Fort Worth burial. In so many ways Branch plants secret codes and shapes perfect symmetries in his reconstruction of events.

These shrewd fictional maneuvers might provide temporary aesthetic pleasure, but they do not provide any lasting consolation or refuge from death. Quite the opposite, they condemn the characters to death sentences in *Libra*. Everett intuits his metafictional bind, realizing as he scripts the shooter that he himself is also a prescribed character: "We lead more interesting lives than we think. We are characters in plots, without the compression and numinous sheen. Our lives, examined carefully in all their affinities and links, abound with suggestive meaning, with themes and involute turnings we have not allowed ourselves to see completely. He would show the secret symmetries in a non-descript life" (*L* 78).

He inscribes these secret symmetries as an author, but he is also inscribed by them as a character.

The same holds true for Branch himself, and he knows it. He is responsible for building this labyrinth, but he is also one of its metafictional inmates. He inserts a coy self-allusion to that effect when describing Oswald's Atsugi incarceration:

> In the prison literature he'd read, Oswald was always coming across an artful old con who would advise the younger man, give him practical tips, talk in sweeping philosophical ways about the larger questions. Prison invited larger questions. It made you wish for an experienced perspective, for the knowledge of some grizzled figure with kind and tired eyes, a counselor, wise to the game. (*L* 99)

Branch has *Libra* in mind as "prison literature," and he has himself in mind as "the artful old con" who knows how this game is played. He might have made a wise counselor for young Lee had they been fellow prisoners in Atsugi—as opposed to fellow prisoners in *Libra*.

In 1988 DeLillo told *Washington Post* reporter Jim Naughton,

> I think Nicholas Branch has reached the point he has because he is so haunted by the story itself and by the people who are part of it," DeLillo says. "I think he is almost immobilized by sadness, compassion, regret and by the overwhelming sense that he is never going to be able to be able to do justice to the enormity of this story.

He added, "'Once you have read in the case I think you do become trapped forever,' he says. 'In fact I'm sure you do. This is certainly the most deeply haunting experience of my life, working on this book'" (Naughton). He ingeniously devised a literary hall of mirrors for depicting this haunting (and haunted) trap. DeLillo created uber-narrator Nicholas Branch who, after years of studying the case as a historian, attempted to break free through fiction. He turned to an ideal model for achieving freedom through art, *A Portrait of the Artist as a Young Man*, and tried to use it as a skeleton key to unlock his cell. The result is endlessly fascinating for readers, and for DeLillo is must be accounted a metafictional masterpiece. But judged by Branch's own standards, *Libra* is a failure, or more precisely "A Portrait of the Failed Escape Artist as an Old Man." "He knows he can't get out. The case will haunt him to the end" (*L* 445). That is, to the end of his life and to the end of the novel—which for a character stuck in a book amounts to the same thing. Near the middle of *Libra* Branch has a revelation: "This is the room of dreams, the room where it has taken him all these years to learn that his subject is not politics or violent crime but men in small rooms." This prompts him to ask, "Is he one of them now? Frustrated, stuck, self-watching, looking for a means of connection, a way to break out" (*L* 181). The answer—irrefutably, pathetically, metafictionally—is yes. He has insinuated himself into the deadly plot and consigned himself to the conspirators' fate. He is one of them, and they are part of him, now and forever, as prisoners of the *Libranth*.

4

"The Martiniad"

Nick Shay as embedded author in *Underworld*

The "Author's Note" at the end of *Libra* asserts, "Any novel about a major unresolved event would aspire to fill some of the blank spaces in the known record. To do this, I've altered and embellished reality, extended real people into imagined space and time, invented incidents, dialogues, and characters" (*L* 458). The novelist exercises his prerogative to forge missing links in history. In *Libra* DeLillo uses this creative license to fill in the blank space on the grassy knoll, identifying Raymo Benítez as the shooter who killed President Kennedy. *Underworld* is even more ambitious in many respects, expanding to a grand historical canvas which encompasses the entire Cold War era. The blank space at the heart of this novel, however, is comparatively small, personal, and idiosyncratic. DeLillo recovers through fiction a notoriously missing relic from baseball history: Bobby Thomson's home run ball from the 1951 game between the New York Giants and the Brooklyn Dodgers, the so-called "Shot Heard 'Round the World."[1] He invents a chain of possession beginning with Cotter Martin, an African American Giants fan who grabs the home run ball. It is then stolen and sold by Manx Martin, Cotter's whiskey-swigging dad. Ultimately, DeLillo has the ball pass down to its current owner, Nick Shay, a waste management executive and ex-Dodgers-fan. These inventions come across as entirely plausible, but their status and function as fictions invite much deeper consideration.

Follow the ball. It leaves Ralph Branca's hand and connects with Bobby Thomson's bat. It sails over Andy Pafko's head into the left field bleachers and into oblivion, only to be recovered through fantasy in *Underworld*.

But: *Whose fantasy is it?* Who invented this compelling but made-up story of what really happened on October 3, 1951? Remember that Marvin Lundy, the obsessive memorabilia collector who sells Nick the ball, claims not to know who first owned it. He can only trace the ball's provenance back to October 4, 1951, when Charles Wainwright first took possession. But the initial link back to the game eludes detection. So who provides that missing link? The obvious answer would be Don DeLillo. Of course, he did in fact compose, arrange, and commit to paper all of the characters, scenarios, and language of the novel. He is the sole author *of* the novel, but he is not the sole author *within* it. Rather, a separate character, distinct from DeLillo, functions as the creative agency behind the story of what happened on that fateful day. Subtle evidence throughout *Underworld* suggests that Nick Shay is the embedded author and implied narrator of the fantasy featuring Cotter and Manx Martin, that is, the October 3, 1951, sequence including the Prologue and the three Manx Martin chapters. Nick is not a "writer" in the sense of one who hammers words onto the page like DeLillo on his old Olympia typewriter. Nonetheless, he does fulfill the author-function in the crucial Cotter and Manx subplot, supplying the vested interest, narrative voice, and intelligent design behind those chapters.

A special reciprocity exists between DeLillo and Nick Shay. The novelist acknowledges their affinity in terms of the reshaping power of language. According to DeLillo in an interview with Maria Moss, Nick Shay thinks like a writer:

> There is this key scene in the book: he sits in a room with a Jesuit priest, and the priest asks him to name the parts of his shoe. This is important for me. He comes from a background where nobody knows these things, where it's not part of one's education. It tells him what he has to do in order to reshape himself, to become a man of the world. It's all about language. Maybe that's why *he very often seems to think like a writer.* (166–67, emphasis added)

Language is the portal through which a writer exerts transformative control over his world and himself. Nick turned to language as a young man to escape the killer he had become. He had long exhibited a capacity for storytelling and myth-making, most notably in his fantasy that his father was whacked by the mob. He sharpens his narrative impulses during his correctional period, where he acquires sophisticated skills of self-reinvention through language. The reformed Nick becomes a responsible citizen and bourgeois husband and father, but his gifts for linguistic reinvention never fade and are reanimated by the Thomson home run ball. He possesses both the motive and the narrative wherewithal to create an explanatory story for his prized souvenir. Nick shares with DeLillo not only an Italian-American Bronx background and Jesuit education, he also shares an inner compulsion to craft fictions from that past—to alter and embellish reality, extend real people into imagined space and time, invent incidents, dialogues, and characters.

Interwoven as a prominent thread within the larger fabric of *Underworld*, Nick's elaborate four-part intratext represents his imaginative attempt to answer otherwise unanswerable questions, about the ball and about himself. Had DeLillo placed Nick's intratext in its entirety at the end of the novel, then its coherence as a separately authored fiction in the present time of the novel would have been obvious, as with Tap's story "The Prairie" appended at the end of *The Names*. However, given *Underworld*'s bricolage techniques and thematic preoccupations with loss, fragmentation, and incomplete recuperation of the past's debris, it is appropriate that Nick's fiction should be cleaved into multiple segments, voices, and perspectives, bending back upon the larger narrative and retrofitted piecemeal as a microcosmic reiteration of the macrocosmos in which it is embedded. These tactics of obfuscation and occlusion work to conceal Nick's identity as embedded author and implied narrator, but his signature is unmistakable in the Cotter and Manx sections once one begins to search for it, hiding in plain sight.

Mise en Abyme: Embedded reflections of the young artificer

A reflection of the creator within his creation (mise en abyme) is already embedded in "Pafko at the Wall," the earlier novella later revised and integrated as Prologue to *Underworld*. Given DeLillo's repeated assurances that he does not plan his novels in advance, it seems highly unlikely that he wrote "Pafko" with an eye already toward repurposing it for *Underworld*. And yet Nick Shay, who is never referenced directly in "Pafko," already casts a shadow in the novella. At the very least, his later presence seems augured in retrospect, through this prescient aside about an isolated Dodger fan:

> There's a sixteen year-old in the Bronx who takes his radio up to the roof of his building so he can listen alone, a Dodger fan slouched in the gloom, and he hears the account of the misplayed bunt and the fly ball that scores the tying run and he looks out over the rooftops, the tar beaches with their clotheslines and pigeon coops and splatted condoms, and he is filled with total fear. The game doesn't change the way you sleep or wash your face or chew your food. It changes nothing but your life. (PWH 49)[2]

Who is this young man? It is tempting to interpret the figure as DeLillo himself, a brief glimpse of the wizard behind the curtain. Indeed, the basic facts of a Bronx teenager who listens to ballgames on the radio matches up with the novelist. But the figure is not autobiographical. As a lifelong Yankees fan who was fourteen years old and at the dentist's office when Thomson homered (Remnick 135), DeLillo sports a personal profile which diverges significantly from the inserted figure. Viewed exclusively within the original context of the novella, no conclusive identification is possible. The solitary Dodgers fan on his Bronx rooftop would have permanently remained an enigma had DeLillo not decoded this cipher in *Underworld*. Within this new context, the Bronx vignette *does* provide a glimpse of the teller behind the tale: Nick Shay.

The identity of the anonymous Brooklyn fan is revealed in the third chapter of *Underworld* when Nick recalls his whereabouts for the "Shot Heard 'Round the World":

> I had a portable radio I took everywhere. The beach, the movies—I went, it went. I was sixteen. And I listened to Dodger games on the roof. I liked to be alone. They were my team. I was the only Dodger fan in the neighborhood. I died inside when they lost. And it was important to die alone. Other people interfered. I had to listen alone. And then the radio told me whether I would live or die. (*U* 93)

Not only is Nick inserted into the October 3, 1951, saga, but he figures in retrospect as a kind of presiding genius, the youth who hovers outside the main action for now but will one day play a central role in the drama as the ultimate possessor of the miraculous ball. DeLillo told Marc Chénetier and François Happe in an interview,

> The ball generates the narrative. Again, this is not something I planned. I did not know that Nick Shay would own the baseball when I began to conceive of him as a character and when I began to write Part 1. It didn't occur to me for maybe three or four chapters into Part 1. It probably seems obvious to the reader that the main character is the guy who owns the baseball; that's why he is the main character. It did not occur to me, it had to occur to me as a revelation. I suddenly said to myself, "This is the guy who owns the ball! How obvious and how wonderful!" And again, this was another moment, like the backward structure of the book, in which I felt I was at the receiving end of instructions from some empyrean place. (105)

The chief catalyst and coalescing agent for the novel's structure is Nick Shay. Having fortuitously discovered his empyrean guide, DeLillo keeps his eye on the ball and his ear attuned to its possessor, following Nick's lead as the October 3, 1951, narrative transitions from the grand overture of the Prologue to what DeLillo has characterized as the "three-part sonata" (Echlin 149) of the Manx Martin chapters. The novelist talks about all the pieces clicking perfectly into place once he recognized that Nick was the ball's owner, and the intuitive rightness of that identification surely seemed ratified by the fact that *Nick was already embedded in the narrative*, like a legitimizing stamp of imprimatur, a preconceived mise en abyme.

FIGURE 4.1 *The famous mise en abyme effect, replicating images of Charles Foster Kane (Orson Welles), in Welles's* Citizen Kane *(RKO, 1941).*

André Gide is generally credited with coining the term mise en abyme in its current narratological sense as an image of the artist reflected in the work of art. In Gide's 1893 *Journals* he observes, "In a work of art, I rather like to find thus transposed, at the level of the characters, the subject of the work itself. Nothing sheds more light on the work or displays the proportions of the whole work more accurately." He gives various examples, from the paintings of Memling, Massys, and Velázquez, to narratives within narratives in *Hamlet, Wilhelm Meister,* and *The Fall of the House of Usher.* Finally he supplies the term through "comparison with the device from heraldry that involves putting a second representation of the original shield 'en abyme' within it" (qtd. Dällenbach 7).

Lucien Dällenbach provides the most thorough typological analysis of literary mises en abyme in his seminal study *The Mirror in the Text.* Dällenbach distills André Gide's initial articulation of the concept down to a concise formula: "The relation of the narrator N to his/her story S [is] the same as that of the narrator/character n to his/her story s" (18). Translating my present argument in terms of this shorthand equation, the relation of DeLillo (N) to *Underworld* (S) is equivalent to the relation of Nick Shay (n) to his imaginary rendition of October 3, 1951, (s). That Dällenbach expresses this relation using the variables N/n and S/s—Nick Shay's initials—is a happy coincidence, one which would not be lost on the author of *The Names.* It is important to stress that N≠n in any straightforward way, neither in Dällenbach's formulation nor in my argument. That is to say, I am not arguing that Nick Shay is simply an avatar for Don DeLillo, any more than Nicholas Branch was in the previous chapter on *Libra*. Rather, I am arguing that DeLillo bears a certain reciprocal *relation* to his fiction, and that he reflects this relation (mise en abyme) by embedding another artificer, Nick Shay, who in turn reflects a proportional relation to his fictional creations Cotter and Manx Martin.

Although mise en abyme is by no means unique to modern literature, it is a key hallmark of the metafictional tradition from which Don DeLillo descends. Steven G. Kellman provides an overview of this tradition in *The Self-Begetting Novel*. He frames the metafictional mise en abyme as essentially a Möbius-strip mutation of the *Künstlerroman*, a novel about the development of an artist: "It is an account, usually first-person, of the development of a character to the point at which he is able to take up his pen and compose the novel we have just finished reading" (3). I do not argue here that Nick Shay is the implied author of the entire novel *Underworld*. Rather, I restrict my interpretation to the Cotter and Manx chapters, arguing that by the end Nick has acquired not only the ball but also the impetus and the requisite abilities to invent an origin myth for it. However, I do not rule out the possibility that some future critic may extend this argument further. Indeed, I will take a first tentative step toward expanding Nick's authorial jurisdiction in the final section of this chapter.

As the previous chapter established, the "self-begetting" interpretive approach is a critical commonplace in Joyce studies. Catherine Morley finds in DeLillo "not a fleeting awareness but a sustained dialogue" with Joyce (178). David Cowart astutely identifies numerous allusions to *Ulysses* in *Underworld*. He compares the cuckolded flâneur Albert Bronzini to Leopold Bloom, the irrepressibly unfaithful Klara to Molly Bloom, and the "ephebe" (young man) Nick to Stephen Dedalus: "The ephebe in this family romance, though apparently not called to art, struggles like Joyce's Stephen with complexes of paternity, duty to the mother, and the remorse of conscience" (Cowart 201). Nick may not be an artist by trade, but he does earn the equivalency of an artist's apprenticeship over the course of *Underworld*, ultimately serving as part-time *Künstler* for DeLillo's *roman*. The budding painter and sculptor Klara Bronzini, still metamorphosing in the artistic chrysalis of becoming Klara Sax, is the first to intuit Nick's Dedalian potential: "At first she thought it might be nice to think of him as the Young Man, like a character in a coming-of-age novel, but she only thought of him in motion, and nameless, and nonfictional" (*U* 747). DeLillo's "Portrait of Nick as a Young Man" is in part the portrait of a killer; but as a mature man Nick's imaginative capacity becomes sufficiently developed to conceive his own portrait of Cotter and Manx Martin. Channeling DeLillo's channeling of Joyce, Nick imagines a day-long odyssey in the life of the ball, of the teeming city of New York, and most importantly of the Martin family. In much the same way that *Ulysses* appropriates Homer as structuring device, so too does *Underworld* appropriate Joyce as literary model for what might, in the Homeric and Joycean spirit, be thought of as "The Martiniad."[3]

Nick Shay's artistic apprenticeship

When we are first introduced to Nick Shay, he hardly comes across as a potential fabulist. In the spring of 1991, as a fifty-seven-year-old waste management executive with a wife, two grown children, and a grandchild on the way, he cultivates a persona of success and no-nonsense stability. He is privately skeptical of Klara Sax's claim that, in the intervening four decades since they broke off their affair, life has taken a turn toward the unreal. Taking stock after their brief reunion in the desert, Nick defiantly tells himself, "I lived in the real" (*U* 82). However, his realist credentials do not hold up to close scrutiny. At important junctures throughout his life he resorts to mythic fabrication to reconceive his relation to the real. Even as a professional waste manager, he regards garbage in terms beyond strict materiality. Characterizing himself as a "cosmologist of waste," he devises an orderly system to make sense of trash: "The Jesuits taught me to examine things for second meanings and deeper connections. Were they thinking about waste?" (*U* 88) The Jesuits instilled in young Nick the Ignatian mandate to find God in all things. Although Nick has apparently drifted away from the Catholic Church, like Stephen Dedalus his mind remains supersaturated with his religious upbringing, predisposing him to view even garbage as suffused with the mysterious aura of buried secrets.

Nick's re-creative impulses are fostered by other inspirational artists engaged in like-minded processes of recuperation. Despite the cocksure bravado of his street-hardened youth, Nick proves unexpectedly sensitive to art. In the spring of 1978, for instance, Nick visits the Watts Towers. He recounts how the grand structure was built by an Italian immigrant, Sabato (aka Simon) Rodia, out of steel pipes, cement, and shards of thousands of found objects. Nick is impressed by the work aesthetically, but it also evokes a profound personal connection to his Italian immigrant father, Jimmy Costanza: "I was standing in the middle of a fenced enclosure in a bungalow slum looking up at the spires of the great strange architectural cluster known as the Watts Towers, an idiosyncrasy out of someone's innocent anarchist visions, and the more I looked, the more I thought of Jimmy" (*U* 276).[4] Nothing we are told of Jimmy's background suggests artistic interest, yet the forty-three-year-old Nick romanticizes his father by recasting him as a modern Daedalus capable of producing the towers. Even as Nick spins out this fantasy, however, he acknowledges its implausibility, as well as its incompatibility with his theory that Jimmy was murdered. Still, the subject of Jimmy always ignites Nick's fire for mythologizing, and he has never been deterred by refutations or appeals to reason. For him, the spirit of his father inhabits Rodia's idiosyncratic edifice: "The work he did is a kind of swirling free-souled noise, a jazz cathedral, and the power of the thing, for me, the deep disturbance, was that my own ghost father was living in the walls" (*U* 277). Mark Osteen rates Nick's response to the Watts Towers as inadequate, observing that Nick "sees his 'ghost father . . . living in the walls' of Rodia's work, but misses an opportunity to see in Rodia's productive recycling of waste an example he should follow" (228). However, if Nick is regarded as the embedded author and implied narrator of the Martin story, then he does eventually learn the lessons that Osteen prescribes. Nick finds in Rodia a model for how to recycle waste in an imaginatively viable way. The Watts Towers teaches him to convert the refuse of his personal rag and bone shop by hauling it up the ladder of art.

FIGURE 4.2 Simon Rodia / Watts Towers *(c. 1950) by Sanford Roth. Los Angeles County Museum of Art, Beulah Roth Bequest (PhA.1993.9.12.12) Digital Image © 2018 Museum Associates / LACMA. Licensed by Art Resource, NY.*

The artist who unquestionably exerts the greatest influence on Nick Shay is Klara Sax. The two had a brief affair in 1952—two bouts of heated sex followed by no contact for forty years. When he reads an article about her during a 1992 business trip to Houston, he impulsively decides to drive into the desert for an impromptu reunion on the site of her latest project. Though their affair was more memorable than either of them admits, their reunion is anticlimactic. The whole trip might have been judged a failure had Nick not driven out to a remote ridge at dawn to view Klara's work in progress, *Long Tall Sally*. The work includes 230 B-52 planes, decommissioned at the end of the Cold War, which Klara has painted vibrant colors and juxtaposed against the vast desert backdrop. Nick is awed by the sight. Klara's artwork delivers the powerful climax missing from their verbal exchange. "I hadn't expected to register such pleasure and sensation," he confesses. "Sometimes I see something so moving I know I'm not supposed to linger. See it and leave. If you stay too long, you wear out the wordless shock. Love it and trust it and leave" (*U* 83).

Nick leaves *Long Tall Sally*, but it doesn't leave him. Klara declines to translate her work into polemics, neither as nostalgic homage nor as anti-war protest. Yet there is no ignoring the epic historical sweep of the project. After all, an artist cannot incorporate a decommissioned bomber into a work of art without inviting contemplation of the plane's former function and of the historically specific reasons for its being put out of service. That said, just as "Pafko at the Wall" assumes an entirely different status and function after it is incorporated as a constituent part of *Underworld*, so too does a B-52 signify quite differently after it has been repurposed and folded into the holistic mass of *Long Tall Sally*. This epiphany marks an important stage in Nick's apprenticeship, providing a prototype for the artistic metamorphosis of detritus on a grand scale. *Long Tall Sally* thus serves as a direct structural inspiration for Nick's omniscient mural of "Longing on a large scale" (*U* 11) in the Prologue of *Underworld*.

Despite its imposing grandeur, Klara's masterwork remains rooted in the personal and intimate. She explains to a French documentary crew that its title is taken from nose art of Long Tall Sally already inscribed on one of the planes.

> She inspired the songwriter or the nose painter or the crew that flew the plane. Maybe she was a waitress in an airman's bar. Or somebody's hometown girl. Or somebody's first love. But this is an individual life. And I want this life to be part of our project. This luck, this sign against death. . . . I want to keep our intentions small and human despite the enormous work we've done and the huge work we have ahead of us. (*U* 78)

As a thirty-two-year-old wife and mother, Klara Bronzini was hardly a "hometown girl" when she had sex with seventeen-year-old Nick, and "first love" would be a hyperbolic exaggeration of their brief fling. But Nick does draw imaginative inspiration from Klara Sax years later, analogous to the inspiration provided by Long Tall Sally to songwriter, painter, and pilot. When he turns his gaze back to October 3, 1951, and reanimates that momentous day in American history, he replicates Klara's ambitious scope, particularly in the Prologue; but he also follows her example by anchoring the historical in the personal, the collective in the individual, and the massive in the modest, especially in the Manx chapters.

To give Nick his full due, he did not simply derive all of his creative sensibilities from other artists. He nurtures an inherent lifelong love for language. His appreciation for the power of words was honed by the Jesuits. His illuminating encounter with Father Paulus, who teaches Nick to name the parts of a simple shoe, is less a vocabulary tutorial than a lesson on perception. The priest instructs Nick how to reconstitute the world simply by learning how to see it clearly and name it accurately: "You didn't see the thing because you don't know how to look. And you don't know how to look because you don't know the names" (*U* 540). Nick's lessons from Father Paulus function as a kind of mystical initiation, teaching him to decode the world's secrets, hidden out in the open. "Everyday things represent the most overlooked knowledge. These names are vital to your progress. Quotidian things" (*U* 542). This initiation also gives Nick, once a seemingly irredeemable thug, the power to devise a new identity through words and narrative. He uses his correctional retreat to Minnesota as a crucible in which to discard his old self and concoct a new one. Language and literature are integral to his self-reinvention:

> All that winter I shoveled snow and read books. The lines of print, the alphabetic characters, the strokes of the shovel when I cleared a walk, the linear arrangement of words on a page, the shovel strokes, the rote exercises in school texts, the novels I read, the dictionaries I found in the tiny library, the nature and shape of books, the routine of shovel strokes in deep snow—this was how I began to build an individual. (*U* 503)

Shoveling snow clears a path for moving forward without impediment, and reading serves an analogous function for Nick, clearing away the clutter of his former self to make way for the new. I have described his transformation in terms of a *Künstlerroman*, but here his tale also unfolds as a kind of meta-*Bildungsroman*, as if he is conscious of being both protagonist and author of a coming-of-age novel:

> The book fits the hand, it fits the individual. The way you hold a book and turn the pages, hand and eye, the rote motions of raking gravel on a hot country road, the marks on the page, the way one page is like the

next but also totally different, the lives in books, the hills going green, old rolling hills that made you feel you were becoming someone else. (*U* 511)

These multiple literary epiphanies allow Nick to understand his place in the world from a new perspective, one where he can assert agency and seize authorial control over his fate.

Nick Shay's myth-making credentials

The defining event of Nick's life was his father's abandonment of the family when he was only eleven years old. Even as Nick matures, the betrayed son remains loyal to a romanticized myth he created as a child to explain his father's absence. Nick observes, "All the mysteries of the family reach their culmination in the final passion of abandonment" (*U* 87). As in Christ's passion, the son asks the father "why hast thou forsaken me?" (Mt. 27:46) With no definitive reply, young Nick answers his own question with myth. He invents a story that Jimmy was "wasted" by mob hit men. His younger brother Matt argues for years against this fantasy: "No one came for him, Nicky. No one got him and took him away. He left because of us basically. He didn't want to be a father" (*U* 203). And yet Matt understands the longing that motivates this necessary fiction. He strikes at the heart of Nick's mythic compulsion when he observes, "The power of an event can flow from its unresolvable heart, all the cruel and elusive elements that don't add up, and it makes you do odd things, and tell stories to yourself, and build believable worlds" (*U* 454–55). *Telling stories and building believable worlds*: here Matt diagnoses Nick's predilection for myth-making more accurately than anyone else.

Having held on to this fantasy deep into adulthood, it is puzzling why Nick suddenly renounces it near the end of *Underworld*. In the Epilogue he confronts his friend Brian Glassic about his affair with Marian and roughs him up. He also finally admits the truth to his wife about his murder of George Manza forty years earlier. Most critically, he finally confronts the ugly truth about his father:

> The earth opened up and he stepped inside. I think it felt that way not only to us but to Jimmy as well. I think he went under. I don't think he wanted a fresh start or a new life or even an escape. I think he wanted to go under. . . . I think he just went under. The failure it brought down on us does not diminish. (*U* 808–09)

This language still echoes mythology, as if Jimmy were abducted like Persephone and taken to the Underworld. Nevertheless, it seems to indicate psychological progress, suggesting Nick finally accepts that his father abandoned his family. What was his breakthrough? What permits Nick after all these years to assimilate the trauma of abandonment? I contend that Nick takes the anxieties once held at bay by the mob-hit story and transfers them to the mythic vehicle of "The Martiniad." This fantasy allows him to work through his father-son tensions and wounds of betrayal by proxy, displacing and substituting his family crisis via the story of Cotter and Manx Martin.

The axis mundi around which Nick builds his mythology is the totemic Thomson home run ball. Nick struggles to articulate his irrepressible desire to possess this relic, but he knows his longing is rooted in loss and misfortune:

> I didn't buy the object for the glory and drama attached to it. It's not about Thomson hitting the homer. It's about Branca making the pitch. It's all about losing. . . . It's about the mystery of bad luck, the mystery of loss. I don't know. I keep saying I don't know and I don't. But it's the only thing in my life that I absolutely had to own. (U 97)

In *On Longing* Susan Stewart argues that a souvenir is inherently incomplete because "the souvenir must remain impoverished and partial so that it can be supplemented by a narrative discourse, a narrative discourse which articulates the play of desire. . . . It will not function without the supplementary narrative discourse that both attaches it to its origins and creates a myth with regard to those origins" (136). She anticipates precisely what Nick attempts to do, namely supply the ball with its missing narrative. However, Stewart also emphasizes that the resulting narrative is ultimately less about the souvenir than about its owner: "It is not a narrative of the object; it is a narrative of the possessor" (136). The ball provides Nick with an expedient substitute for his true object of desire: an origin myth that restages the prelapsarian paradise and fall from grace of a son betrayed by his father.

Nick revises his old myth about Jimmy, replacing it with a new myth about the Martins. A point that cannot be stressed enough is that *Cotter and Manx are never explicitly referred to outside "The Martiniad" chapters.* The only character who even comes close to such an allusion is Charles Wainwright, Sr., who recalls buying the ball from "a guy who claimed it was the very object Branca had hurled and Thomson had heroically struck" (U 529). That's it. Wainwright's son Chuckie, the only other eyewitness who might have identified Manx, has even hazier recollections: "Vague names from his unstable childhood. The memory of the baseball itself, the night of the baseball—vague and unstable and dim" (U 612). So: "a guy," who may or may not be Manx Martin, is the sole reference to the father, and there is not so much as a nod in the direction of Cotter Martin. Outside the chapters set during October 3, 1951, it is as if the Martin men disappear from history. In fact there is no independent verification in *Underworld* that

Cotter or Manx Martin ever possessed the ball *or that either even existed*. Nick says his precious relic serves "to commemorate failure. To have that moment in my hand when Branca turned and watched the ball go into the stands—from him to me" (*U* 97). But Nick has no factual knowledge of the first or second pair of hands that allegedly grasped the ball: from him (to X) to me. He purchases the souvenir with a gaping hole in its provenance. He fills this hole in history with fiction. Nick creates an origin myth of Cotter and Manx. He needs the ball because he needs the story it allows him to tell.

Stylistic signatures in "The Martiniad"

The Martin chapters are clearly marked as distinct from the rest of the novel. The three Manx chapters are visually partitioned off with black pages. The October 3, 1951, sections are also the only subplot moving forward in time, as opposed to the backward temporal trajectory of the rest of *Underworld*. DeLillo stressed the special status of this intratext to Kim Echlin:

> Those black pages are not a proper part of the book that precedes them and the part that follows them. *Manx is not part.* His chapters come after Chapters One, Three, and Five. *He's not part of those chapters, he's different.* And then at the end of the last Manx Martin chapter, suddenly these two conflicting streams lock together because on the day after he sells the baseball, Part Six begins. And then the Manx chapter becomes part of the larger chronology of the book. (149, emphasis added)

Manx is not part, he's different. He is a special case; and we can add, so is Cotter, since there is no separating the two. The four Martin chapters mark a discrete independent narrative, albeit one chopped up and rationed out in the larger novel. But the narrative continuity remains unbroken; for instance, notice that Cotter's perspective prevails throughout the Prologue and well into the first Manx chapter. Up until the gap on page 148, the nominal "Manx Martin 1" chapter is told entirely from Cotter's point of view, inextricably linking the first and second stages of the October 3, 1951, odyssey as surely as Stephen's "Telemachiad" flows ineluctably into Bloom's "The Wanderings of Ulysses." Furthermore, it is telling that the Prologue introducing Cotter is followed immediately by a first-person section from Nick, and all three of the Manx chapters are preceded by Nick chapters. Cotter and Manx constitute a single, separate narrative stream, and Nick is the conduit through which that stream is channeled into the larger narrative.

"The Martiniad" is also stylistically distinct for being told in present tense, a surprising but significant choice. Although this subplot is chronologically the oldest in the novel, it is conveyed as if unfolding in the present, right now. Interestingly, one of the more significant alterations in transferring

"Pafko at the Wall" to _Underworld_'s Prologue is the revised time signature at the end. The original novella concludes, "It is all falling indelibly into the _now_" (PWH 70, emphasis added). John Duvall argues, "the 'now' is now our now, our present as much as that of DeLillo's Russ Hodges" (305). This interpretation holds up in the original text, but it gets lost in translation to the Prologue, which instead concludes, "It is all falling indelibly into the _past_" (U 60, emphasis added). This new ending resituates October 3, 1951, from the _now_ into the _past_. But then why tell this distant tale in present tense? If Nick is factored in as the agent behind this narrative reenactment, then the time signature becomes more legible. For it is only by the end of _Underworld_, in the present time of the novel, after Nick has completed the full arc of his development as a mature adult and would-be artificer, that he is capable of imagining the origin myth of "The Martiniad" into being. Therefore, although the story's _action_ is set in 1951, the story's _narration_ comes last in _Underworld_, beget through Nick's imagination in the 1990s of the novel's present.

Nick's shadow is retrospectively detectable from the very first sentence. A new opening line that did not appear in "Pafko" is inserted at the beginning of the Prologue: "He speaks in your voice, American, and there's a shine in his eye that's halfway hopeful" (U 11). Elsewhere DeLillo experiments with that rarest of narrative voices, second-person, as in the opening scene of _Running Dog_ (RD 3–4). But nowhere are his experiments with the second-person "you" more extensive or suggestive than in _Underworld_, where the technique is associated at several points with Nick Shay. During his first-person narrative, Nick occasionally lapses into the second-person "you" in reference to himself, capturing a sense of detachment from his own actions. For instance, upon killing George Manza he reflects, "Because you were the shooter and the witness both and you can separate these roles. The second was helpless to prevent the first from acting" (U 510). This declaration of self-detachment, issuing from a second-person hinterland located somewhere between first-person subjectivity and third-person objectivity, is symptomatic of Nick's narrative consciousness: "And there were times when you detached yourself from the steepest breathing, even, and felt a kind of white shadow, a sliding away into a parallel person, someone made of mind-light, who seemed to speak for you" (U 553). Nick's split-off "parallel person," one "who seemed to speak for you," is directly echoed in the opening invocation: "He speaks in your voice"—"He" being the shadow-self Cotter, and "your voice" being Nick's self-address, the inner murmur of his narration.

To speak in terms of fractured identity may suggest a desire for reunification, to reintegrate the self into wholeness again. However, in Nick's case it is essential that he maintain his critical distance from Cotter. While empathizing deeply with this fantasy figure, he also needs to regard Cotter safely at arm's length, which explains his choice of third-person narration in the Martin chapters instead of first- or second-person (in concert with other distancing effects: black instead of white, Giant instead of Dodger, Harlem instead of the Bronx, etc.). The buffer of third person provides Nick the necessary insulation to confront difficult truths from his own experience but to tell them slant, through projection, deflection, and sublimation. At one revealing point Nick explicitly alludes to these tactics in terms of narrative voice. He reflects upon "a fellow executive" (perhaps a veiled reference to himself) who harbors "a secret linger of childhood, the game he played inside himself." As an expert player of this game, Nick knows the rules: "He was spying on himself. The third person watches the first person. The 'he' spies on the 'I.' *The 'he' knows things the 'I' can't bear to think about*" (*U* 119, emphasis added). This description succinctly captures the literary strategy Nick employs in the Martin chapters, spying on himself through the guise of another, placing first the "he" of Cotter, and subsequently the "he" of Manx, under surveillance in order to work through "things the 'I' can't bear to think about" except through the mediation of fiction.

The names featured in Nick's intratext are highly suggestive as well. Stemming from his language lessons about the shoe, Nick remains acutely attuned to specialized vocabulary for quotidian objects: "I used to tell my kids when they were small. A hawser is a rope that's used to moor a ship. Or, The hump in the floor between rooms, I used to say. This is called the saddle" (*U* 102). He might well have added to this list a "*cotter*," sometimes called a "cotter pin" or "cotter key." A cotter is literally a linking device, a split pin used to link two parts of a mechanism together; in its verb form, "to cotter" means to fasten, fit closely, or bind together. Figuratively speaking, this is the precise function Cotter Martin serves for Nick Shay: Cotter is the missing link in the ball's provenance, the fastener joining the past to the present and the end of the novel to the beginning, and the key to unlocking formative episodes from Nick's youth.

The name Manx is even stranger than Cotter, but no less suggestive. Manx's catlike qualities allow him to abscond with his son's prize ball. Manx also connotes a language, sometimes called Manx Gaelic, the language once native to the Isle of Man. Manx is particularly appealing in the present context as something of a dead language; it was declared extinct in 1974 after the death of the last native speaker. The Manx language has since been revived by being taught in school on the Isle of Man, but UNESCO still categorizes it as "critically endangered," one step away from extinction.[5] In *Underworld* the past functions for all practical purposes as an alien country with a dead language, despite the longing of characters to book passage on the next ship to Byzantium or the next train to the Polo Grounds. Fiction opens an avenue to return vicariously to the past and revive its dead language, and in that sense Manx Martin is the last native speaker of October 3, 1951. Another clue to his strange name may be gleaned from Klara Sax. Her own distinct surname is borrowed from her father, who would sometimes change

"Sachs" to "Sax" as a business ploy to disguise his Jewishness. She recalls, "And how curious, what a distance he sought to travel from the gratifying sound of that *c-h* with its breadth of reference, its guttural history and culture, those heavy hallway smells and accents—from this to the unknown *x*, mark of mister anonymous" (*U* 483). Nick need not know this anecdote about Klara's father to be familiar with the convention of using an "X" as a signature, at once a marker and an erasure of one's identity (e.g., Malcolm X). Klara speaks of her father's *x* as an attempt to hide one racial identity behind another, and that is essentially how Nick uses the convention, too. He hides his own father Jimmy behind the guise of Manx, the mysterious Mister X—*Man X*.

Familial conflict and wish-fulfillment fantasy in "The Martiniad"

The Prologue is painted from a broad palette, but Nick's primary colors are sons and fathers drawn in black and white. Several nominal "-sons" are featured, including Bobby Thom*son*, Jackie Glea*son*, and Bill Water*son*. The first two are familiar celebrities, but the latter plays the most prominent role in illustrating the fault lines dividing fathers from sons. After jumping the turnstile and eluding the security guards, Cotter finds an empty seat in the leftfield stands beside Bill Waterson, a white Giants fan who has taken the day off from his construction firm (here is a man who knows a "cotter" when he sees one) to witness the big game. He instantly warms up to Cotter, buying him a bag of peanuts, shooting the breeze, luxuriating in the spectacle—in short, performing all the traditional functions of a father with his son at a ballgame, the part Manx conspicuously fails to play for Cotter. "That's the thing about baseball, Cotter," Waterson waxes in full paternal mode. "You do what they did before you. That's the connection you make. There's a whole long line. A man takes his kid to a game and thirty years later this is what they talk about when the poor old mutt's wasting away in a hospital" (*U* 31). Like Joyce in *Ulysses*, Nick employs a form of metempsychosis, morphing fathers and sons past and present into one another, forming a long continuous line of connection leading to and from baseball. Baseball has traditionally provided an idyllic and quintessentially American setting for cementing the bonds between fathers and sons. However, the Prologue dramatizes the precariousness of this connection and ultimately stages its dissolution. The Giants' improbable victory should have "cottered" Bill and Cotter together, but their makeshift alliance across the divisions of race, age, and class quickly dissolves. Cotter seizes the home run ball only to realize that his competitor for the prize had been "good neighbor Bill flashing a cutthroat smile" (*U* 49). The older man's affability is suddenly replaced by rivalry, reproach, and menace when Cotter refuses to surrender the ball. The smiling predator pursues his prey deep into Harlem before finally conceding that he cannot win on Cotter's home turf. Cotter emerges from the Prologue as momentarily victorious, but his success proves short-lived. He thinks that he has secured the ball by sliding in "safe at home," but Nick's experiences tell him that the domestic sphere is a false sanctuary. Cotter escapes his surrogate father in the streets only to encounter an even greater threat from his actual father at home.

The core father-son conflict between Manx and Cotter is drawn from Nick's repressed relationship with Jimmy Costanza. Like Jimmy, Manx Martin is an undependable, incorrigible, and remote father and husband, dirtying his hands in a number of shady dealings. From the moment Manx slinks onto the scene, he is up to no good, sneaking home to avoid detection by the janitor (from whom he stole and hocked some shovels) and by his wife (since he is late for dinner and drunk again). Cotter is wary of Manx and accustomed to being disappointed by him, but at fourteen he still remains innocent and needy enough to look up to the man, especially on this night when he has such exciting news. The eager son confides his secret to his father, how he skipped school, attended the game, and emerged with the miraculous ball. Manx immediately begins scheming to turn a profit on the ball, but Cotter states his opposition defiantly: "I don't want to sell it. I want to keep it" (U 146). So instead his ruthless father simply steals the ball from his sleeping son's room. Adding insult to injury, Manx exploits baseball's promise for cottering fathers and sons together as a gimmick to unload the ball. Scouting out the crowd gathered that night at Yankee Stadium to buy World Series tickets,

He gets an idea. He gets it from the crowd. He ought to be looking for fathers and sons.

Get the man to do it for the boy.

Appeal to the man's whatever, his rank as a father, his soft spot, his willingness to show off a little, impress the boy, make the night extra special. (U 643)

As if it were not bad enough that Manx steals the ball from his son, Nick magnifies Manx's betrayal by having him sell it to another father, Charlie Wainwright, so that he can give it to his son, Chuckie, who doesn't even want the damn thing. Granted, if a transaction like this had never taken place, then Nick could never have gained access to his most precious possession. But it is so perfectly telling that this unholy relic, already infused with the spirit of loss and misfortune for any Dodger fan, should also inherit the family curse of betrayal in changing hands from Manx to Wainwright. Forged in Nick Shay's haunted mind, this origin myth for the ball springs from the central animating tensions and unanswered questions that shaped his character ever since his own father went out for Lucky Strikes and never came back.

Without in any way justifying or minimizing the traitor's actions, there are some noteworthy distinctions between Manx's betrayal of Cotter and Jimmy's betrayal of Nick. The most important difference is that *Manx returns home*. After selling the ball, Manx considers skipping out on his family: "It occurs to him further than he could take a Greyhound bus out of here, ride that skinny dog into the sweet distance" (*U* 654). But he ultimately chooses a different path than Jimmy chose. He feels a passing tug of guilt for what he has done, but rather than pushing him away from his family, his seller's remorse sends him home to try and make it right. "Make the boy feel better about things" (*U* 654). This turn of events constitutes a double wish-fulfillment fantasy for Nick, one where the father feels guilty for his offenses, and one where some inner compulsion—guilt, responsibility, atonement, might as well call it love—drives him home. The final Manx chapter ends with the prodigal father returning to face his son.

Nick's narrative adjustment in the first Manx Martin chapter, switching from the son's perspective to the father's, makes this crucial plot twist possible. In an effort to understand the father's betrayal, Nick vicariously follows in his shoes, sees through his eyes, and speaks in his voice. From a psychological perspective, he can give voice to these chapters so effectively because he knows firsthand what it is like to be a betrayed son. But he also knows from personal experience what it is like to be a remote father. At the Staatsburg correctional facility Dr. Lindblad asks him if he wants a family of his own someday, to which he replies, "'I don't know. Haven't thought about it. No,' I said. 'I don't think so. Kids? I don't want kids. I don't want to be a father. . . . After what I've done? I don't think I should be a father. Do you?'" (*U* 509) In 1965 he tells an old friend at a bar, "I'm not the marrying type. I don't see myself married. I don't feel marriage bound. I don't even think about it" (*U* 618). He is likewise resistant to the idea of a family: "Children. This was remote to me. . . . Marriage remote. Fatherhood a vague regret somewhere in the kitchen smell of another country" (*U* 636). Even after he marries Marian and they have Lainie and Jeff, a fundamental part of him remains alienated from family life. He confesses years later to Big Sims, "How close I am, some of the time, I sometimes think, as much as I love them all, to feeling like an imposter. Because it has not fucking, ever, been something I am comfortable with" (*U* 339). Nick privately acknowledges his chronic sense of detachment, his impulse to hedge his emotional bets rather than go all in, and he recognizes this condition as congenitally inherited from his father: "I've always been a country of one. There's a certain distance in my makeup, a measured separation like my old man's, I guess, that I've worked at times to reduce, or thought of working, or said the hell with it" (*U* 275). He doesn't have to speculate on Manx's temptation to cut ties and leave; Nick knows the feeling firsthand. Nevertheless, he ultimately chooses to follow through on his family commitments, and in that sense Manx does not resemble Jimmy Costanza so much as Odysseus, Leopold Bloom, and Nick Shay—embattled husbands and fathers who returned home in the end. Nick's surname comes from his mother, not his father; and as Peter Boxall reminds us, the name "Shay" is homophone for "*chez*," the French word for home (190).

Paradoxically, Nick's increased identification with Manx comes at Cotter's expense, as if father and son are locked in a zero-sum game. In order to fully inhabit the fictional perspective of the father he has become, Nick must first divest himself of the son he once was. Indeed, Cotter recedes entirely from both the microtext of "The Martiniad" and the macrotext of *Underworld*, never heard from again after October 3, 1951. However, as embedded author and implied narrator, Nick does confer one last gift upon Cotter: sleep. Nick effectively dramatizes Cotter's fall from grace, but he concludes before the dawn of October 4, 1951, the first day of the rest of the young man's postlapsarian life. Cotter remains suspended forever on the threshold between innocence and experience, poised at the precipice, not yet conscious of the fall. Nick does not need to imagine Cotter's impending fall because he already lived it himself.

Nick's fall is no felix culpa, but it is worth noting that his fall was not irredeemably tragic. After bottoming out in 1952 as a killer, he gradually clawed his way up to respectability and self-actualization, reinventing himself as a flawed but relatively successful husband, father, and waste management executive. His most mature achievement, however, comes in the form of "The Martiniad." Through this fantasy reenactment of October 3, 1951, Nick imaginatively reconceives the past and finds a creative outlet for dealing with his father's abandonment. Thomson's miraculous home run ball demands an explanatory story, and Nick is ideally suited to provide one.

Out of the many scenarios he might have invented to account for the ball's descent through history, he chooses a version of events that permits him to revisit the formative crises of his own past. Nick balances his need to know more and understand better his father's betrayal with his need to insulate himself from the full impact of that trauma. He confronts disillusioning truths about Jimmy Costanza and about himself through the guise of Manx Martin. But he also exercises creative prerogatives to soften the blows of his past, indulging the fantasy that the absent father returns home and that the betrayed son never awakens into the postlapsarian world of harsh experience. Unfortunately, Nick did awaken into that world. The crash-landing from that fall reverberates throughout his youth and leads him initially down a path of destruction. However, through a lifetime of concentrated effort, he gradually acquires the skills necessary to reconstruct himself. By the end, like Sabato Rodia, Klara Sax—and Don DeLillo—Nick Shay becomes capable of transforming the wasted fragments of his past into art.

Cottering Epilogue to Prologue

The imagery of falling and soaring dominates the conclusion of *Underworld*, in the gruesome death of Esmeralda Lopez (hurled from the roof of a Bronx tenement), in her quasi-miraculous resurrection as an angel (her apparition visible whenever the passing train lights shine upon a certain billboard), and in the posthumous transcendence of Sister Edgar (dispersed into cyberspace). A full account of *Underworld*'s conclusion lies beyond the scope of the present chapter. But in closing I wish to reconsider certain subtle implications in the Epilogue which suggest that Nick's authorial purview may extend beyond the Martin chapters. Nick ostensibly recedes from the novel midway through the Epilogue, much as Cotter recedes midway through the first Manx Martin chapter. However, the narrative after Nick's exit contains multiple allusions to a guiding and personally invested agency behind the narration.

The story of Esmeralda's rape and murder, her billboard apparition, her transformative impact on the crowds who gather to adore the vision, and Sister Edgar's cyber-ascension are collectively headed with the web address "*http://blk.www/dd.com/miraculum*" (*U* 810). Nick reports that his son Jeff "visits a website devoted to miracles. . . . Jeff tells us this and smirks shyly, either because he thinks it's funny or because he thinks it's funny and believes it" (*U* 806). Much of the critical commentary on the conclusion has concentrated on whether DeLillo is being sincere or ironic in these overtly religious invocations of transcendence. Less attention has been paid to the narrative agency of this section. And yet someone is clearly telling this story, and that narrative presence shines through as mysteriously as the apparition of Esmeralda. The brief but hideous subsection detailing Esmeralda's rape and murder is headed "*Keystroke 1*," implying that someone has clicked on a hyperlink on the Miraculum website to learn more about that aspect of the story. Subsequent references—"when you enter a name-search the screen reads *Searching*. . . . and the screen reads *Searching*. . . . Screen reads *Searching*" (*U* 817–18)—unmistakably gesture toward someone doing the searching, as does the subsequent subheading "*Keystroke 2*" (*U* 824). *Who is the searcher?*

Jesse Kavadlo observes, "The sequence is narrated in such a way that the reader isn't sure whether the story is part of the novel or a story-within-a-story" (111). He describes a dynamic wherein the external reader of *Underworld* encounters an internal reader of the website within *Underworld*. Kavadlo identifies this embedded reader as "presumably Jeff, Nick Shay's adolescent son" (111). Like father, like son. If Jeff is indeed the mediating agency through which we receive the closing stories of the billboard angel Esmeralda and the cyber-angel Edgar, the son serves a function analogous to the one played by his father vis-à-vis the Martins. Furthermore, this construction posits the Epilogue as a counterbalance to the Prologue and

Manx Martin chapters. Nick and Jeff do not seem especially close, but at least they are capable of peaceful cohabitation beneath the same roof and within the same chapter, unlike the Martins, who are disaggregated into four chapters and poised for the fall of a house divided.

Without disavowing that interpretation, I must also acknowledge that certain stylistic signatures at the end of the novel once again harken back to Nick Shay's voice. The closing crescendo is formulated in the telltale second-person voice most associated with Nick. "And you can glance out the window for a moment, distracted by the sound of small kids playing a made-up game in a neighbor's yard, some kind of kickball maybe, and *they speak in your voice* . . ." (*U* 827, emphasis added). Surely "they speak in your voice" is meant to circle back to the beginning and connect the final page with the first: "He speaks in your voice, American, and there's a shine in his eye that's halfway hopeful" (*U* 11). The second half of that opening sentence with its halfway hope also effectively links with the novel's closing benediction of "Peace" (*U* 827). Young Cotter may have scant cause to be hopeful, except within the ephemeral sanctuary of sleep; but the mature Nick, awakening to the voices outside his window and animating the voices inside his head, becomes capable through his imaginary tale about the Martins of achieving some measure of peace. Finally, and most tellingly, the opening line of the novel's last page features this single-sentence paragraph: "*Fasten, fit closely, bind together*" (*U* 827, emphasis added). What else can this be, what other function could this sentence serve, but *to define the word "cotter"*? Here is the linchpin binding the Epilogue with the Prologue, embedded on the final page and hiding in plain sight. The conclusion of *Underworld* thus forges one final imaginative link allowing Cotter Martin and Nick Shay to speak in each other's voice.

5

The artistic gestation of Klara Sax

The Prologue of *Underworld*, called "The Triumph of Death," takes its title from a painting by Pieter Bruegel the Elder. *The Triumph of Death* is a ghastly depiction of a battlefield where the forces of death lay siege to humanity.

Bruegel's image of *Death* paradoxically enters the novel through the pages of *Life*. A reproduction of Bruegel's painting appeared in the October 1,

FIGURE 5.1 The Triumph of Death *(c. 1562) by Pieter Bruegel the Elder. Oil on panel. Museo del Prado, Madrid, Spain.*

1951, issue of *Life* magazine, and this littered page drifts into the hands of J. Edgar Hoover at the Polo Grounds. Hoover is attending the legendary Dodgers-Giants game on October 3, 1951, discussed in depth in the previous chapter. The intrusion of Bruegel's macabre image amid the teeming throng of animated fans at the Polo Grounds establishes a tension between Life and Death from the start of the novel. No character is better positioned to appreciate this tension than Hoover, who has been informed that, unbeknownst to the clamoring crowd around him, the Soviets have just tested a nuclear weapon on that same fateful day. Even as one of the greatest moments in American sports history is unfolding, a far more significant and foreboding "Shot Heard 'Round the World" has been fired in America's escalating Cold War with the Soviet Union. The Prologue uncovers the seeds of death buried beneath the pageantry of American life.

However, *Underworld* is also teeming with life, and the genesis for much of its creative energy comes from art. A counterbalance to the Prologue's *Triumph of Death* is offered in the first chapter through a very different artwork, *Long Tall Sally* by Klara Sax. Her story in *Underworld* represents the Triumph of Life and Art. DeLillo's detailed study of Klara Sax stands out as his most fully realized and most lovingly rendered portrait of an artist. Klara epitomizes the life-giving potential of art, and, through her, DeLillo expands the possibilities of his own fiction. Asked in his first interview about the novels that most inspired him, he responded,

> The books I remember and come back to seem to be ones that demonstrate the possibilities of fiction. *Pale Fire*, *Ulysses*, *The Death of Virgil*, *Under the Volcano*, *The Sound and the Fury*—these come to mind. There's a drive and a daring that go beyond technical invention. I think it's right to call it a life-drive even though these books deal at times very directly with death. No optimism, no pessimism. No homesickness for lost values or for the way fiction used to be written. These books open out onto some larger mystery. (LeClair 10)

Underworld earns a place on the top shelf alongside those great works as DeLillo's most daring achievement. The novel deals directly with death but is charged with life. The primary engine of *Underworld*'s life-drive is Klara Sax.

Nothing thrown away in DeLillo's *Underworld* is ever lost. Everything gets recycled over the course of the novel. Take, for instance, Klara Sax's great throwaway line in her Part One encounter with Nick Shay. After not seeing one another for forty years, Nick impulsively decides to visit Klara in the desert on the site of her greatest art project. They exchange a few words, neither of them sure how to navigate this unlikely reunion. Then the seventy-two-year-old Klara lights a cigarette and quips, "I'm not pregnant so I can do this" (*U* 73). The first-time reader is merely amused, but the experienced re-reader of DeLillo can trace the palimpsest of intratextual references that lie behind this gesture. Flip forward almost seven hundred pages and flash back four decades, and we arrive at the first encounter between seventeen-year-old Nicky and thirty-two-year-old Klara Bronzini on a Bronx stoop, a flashpoint ignited by a cigarette:

"You wouldn't think of saving me a drag, would you, on that cigarette?" She looked at him, taking in the question.

"Hate to ask," he said.

She looked at him, taking in the damp shirt and scuffed dungarees, the way he held the crate at belly level, forearms veined beneath the rolled sleeves.

"One drag could mean the difference," he said, "between life and death."

She said, "In which direction?"

He smiled and looked away. Then he looked at her and said, "When you need a smoke, does it matter?" (U 731)

And so the spark is lit. This flirtatious scene is followed a week later by sultry sex in Klara's apartment, followed soon thereafter by a second and final hook-up. Then no contact for forty years until the impromptu desert reunion.

Sometimes a cigarette is not just a cigarette. Contrary to the warning labels, DeLillo's cigarettes promote fertility. Just look at that pregnant weight young Nick is holding belly level in their first encounter. I am not suggesting that Nick literally impregnated Klara Bronzini back in 1952—what an amazing difference that would have made in both of their lives—but I am asserting that Klara's line in 1992, "I'm not pregnant so I can do this," is pregnant with personal and artistic significance. Young Nick refers to a smoke as a matter of "life and death," two subjects about which he knows very little at that point (oh, but he will learn). He doesn't realize that the woman to whom he directs this line is seriously teetering on the brink between life and death and could tip either direction. David Bell represents one side of the artistic scale, a mother-haunted would-be artist who retreats from life in a fantasy of getting unborn. Klara represents markedly different impulses. She was a wife and mother who longed to become an artist, but in the context of 1950s America she found it impossible to reconcile those roles. Underworld regresses back through the gestational stages in which the Bronx homemaker Klara Bronzini became reborn as the famous artist we first meet in 1992. Nick Shay certainly played his unwitting role in making that transition possible, but it is important not to misconstrue his paternity. He did not sire Klara with an artistic vocation; she does not owe her career to having sex with Nick. If anything the opposite is closer to the truth, since Nick was partially inspired by Klara's ambitious art project to conceive his own artistic effort, "The Martiniad" examined in the previous chapter. The birth and gradual evolution of Klara's art and identity are largely matters of auto-genesis, of self-reinvention. Nonetheless, a multitude of generative influences do contribute to nurture the transformation of Klara Bronzini into Klara Sax. The irony of "I'm not pregnant so I can do this" isn't just that it's delivered by a post-menopausal elderly woman, but that in a sense she *is* pregnant, her imagination is again fertile with new artistic growth. As DeLillo shows in three distinct trimesters—"Long Tall Sally" (Part One) in 1992, "Cocksucker Blues" (Part Four) in 1974, and "Arrangement in Gray and Black" (Part Six) in 1951–52—Klara periodically reconceives herself as both a woman and as an artist.

Creation

When the reader is first introduced, and Nick is reintroduced, to Klara Sax in Part One, she is already a legendary figure in the art world. Her grandest project of all is underway in the desert of the American Southwest. *Long Tall Sally* is an ambitious project which aims to appropriate 230 decommissioned B-52 planes no longer needed after the Cold War. Klara and her numerous assistants are hard at work repainting these discarded relics in flamboyant colors and repurposing them as constituent parts in a massive environmental artwork. When Nick arrives, Klara is surrounded by a French television crew shooting a documentary about the project. She insists that her motives are chiefly aesthetic rather than political. She tells the French, "This is an art project, not a peace project. This is a landscape painting in which we use the landscape itself. The desert is central to this piece. It's the surround. It's the framing device" (*U* 70). Still, there is no getting around the military function once served by the B-52 castoffs. She recalls years ago sailing off the coast of Maine with her second husband. From that vantage she could occasionally glimpse the distant lights of B-52s flying overhead. She tells the French,

> War scared me all right but those lights, I have to tell you those lights were a complex sensation. Those planes on permanent alert, ever present you know, sweeping the Soviet borders, and I remember sitting out there rocking lightly at anchor in some deserted cove and feeling a sense of awe, a child's sleepy feeling of mystery and danger and beauty. I think that is power. I think if you maintain a force in the world that comes into people's sleep, you are exercising a meaningful power. (*U* 75–76)

This awe for the sublime power represented by the B-52s threatens to devolve into nostalgia for the Cold War, a charge that is sometimes lodged against *Underworld*.[1] However, Klara's art project is not an homage to America's military might, nor is it a monument for the United States' alleged victory in the Cold War. Both Klara's and DeLillo's art rejects such triumphalism, at least insofar as it applies to any notion of the United States defeating the Soviet Union. According to Klara, if there is triumph to be found at the end of the Cold War, it lies in the fact that thousands of nuclear weapons manufactured by both superpowers, a deadly arsenal cumulatively capable of killing all the world's inhabitants many times over, were ultimately not exploded. Klara is not completely naïve in her rendition of history; she acknowledges, for instance, "Many things that were anchored to the balance of power and the balance of terror seem to be undone, unstuck" (*U* 76). Here she seems to anticipate the rise of new international terrorist threats after the fall of the Soviet Union and the relaxation of Cold War tensions which once sustained a degree of geopolitical equilibrium. Nonetheless, Klara does find legitimate cause for relief that the hard rain didn't fall: "I've thought hard about the weapons they carried and the men who accompanied the weapons and it is awful to think about. But the bombs were not released. You see. The missiles remained in the underwing carriages, unfired. The men came back and the targets were not destroyed" (*U* 76). The pregnancy metaphor is evident here, too: the bulging missile loads in the bellies of those planes were never released; the threat of global annihilation was not delivered; the nuclear spawn of death lay stillborn.

The point is not so much that DeLillo endorses Klara's view on this matter, any more than he endorses Hoover's opposing view in the previous

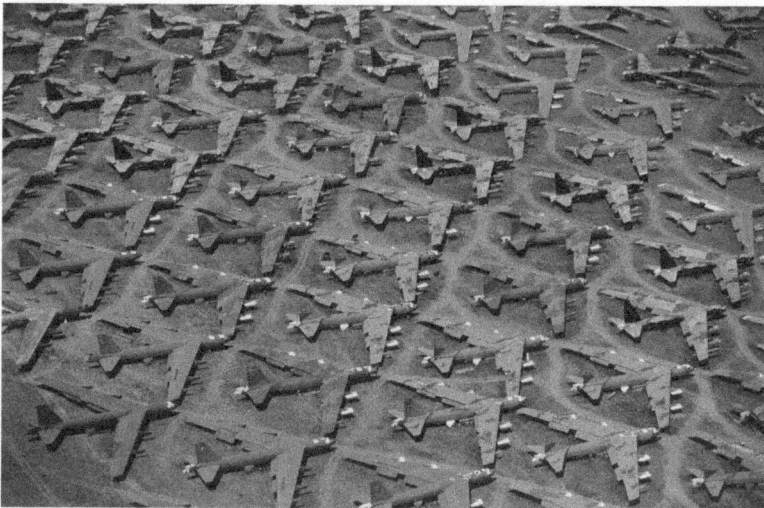

FIGURE 5.2 *The B-52 Boneyard outside Tucson, Arizona, which inspired DeLillo's invention of Klara Sax's* Long Tall Sally. © *Alex S. MacLean, courtesy Landslides Aerial Photography.*

section, but that he juxtaposes them against one another. Along with being a richly drawn, complex character, Klara serves a thematic function within the larger framework of the novel, pulling on her side of the rope for Life against Death. *Underworld* is animated throughout by several contrapuntal tensions (e.g., America and Soviet Union, whites and blacks, fathers and sons, mothers and daughters, East and West, city and desert, world and underworld, etc.), all yin-yang variations of what Hoover labels in the Prologue as Us and Them: "And what is the connection between Us and Them, how many bundled links do we find in the neural labyrinth? It's not enough to hate your enemy. You have to understand how the two of you bring each other to deep completion" (*U* 51). In an aesthetic sense, DeLillo mirrors the binary logic and replicates the equilibrium once maintained by the two superpowers within the structure of his Cold War elegy. When Nick catches his first glimpse of *Long Tall Sally* from a desert bluff at sunrise, he immediately appreciates the holistic effect of the piece: "She wanted us to see a single mass, not a collection of objects. She wanted our interest to be evenly spaced. She insisted that our eyes go slowly over the piece. She invited us to see the land dimension, horizonwide, in which the work was set" (*U* 83–84). DeLillo aims for a similar effect in his most ambitious novel. As in *Americana* and *Libra*, the individual stories are set against a larger national backdrop and are part of a broader cultural analysis. *Underworld* features dozens of memorable characters and evocative scenes, covering the vast and tumultuous sweep of the second half of the twentieth century. These individual parts are fascinating in and of themselves, but they must ultimately be appreciated as constituent pieces of a larger work governed by aesthetic concerns beyond the sphere of a single character, setting, or time.

Klara's function rests squarely on the side of life and art. She weds these forces by accentuating the individual human dimension of her epic project. The title *Long Tall Sally* comes from a voluptuous woman painted on the nose of one of the B-52s:

> She inspired the songwriter or the nose painter or the crew that flew the plane. Maybe she was a waitress in an airman's bar. Or somebody's hometown girl. Or somebody's first love. But this is an individual life. And *I want this life to be part of our project*. This luck, *this sign against death*. Whoever she is or was, a waitress bedraggled you know, hustling a ketchup bottle across the room, and never mind the bomb, I want to keep our intentions small and human despite the enormous work we've done and the huge work we have ahead of us. (*U* 78, emphasis added)

Klara's explanation for the TV crew weaves together the major themes of her work and affirms her role as chief advocate for creative life forces within DeLillo's novel. David Bell epitomizes one prominent tendency among artists in DeLillo's *Künstlerromans*, an impulse toward withdrawal, contraction, silence, and oblivion. Taking all of DeLillo's works into consideration, this trajectory is by far the most common, including the all-male fraternity of rocker Bucky Wunderlick in *Great Jones Street*, math genius Billy Twillig in *Ratner's Star*, novelist Bill Gray in *Mao II*, and environmental artist Alex Macklin in *Love-Lies-Bleeding*, not to mention all DeLillo's other "men in small rooms" who exile themselves away from the world to plot the annihilation of others and/or themselves. Klara Sax, on the other hand, follows a rare but magnificent alternative trajectory. Her life and her art represent a series of expansions, with each stage of her development reaching farther and encompassing more. Of course, DeLillo cannot be satisfied with a straightforward success story of growth, attainment, and triumph. Klara had to give up a lot along the way in her pursuit of art. And DeLillo's backward chronology has the paradoxical effect of presenting Klara as getting smaller and becoming more confined as the novel progresses, like a butterfly curling back into her chrysalis. Nevertheless, the overall effect of *Underworld*'s portraits of Klara as an old, middle-aged, and young woman is a soaring creative achievement, a time-lapse document of an artist being born.

DeLillo seems to have drawn partial inspiration for Klara Sax from the groundbreaking and iconoclastic New York artist Louise Nevelson. Both women harbored artistic aspirations from a young age, but both found their creativity stifled as young wives and mothers. Nevelson eventually broke free from her family and from conventional gender expectations to pursue a life devoted to art. In her memoir *Dawns + Dusks* she describes her gravitation toward art as both a desperate act of self-preservation and a life-affirming process of self-discovery:

> I didn't make sculpture to share my experience. I was doing it for myself. I did it because I knew I was in a spot, and I had to move out of it to survive. Almost everything I had done was to understand this universe, to see the world clearer. I think that ultimately what drove me so desperately was . . . I could only understand through working. That means, through myself. (76)

Nevelson's earliest works were modest in scale and received little attention from the male-dominated New York art world. However, by the late 1950s she began developing a distinct style, working with discarded wooden objects and combining them together into massive monochromatic installations.

Reviewing Nevelson's breakout 1958 exhibit *Moon Garden + One*, Emily Grenauer of the *New York Herald Tribune* observed,

> On entering the gallery, one feels first a breathless, imageless stir. . . . This is a nether world Nevelson has conjured out of her enormous imagination, technical ingenuity and surging creativity. . . . The important thing is that as we allow it to envelop us we feel it, still, as a world we can enter along with the artist, a cave of the heart, a dark place of dreams and loneliness. (qtd Wilson 183)

FIGURE 5.3 Sky Cathedral *(1958) by Louise Nevelson. Painted wood.* © *2018 Estate of Louise Nevelson / Artist Rights Society (ARS), NY. Gift of Mr. and Mrs. Ben Midwoff. Digital Image* © *2018 The Museum of Modern Art / Licensed by SCALA / Art Resource, NY.*

Moon Garden + One points the way toward Klara Sax's early artistic sensibilities through its use of scrap materials with domestic associations and its rejection of all bright colors. The vaunting scale of works like *Sky Cathedral* also gesture toward Klara's later more ambitious *Long Tall Sally*. Indeed, by the end of her career Nevelson had outgrown the confines of gallery space and turned her attention to giant steel sculptures commissioned for highly visible public spaces. For instance, in 1977 she completed *Sky Tree*, a 54-foot tall steel sculpture at the Embarcadero Center in San Francisco. And in 1978 Nevelson installed one of the largest wood sculptures she ever made, *Sky Gate—New York*, in the mezzanine lobby of the North Tower of the World Trade Center—where it remained overlooking the plaza until September 11, 2001, when it was destroyed in the collapse of the Twin Towers.

FIGURE 5.4 Sky Tree *(1977) by Louise Nevelson. Black Cor-Ten Steel. Embarcadero Center, San Francisco. © Bryan Costales.*

As titles like *Sky Cathedral*, *Sky Tree*, and *Sky Gate* indicate, flight is a recurring preoccupation of Nevelson's work, as it is in Klara's B-52 project. Explaining the allure of flight for an early piece called *Winged City*, Nevelson added a note to the base of the sculpture which in part reads, "I believe the first consciousness, the first human was aware of flight. All our heritage . . . expressed in literature, spiritual messages, mythology, the visual arts, has been winged" (qtd Wilson 161). Furthermore, the theme of creation—as artistic genesis, as metamorphosis, and as rebirth—is central to both Klara Sax and Louise Nevelson. Nevelson proclaimed in her memoir:

Creation itself is a dimension, you see. Creation itself. The word *creation* is like the earth, the volcanoes, the mother who has her labor pains, and this rain, whatever, all the emotions in the ocean, the turmoil. Creation is there. It isn't where the water's clear. Creation means you are in the labor pains of something, in the great activity. I think creation is living. (115, emphasis in original)

Metamorphosis

The metamorphosis motif is prominent throughout Part Four of *Underworld*. The summer of 1974 finds Klara Sax in a fallow period. "She was fifty-four now, let that number rumble in your head—fifty-four and between projects and humanly invisible and waiting to go back to work, to make and shape and modify and build" (*U* 372). She is not only between projects but also between stages of her artistic career. Of course, just like the phrases "between jobs" or "between meals," one can only nervously hope that another job or meal awaits somewhere, somehow in the not-too-distant future. There are no guarantees. But Klara is a mature enough artist to have learned that there is no speeding up the gestational process of inspiration. It will come, if at all, in its own time. "It wasn't quite time for her to go back to work but it was beginning to be the time. Something in her skin began its anxious leap, some need to handle and shape, only deeper really—some need so whole she could sit alone in the loft and be a little wary of it" (*U* 397). Until then, she drifts through the summer of 1974, what she dubs "the rooftop summer": "This was Klara Sax's summer at the roofline. She found a hidden city above the grid of the fever streets" (*U* 371). Again, Klara's perch above the city is not arbitrary. DeLillo places her there as a counterpoint to the underground art scene and the underworld imagery he weaves throughout the other subsections of "Cocksucker Blues" (named for an underground documentary about the Rolling Stones on tour). But the rooftop view from countless cocktail parties that summer also plays a part in Klara's slow transformation. The view is defamiliarizing, showing her the city from an unfamiliar angle, rendering perspectives she's never seen or heeded before. Her placement on high also prompts her to reflect on her life, as if the synoptic view covers both space and time. She looks back on her youth as Klara Sachs, her married life as Klara Bronzini, and her growth into artistic prominence as Klara Sax. She also tries to look ahead into the hazy horizon of her artistic future.

The reader has a clearer view of her future than Klara does. Therefore, we are in a position to see how the experiences of 1974 contribute to the development of the artist she becomes by 1992. It's a long way from 1974 to 1992 and from New York to the desert, not only in space and time but also in aesthetic sensibility. The kind of work Klara had produced prior to 1974, and the kind of artistic principles she expounds within this section, are at odds in many ways with *Long Tall Sally*. She first became recognized for work that earned her the dubious nickname "the Bag Lady": "There were a few of us then. We took junk and saved it for art. Which sounds nobler than it was. It was just a way of looking at something more carefully. And I'm still doing it, only deeper maybe" (*U* 393). In one sense, this technique of converting junk into art, sifting through the detritus of the past and reclaiming it for aesthetic use, is exactly what Klara does in *Long Tall Sally*. However, her sense of scale, purpose, and specific technique were radically different early in her career. "For a while she used house paint, radiator paint. She liked rough surfaces, flaked paint on metal, she liked puttied window frames, all the gesso textures, the gluey chalks and linseeds that get mixed and smeared, that get *schmeered* onto a weathered length of wood" (*U* 471, emphasis in original). Her previous emphasis upon humble domestic objects is worlds apart from the grand metallic sheen of mass-produced military weaponry. "The Bag Lady" deliberately eschewed conventional beauty or virtuosity, preferring grainy textures and haphazard applications.

DeLillo draws heavily upon Louise Nevelson's early work for Klara's "Bag Lady" period. In fact Klara explicitly mentions Nevelson as a mentor in this section of the novel (*U* 386-87). Nevelson established her reputation in the 1950s by using rough-hewn scraps and discarded domestic remnants as raw material for her art. She recalled in *Dawns + Dusks*,

> That was when I began using found objects. I had all this wood lying around and I began to move it around, I began to compose. Anywhere I found wood, I took it home and started working with it. It might be on the streets, it might be from furniture factories. Friends might bring me wood. It really didn't matter. (76)

Although Nevelson's approach was sometimes dismissed as "scavenger art," she preferred to think of it as "resurrection": "I feel that what people call by the word *scavenger* is really *resurrection*. You're taking a discarded, beat-up piece that was no use to anyone and you place it in a position where it goes to beautiful places: museums, libraries, universities, big private houses" (81, emphasis in original). She went on to explain that

> when you do things this way, you are really bringing them to life. You know that you nursed them and you enhance them, you tap them and you hammer them, and you know you have given them an ultimate life, a spiritual life that surpasses the life they were created for. That lonely, lowly object is not used any more for what it was—a useful object. It becomes a work of art. (83)[2]

FIGURE 5.5 *Louise Nevelson, portrait by Lynn Gilbert (1976), commissioned by Pace Gallery, photographed in her studio.* © *Lynn Gilbert, courtesy of Lynn Gilbert.*

Klara Sax adopts a similar recombinational aesthetic, one also employed by the covert author Nick Shay and the overt author Don DeLillo in *Underworld*. Like Nevelson, Klara was also suspicious of color back then: "She'd been pulling color out of her work for years. . . . It felt right for her to pull it out" (*U* 376). As the reader knows, Klara will later disavow this monochromatic asceticism in favor of vibrant color. The elder Klara tells the French,

> I want to say in this passage from small objects to very large ones, in the years it took me to find these abandoned machines, after all this I am rediscovering paint. And I am drunk on color. I am sex-crazed. I see it in my sleep. I eat it and drink it. I'm a woman going mad with color. (*U* 70)

But this evolution still remained on the distant horizon during the rooftop summer of 1974.

The unabashed expansiveness of Klara's later development involves bursting out of the self-imposed restrictions that kept her earlier art restrained and modest. Back in 1974, she still maintained very strict scruples about artistic hubris: "She had to watch for ego creeping in. She had to ask herself would you do this piece a truer way if you worked in a stunted garret somewhere. She tried to scale her work to the human figure even though it wasn't figural. She was wary of ego, hero, heights and size" (U 374–75). These views led her to distrust the vaunting ambition of other artists who gave unchecked expression to exuberance. Klara rejected "Art in which the moment is heroic, American art, the do-it-now, the fuck-the-past—she could not follow that. She could look at it and respect it, envy it, even, in a way, but not, herself, place hand to object and make some furious now, some brilliant jack-off gesture that asserts an independence" (U 377). This is a brilliant send-up of the testosterone-fueled bravado of the male-dominated New York School of painters that burst on the art scene at the same time Klara was coming up.[3] There is also an unmistakable element of self-parody here, since DeLillo's own megaton American epic *Underworld* might likewise be rated a "brilliant jack-off gesture that asserts an independence." But what then of Klara's own masterpiece *Long Tall Sally*? Klara certainly extracts the testosterone from her magnum opus. Painting decommissioned B-52s in flamboyant colors and posing them together in chorus lines seems less a brilliant jack-off gesture than a colossal drag show. Her monumental emasculation of these weapons of mass destruction is akin to Vietnam War protesters sticking flowers in the rifles of soldiers sent to subdue them, but on a much grander scale. Ultimately, the massive scope of *Long Tall Sally*, the unrestrained and irrepressible audacity of the gesture, puts it on a par with the artistic ambitions of a Jackson Pollock or a Don DeLillo.

How did Klara traverse such vast distances to get from the Bag Lady to the impresario of *Long Tall Sally*? DeLillo's mise en abyme approach of embedding reflections of the artist is replicated in several instances by Klara, who mirrors a number of influences from 1974, reconceiving her subsequent self-image and art in the process. The artist with whom she interacts most is Acey Greene. In a novel filled with binary oppositions, Acey is Klara's photographic negative. She is young, black, lesbian, and prolific as a figural painter.[4] "This was supposed to be a postpainterly age, Klara thought, and here was a young woman painting whole heat, a black woman who paints black men generously but not without exercising a certain critical rigor" (U 393). Acey made her first mark in the art world through a series of portraits of Chicago gang members. In the summer of 1974 she transitions to an entirely new series: variations on the image of buxom B-movie starlet Jayne Mansfield. Acey is bold and subversive, and her latest evolution proves that she is unwilling to be confined to narrow racialized categories in her subject matter. Acey and Klara couldn't be more dissimilar in terms of personal and aesthetic style, as well as choice of subjects and medium. But Klara admires Acey, even as envy gnaws at her over her friend's level of productivity and ascendant success. "What Klara admired most was the seeming ease of address, the casually ravishing way Acey laid down paint" (*U* 394). Klara will eventually try to emulate this less tortured approach in her own artwork. She also takes to heart some of Acey's criticism of Klara's early junk-art phase. "It's not my thing. Maybe I don't trust the need for context," Acey complained.

> Because I understand up to a point. You take your object out of the dusty grubby studio and stick it in a museum with white walls and classical paintings and it becomes a forceful thing in this context, it becomes a kind of argument. And what it is actually? Old factory window glass and burlap sacking. It becomes very, I don't know, philosophical. (*U* 393)

Context remains important to Klara; witness the crucial framing device of the desert landscape in *Long Tall Sally*. Nonetheless, Klara does adapt her work in light of Acey's critique, employing a less philosophical and more visceral approach in *Long Tall Sally*, one where the artwork is integrated more organically with its surrounding environment.

Klara Sax has much to learn in terms of ethos, ethic, and camaraderie from Acey Greene.[5] However, there are limits to how much practical craft she can pick up from a canvas painter, since Klara has resolutely moved past that medium in favor of object-based arts. Her stronger 1974 influences come from less conventional sources. Ismael Muñoz (aka "Moonman 157") is literally an underground artist: he is a graffiti writer from the Bronx who tags subway trains. Klara never actually meets him, though she does descend into the subway with her art dealer friend Esther Winship in search of his work. "The kid's a goddamn master," assures Esther (*U* 377). When Klara finally sees his work, she agrees:

> Klara had to admit this particular kid knew how to make an impact. The train came bopping into the old drab station like some blazoned jungle of wonders. The letters and numbers fairly exploded in your face and they had a relationship, they were plaited and knotted, pop-eyed cartoon humanoids, winding in and out of each other and sweaty hot and passion dancing—metallic silver and blue and cherry-bomb red and a number of neon greens. (*U* 395)

This would become part of Klara's "sex-crazed" color palette in *Long Tall Sally*.

Moonman 157 is DeLillo's composite representative for dozens of renegade graffiti writers who left their marks all over New York City beginning in the late 1960s.[6] In *The History of American Graffiti*, Roger Gastman and Caleb Neelon chronicle the birth of the movement:

In the late 1960s and early 1970s, totally unaware of graffiti elsewhere, a generation of young New Yorkers began to write their street names—names like TAKI 183, LSD OM, DINO NOD, SUPER KOOL 223, STAY HIGH 149, PHASE 2, PHIL T GREEK, SNAKE, and JUNIOR 161—in ever-increasing volume. America was in turmoil, and New York City was in crisis . . . . But this generation of young people . . . realized that they could speak to the entire city by painting the one thing that crossed every boundary of class, borough, race, and neighborhood: the New York subway system. (20)

The so-called "King of Graffiti" in the early 1970s was TAKI 183, whose tag could already be found all over the city. TAKI 183 wrote the Foreword to Gastman and Neelon's book, where he recalled,

Some people said that the July 21, 1971, article about me in the *New York Times*, "Taki 183 Spawns Pen Pals," was what ignited the graffiti art movement in New York because it was the first local story about this idea of writing your name everywhere. I don't know if it's true that the article inspired other kids, since none of the teenagers I was hanging around were reading the *New York Times*, but I think that article did kind of plant the flag that graffiti had arrived. (17)[7]

FIGURE 5.6 *Graffiti on a subway car on the Lexington Avenue line in New York City, July 1974. Photo by Jim Pickerell for the Environmental Protection Agency, courtesy of the National Archives and Records Administration.*

New York was divided at the time between outraged citizens, led by Mayor John Lindsay, who regarded graffiti as a civic scourge of vandalism, and art supporters who hailed graffiti as a major new avant-garde movement. Despite attempts by advocates like Hugo Martinez, who organized United Graffiti Artists in 1972 to provide supplies, studio space, and public advocacy for the burgeoning movement, most graffiti writers were as wary of their supporters as they were of their detractors. As TAKI 183's Foreword suggests, he and his peers were not bourgeois subscribers to the *New York Times*; and they certainly weren't affiliated with New York's revered but exclusive art institutions.

> One thing is clear: Young graffiti writers such as CRASH certainly were not getting their inspiration from the city's museums or art institutions. "When you grow up in the projects or in a place like the South Bronx, art museums don't come into your life," CRASH explains, "You don't think about that at all. . . . I grew up poor enough that we would share sneakers. . . . So growing up in that [environment], museums are, like, the last thing you think of." (Gastman and Neelon 23)

Graffiti writers found inspiration from popular culture and sought validation primarily from one another. Though they certainly hungered for notoriety, their stamp of legitimacy did not come from exhibits at the Museum of Modern Art (MoMA) or The Metropolitan Museum of Art, but rather from mobile metal murals hurtling down the IRT from the Bronx to Manhattan with masterpieces emblazoned for the whole city to see.

The first book on graffiti was published by photographer John Naar in 1974, and Norman Mailer penned the accompanying text. The iconoclastic author was the perfect choice. If anyone could relate to an insatiable hunger for notoriety or recognize a "brilliant jack-off gesture" when he saw one, it was Norman Mailer. In his essay "The Faith of Graffiti," he faithfully captures the insurrectionary spirit and illicit thrill of subway graffiti:

> And when the cops are out of sight and a train is coming in, they whip out their stash of paint from its hiding place, conceal it on their bodies, and in all the wrappings of oversize ragamuffin fatigues, get on the cars to ride to the end of the line where in some deserted midnight yard, they will find their natural canvas which is of course that metal wall of a subway car ready to reverberate into all the egos of all the metal of New York, what an echo that New York metal will give into the slapped-silly senses of every child-psyche who grew up in New York, yes, metal as a surface on which to paint is even better than stone.

As important as any of his visual inspirations, Moonman 157 provides Klara Sax with a model for art-as-vandalism, a defiant assertion of independence and selfhood in the face of the state's pristine, mass-produced instruments of uniformity and control. Tellingly, Klara locates a "graffiti instinct" at the heart of *Long Tall Sally*, explaining to the French TV crew,

> See, we're painting, hand-painting in some cases, putting our puny hands to great weapons systems, to systems that came out of the factories and assembly halls as near alike as possible, millions of components stamped out, repeated endlessly, and we're trying to unrepeat, to find an element of felt life, and maybe there's a sort of survival instinct here, a *graffiti instinct*—to trespass and declare ourselves, show who we are. The way those nose artists did, the guys who painted pinups on the fuselage. (*U* 77, emphasis added)

Granted, Klara's project constitutes an act of trespassing only in the abstract; in truth, her work is completely sanctioned by the government, with the artist dictating the specific terms of the agreement. In that sense, her appropriation of Muñoz's techniques and sensibility has sanitized out the hazardous conditions and legal risks he took in tagging subway cars. Like Moonman's underground rivals at the time, Klara is guilty of biting his style. But she does preserve intact the radical estrangement of graffiti. In the words of sculptor Claes Oldenburg, "You're standing there in the station, everything is gray and gloomy and all of a sudden one of those graffiti trains slides in and brightens the place like a big bouquet from Latin America" (qtd Mailer). Both Klara and Moonman take giant metallic vehicles which are quite familiar in one context and then profoundly transvaluate them through painting. By retraining perception, first his or her own and then that of the spectator, an artist has the capacity to reinvent reality, to change the way we see and comprehend the world and our relation to it. This is the effect of Klara's defamiliarized planes as well as Moonman's defamiliarized trains. Young Muñoz describes it as an effort to "get inside people's heads and vandalize their eyeballs" (*U* 435). Klara is inspired by his example to attempt a kindred effect in *Long Tall Sally*.

Klara's most moving experience with an artwork in 1974, and her most instructive as well, comes from the Watts Towers. Italian immigrant Sabato Rodia devoted over thirty years to building his idiosyncratic masterpiece out of wire, steel rods, concrete, everyday objects, and shards of refuse. The reader encounters this marvel of ingenuity and individualism two hundred pages earlier (albeit four years later in terms of narrative chronology) when Nick Shay visits the site. Klara and Nick have long since lost contact with one another, but DeLillo sets up these two scenes in conversation with one another, juxtaposing their reactions and inviting dialectical comparison. As an experienced object-based artist herself, Klara Sax is in a much better position than Nick to appreciate the enormity of Rodia's achievement in the Watts Towers. She is awestruck and gropes for purchase on how to comprehend it all. "She didn't know what this was exactly. It was an amusement park, a temple complex and she didn't know what else. A Delhi bazaar and Italian street feast maybe. A place riddled with epiphanies, that's what it was" (*U* 492). In essence Rodia was a junk artist like Klara. He took humble, broken, discarded objects and re-envisioned them through artistic eyes. Where he radically departed from her—and where he blows her mind— is expanding this vision beyond the quotidian to the epic. "She had no idea. She didn't know a thing so rucked in the vernacular could have such an epic quality" (*U* 492). More than any other work she encounters in 1974, the Watts Towers provides Klara with the key to unlocking the artistic potential she will ultimately realize in *Long Tall Sally*. Rodia points the way forward, even if it will take a long gestation period before Klara eventually solves the riddle of this artistic epiphany. "She was weak with sensation, weak with seeing and feeling. She touched and pressed. She looked up through the struts of the tallest tower. Such a splendid independence this man was gifted with, or likely fought for, and now she wanted to leave. She didn't need to stay any longer" (*U* 492). She is wary of her impulse, exposed by Acey, to overthink and philosophize her artistic responses. She wants to limit her exposure to the Watts Towers so that the experience remains purely visceral and unassimilated. In that respect her response mirrors that of Nick when he first glimpsed *Long Tall Sally* in 1992: "Sometimes I see something so moving I know I'm not supposed to linger. See it and leave. If you stay too long, you wear out the wordless shock. Love it and trust it and leave" (*U* 83).

FIGURE 5.7 Watts Towers (1962), Los Angeles, CA. *Photograph by Seymour Rosen. © SPACES – Saving and Preserving Arts and Cultural Environments.*

The reader is invited to linger longer, however, and to make connections that escape detection by the characters. Klara never explicitly mentions her father in response to the Watts Towers, and yet it becomes increasingly clear that, like Nick, she is father-haunted. Virginia Woolf famously asserted in *A Room of One's Own*, "Women have served all these centuries as looking-glasses possessing the magic and delicious power of reflecting the figure of man at twice its natural size" (35). The magnified image of Klara's father is reflected in her art, but with an inversion of Woolf's metaphor. Klara's art is made smaller through its reflection of her father; or, to put it another way, her art is a mirror which magnifies her father's failures and compels her to reflect them. To most observers it would seem that Klara has advanced far beyond the conditions of her upbringing. She has become an artist of some renown, she gets invited to all the right openings and parties, and she exercises a degree of autonomy unthinkable for a woman in the world from which she emerged. Nevertheless, her experiences during the downtime of 1974 teach her to recognize the ways in which her art is still rooted in and limited by her background. Reconsidering her abiding preference for humble objects, gritty surfaces, and smearing techniques, she realizes, "it took her years to understand how this was connected to her life, to the working-class grain, . . . and how the flowoff of drips and trickles became elements of memory, and the aluminum paint on the whistling radiators, and the paint her father carried home to recoat the kitchen chairs" (*U* 472). She concedes that her domestic subjects and her medium of expression are inheritances from her father.

Here again, Klara Sax bears a close resemblance to Louise Nevelson. Curator Brooke Kamin Rapaport asserts that Nevelson's early reputation as "The Forager" who worked with discarded wood was actually an homage to her father who worked in lumber:

She continued to physically assemble the piece of wood herself, initially in intimate scale, ultimately in room-size environments. And wood was hers—a material that she could command viscerally because of childhood associations with her father's work as a lumberman. After abandoning traditional family roles as wife and mother, and following trials with other artistic media, Nevelson found her life's work in foraged wood. This material, coupled with her ability to sever her home life from her artwork, was Nevelson's salvation. (11)

Like Nevelson, Klara is torn, personally and artistically, between keeping faith with her past and breaking free from it. On some level from the very start, she has been trying to work past or undo that influence. Klara admits, "At some point she realized she was putting down paint mainly to take it off, scrape it with a kitchen tool—she liked the veiny residue" (*U* 472). This gesture, schmeering on paint in tribute to her father only to scrape it off, suggests that she is trying to rid herself of her father's influence, trying to find her own self-image hidden beneath his reflection. Though Klara is sufficiently ambitious to become an artist and to seek acclaim, her aspirations are artificially limited by an unspoken vow not to disrespect her father's memory by becoming more successful than him. "And her radius of endeavor, her smallish ambition, what she saw as a clustering in her work, a familial thing, determinedly modest. She was only now beginning to wonder if she wanted to ensure herself a life unlaureled, like her father's" (*U* 472).

It is not until 1974 when she's between projects that she finally begins to acknowledge "how guarded she was about certain accomplishments, not other people's but her own—how distrustful and slightly shamed. She needed to be loyal to the past, even if this meant, most of all if this meant incorporating her father's disappointments, merging herself with the many little failures amassed like faded keepsakes" (*U* 473). Even her *nom de plume*, Klara Sax, is tied to her father's secret shames. Her family's name is Sachs, but her father would sometimes assume the name Sax on business trips in an effort to conceal his Jewish identity (*U* 483). Klara's adoption of the signature Sax is perfectly appropriate, since her art remains both inscribed and proscribed by her father's limitations.

Her various artistic influences in 1974 finally provide Klara with external models and internal wherewithal to climb out of her father's shadow. In doing so, however, she is still able to honor her father by using his own stifled fantasies as raw materials for her magnum opus. She summons up distant memories of her father's dreams of the American West:

> She thought of his View-Master reels of the Grand Canyon and the great West, the unreachable spaces he clicked into place on his stereoscope, and she recalled so clearly the image of the Hopi scout posed on the edge of some rimrock, and whatever it was out there in the 3-D distance, the Painted Desert or Zion Park, and how her own smallness, her unnoticeability was precisely the destiny she'd assigned herself. (*U* 473)

This memory strongly prefigures her eventual project out in the desert, revealing multiple layers of personal significance to a work that would seem for the uninitiated to emerge chiefly from historical and meta-artistic commentary. Like so many American journeys westward, Klara goes in search of a new self. But she still carries the baggage of the past with her, including the unrealized dreams of her father. Making *Long Tall Sally* is at once a rejection and an apotheosis of her upbringing. The rooftop summer of 1974 regularly affords Klara synoptic views of Manhattan, but her flight back from California provides an even more magnificent and fateful view of the future: "She didn't know the West and she'd never flown above it in weather so clear. It looked young and untouched, it had the strangeness of worlds we'd never seen, it was not ours from up here, it was too flowingly new and strange—we hadn't settled it yet" (*U* 494). She depicts the West like a tabula rasa, and indeed it will eventually serve as her greatest canvas, though one deeply imprinted by the past she brings with her from back East.

Klara still can't quite see it, how this desert view will coalesce with her memories and influences, her father's unrealized dreams, and her unrealized artistic ambitions. One more key obstacle must be overcome, or at least acknowledged and accepted, in order for the great new work to commence. Klara's personal sense of guilt and failure is not all inherited second-hand from her father; much of it is rooted in her firsthand responsibility for breaking up her family. Her twenty-five-year-old daughter Teresa visits during the summer of 1974, and the mutual tension is palpable. Klara confides to Acey, "I broke up a family, yes. I went away, I came back, I took my daughter for a while. She was better off with her father and I understood that but it consumed me, being separated like that. I had a very bad time. Of course we all did" (*U* 389). So much of Nick Shay's adult life is consumed by the primal abandonment from his father. DeLillo balances his depiction of family crisis by telling another version from the parent's perspective, in this case from the mother's perspective, the one who walked away. Klara's deepest parental scars come from the damage she inflicted on her child: "Teresa doesn't hate me. Maybe worse. I think she hates herself. She was part of the failure somehow. Let's not talk about this" (*U* 390). Needless to say, one does not necessarily have to choose between having a family and becoming an artist. However, it is clear Klara did become convinced at some point that a life devoted to art was impossible in the specific context of her 1952 Bronx home life. She made her decision and lives unapologetically with the consequences. But if the idea was to neatly partition off that previous chapter of her life from the art she subsequently pursued, she has failed. If the image of Klara's father is always visible in her art, the invisible motor behind her art, driving her to produce and succeed, is the dissolution of her family. That motor has stalled in 1974, and Acey Greene perceptively diagnoses the root problem:

You worry about the work you're not doing because you feel deeply obliged to justify. I think you're always justifying in your mind. And you also worry about the work you've done because considering what you gave up and took away, considering the damage you caused, if we tell it like it is, child, you need to convince yourself your work is good enough to justify this. (*U* 485)

Klara could never have become the artist she did within the confines of her former life. But she also struggles in 1974 to rid herself of the final remnants of that old skin so that she can fully inhabit a new artistic identity. Given the pain she both endured and inflicted in order to emancipate herself, it may seem puzzling that DeLillo ends Part Four with Klara getting remarried, this time to Carlo Strasser, a man she barely knows. In Part One she confessed to Nick that she had been "completely reckless when it came to marriage": "I've married out of impulse, out of a cozy evening with a nice wine" (*U* 72). She seems especially to be referring to the Strasser marriage, though there were other precedents, too. In the context of the 1974 rooftop summer, her wedding seems like a recklessly impulsive act, maybe little more than a bored excuse to throw a season-ending party. But there's no ignoring the fact that this gesture also risks looking like capitulation. The lingering guilt of breaking up her family has manifested into a creative blockage, an impediment to her artistic fertility. At this point in her life, not knowing (as the reader does) what her future holds, Klara may seem to be throwing in the towel, effectively saying, "I gave art a chance and it worked for a while, but now I'm all used up as an artist and am ready to focus on being happy in my life, in a relationship, in a family."

There's much more to it than that, however. She must know that this stunt of marrying Carlo Strasser is destined from the start to be a short-lived lark. It cannot work. She's not reverting to married life and rejecting art. She is recreating a simulation of the conditions in which she first broke free to become an artist. Klara may not be so cruelly calculating as to intentionally marry a man just to break up with him, to flee from the arms of her husband on the gossamer wings of art. On a subconscious level, however, that's exactly what she's doing. She has absorbed all the influences she needs from 1974. She's pregnant again with inspiration, even if she's not showing yet. The final preparatory step she needs is achieving the familiar conditions of flight. She builds a domestic nest at the end of Part Four so that she has the proper perch for escape, a launching pad back into art.

Death and rebirth

DeLillo captures the first gestational stage of Klara's artistic career in Part Six, "Arrangement in Gray and Black," spanning the fall of 1951 through the summer of 1952. Later in life, Klara occasionally lapsed into nostalgia for these early years. In 1992 she told Nick, "Sometimes I think everything I've done since those years, everything around me in fact, I don't know if you feel this way but everything is vaguely—*what*—fictitious" (*U* 73). The changes in her life over the ensuing forty years were so dramatic as to seem unreal, or as if it had happened to someone else. Reminiscing with Acey in 1974, "Klara talked about her early days painting, trying to paint, and how it was small-scale hell in a number of ways but was beginning, now, to seem late bohemian and sort of pastel-edged until she made herself remember more rigorously" (*U* 474).The pastels of rosy hindsight are replaced with a much grimmer arrangement in gray and black by Part Six.

On the surface, things don't seem so bad. Klara Bronzini is in a stable marriage with a science teacher, Albert. She is a homemaker in the Bronx, raising their young daughter Teresa and caring for Albert's dying mother. When she has time, she also has a spare room in the apartment set aside for painting. Klara isn't exactly miserable, and she's even occasionally content. However, she suffers from the urban strain of what her contemporary Betty Friedan famously described in *The Feminine Mystique* as "The Problem That Has No Name":

> The problem lay buried, unspoken, for many years in the minds of American women. It was a strange stirring, a sense of dissatisfaction, a yearning that women suffered in the middle of the twentieth century in the United States. Each suburban wife struggled with it alone. As she made the beds, shopped for groceries, matched slipcover material, ate peanut butter sandwiches with her children, chauffeured Cub Scouts and Brownies, lay beside her husband at night—she was afraid to ask even of herself the silent question—"Is this all?" (15)

Louise Nevelson found herself similarly stifled, and many years later she still grappled for words to describe her domestic condition and her desperate need to escape it through art. In an interview for *Monumenta* magazine in 1974—the same year as Klara's rooftop summer—Nevelson mused,

> I think somewhere I rejected the whole experience of family and husbands. I got married because at the time I didn't quite trust my beliefs in myself. . . . [Marriage was] too confining ultimately for my kind of living. . . . It takes so much of life away, and destroys my concentration. I want to live fully through my work. I want to live with great intensity. I want to be aware as much as possible of the livingness of life. . . . This way . . . my life is totally mine. And nobody has a claim on me. (qtd Wilson 308–9)

For her part, Klara tries to reserve a small corner for herself and her art in her cramped 1952 Bronx apartment by claiming "a room of her own." In Randy Laist's words, "She has set up the spare room as a room of her own in which she can close the door on her domestic obligations and paint" (144). There is potential for artistic growth in this painting space, and in retrospect we can see that room as her first chrysalis. But it needs to be emphasized that the spare room did not feel that way to Klara at the time. When we meet her in late 1951, she feels stymied and directionless. Her painting room feels less like a foothold for her imagination than a quarantine for her creativity; less Virginia Woolf's *A Room of One's Own* than Doris Lessing's "To Room Nineteen." Albert merely humors her with the makeshift studio, regarding her painting as little more than a precocious hobby. "Give it time," he counsels when she considers giving the room away to their daughter. He adds patronizingly, "And anyway where do you expect to get with it? Do it for the day-to-day satisfaction. For the way it fills out the day" (*U* 748). It is unfathomable to him that she could take this hobby seriously, let alone secretly regard it as a vocation more sacred than her duties as wife and mother.

Truth be told, Klara is not yet fully convinced that she is cut out to be an artist. She is unsparingly critical of her work. "Painters are supposed to have a line. Klara thought she had a scribble. . . . After a while she went into the spare room and stood by the easel and looked at what she'd done. What had she done? She decided she didn't want to know" (*U* 712). Not only does she paint in the spare room, but the room is also the subject of her paintings. "Klara went into the spare room and restacked all the canvases and stood looking at the sketches she'd done. The door, the doorknob, the walls, the window frame" (*U* 690). She teaches painting to neighborhood children, and doubtlessly such exercises are part of the curriculum. Many apprentice artists painstakingly hone their craft through such detail studies. For Klara, however, her limited subject matter signifies a growing awareness of the restrictive limitations placed upon her as wife and mother, lowering the ceiling of her aspirations as an artist. She is painting what she knows best and that is confinement. She is in effect painting her own prison cell.

Friedan is spot on in labeling this ubiquitous sense of dissatisfaction as "The Problem That Has No Name." Klara has no language to understand or express her gradual suffocation. She cannot yet articulate her existential crisis into the question, "Is this all?" Poor Albert is even more clueless. He is perfectly satisfied with his little nuclear family:

> This was happiness as it was meant to evolve when first conceived in caves, in mud huts on the grassy plain. Mamelah and our beautiful bambina. And his own mother, ghastly ill but here at last, murmurous, a strong and mortal presence in the house. And Albert himself in the hot bath, back from the hunt, returned to the fundamental cluster. (*U* 681)

Klara does not share his enthusiasm, and he senses that she wants more. But what does she want? Klara claims she wants *less*: "She didn't want more, she wanted less. This was the thing her husband could not understand. Solitude, distance, time, work. Something out there she needed to breathe" (*U* 747). She wants to breathe in the air of freedom, self-determination, and life lived on her own terms, the air Louise Mallard breathes in at the window in Kate Chopin's "The Story of an Hour." Instead, the air she breathes in her Bronx apartment stinks of death. Tellingly, the differences between Albert and Klara come through most clearly when they are talking not directly about their marriage but about art. Strolling the streets one day and watching kids play, Albert is reminded of Bruegel's painting *Children's Games*. He mentions this painting to Klara, but she has a starkly different response:

> "Do you know the old painting," he said, "that shows dozens of children playing games in some town square?"
>
> "Hundreds actually. Two hundred anyway. Bruegel. I find it unwholesome. Why?"
>
> "It came up in conversation."
>
> "I don't know what art history says about this painting. But I say it's not that different from the other famous Bruegel, armies of death marching across the landscape. The children are fat, backward, a little sinister to me. It's some kind of menace, some folly. *Kinderspielen*. They look like dwarves doing something awful." (*U* 682)

Unlike her husband, Klara has a very dark view not only of *Children's Games* but also of children in general—hardly a ringing endorsement of child-rearing from this disenchanted young mother. The reference to Bruegel also invites the reader to contrast this scene with the early pages of the novel. Septuagenarian Klara Sax is a vibrant advocate for life and art, the counterforce to "The Triumph of Death." Forty years earlier, however, Klara Bronzini's limited possibilities filled her with morbid hopelessness. She felt much closer to death when she was a thirty-two-year-old wife and mother than when she was a liberated seventy-two-year-old artist.

FIGURE 5.8 Children's Games *(1560) by Pieter Bruegel the Elder. Oil on panel. Kunsthistorisches Museum, Vienna.*

Her most direct exposure to death in Part Six comes through the vigil over her dying mother-in-law. Albert's mother suffers from myasthenia gravis and occupies the space next to Klara's painting room. One might expect this proximity to death in the apartment's cramped quarters to weigh heavy on Klara, but she actually enjoys spending time with the old woman. "Klara did not tell Albert that she found an odd comfort, at times, to sit with his mother. . . . Her skin was getting browner, her hair whiter, hands spotted and blotched, but there was still something strong about her, something Albert seemed to fear, a judgment, a withering conviction of some kind" (*U* 713). She admires the woman's strength and solemnity, and she senses a special aura of premonition about the woman: "She looked a little like a vision, or someone waiting for a vision" (*U* 687). What does the old mother see? What mystery lies behind those eyes? Klara wonders, but at this point she is scarcely capable of seeing through her own eyes. Everything is detached, remote, other. She is like Echo to David Bell's Narcissus; as he put it, "The only problem I had was that my whole life was a lesson in the effect of echoes, that I was living in the third person" (*A* 58). Klara steps outside of herself to view her life with the remorseless clarity of a painter preparing a canvas. She sees herself in the room with her mother-in-law as if studying an Edward Hopper tableau: "How strange it was to find herself here, listening to Perry Como with a woman she didn't know, who was dying, and with everything else as well, this chair, that lamp, this house and street, and to wonder how it happened" (*U* 713). In 1992 Klara waxed nostalgically to Nick, claiming that life had never been so real since she left the Bronx. She misremembers. She didn't feel at all substantial and grounded in her life in 1952. She felt completely estranged, wondering how she got there and hoping that she might somehow escape before she became the old woman dying in a room.

Art becomes her ticket out. One can begin to see the first flickers of that epiphany in Klara's reflections on Whistler's Mother. James Abbott McNeill Whistler's famous portrait of Anna Whistler, usually referred to as "Whistler's Mother," is actually titled *Arrangement in Grey and Black No. 1*. DeLillo takes his title for Part Six from this painting, signaling its significance as a beacon for Klara. Her thoughts about motherhood, mortality, and art all converge in her meditations on this painting, compressed by DeLillo into a single intoxicating sentence:

She had a small print of a Whistler, the famous Mother, and she hung it in a corner of the spare room because she thought it was generally unlooked at and because she liked the formal balances and truthful muted colors and because the picture was so clashingly modern, the seated woman in mobcap and commodious dark dress, a figure lifted out of her time into the abstract arrangements of the twentieth century, long before she was ready, it seemed, but Klara also liked looking right through the tonal components, the high theory of color, the theory of pain itself, perhaps— looking into the depths of the picture, at the mother, the woman, the mother herself, the anecdotal aspect of a woman in a chair, thinking, and immensely interesting she was, so Quaker-prim and still, faraway-seeming but only because she was lost, Klara thought, in memory, caught in the midst of a memory trance, a strong and elegiac presence despite the painter's, the son's, doctrinal priorities. (*U* 748)

What does Klara see when she looks at Whistler's Mother? One must peel off several layers of paint to see the full picture. On one level she sees Whistler. She recognizes what he is attempting to do theoretically with the piece, taking a conventional subject matter, defamiliarizing it through modernist techniques, and reinvigorating the image for avant-garde purposes. On another level she sees an avatar for her mother-in-law, an inscrutable older woman in the inky cloak of mourning surrounded by an aura of mystery. Klara may also see a vision of her potential future self: a woman stuck in a room, going nowhere, utterly defined and confined within the frame of others' views, expectations, and needs.

FIGURE 5.9 Arrangement in Grey and Black No. 1 *(better known as* Whistler's Mother*) (1871) by James Abbott McNeill Whistler. Oil on canvas. Musée d'Orsay, Paris.*

When each layer of paint is scraped away, however, what is left is a clean slate, which always holds out the promise for starting anew. Klara recognizes that the son has appropriated his mother's image in the painting, turning her into a projection screen for his own aesthetic agenda. But she also recognizes that something essential gets lost in the conversion. She looks past the son's theoretical approach to concentrate on "the mother, the woman, the mother herself, the anecdotal aspect of a woman in a chair, thinking, and immensely interesting she was" (*U* 748). And what does Anna Whistler see? Peter Boxall speculates that she is gazing into the past:

> Like the angel in Paul Klee's painting *Angelus Novus*, the mother in Whistler's painting turns her back to the future, and looks longingly, elegiacally, to a lost era from which she has been displaced. The painting contains a lurching gap, a gulf between the lost age to which this woman belongs, and the 'abstract arrangements' that produce and are produced by a modernist revolution in ways of seeing. (209)

This is a convincing interpretation of the painting. Within the context of *Underworld*, however, the pivotal question is "What does Klara Bronzini see when gazing at the gaze of Anna Whistler?" Whistler's mother may see the past, but I think Teresa's mother sees the future, or at least she's beginning to point her gaze in that direction.

Soon after 1952 she left her family and abandoned canvas painting. These two emancipatory acts are related, and her meditations on Whistler's Mother help induce her first rebirth spasms. Klara not only gives up painting traditional canvases, she also gives up figural representation in her art. Why? Whistler's Mother exposes certain limitations of that medium to her. One can study the figure of another, one can gaze at the mother's gaze, but ultimately her inner consciousness resists penetration from without. She remains an insoluble mystery, as do we all. As Beckett put it in his book on Proust, "We are alone. We cannot know and we cannot be known" (540). Whistler strikingly captures his mother transfixed in thought, but the depth and content of her thoughts remains resolutely off limits. Art that attempts to penetrate the subjectivity of others only ends up bouncing back reflected images of the artist. The expression of subjectivity through two-dimensional reflection proves an artistic dead-end for Klara. This revelation is the turning point for an artistic paradigm shift away from subjects toward objects, forgoing paintings of people or even paintings of doors, mattresses, and window frames in favor of making art out of three-dimensional objects, laying her hands on things themselves rather than replicating images. This will become the first stage of Klara's artistic metamorphosis. It hasn't happened yet in 1952, but it is coming, and we have seen where it leads. The seeds for that revelation are planted in Part Six, and Whistler's Mother serves as one key fertilizing agent.

The other is Nick Shay. When Klara sticks that lit cigarette in his mouth, she lights the fuse on a brief but explosive affair that will blow her family life to bits. She didn't know that at the time, but even if she had she might have done it just the same. There is no special magic in seventeen-year-old Nick Shay. To put it in the crude terms in which Nick thinks and speaks in 1952, he's young, dumb, and full of cum. He is no knight in shining armor come to rescue a damsel in distress; he's a horny teenager looking to score. Nonetheless, he serves an absolutely critical function in Klara's transformation, even if another man could have served the same function just as well. In fact, had Nick been more mature and more appealing he might have been less effective as a catalyst for change, simply because Klara might have been tempted to jump out of one restrictive relationship and into another. There's never any threat of that here. Nick is just in it for the sex. And what is Klara in it for? Years later Acey Greene helps her understand the significance of the affair:

> "Yes, well, maybe it's true. Seventeen's a man," Klara said. "And I've asked myself was the thing more important than I was willing to admit?"
> "In other words did it show you a way out?"
> "Did it point a way out?"
> "Which you didn't want to think about at the time." (U 484)

The affair pointed Klara toward the exit, the escape route out of her stultifying life as a Bronx homemaker and toward the freedom necessary to begin her new life as an artist. At least that's the way Klara begins to reconstruct the narrative in 1974. But what did the fling mean in 1952 as it was happening? Nick and Klara had sex on two separate occasions only, a hello-fuck and a goodbye-fuck to put it again in Nick's lingo. DeLillo neatly cleaves the affair into two episodes, depicting the first sex scene from Klara's perspective and the second from Nick's.

"Six days later, or seven, she came out of the flat and locked the door. There was someone on the stoop looking in through the vestibule. She knew exactly who it was and what he was here for and she made a gesture that was either a shrug or a come-on" (U 732). So begins the first episode from Klara's point of view. In one sense her perception is acutely hypersensitive. Even though she has only met Nick once, and even though she's never had an affair before, she intuits immediately without a single word exchanged that he is here for sex. In another sense, however, Klara is coolly detached from the scene. Even in this most carnal of experiences, she sort of goes out of body again, viewing events from the outside rather than fully inhabiting the experience internally. The first clue to her detachment is the line "she made a gesture that was either a shrug or a come-on" (U 732). Well, which is it? One might well expect Nick not to know if Klara will welcome his advances or spurn them. But apparently she's not even sure herself. Is her gesture meant careful examination of Whistler's Mother takes place immediately before the final sex scene with Nick, where he is essentially forced to learn similar lessons. His focus is almost entirely superficial, like an object lesson on the male gaze. He enumerates her physical features: her twisted smile, buggy eyes, pale skin, with particular and recurring emphasis on "the ass and tits and bush" (*U* 749). "A naked woman was amazing" Nick guilelessly observes, and he concedes, "She knew how to be naked" (*U* 750). DeLillo is not simply emphasizing Nick's superficiality, but also the impenetrability of surfaces. Nick has been inside Klara's body, but he is barred access to the inner sanctum of her mind, much as Whistler and Klara are left on the outside looking into the gaze of the mother. To solidify the connection, DeLillo installs the seminal image above the mattress. Nick observes, "It just happened. It happened bang and that was it, with Whistler's fucking Mother hanging on the wall" (*U* 751). Nick wants to know Klara and mistakenly assumes that he does. As this final afternoon together winds down, he thinks, "Never mind the body. He's never looked at a woman's face so closely. How he thinks he knows who she is from her face, what she eats and how she sleeps, from the lookaway smile and the uncombed hair, the hair over the right eye, how her face becomes everything she is that he can't put into words" (*U* 752). These are unusually tender sentiments from the hardened street-wise Nick. Unfortunately for him, his longing to connect with her comes precisely when she's informing him that it's over. "Nick, you can't come here anymore. It's too completely crazy. No more, okay? We did it and now we have to stop doing it" (*U* 752).

Because the scene is depicted from Nick's perspective, we have no privileged insights into Klara's abrupt decision to break it off; of course, even when we did have access to her private thoughts, her motives were equally mysterious. Belated remorse, fear of detection, and creeping disaffection might all be factors. On the other hand, ending the relationship in full prime, before either of them grows to regret it or even fully understands it, can be one way of honoring the experience. Nick and Klara both independently endorsed such a stance in their respective responses to art. The fifty-seven-year-old Nick's reaction to *Long Tall Sally* is worth repeating in this context: "Sometimes I see something so moving I know I'm not supposed to linger. See it and leave. If you stay too long, you wear out the wordless shock. Love it and trust it and leave" (*U* 83). And so, as instructed, the seventeen-year-old Nick leaves: "He picked up the pants and got dressed and left her naked on the mattress, seated sort of leaning to one side, legs together and bent, blowing smoke away from her face with the hand that held the cigarette, and he didn't think of looking back" (*U* 752). If only the past could be left behind so easily and decisively.

When seventy-two-year-old Klara fires up a smoke and blithely announces, "I'm not pregnant so I can do this" (*U* 73), it's as if she's reigniting the flame from those cigarettes forty years earlier, the first that introduced Nick and

Klara, and the last which she was smoking as he walked out the door. No, she wasn't pregnant with child. By the time Nick left her painting room in 1952, however, all of the necessary conditions for her artistic rebirth were in place. Neither of them knew where their lives were headed at the time, but the reader knows full well and is finally in a position to reconstruct the full gestational process. In a strangely beautiful and retroactively prophetic passage, Nick intuits Klara's metamorphosis taking shape as they have sex one last time:

> She looked like she'd been raised naked in this room, a skinny girl when she was a girl, probably, and skinny in a certain way, with a little bulgy belly and ashamed of her feet, but grown out of shyness and wrong proportions now, and being married of course, used to being seen, and she didn't have curves and swerves but was good-looking naked, and stuck to him when they fucked like a thing fighting for light, a great wet papery moth. (*U* 750)

In a single magnificent sentence, the stages of Klara's development from childhood through adulthood are recapitulated in sequence, leading up to this pristine moment, where she's naked in the room as if freshly delivered. That gorgeous final image of her "fighting for light, a great wet papery moth" pushes the transformation further, as if she is emerging from a cocoon and ready to take flight.

She may once have retreated into her solitary room to escape from the world and her life, a solipsistic move inward followed by several of DeLillo's artist characters. However, Nick helps dispel that solitude. She does not leave the painting room to rush into his arms, which would have been a huge mistake on his part and a banal cliché on DeLillo's part. Instead she leaves the room, the apartment, the family, and the conventional expectations of a 1950s homemaker in pursuit of art and a new life. Rather than collapsing inward toward oblivion, the housewife Klara Bronzini converts her tomb into a womb and is reborn as the artist Klara Sax, the triumphant life-force of *Underworld*.

to be a flirtatious invitation into the apartment? Or a shrug, as if to ask, "What are you doing here?" Or it could be a shrug of passive resignation, as in, "Ah, what the hell, might as well." Klara wonders herself what she's doing, but apparently she's been left out of the loop. As clothes come off and erotic heat rises, she keeps waiting for panic or ecstasy or outrage to seize her, but the expected emotions and standard-issue admonitions never arrive. Early in the encounter, "She kept waiting to feel crazy but didn't" (*U* 732). Even after she hauls out a mattress and they have sex, her inner voice is conspicuously silent: "When he went to find the toilet, she thought she'd feel strange and crazy and out of her mind, finally, but she just sat on the mattress smoking" (*U* 733). Does she fall madly in love with Nick? Not a bit of it. Is she racked with guilt over cheating on her husband? No. She expects to be and is curious why she isn't, but there it is. On a subconscious level she's already embracing the inevitable consequences of this self-sabotage of her marriage, though she keeps that knowledge at bay.

Klara resists directly linking sex with Nick to her desire to leave her family in pursuit of art, but DeLillo asks the reader to make precisely that connection. A crucial clue is provided by the location: "She thought as long as she kept him in this one room, no one could say there was something crazy going on. This was the spare room, the paint room. She wasn't supposed to be naked here but aside from that, her feet cold on the bare floor, there was nothing awfully strange happening here" (*U* 732). Klara has spent countless hours here, painting detailed studies of the room itself, and getting nowhere. But this blatantly transgressive act—inviting a strange young man into her home and having sex with him in the painting room—activates something latent in the room and in Klara. She literally begins to see the room in a new light: "The room was beautiful in this light, shadow-banded, all lines and gaps, claire-obscure" (*U* 733). As Boxall keenly observes, "Klara's painting of the room acquires its focus when blank repetition gives way to a kind of disjunction, to a kind of erotic disruption or disturbance that opens a crack in the wall" (208). She has struggled to see the work she's produced so far in this room as legitimate art, but she is instantly capable of viewing what she does with Nick in this room in an artistic light: "Then they were everywhere at once again, looped about each other, everything new for the second time, and she closed her eyes to see them together, which she could almost do for the sheerest time, bodies turned and edged and sidled, one way and the other, this and that concurrent, here but also there, like back-fronted Picasso lovers" (*U* 733). The "crack in the wall" described by Boxall soon spreads like a chasm to engulf her old life, but her new life will be devoted to making art out of the shattered remnants.

The second sex episode paradoxically emphasizes Klara's impenetrability. Whistler's Mother taught Klara important lessons about the strict limitations of understanding another person, of penetrating the surface to access someone's inner thoughts and mysterious motives. Tellingly, her

The other is Nick Shay. When Klara sticks that lit cigarette in his mouth, she lights the fuse on a brief but explosive affair that will blow her family life to bits. She didn't know that at the time, but even if she had she might have done it just the same. There is no special magic in seventeen-year-old Nick Shay. To put it in the crude terms in which Nick thinks and speaks in 1952, he's young, dumb, and full of cum. He is no knight in shining armor come to rescue a damsel in distress; he's a horny teenager looking to score. Nonetheless, he serves an absolutely critical function in Klara's transformation, even if another man could have served the same function just as well. In fact, had Nick been more mature and more appealing he might have been less effective as a catalyst for change, simply because Klara might have been tempted to jump out of one restrictive relationship and into another. There's never any threat of that here. Nick is just in it for the sex. And what is Klara in it for? Years later Acey Greene helps her understand the significance of the affair:

"Yes, well, maybe it's true. Seventeen's a man," Klara said. "And I've asked myself was the thing more important than I was willing to admit?"
"In other words did it show you a way out?"
"Did it point a way out?"
"Which you didn't want to think about at the time." (U 484)

The affair pointed Klara toward the exit, the escape route out of her stultifying life as a Bronx homemaker and toward the freedom necessary to begin her new life as an artist. At least that's the way Klara begins to reconstruct the narrative in 1974. But what did the fling mean in 1952 as it was happening? Nick and Klara had sex on two separate occasions only, a hello-fuck and a goodbye-fuck to put it again in Nick's lingo. DeLillo neatly cleaves the affair into two episodes, depicting the first sex scene from Klara's perspective and the second from Nick's.

"Six days later, or seven, she came out of the flat and locked the door. There was someone on the stoop looking in through the vestibule. She knew exactly who it was and what he was here for and she made a gesture that was either a shrug or a come-on" (U 732). So begins the first episode from Klara's point of view. In one sense her perception is acutely hypersensitive. Even though she has only met Nick once, and even though she's never had an affair before, she intuits immediately without a single word exchanged that he is here for sex. In another sense, however, Klara is coolly detached from the scene. Even in this most carnal of experiences, she sort of goes out of body again, viewing events from the outside rather than fully inhabiting the experience internally. The first clue to her detachment is the line "she made a gesture that was either a shrug or a come-on" (U 732). Well, which is it? One might well expect Nick not to know if Klara will welcome his advances or spurn them. But apparently she's not even sure herself. Is her gesture meant to be a flirtatious invitation into the apartment? Or a shrug, as if to ask, "What are you doing here?" Or it could be a shrug of passive resignation, as in, "Ah, what the hell, might as well." Klara wonders herself what she's doing, but apparently she's been left out of the loop. As clothes come off and erotic heat rises, she keeps waiting for panic or ecstasy or outrage to seize her, but the expected emotions and standard-issue admonitions never arrive. Early in the encounter, "She kept waiting to feel crazy but didn't" (*U* 732). Even after she hauls out a mattress and they have sex, her inner voice is conspicuously silent: "When he went to find the toilet, she thought she'd feel strange and crazy and out of her mind, finally, but she just sat on the mattress smoking" (*U* 733). Does she fall madly in love with Nick? Not a bit of it. Is she racked with guilt over cheating on her husband? No. She expects to be and is curious why she isn't, but there it is. On a subconscious level she's already embracing the inevitable consequences of this self-sabotage of her marriage, though she keeps that knowledge at bay.

Klara resists directly linking sex with Nick to her desire to leave her family in pursuit of art, but DeLillo asks the reader to make precisely that connection. A crucial clue is provided by the location: "She thought as long as she kept him in this one room, no one could say there was something crazy going on. This was the spare room, the paint room. She wasn't supposed to be naked here but aside from that, her feet cold on the bare floor, there was nothing awfully strange happening here" (*U* 732). Klara has spent countless hours here, painting detailed studies of the room itself, and getting nowhere. But this blatantly transgressive act—inviting a strange young man into her home and having sex with him in the painting room—activates something latent in the room and in Klara. She literally begins to see the room in a new light: "The room was beautiful in this light, shadow-banded, all lines and gaps, claire-obscure" (*U* 733). As Boxall keenly observes, "Klara's painting of the room acquires its focus when blank repetition gives way to a kind of disjunction, to a kind of erotic disruption or disturbance that opens a crack in the wall" (208). She has struggled to see the work she's produced so far in this room as legitimate art, but she is instantly capable of viewing what she does with Nick in this room in an artistic light: "Then they were everywhere at once again, looped about each other, everything new for the second time, and she closed her eyes to see them together, which she could almost do for the sheerest time, bodies turned and edged and sidled, one way and the other, this and that concurrent, here but also there, like back-fronted Picasso lovers" (*U* 733). The "crack in the wall" described by Boxall soon spreads like a chasm to engulf her old life, but her new life will be devoted to making art out of the shattered remnants.

The second sex episode paradoxically emphasizes Klara's impenetrability. Whistler's Mother taught Klara important lessons about the strict limitations of understanding another person, of penetrating the surface to access someone's inner thoughts and mysterious motives. Tellingly, her

6

Performing self-dialogue in "The DeLillo variations"

The eccentric genius Glenn Gould is one of the guiding muses in Don DeLillo's contemplative 2004 essay, "Counterpoint: Three Films, a Book, and an Old Photograph." Gould first earned international acclaim in the mid-1950s for his recording of Bach's *Goldberg Variations*. This notoriously complex piece is structured as a variation set: Bach establishes an aria, follows it with thirty variations on the initial theme, and returns to the beginning with an aria da capo. The filmmakers of *Thirty Two Short Films about Glenn Gould* likewise adopt a contrapuntal approach for their character study of the mercurial artist. DeLillo constructs his "Counterpoint" essay in similar fashion, using juxtaposition and variation to develop thematic relationships between solitude, madness, art, and death in the lives and works of Gould, Thelonious Monk, and Thomas Bernhard.

DeLillo's own oeuvre invites contrapuntal consideration as well. Early in his career, he seemed determined to reinvent himself with every novel, experimenting with one subgenre after another: the artistic apprenticeship novel (*Americana*), sports (*End Zone*), music (*Great Jones Street*), science fiction (*Ratner's Star*), and cloak-and-dagger thrillers (*Players* and *Running Dog*). The mature works of DeLillo's mid-career—*The Names*, *White Noise*, *Libra*, *Mao II*, and his magnum opus *Underworld*—cemented his reputation as the most penetrating literary chronicler of late twentieth-century American life. Throughout his diverse canon, DeLillo returned again and again to certain predominant themes, and in his twenty-first-century, post-*Underworld* work for page and stage, these recurring preoccupations have crystallized into urgent obsessions. The late DeLillo aesthetic focuses unblinkingly on the role of the artist to interrogate and mediate time, identity, and mortality. But to say that DeLillo returns obsessively to these core themes is not to say that his work has become redundant or predictable.

In fact, what is most remarkable is the striking variety and medium-specific nuance he brings to bear on each new variation upon his themes. In "Counterpoint" DeLillo observes, "Gould's second recording of the *Goldberg Variations* was made twenty-six years after his first rendition and is somber and slower, far more contemplative. He is not only reimagining Bach but engaging in a form of corrective *self-dialogue*" (CP 44, emphasis added). The same dynamics of self-dialogue animate DeLillo's late work. Taking my cues from DeLillo, Gould, and Bach, the present chapter takes a contrapuntal approach to three late works, the essay "Counterpoint" (2004), the novella *The Body Artist* (2000), and the play *Love-Lies-Bleeding* (2005). DeLillo uses the medium-specific conditions of printed prose and performed drama to explore his signature obsessions in strikingly different ways. Each of these reflexive self-dialogues is provocative in its own right. However, apprehended in counterpoint, what we might collectively think of as "The DeLillo Variations" constitute an important triptych within his late oeuvre. Performance art is central to all three works; indeed, DeLillo's increasing attention to performance constitutes one of the central features of his late aesthetic.[1]

"Counterpoint"

"Counterpoint: Three Films, a Book, and an Old Photograph" appeared in the journal *Grand Street* four years after the publication of *The Body Artist* and several months before the stage premiere of *Love-Lies-Bleeding*. This work of creative non-fiction serves effectively as a thematic bridge between the other two fictional works. The three movies referenced in the title are *The Fast Runner* (based upon an Inuit legend about Atanarjuat), *Thirty Two Short Films about Glenn Gould* (a film including dramatic enactments by an actor and interviews with people who knew the enigmatic virtuoso), and *Straight No Chaser* (a documentary about jazz innovator Thelonious Monk). The titular book is *The Loser*, a novel about Glenn Gould by the relentlessly intense Austrian writer Thomas Bernhard. The old photograph refers to an image hanging on the wall of DeLillo's writing room. The shot was taken in 1953 by photographer Bob Parent at the Open Door in the Village. It captures the Mount Rushmore of the 1950s New York jazz scene: Monk on piano, bassist Charles Mingus, drummer Roy Haynes, and saxophonist Charlie Parker.[2] The essay riffs back and forth between these eclectic artists, developing motifs close to the heart of DeLillo's own work.

The essay's most emblematic photo depicts a naked runner sprinting across a frozen white landscape, fleeing for his life from a distant pack of pursuers. "In *The Fast Runner*, Atanarjuat, racing, naked, is a man reacting to a primal danger; there are other men who want to kill him. But he may also resemble an individual trying to reestablish his sense of isolation,

FIGURE 6.1 *Jazz Musicians play at Open Door, New York. Charles Mingus (bass), Roy Haynes (drums), Thelonious Monk (piano), and Charlie Parker (saxophone). September 13, 1953. Photo by Bob Parent, courtesy Getty Images.*

his natural place in the landscape" (CP 46). From the beginning, most of DeLillo's works have featured at least one major figure who feels hounded into retreat by a hostile world. In his first published interview, he was asked by Tom LeClair about the tendency of his characters to withdraw from the world. He explained, "They feel instinctively that there's a certain struggle, a solitude they have to confront. The landscape is silent, whether it's a desert, a small room, a hole in the ground. *The voice you have to answer is your own*" (8, emphasis added). Ascetic withdrawal into meditative isolation is, according to DeLillo, a fundamental precondition to producing art. He identifies this same impulse in Glenn Gould, a Canadian by nationality and a lone wanderer of the metaphysical North.[3] According to DeLillo, "The artist is an adept of solitude living at the edge of that psychic immensity, the otherworld of ice and time and wintry introspection" (CP 38). Following a compass that always points away, an inner compulsion toward solitude so crucial to artistic achievement, involves great personal risk. The ascetic places himself at odds with society, a stance DeLillo defines in terms of *counterpoint*: "In older cultures, the solitary man is a malignant figure. He threatens the well-being of the group. But we know him because we encounter him, in ourselves and others. He lives in counterpoint, a figure in the faint distance. This is who he is, lastingly alone" (CP 47, 49). The group may feel threatened by the individual's secession, and the loner is also threatened by the corrosive effects of prolonged isolation. Solitude can foster genius, but it can also breed madness and crippling loneliness. As DeLillo notes, "The prisoner is thrown into solitary. He is alone, confined, sequestered. This is the harshest punishment the state allows, short of outright execution" (CP 46). DeLillo's vacillation between a romanticized image of the remote artist and a cautionary image of the indigent prisoner serves to remind that quests which begin on the mountaintop in search of enlightenment can end in the madhouse of psychic disintegration and self-annihilation.

The voice you have to answer is your own. DeLillo's opinion has not altered since he made that declaration to LeClair, though his estimation of the cost for this self-dialogue has increased with age. At the heart of "Counterpoint," DeLillo launches into a verbal jazz solo riffing on various dead-end attempts to explain away or pathologize the solitary lives led by Gould, Monk, and Bernhard:

> First there is the gradation of language, a sense of deepening threat played out in the terms themselves. Introspection, solitude, isolation, anxiety, phobia, depression, hallucination, schizophrenia. Then there are the human referents. He is free from convention; or there is something scanted in his humanity; or he is trapped in a modern context, bearing some taint of estrangement that makes him uneasy in the world; or it's a result of upbringing maybe; or he's a goddamn genius—leave him alone; or the matter is strictly clinical, a question of brain chemistry; or it's a natural state in fact, some dread that lingers in the early brain, the snake brain, outside the slanted limits of all the things he has shored against it. (CP 49)

FIGURE 6.2 *Atanarjuat (Natar Ungalaak) flees from pursuers in Zacharias Kunuk's* Atanarjuat: The Fast Runner *(Odeon Films, 2001).*

But for all these pigeonholing rationalizations, DeLillo distills the artist's solitary quest down to a single driving question: "How close to the self can we get without losing everything?" (CP 49)

Who or what or where is "the self"? How does one get close enough to it to risk losing everything? The postmodern era with which DeLillo is most commonly associated has little truck with antiquated absolutes like the essential, unified self. However, this does not prevent several characters in his recent work from reopening the closed subject of the Subject, the True Self. For instance, war theoretician Richard Elster is introduced into the novel *Point Omega* through his observations on the "true life": "The true life is not reducible to words spoken or written, not by anyone, ever. The true life takes place when we're alone, thinking, feeling, lost in memory, dreamingly self-aware, the submicroscopic moments" (*PO* 17). Later Elster describes the true life like a Proustian epiphany of the self's confrontation with its own mortality: "A moment, a thought, here and gone, each of us, on a street somewhere, and this is everything. . . . It's what we call self, the true life, he said, the essential being. It's self in the soft wallow of what it knows, and what it knows is that it will not live forever" (*PO* 63). Delfina Treadwell, the confession-seeking, death-dealing talk show host in the play *Valparaiso*, invokes the concept more crudely and succinctly: "Then call it the self. I want your naked shitmost self" (*V* 91). Of course, Elster and Delfina are dubious sources of knowledge, so we shouldn't necessarily take their words for it. DeLillo's depiction of identity is more complex, contingent, elusive, diffuse, and, most interestingly in the present context, more *performative*.

His most revealing commentary with respect to the dangerous pursuit of self comes in his reflections on fellow novelist Thomas Bernhard. DeLillo makes no claims to membership among the madmen-geniuses he studies in "Counterpoint." But he does know a thing or two about writing, so he speaks with hard-won authority when he turns from Gould's classical music and Monk's jazz to Bernhard's novel *The Loser*. He pushes a provocative line of inquiry: "To what extent is Bernhard himself speaking to the reader?" (CP 41). The answer is implied in the asking: Bernhard expresses himself to the reader through the guise of his narrator. Here DeLillo the reader commits the very offense that DeLillo the novelist has consistently discouraged in numerous interviews; namely, he equates the novel's narrator and characters as mouthpieces for the novelist himself. In so doing, DeLillo indirectly sheds light on his own creative process and that of the artist characters who preside over several of his works. "There are shadings of identity among author, narrator, and character. There is the doubling of Bernhard/Gould and also the split between Bernhard the pianist and Bernhard the novelist" (CP 41). These shadings of identity between the artist and his/her creations, the propensity of art to reflect and replicate the artist—one's self-image, fantasies, fears, and obsessions—is fundamental to understanding multiple DeLillo works for page and stage.

It is particularly telling that DeLillo identifies this aesthetic of projection, reflection, and deflection not by pointing to it in his own work (where it is manifestly evident), but by locating it in the work of an artist he admires (Bernhard), who was himself identifying with another artist they both admired (Gould). Most enlightening of all, DeLillo conceptualizes this relationship between creator and creatures in terms of *acting*: "Where is the novelist? He is sitting in a room in Vienna or Salzburg writing lines for a narrator who is not him, but is him, but isn't. In the end the narrator is an uncredited actor playing Thomas Bernhard in much the same way that a flesh-and-blood actor plays Glenn Gould in *Thirty Two Short Films*" (CP 42). The sequestered novelist draws closer to the self by creating and acting out the roles of other selves, a performance of self-dialogue. As Samuel Beckett described the primal creative impulse in *Endgame*, "Then babble, babble, words, like the solitary child who turns himself into children, two, three, so as to be together, and whisper together, in the dark" (126). *The voice you have to answer is your own.* Through his penetrating meditations on the art of others in "Counterpoint," DeLillo provides his clearest articulation of the performative aesthetic that animates his late work, an approach he had already begun developing in the earlier novella *The Body Artist*, and a method he subsequently returned to in variant form in the play *Love-Lies-Bleeding*.

The Body Artist

Readers enter the novella in medias res amid breakfast banter between a husband and wife. We cannot appreciate the significance of this encounter until the obituary appended at chapter's end. The breakfast scene chronicles the final morning Lauren Hartke spent with Rey Robles, her filmmaker husband who committed suicide later that same day. Lauren is identified as "the body artist" at the conclusion of Rey's obituary (*BA* 31). In retrospect there are several prior indications establishing her habits of mind as a performance artist. She doesn't simply browse the newspaper; she absorbs the stories and is gathered into the lives of people she reads about. "She tended lately to place herself, to insert herself into certain stories in the newspaper. Some kind of daydream variation" (*BA* 16). "Variation" here connotes contrapuntal experiments in rearrangement like those expressed musically in the *Goldberg Variations*. At times it is difficult to determine who is rearranging whom. Is Lauren projecting herself into the lives of others? Or is she hyper-receptive to being acted upon by the experiences and voices around and within her? "She had a hyper-preparedness, or haywire, or hair-trigger, and Rey was always saying, or said once, and she carried a voice in her head that was hers and it was dialogue or monologue . . . a voice that flowed from a story in the paper" (*BA* 18). The boundary separating Lauren from others is porous, dappled with shadings of identity, where "an incident described in the paper seemed to rise out of the inky lines of print and gather her into it" (*BA* 20), and where "there are people being tortured halfway around the world, who speak another language, and you have conversations with them more or less uncontrollably until you become aware you are doing it and then you stop" (*BA* 21). Ink is to Lauren what drink is to an alcoholic: one story and she's besotted with voices. Mark Osteen has described *The Body Artist* as "DeLillo's most penetrating analysis of the process of artistic generation" (65). One wonders how closely Lauren's process of creative inspiration mirrors that of her author. Certainly the two share common talents, including a finely tuned ear for speech, a willingness to allow new work to develop slowly at its own pace, and an openness to following different paths and shapes dictated by the characters. However, a fundamental difference is announced in the title. DeLillo is a word artist of language, but Lauren is a *body* artist. Her body is her medium of expression.

Lauren maintains a rigorous training ritual to prepare her body for art. She stretches and strains her muscles, sands her skin, waxes off her body hair, and applies bleaching cream to her skin. "This was her work, to disappear from all her former venues of aspect and bearing and to become a blankness, a body slate erased of every past resemblance" (*BA* 86). In the wake of Rey's suicide, one might interpret her austere measures as symptomatic of unresolved grief; she is slowly dwindling to nothing, annihilating her past and erasing her identity. However, her training regimen was well established long before Rey's death. Her discipline and commitment cannot merely be dismissed as melancholia. She certainly suffers for her art, but she also makes an art of suffering. Lauren is a composite of performance artists like Carolee Schneemann, Laurie Anderson, Karen Finley, and especially Marina Abramović. Lauren also recalls Kafka's hunger artist, whose influence is palpable throughout *The Body Artist*, and anticipates "The Starveling" from DeLillo's later short story. Lauren's self-erasure serves a practical function. She aspires to become a blank cipher or tabula rasa in preparation for reinscribing her "body slate" with new characters. In that sense her process seems comparable to a painter priming a new canvas, or DeLillo rolling a clean page into his Olympia typewriter.

The example of Serbian performance artist Marina Abramović is particularly instructive. She first gained notoriety for a series of *Rhythm* pieces in the early 1970s. Each piece tested the limits of her personal endurance and pain threshold, while also piercing the boundary between artist and audience. For instance, in *Rhythm 0* (1974) she spent six hours in Studio Morra in Naples and surrendered herself to the whims of her audience. She placed 72 objects on a table. Her instructions to the audience said: "I am the object. / During this period I take full responsibility" (68). Over the course of the performance (8:00 p.m. to 2:00 a.m.), she was stripped, cut, stuck with pins, written upon, picked up and carried around, and manipulated to point a pistol at herself. In her memoir *Walk Through Walls* Abramović reflects, "What had happened while they were there, quite simply, was performance. And the essence of performance is that the audience and the performer make the piece together. I wanted to test the limits of how far the public would go if I didn't do anything at all." (71). Like DeLillo, Abramović invokes the mirror as an emblem for her self-reflexive art: "Human beings are afraid of very simple things: we fear suffering, we fear mortality. What I was doing in *Rhythm 0*—as in all my other performances—was staging these fears for the audience: using their energy to push my body as far as possible. In the process, I liberated myself from my fears. And as this happened, *I became a mirror for the audience*—if I could do it, they could do it, too" (71, emphasis added).

Abramović uses the mirror in other pieces to link art to mortality, playing with the paradox of "live" performance inspired by death much like Lauren in *The Body Artist*. An exemplary piece in this respect is her *Cleaning the Mirror* series of video performances, displayed at Modern Art Oxford in 1995. As she describes it, "In one of the *Cleaning the Mirror* pieces, I lay naked with a (very realistic) skeleton model on top of me for ninety minutes, breathing easily, the skeleton rising and falling gently with every breath I took. In another piece I sat with the skeleton on my lap and, using a hard scrub brush and a pail full of soapy water, spent three hours furiously scouring

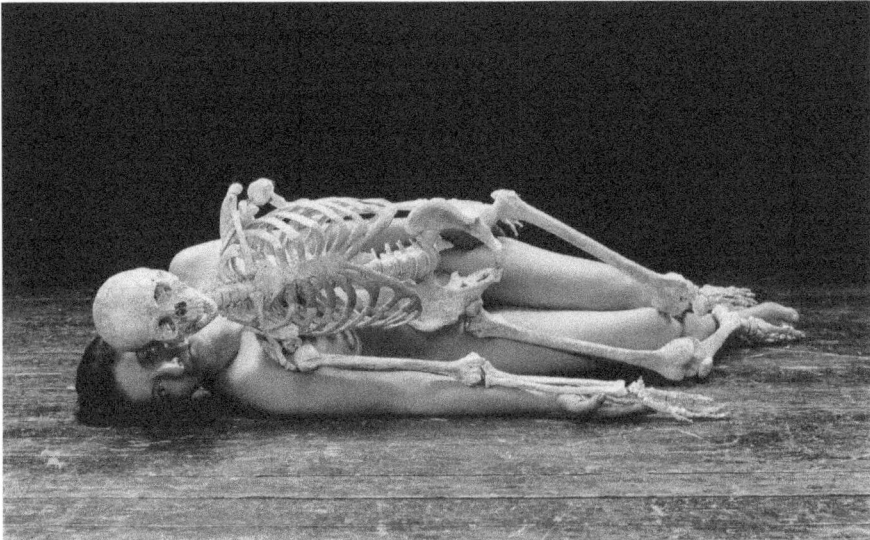

FIGURE 6.3 Self Portrait with Skeleton *(2002–05) by Marina Abramović.* © *2018 Marina Abramović. Photo Attilio Maranzano, courtesy Marina Abramović Archives / Sean Kelly Gallery / Artist Resource Society (ARS), New York.*

its every nook and cranny" (Abramović 227). The title phrase "cleaning the mirror" refers to the dead skeleton as a mirror of the living artist interacting with it. The piece was inspired by the rituals of Tibetan monks in prolonged contemplation of their own mortality. The website LIMA, which preserves and distributes digital works by Abramović and other performance artists, has this to say about *Cleaning the Mirror 1*:

> Close-ups of Abramović's hands and the body parts of the skeleton exhibit a kind of "family-likeness" between the two. The boundaries between the actor and the "object" acted upon start to blur; the dead and the alive start to intermingle. As for Abramović *the skeleton metaphorically represents* ". . . *the last mirror we will all face*," death and temporality are the major themes addressed in this work. (LIMA, emphasis added)

Cleaning the Mirror dramatizes the artist's meditation upon death while simultaneously inviting the spectator to do the same.

Abramović's most famous performance, and the apotheosis of her self-reflexive mirroring relationship with her audience, is *The Artist Is Present*. As part of a career retrospective at MoMA in New York, Abramović was in residence seven hours a day for three months. She sat in a simple chair across an unadorned table from another simple chair; at one point during the run the table was removed and the performance space was pared down to two facing chairs. "The rules were simple: Each person could sit across from me for as short or as long a time as he or she wished. We would maintain eye contact. The public was not to touch me or speak to me" (Abramović 309). The daily performances began on March 14 and ended some 736 hours later on May 31, 2010. Over 1,500 audience members sat across from Abramović, some for only a minute, others for multiple hours. The entire performance was on display to the public and was documented through film and photography. The crowds grew steadily over the course of the three months, culminating in an audience of 17,000 on the final day (318). Despite the teeming attendance, the piece remained an intimate one-on-one encounter between the artist and each individual she encountered.

One of the most moving moments from the performance—and one of the most self-reflexively rich—came on the first day, when Ulay sat across from Abramović. The two artists had collaborated on numerous groundbreaking performances in the 1970s and 1980s, mining the depths of their personal relationship for material. But after an acrimonious breakup the two had not seen each other for many years before Ulay arrived at MoMA on March 14, 2010. The resulting encounter between artist and artist-turned-audience-member left both Abramović and Ulay visibly shaken. It also captured the spirit of *The Artist Is Present* better than any other encounter could have.[4] The artist is present, but so is the audience, and both are necessary participants as co-creators of performance art. The two mirror each other, but not in a hierarchical relationship where one is active subject and the other passive object. Human energy is transmitted from and transferred to both sides to complete the artistic circuit. Emotional investment and psychic labor is required on both sides of the mirror for this kind of performance to succeed. Looking back on *The Artist Is Present*, Abramović recalls, "What I found, immediately, was that the people sitting across from me became very moved. From the beginning, people were in tears—and so was I. *Was I a mirror?* It felt like more than that. I could see and feel people's pain" (309, emphasis added).

Lauren Hartke is likewise super-sensitive to pain, her own and that of others, and she uses it to fuel her deeply personal performance art. Although she seemingly aspires to the pristine condition of blank "body slate," she cannot ultimately be reduced to the same object status as a canvas or a piece of paper. This body artist is a living, feeling subject. Corporeality and mediation emerge as major sources of tension in *The Body Artist* after Rey's death. The quotidian breakfast scene which opens the novel may seem unremarkable at first, but it establishes that Lauren was *not* a solitary artist so long as she had Rey. She has her voices too, yes, her inner murmur and the vicarious voices she weaves together in "daydream variation." But as DeLillo subtly emphasizes in the breakfast scene, Lauren experiences most people and events at a distant remove. She encounters others via the newspaper in narratives that are already mediated. The singular, sustaining

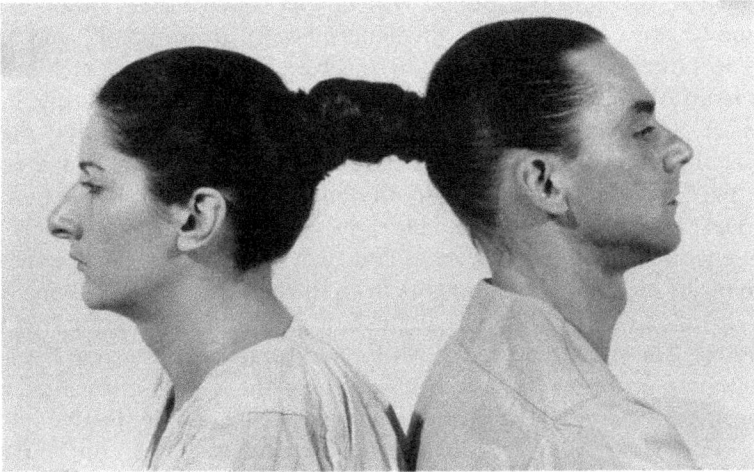

FIGURE 6.4 Relation in Time *(1977) by Marina Abramović/ Ulay (Uwe Laysiepen). 17-hour performance, Studio G7, Bologna, Italy. © 2018 Marina Abramović / Ulay, courtesy Marina Abramović Archives / Sean Kelly Gallery / Artist Resource Society (ARS), New York.*

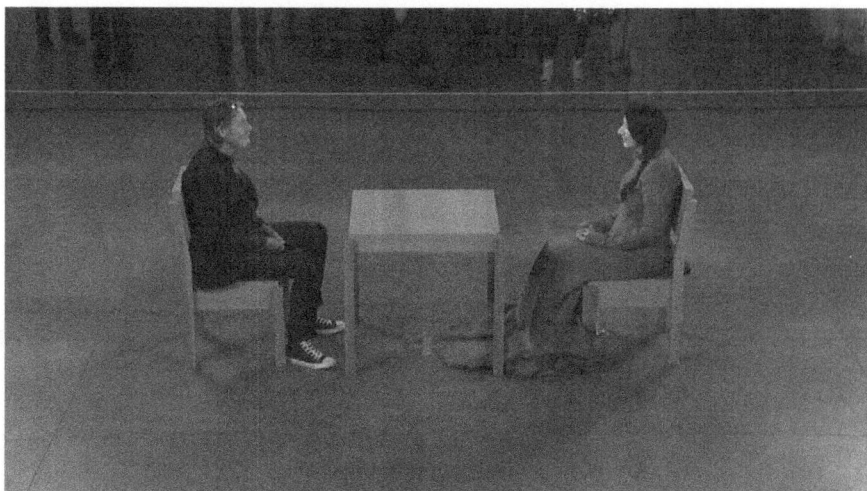

FIGURE 6.5 *Ulay reunites with Abramović in* Marina Abramović: The Artist Is Present, *directed by Matthew Akers and Jeff Dupre (Show of Force, 2012).*

exception is Rey. She is grounded by direct contact with the material body of her husband. *The Body Artist* is DeLillo's shortest novel, a quite conscious gesture scaling down from his longest and grandest novel *Underworld*. But it is also his most sensual, crackling with supercharged physical sensations. For instance, when Rey lights up a cigarette at the kitchen table, it sends Lauren into sensual reverie:

> It was agreeable to her, the smell of tobacco. It was part of her knowledge of his body. It was the aura of the man, a residue of smoke and unbroken habit, a dimension in the night, and she lapped it off the curled gray hairs on his chest and tasted it in his mouth. It was who he was in the dark, cigarettes and mumbled sleep and a hundred other things nameable and not. (*BA* 21–22)

Rey helps to anchor Lauren bodily in the material world, and she suddenly becomes unmoored after his suicide.

Enter Mr. Tuttle. After Rey's suicide Lauren returns to their rental home and discovers a small male of indeterminate age and aspect. She nicknames him "Mr. Tuttle" after an awkward science teacher from high school. The silliness of the name bears no resemblance to the seriousness of his impact on Lauren. Perhaps DeLillo intended "Mr. Tuttle" as a rough homophone for "Mortal" or "Mortality," for Lauren soon associates him with her dead husband. Not that he looks or acts like Rey at first. She initially mistakes him for a sandy-haired child. Even after she concludes that he is older, he retains the air of a sleepy foundling, a perversely inscrutable variation on Goldilocks. It is his voice that eventually binds him to Rey. When Mr. Tuttle first attempts to speak in his own voice, his stilted gibberish is barely decipherable. His first words, "It is not able" (*BA* 45), sound less like a Zen koan and more like a poor imitation of "E.T. phone home." At one point Lauren wonders half-jokingly, "Am I the first human to abduct an alien?" (*BA* 85) But she snaps to attention when she discovers that Mr. Tuttle can recite entire monologues and dialogues involving Rey. At first she suspects he was eavesdropping on conversations and memorizing them with pitch-perfect mimicry: "This was not some communication with the dead. It was Rey alive in the course of a talk he'd had with her, in this room, not long after they'd come here. She was sure of this" (*BA* 63). Later she suspects Mr. Tuttle is capable of channeling her dead husband in the present, conjuring him from the dead. "It was Rey's voice all right, it was her husband's tonal soul, but she didn't think the man was remembering. It is happening now. This is what she thought. She watched him struggle in his utterance and thought it was happening, somehow now, in his frame, in his fracted time, and he is only reporting, helplessly, what they say" (*BA* 89).

Is Mr. Tuttle the hallucination of an unhinged mind? Is he a warped external projection of Lauren's inner fantasy to reunite with Rey? David Cowart observes, "So far as the reader of knows, only Lauren ever lays eyes on or converses with her visitor" (204). He further speculates that "in Mr. Tuttle Lauren encounters, as a projection of her own unconscious, the artist in herself, temporarily obtunded or disoriented by late catastrophe" (206). To be sure, no rational explanations adequately account for this strange visitor, or even confirm his existence. Yet Lauren is drawn inexorably to Mr. Tuttle, not as a ghost or a delusion, but as a substantial corporeal being. She regards him as a portal through which she might reestablish a carnal connection with Rey. In one of the most revealing scenes in *The Body Artist*, Lauren expresses her desire to physically enter Mr. Tuttle, or be entered by him, as a means of reuniting with Rey:

> Rey is alive now in this man's mind, in his mouth and body and cock. Her skin was electric. She saw herself, she sees herself crawling toward him. The image is there in front of her. She is crawling across the floor and it is nearly real to her. She feels something has separated, softly come unfixed, and she tries to pull him down to the floor with her, stop him, keep him here, or crawls up onto him or into him, dissolving, or only lies prone and sobs unstoppably, being watched by herself from above.
>
> She could smell his liniment on her body, his muscle rub, and then he was all through talking. (*BA* 89–90)

This passage captures Lauren's abject desperation, her physical need, her loosening grip on the distinctions between fantasy and reality, and her identity dissociation. But notice an important rhetorical move here: "She saw herself, she sees herself crawling toward him." The narrative voice abruptly shifts from past- to present-tense verbs and continues on in that new temporal mode for the rest of the paragraph—only to plummet back into past tense in the final sentence, after the spell is broken. This passage signals one of DeLillo's primary preoccupations in *The Body Artist* and in much of his twenty-first-century work: *Time*.[5]

The novella opens with the line: "Time seems to pass" (*BA* 9). The present verb tense is again notable, but more striking still is the verb itself. Time only *seems* to pass? DeLillo began testing the boundaries of time and space in his fiction as far back as the mid-1970s in *Ratner's Star*. In recent years the relationship of time and space has become a recurring preoccupation. Samuel Chase Coale has studied the Harry Ransom Center's archival material and found abundant evidence of DeLillo's interest in quantum theory and physics. "There were his interpretations of and quotations from articles on Einstein, Bohr, Heisenberg, Schrödinger, and others" (Coale 5). He connects the opening of *The Body Artist* with a manuscript note quoting Hermann Weyl: "The objective world simply is; it does not happen" (7). The idea here is that time does not unfold gradually in a chronological sequence of moments but instead already exists all at once on what we might conceive of spatially as an infinite plane, encompassing all past, present, and future. The implications of this concept are significant for art. In aesthetic terms it refutes and conflates Lessing's classic distinction in *Laocoön* between the *nacheinander* (the temporal nature of arts that develop in time like music, poetry, and drama) and the *nebeneinander* (the spatial nature of arts that are entirely present all at once like painting and sculpture). DeLillo is essentially applying modern physics' understanding of the space-time continuum to the novel. Think of time as a book. All the things that happen in that book have already been committed to print. At any given moment in the reading experience, future events one has not yet read are already fixed (just flip ahead and see), while events that have previously happened continue to exist unaltered (flip back and they're still there). These bedrock truths apply to all books, but few novelists exploit this space-time dimension as deftly as DeLillo.

His clearest articulation of the quantum theories undergirding his late work came in a 2003 radio interview with Michael Krasny. The interviewer asked about the subject of déjà vu in *White Noise*, and DeLillo began to open up about his broader theories on time. "Time is a great mystery to most people, including philosophers, cosmologists, and others. . . . It occurs to me, and I think it has occurred to physicists who work in this particular area, that it may well be that time exists—past, present, and future—simultaneously. And that it is simply a question, for the sake of our self-protection, of completely reformulating the nature of time in order to survive." DeLillo posed the questions, "Is it possible that the experience of déjà vu is somehow connected with the idea that time exists in one continuum, and that it is just a question of our gaining access to it? Is it possible for us to gain access to the future? Does déjà vu suggest that we are able to do this, that there is some kind of leakage from the future into our current sense of perception?" Krasny asked what DeLillo's instincts as a novelist told him with respect to time as a single pre-existing continuum, and his reply was fascinating:

> I think there is much on this subject that we simply haven't been able to understand. It's the way in which we construct our own universe. The way that the universe itself is totally different, we are told, from our perceptions of it. We create the universe in a way; we create the world around us. And I don't know that anyone can attempt to discuss this in any great, accurate detail. But it seems to be a fact, if we can use the word "fact," not that it doesn't exist, but that it exists in a way that may be totally alien to the ability of humans to survive it. (Krasny)

As an artist, DeLillo has long been a creator of worlds, and he often writes about artist characters who are themselves creators of worlds inside worlds. But here DeLillo radically extends his understanding of creation to include all of us. Each human effectively creates a variation of the world through individual perceptions. Furthermore, we distort time and space because we could not survive staring into the Medusa's head of a space-time continuum which retains our ineluctable past, augurs our inevitable future, and contains our unavoidable death.

Mr. Tuttle is a creature fully steeped in this alternate understanding of time. He finds himself stranded in our alien world and struggling to adapt, like a Tralfamadorian stuck in the amber of human time. The first hint of Mr. Tuttle's different temporal bearings comes through his inability to grasp verb tense. He observes, "It rained very much," but Lauren corrects him: "It will rain. It is going to rain" (*BA* 46). He apprehends past, present, and future equally and at once, rendering meaningless distinctions between what has happened, what is happening, and what will happen. She gradually speculates, "Maybe this man experiences another kind of reality where he is here and there, before and after, and he moves from one to the other shatteringly, in a state of collapse, minus an identity, a language . . . . She thought maybe he lived in a kind of time that had no narrative quality" (*BA* 66, 67). Time that has no narrative quality is time that doesn't happen but merely is. Connecting Mr. Tuttle's worldview with the opening passage of *The Body Artist*, Lauren reflects, "Time is supposed to pass, she thought. But maybe he is living in another state. It is a kind of time that is simply and overwhelmingly there, laid out, unoccurring, and he lacks the inborn ability to reconceive this condition" (*BA* 79). Lauren resists Mr. Tuttle's relationship with time. Yet she is so mired in grief and thwarted desire that she is gradually forced to reconsider the existence of time that does not pass.

Ultimately Lauren learns to work through her suffering and assimilate Rey's death. Art is crucial to that process. Mr. Tuttle becomes the principal muse and culminating character for a new work of performance art. During her interrogations of Mr. Tuttle, Lauren began recording their conversations, which eventually served as a kind of artist's journal guiding her toward the development of *Body Time*. As this suggestive title indicates, Lauren brings her distinct connection with the body into contrapuntal dialogue with Mr. Tuttle's distinct connection with time. DeLillo includes a review of the piece by Lauren's friend and theater critic Mariella Chapman titled "Body Art In Extremis: Slow, Spare and Painful." The reviewer observes, "Hartke clearly wanted her audience to feel time go by, viscerally, even painfully" (*BA* 106). Lauren explains, "Maybe the idea is to think of time differently . . . . Stop time, or stretch it out, or open it up. Make a still life that's living, not painted" (*BA* 109). The idea of a "still life that's living" perfectly captures the demands Lauren makes of her body, manipulating herself like an organic canvas for portraying various characters. As Chapman describes it, "Hartke is a body artist who tries to shake off the body—hers anyway. . . . Hartke's work is not self-strutting or self-lacerating. She is acting, always in the process, of becoming another or exploring some root identity" (*BA* 107). Paradoxically, the more Lauren removes her ego from her art and just gets out of the way, the more she surrenders herself to other bodies and voices and allows them to speak and move through her, the closer she comes to reintegrating her shattered identity.

Commenting upon the novella's experiments with identity, Mark Osteen observes, "*The Body Artist* also traffics in metempsychosis: both the literary kind, whereby patterns and motifs from previous texts are revived, and the human kind, whereby human beings return to life in altered forms" (65). Focusing upon *The Body Artist*'s experiments with time, David Cowart argues, "Mr. Tuttle is not unique in either his shuttling backward and forward in time or his ability to act as a recording device to replicate or reproduce the world's discourse. The literary artist can do these things as well—and in narrative that need not proceed in a linear fashion" (205). Both critics are right in terms of DeLillo's literary achievement, but Lauren's achievement within the novella hinges upon the specifically *performative* nature of her art as distinct from the literary. DeLillo once admitted in an interview with Adam Begley, "When my head is in the typewriter the last thing on my mind is some imaginary reader. I don't have an audience; I have a set of standards" (91). By contrast Lauren, who seeks to restore her severed physical connection to the world which she lost when Rey died, relies upon the presence of an audience as an essential component to her performance art. The relation of live performance to time is crucial, a temporal relation that is significantly different from printed fiction. One doesn't have to be a ghost, a space-time alien, or a supernatural foundling to inhabit a reality that simultaneously encompasses past, present, and future: one can be a performing artist. Each performance takes place on a fixed stage and "seems to pass" in the singular, unprecedented, unrepeatable *now*. And yet, no matter how fully the performer immerses herself in the now, there is no escaping the fact that a version of tonight's now happened last night, and another version will happen again tomorrow night. Though a hundred incremental changes could differentiate Saturday's performance from Friday and Sunday, the physical stage and the written script generally remain fixed. Thus, the conditions of stage performance constitute a relatively stable space-time continuum encompassing past, present, and future.

Love-Lies-Bleeding

DeLillo has worked in the performing arts as a playwright, though he has not achieved nearly the same level of critical and popular acclaim in this medium. His full-length plays *The Day Room* (1986), *Valparaiso* (1999), and *Love-Lies-Bleeding* (2005) have all received multiple productions and generally positive, if muted, receptions.[6] Of these plays, the latter work about the dying artist Alex Macklin is his most accomplished, though also his least understood. DeLillo directed the first staged reading of the play in 2005 with the Boise Contemporary Theater (BCT) company, and the following year the BCT mounted a full production directed by Tracy Sunderland. In 2006 the renowned Steppenwolf Theatre of Chicago put the play on to more mixed reviews. For instance, Tony Adler snarkily voiced the gripes of many detractors:

> As a playwright, Don DeLillo makes an excellent novelist. This isn't as damning as it sounds. There's some merciless, meticulous writing in DeLillo's new *Love-Lies-Bleeding*. The language is interesting for the way it traps anguish in frozen, formal diction. The characters each have their own weight and mass. The premise provides an elegantly simple mechanism for exploring primal issues. It's all very strong. It just doesn't belong on a stage. (Adler)

Adler rehashes familiar complaints about static, verbose fiction writers who try and fail to translate their talents from page to stage, and then he sends DeLillo's would-be audiences across town to see a better show:

> Coincidentally, you can find out how a real playwright handles the same formal challenge by seeing Edward Albee's *Three Tall Women*, currently at the Apple Tree Theatre. Albee takes a comatose old lady and divides

her up into her young, middle-aged, and dying selves, giving them rein
not only to argue with one another but to scare the old lady's son as he
observes his deathbed vigil. The result is funny, profound, and visually
dynamic. Theatrical. (Adler)

The reviewer is right to compare DeLillo and Albee's formal challenges—
staging a death by splitting the dying person into three selves—but he
ignores the metadramatic dimensions of *Love-Lies-Bleeding* which prevail
in DeLillo just as surely as in Albee. Critics and audiences have generally
been so distracted by the topical euthanasia plot that they have failed to
appreciate *Love-Lies-Bleeding* as a bold theatrical experiment in time and
self-dialogue.

DeLillo uses the same term to describe Alex Macklin that he applied to
Lauren Hartke's body art: *in extremis*. That is, at the furthest extreme of
life, in the final agony at the brink of death. Having suffered two massive
strokes, the seventy-year-old Alex can no longer speak or walk. But his
younger selves—the sixty-nine-year-old Alex (featured in Act One, Scene
One and Act Three, Scene Nine) and the sixty-four-year-old Alex (featured
in Act Two)—still exist at other points in the space-time continuum and

FIGURE 6.6 *The son Sean (played by Matthew Cameron Clark) talks to his catatonic
father Alex Macklin (played by Stitch Marker) in the 2006 Boise Contemporary
Theater production of* Love-Lies-Bleeding, *directed by Tracy Sunderland.* © *Jeremy
Winchester.*

remain capable of speech and movement. DeLillo never explicitly spells this division out in the dialogue of the play. Instead he uses the medium-specific tools of theater to communicate this concept. The stage directions note, "Two actors appear as Alex. One plays the character in three episodes that precede the main action. The other plays Alex *in extremis*, a helpless figure attached to a feeding tube" (*LLB* 1). Alex *in extremis* sits separately on the side of the stage in distinct lighting. He occupies the same stage at the same time while an episode from his past is reenacted in the opening scene. Unlike Albee's *Three Tall Women*, the three Alexes never directly interact with each other in *Love-Lies-Bleeding*. In the first scene neither the seventy-year-old catatonic Alex nor the sixty-nine-year-old partially incapacitated Alex overtly acknowledges the other's presence. Nevertheless, the audience is made visually aware of their simultaneous presence. We are effectively positioned to see through the temporal perspective of Mr. Tuttle. This dramaturgical precedent establishes the conceptual paradigm for understanding the entire play.

Alex Macklin is the embedded author of *Love-Lies-Bleeding*. He is the demiurgic descendent of the two Nicks, Branch and Shay, and a forefather of *Zero K*'s Jeff Lockhart. The stage represents Alex's solipsistic inner world, and all the action is filtered through his perspective. Alex may be the one giving life to the play, but his gaze is fixed squarely upon his death. *Love-Lies-Bleeding* is ostensibly a play about euthanasia, but this is actually a MacGuffin, a narrative contrivance which obscures DeLillo's deeper interests. Instead of replicating the popular paradigm for approaching euthanasia, DeLillo begins from a self-reflexive premise: What might these ethically provocative and personally wrenching end-of-life decisions look like from the perspective of a dying artist? What goes on in the mind of a creator at the end of life? The play dramatizes the dying reveries of Alex Macklin, a seventy-year-old man who is physically immobilized and incommunicative. Yet Alex is still lucid enough to be aware of his dilemma and curious enough to meditate upon his own mortality, to remember previous encounters that have shaped his attitudes toward death, to enact debates and fantasize potential scenarios whereby an ensemble cast of his loved ones collaborate to enact his end. In an interview promoting his first produced play, *The Day Room*, DeLillo reflected upon the intrinsic connection between the craft of acting and the human propensity for denying death:

I began to sense a connection, almost a metaphysical connection, between the craft of acting and the fear we all have of dying. It seemed to me that actors are a kind of model for the ways in which we hide from the knowledge we inevitably possess of our final extinction. There's a sense in which actors teach us how to hide. There's something about the necessary shift in identity which actors make in the ordinary course of their work that seems almost a guide to concealing what we know about ourselves. (Rothstein 21)

By the time DeLillo progresses to *Love-Lies-Bleeding*, he interrogates the links between acting and mortality with increased precision, sophistication, and metatheatrical self-awareness—as a playwright, that is, and not merely as a moonlighting novelist. *Love-Lies-Bleeding* experiments with using theatrical performance as a vehicle for confronting death, not just avoiding it, in ways that acknowledge both the fear and the allure of death under conditions *in extremis*.

The first scene turns back the calendar a year, just after Alex had suffered his first stroke. The sixty-nine-year-old Alex fixates upon the first dead body he ever saw as a child, a man on a New York subway train. He recalls to his wife Lia: "Gray like an animal. He belonged to a different order of nature. The first dead man I'd ever seen and there's never been anyone since who has looked more finally dead" (*LLB* 8). What was becoming clear to Alex after his first stroke, and what is manifestly evident for Alex *in extremis* after the second stroke, is that he, too, will eventually become a gray, lifeless animal. As an eleven-year-old kid, he received his first premonition of death, and the play dramatizes his fulfillment of the prophecy.

Viewed from a perspective that comprehends time as always already existing, Alex is both always alive and already dead; it's just a question of what position he occupies in the space-time continuum at a given point. Here Murray Jay Siskind's theories on déjà vu in *White Noise* are apropos for *Love-Lies-Bleeding*. "Why do we think these things happened before?" Murray asks. "Simple. They did happen before, in our minds, as visions of the future. Because these are precognitions, we can't fit the material into our system of consciousness as it is now structured." Murray theorizes that in déjà vu "we're seeing into the future but haven't learned how to process the experience. So it stays hidden until the precognition comes true, until we come face to face with the event. Now we are free to remember it, to experience it as familiar material." This phenomenon is felt most sharply with respect to our inevitable mortality: "Most of us have probably seen our own death but haven't known how to make the material surface. Maybe when we die, the first thing we'll say is, 'I know this feeling. I was here before'" (*WN* 145–46). Seventy-year-old Alex is in a position to look back at the dead man on the subway and appreciate this as a premonition of his own death. He's been here before. *Love-Lies-Bleeding* is a dramatic staging of what Alex *in extremis* sees when he goes back to the future of his death.

Does Alex see a preordained future, or does he creatively construct it? That is, does Alex flip ahead to read a script already etched in the stone of time? Or does he use his imagination to invent that script—a subjective fantasy of what his loved ones might say and do to hasten his death, and a self-dialogue with his former and future selves? The most honest answer is that DeLillo invites both interpretive possibilities, mutually exclusive though they are, and allows both to remain open. As an artist, as a creator of worlds, DeLillo equips his artist-figures with the same creative license to generate their own worlds. Following the example of Beckett, who transformed the theater space into a mindscape in plays like *Endgame*, *Not I*, *Footfalls*, and *Rockaby*, *Love-Lies-Bleeding* is a self-contained solipsistic fantasy world of Alex's own device.

The self-reflexive dimension of the play becomes most evident in Act Two. Set six years prior to the main action, Act Two features sixty-four-year-old Alex in full health and top form, flirting with his ex-wife Toinette and discoursing on his latest artwork. He reluctantly explains to her why he has a crew blasting into a desert mountain:

A room, a cube. I don't have a name for it. First we cut a passage in. A tough narrow entranceway, cramped, with jutting rock. . . . A chamber, a cubical room. Fashioned out of solid rock. Precise dimensions. A large empty room. Six congruent square surfaces. Painted. Ocher and amber. Old colors. Burnt brick. Lampblack. All six surfaces, every square inch. (*LLB* 59)

FIGURE 6.7 *Toinette (played by Lynn Allison) reunites with pre-stroke Alex (played by John Patrick Lowrie) in the 2006 Boise Contemporary Theater production of* Love-Lies-Bleeding, *directed by Tracy Sunderland.* © *Jeremy Winchester.*

On one level, this artwork represents the apotheosis of DeLillo's classic "men in small rooms" conceit. On another level, the project fits within a much older tradition of cave art. In an earlier scene (chronologically later), Alex's wife Lia recalls his deep admiration for the cave temples of Ajanta in India (*LLB* 37). On the meta-level of self-dialogue, Alex's room also harkens back to the caves of *Ratner's Star*. There Jean Sweet Venable connects ancient cave art to a primal confrontation with death:

> Wondering what it would take to "remember through" the ochre and soot of cave art to the very reason why these earliest of artists descended to the most remote parts of caves and applied their pigments to nearly inaccessible walls, the intricate journey and the isolated site being representative perhaps of the secret nature of the story told in the painting itself, all fiction, she thought, all fiction takes place at the end of this process of crawl, scratch and gasp, this secret memory of death. (*RS* 394)

Alex seems to have been remembering his death for much of his life, and there is no mistaking the morbid implication of his underground room as a self-constructed grave. Toinette reminds him that this idea has been germinating within him for years. She recalls him talking in bed about "Art that's hidden in a mountain. An incredible, you said, sort of stone enclosure that you would drench with paintings of your dreams" (*LLB* 60). Alex harbors doubts about his plans, fretting

> Should the room be painted at all? I have my doubts. I always have my doubts. The paint's a mistake. The paint is excess. A bare room inside a mountain. . . . I want to throw off doubt, stop thinking, stop caring, just be, just work. Throw off who I am, goddamn it. A bare room without a signature. (*LLB* 61)

If Alex is digging his own grave, he seems determined to make it an unmarked one. Like Lauren Hartke, he struggles to remove ego as an obstacle to realizing his art. He longs to erase the epitaph from his headstone, detach the dreamer from the dream. In Act Three Lia laments, "What powerful work he had it in mind to make. Untitled, unfinished. But not nothing" (*LLB* 83). This eulogy implies that Alex's greatest work was never completed.

Or was it? A variation of Alex's artistic vision to construct an inner sanctum for his dreams may ultimately be realized, not inside a desert mountain, but in the theater itself. The hermetically sealed auditorium lends itself to appropriation as solipsistic dreamscape. Bert O. States famously characterized the phenomenology of theater as "great reckonings in little rooms."[7] The little room that hosts a production of *Love-Lies-Bleeding* is capable of housing no less than the psychic immensity of Alex Macklin's mind reckoning with death. *M'illumino d'immenso*. Alex and Toinette mull over possible English translations of this verse from Giuseppe Ungaretti. "I glow, I shine, I bathe myself in light," begins Alex. "I turn luminous in this vast space." Toinette counters, "Do we want space in the physical sense? Or spiritual immensity? Something unnamable." But Alex cautions, "Let's not get too ambitious. We'll keep it local. This space and this light" (*LLB* 64). In the literal and the metatheatrical senses, *this* space and *this* light is a phenomenological self-reference to the performance conditions on stage as those lines are being delivered, a stage coterminous with Alex Macklin's mind.

One might reasonably expect a euthanasia play to culminate in the death of the patient. *Love-Lies-Bleeding* does stage Alex's death in Act Three, Scene Eight. However, the play then continues onward with two more scenes. As in several of his novels, DeLillo favors a narrative trajectory that bends back on itself, connecting the end with the beginning. Scene Nine continues that pattern by returning to the opening exchange between Alex and Lia. Once again Alex reflects upon the dead-sitting figure on the subway, while the dimly lit Alex *in extremis* sits apart on the periphery. DeLillo does note *"feeding tubes not visible"* for the sitting figure (*LLB* 92), which potentially indicates that the sitting figure is now dead. This interpretation jives with Alex's reported death in Scene Eight, yet it is difficult to reconcile his death with the continuation of his memory in Scene Nine. An alternative is that the sitting figure occupies some shadowy zone between life and death—"No longer and not yet," as Sean once put it (*LLB* 48), a quotation from Hermann Broch's *The Death of Virgil*. Perhaps the most harrowing possibility is that, as in Beckett's *Play*, physical death does not mark the end of consciousness but only the beginning of a new phase, where the body wastes away but the mind motors on unabated, ceaselessly revolving laps around the remembered past life.

The Cartesian split of mind and body, and the widening chasm separating them, emerges as one of Alex's chief preoccupations after his first stroke. Lia persistently tries to reassure her husband, insisting "Your mind is strong" (*LLB* 94) and "Your mind is alive" (*LLB* 95). She also continues to stimulate him sensually, reminding him "You can feel my hand on your body" (*LLB* 94) and "My breath on your face. That's what you feel and who you are, now, this instant. You need to hold hard" (*LLB* 95). But Alex feels increasingly unmoored from the present, alienated from his body and pulled irresistibly backwards in his mind. He tells Lia, "Everything's collapsing backwards. I can't feel what's here. . . . Everything's running backwards now. This is what consciousness is beginning to mean. Objects in rooms in dying light. I live in old objects, things turned gray" (*LLB* 94). This reflection echoes his description from the first scene of the dead man on the subway: "Gray like an animal. He belonged to a different order of nature. The first dead man I'd ever seen and there's never been anyone since who has looked more finally and absolutely dead" (*LLB* 8). Now the "gray animal" of death is devolving

FIGURE 6.8 *A field of the dead speaking from urns in Anthony Minghella's 2001 film adaptation of Samuel Beckett's* Play *for the* Beckett on Film *project (Blue Angel Films).*

further down the order of nature, down to gray "Objects in rooms in dying light." In short, Alex is becoming divested of his humanity, following his death drive back to the inorganic state, becoming less a man and more a lifeless object—less a character and more a prop. As he bluntly puts it to Lia, "I'm carrying around a corpse and we both smell him" (*LLB* 94).

Alex's premonition of what he will become is followed by a stark depiction of what the sitting figure is now. The script for the final Scene Ten reads in its entirety: "*The sitting figure in isolation. / Black*" (*LLB* 97). For all its simplicity and silence, this closing image is rich with suggestive possibility. The directions do not specify if the sitting figure is alive or dead, presumably leaving that choice to the discretion of each production. Playing him as alive would lend credence to the interpretation that Alex is the source and site of the preceding action, although playing him as dead certainly does not negate that interpretation. Even if the production sends signals that Alex is deceased, this still leaves open the question of how best to understand that death. To the extent that Alex longed for release, longed to be unfastened from the dying animal of his body and reprieved from physical and mental suffering, he seems to have gotten his wish: his life—and the play—have reached the end. From the standpoint of his abiding fantasy of regression into a womb-tomb of perfect solitude and silence, the final image would seem to represent an ideal consummation of both his life and his art.

However, such definitive resolutions ring false. Had DeLillo wanted to tie up the loose ends of the dramatic conflict so tidily, he could have proceeded straight from the report of Alex's death in Scene Eight to the closing vignette of the sitting figure in perfect repose. Instead, he inserts Scene Nine, a fretful scene that highlights the growing disconnect between the mind and body, implying that relief to one by no means guarantees relief to the other. Furthermore, the backward propelled inertia of the scene suggests less the end of a line, a terminal destination, and more a cyclical orbit, a return to the beginning for another circuit. Indeed, this latter trajectory is far more consistent with the metatheatrical paradigm DeLillo establishes from the start and applies rigorously throughout *Love-Lies-Bleeding*. For no ending is truly "the end" in theater. Beckett notoriously draws attention to this bedrock principle in *Play* by inserting my favorite stage direction of all time at the end of the script: "[*Repeat play*.]" (317) And they do. The "dead" characters (performed by live actors buried up to their necks in urns) start from the top and launch into a second performance of the entire play. For unprepared spectators, the gradual realization that they have heard these words before, that this bizarre play has rewound to the beginning and started over, is both startling and horrifying. How long will this go on? How many times will the play be repeated? Will I be stuck in my chair, as the characters are stuck in their urns, mutually bewildered and disoriented forever? In theory Beckett's *Play* forms a Möbius strip that could go on ad infinitum, or at least until the actual deaths of the actors playing the characters. In practice, however, the play is only repeated once—enough to make its point that plays never really end in the theater.

In his interview about *The Day Room*, DeLillo told Mervyn Rothstein, "It seemed natural to me beginning a play that theater itself would be one of the subjects I was interested in" (21). Elaborating upon the metadramatic elements that appealed to him, he added, "I'm interested in the way the play forms a kind of unending circular structure—it bends back on itself" (23). By the time he conceived *Love-Lies-Bleeding* almost twenty years later, DeLillo had matured as a playwright fully capable of self-reflexively exploiting the infinite loop of dramatic time. Tonight's performance may have ended, but the play itself remains frozen in suspension, reset and ready to be activated again. Come back tomorrow night, and we'll do it all over again. All plays share this inherent cyclical nature, but few draw reflexive attention and exploit this fact as much as Beckett's *Play*—or Don DeLillo's *Love-Lies-Bleeding*.

The closing image of Alex as a sitting figure in solitude, fading into black, is essentially the same position and condition he occupied from the start. Indeed, if the entire play has represented an interior drama playing out in his mind, he may have been sitting physically undisturbed the whole time. The audience enters tonight's performance through Alex, and perhaps the final vignette points the way toward exiting Alex before we exit the auditorium. In any case the sitting figure returns full circle to a resting position, prepared effectively for tomorrow night's performance, where he will revolve through his memories, fears, and fantasies again, reliving his life and death before a new audience.

* * *

In the liner notes to his *Goldberg Variations*, Glenn Gould addressed what he considered to be the timelessness of the piece, not in terms of its enduring legacy, but in terms of the internal structure of Bach's variation form. Gould proclaims, "the theme is not terminal but radial, the variations circumferential not rectilinear," resulting in "music which observes neither end nor beginning, music with neither real climax nor real resolution." These observations apply equally well to DeLillo's performance-based self-dialogues in "Counterpoint," *The Body Artist*, and *Love-Lies-Bleeding*. His works for page and stage revolve around a persistent set of core themes in a radial, circumferential manner. His agenda is not to resolve the irresolvable themes of time, identity, death, and the function of art. Rather, through relentless performances of self-dialogue, he returns again and again to enact themes from his previous work and to rearrange them into inventive new combinations: "The DeLillo Variations."

7

Art stalkers

Throughout his career Don DeLillo has remained persistently engaged with art, artists, and the creative processes through which various artworks are made. In his late work his focus has increasingly shifted toward the other end of the artistic transaction, examining the reception processes through which artworks are perceived, assimilated, deconstructed, and reconstructed to suit the needs of individual viewers. DeLillo is particularly interested in characters drawn to engage repeatedly with the same artworks or art venues. Driven by shadowy forces they scarcely understand or control, these compulsive characters return day after day to a museum, gallery, or cinema where they can gaze once again upon the objects of their obsessive desire. Although their obsessions are diverse, sometimes perverse, and always imagined as private, these intimate artistic encounters all take place in public spaces. Such conditions provide the basic components of a self-reflexive scenario to which DeLillo himself is continually drawn: a male predator gazes upon a female spectator gazing at an artwork, stalking his prey back and forth between the presumed sanctuary of the art venue and the vulnerable world outside.

DeLillo's first passing reference to this scenario comes in *The Names* (1982), where a woman complains, "I don't like museums. Men always follow me in museums. What is it about places like that? Every time I turn there's a figure watching me" (*N* 147). DeLillo again alludes to the eroticized potential of museums in his play *The Day Room* (1986). During a sexually charged seduction scene in a motel room, Lynette mentions that she is routinely propositioned by men in museums: "They think I won't mind, surrounded by serious art. . . . I'm supposed to believe if a man is in a museum, he is wonderfully sensitive and intelligent. We have sensitive things to say to each other. An afternoon of intelligent sex is sure to follow" (*DR* 80–81). According to these characters, museums are ideally suited for scoping out and picking up women. DeLillo exposes institutional conditions for viewing art which are latent with sexual permissiveness and conducive to exploitation. In their book *Crimes of Art + Terror*, Frank Lentricchia and Jody McAuliffe call into question "the virtually unavoidable sentimentality that asks us to believe that art is always somehow humane and humanizing, that artists, however indecent they might be as human beings, become noble when they make art, which must inevitably ennoble those who experience it" (9). DeLillo's art stalkers deflate such pieties, dramatizing scenarios where art is manipulated as sexual bait. His first extensive treatment of the theme came in the short story "Baader-Meinhof" (2002), which was followed by a condensed allusion in *Falling Man* (2007), both told from the perspective of women who are threatened in galleries by shady male figures. He then significantly reimagined the scenario in *Point Omega* (2010) and "The Starveling" (2011), both told from the male perspective of an art stalker, the former in the mode of deadly noir, the latter as pathetic farce.[1]

DeLillo keeps coming back to this scenario, much as his characters keep returning to the scene of the art/crime. In fact, this tendency toward perpetual return is the crucial animating dynamic common to all of DeLillo's art stalker stories. Characters arrive on site, brood in deep meditation, and then return to the world outside, only to gravitate back to the museum, gallery, or cinema the following day, resuming the vigil (or the hunt). This *fort-da* oscillation is symptomatic of repetition-compulsion within each narrative.[2] It also invites correspondent recursive strategies from the reader, in effect falling into step with the characters and compulsively coming back for more. The present essay represents one such case in point. The most conventional approach to examining DeLillo's art stalkers would be to develop the analysis chronologically, tracing a linear progression from the earliest manifestation through the most recent. However, in initially attempting to orient my argument in this direction, my critical impulses kept drawing me back to DeLillo's haunting "Baader-Meinhof," his first full treatment of the theme. Finally, I recognized that this urge mirrors the tendency of both DeLillo and his characters for returning to the work of art that first inspired and disturbed the imagination, a melancholic circuit that rejects moving on in favor of coming back. Instead of resisting this repetitive urge, I have adopted it as the interpretive approach most appropriate to DeLillo's oscillating narratives. The following study will therefore move back and forth between his first full expression of the art stalker motif and subsequent reiterations, wandering from wing to wing of the "DeLillo Gallery" as it were, contemplating variations upon the theme, but always coming back to the primary confrontations and perceptual frameworks established in "Baader-Meinhof."

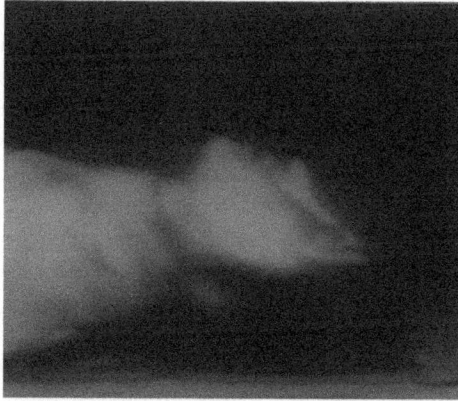

FIGURE 7.1 Dead *(1988) by Gerhard Richter. Oil on canvas.* © *Gerhard Richter, courtesy Atelier Richter, Cologne, Germany.*

"Baader-Meinhof" 1

The first scene of "Baader-Meinhof" is set in an exhibition gallery at MoMA in New York, where Gerhard Richter's *October 18, 1977*, is on display. This series of fifteen canvases depicts several scenes from the lives and deaths of the Red Army Faction (RAF), sometimes referred to as the Baader-Meinhof gang, led by Andreas Baader, Ulrike Meinhof, and Gudrun Ensslin.[3] The RAF was strongly opposed to what they saw as the imperialist war in Vietnam, the crypto-fascist policies of the West German government, the vacuous materialism of the German "Economic Miracle," and the narrow-minded shackles of bourgeois morality. The group used terrorist tactics to wage urban guerilla warfare on the West German state. The climax of their campaign was the "German Autumn" of 1977, ending in the coordinated suicides of Baader, Meinhof, Ensslin, and other imprisoned RAF leaders on October 18, 1977.[4] Appalled, fascinated, and haunted by the bloody cataclysm, Gerhard Richter responded eleven years later with *October 18, 1977*, a series of oil paintings based upon black and white photographs from the German Autumn. Richter's series draws renewed attention not only to the Baader-Meinhof group but also to the perceptual mechanisms of art's mediated gaze. By working from photos, Richter chooses from the start to position his gaze one remove from the actual persons and events he depicts. He incorporates images from a different medium, captured by someone else with a different agenda and sensibility, and interjects an additional frame of reference onto the canvas. Richter's trademark distortion brings the transformative gaze of the artist even further to the fore, rendering the images unclear, destabilized, elusive, and thus thwarting the spectator's efforts to either romanticize or fetishize the figures on display. In effect, what one sees in *October 18, 1977*, becomes secondary to how one sees it, how that perception is refracted through multiple mediating gazes.

DeLillo adopts a number of Richter's techniques for his own literary approach to the Baader-Meinhof group. Although he certainly could have written a story directly about the RAF, he chooses instead to focus on shadowy paintings of the group, thus placing himself at a remove even more distant—culturally, historically, and phenomenologically—than Richter's vantage. He channels his response through a fictional woman's perspective and then further complicates the perceptual matrix by introducing yet another frame of reference from an unnamed male visitor lurking behind the woman. In fact, the opening passage of the story focuses not on the paintings but on the disturbing incompatibility of one frame of reference with another: "She knew there was someone else in the room. There was no outright noise, just an intimation behind her, a faint displacement of air" (BM 105). The man's unnerving presence disrupts her private communion, a disturbance rendered all the more creepy by the suspicion that he is gazing at her more than at the paintings. From the outset then, DeLillo's primary emphasis in "Baader-Meinhof" is less on the RAF or Richter's series than on the competing perceptions and agendas of two visitors drawn to the museum for starkly different reasons.

The opening scene marks the third consecutive day that the woman has returned to view the Baader-Meinhof paintings. What does she see when she looks at these paintings? And what compels her to keep coming back to look again? In part she is drawn to images of death: "And this is how it felt to her, that she was sitting as a person does in a mortuary chapel, keeping watch over the body of a relative or a friend" (BM 105). DeLillo is renowned for careful ekphrastic descriptions of artworks, and the opening scene includes several such translations of images into words. He even takes the unusual step in *The Angel Esmeralda* to include a reproduction of one of these images, something he had only done in one previous book, *Mao II*. The visual image, one of three blurry profiles of the dead Ulrike Meinhof in profile, serves as preface to the story (BM 103) and as focal point for the woman's contemplation: "The woman's reality, the head, the neck, the rope burn, the hair, the facial features, were painted, picture to picture, in nuances of obscurity and pall, a detail clearer here than there, the slurred mouth in one painting appearing nearly natural elsewhere, all of it unsystematic" (BM 105). Both the visual and verbal renditions of Meinhof are spare, obscure, and "unsystematic," in the sense that there is no symbolic embellishment, no political editorializing, no fixed intentionality, and no implied proper stance for viewing and interpretation. The burden of making sense of these deathly images, if any sense can be made, falls squarely on the spectator.

In his influential lecture "The Creative Act," Marcel Duchamp examines "the two poles of the creation of art: the artist on the one hand, and on the other the spectator" (77). Duchamp characterizes art not as a finished manifestation of the artist's vision, but as a process of "esthetic osmosis" between artist and spectator, where the latter supplies the missing link in the work's transubstantial chain of subjective reactions. Duchamp terms this missing value the "art coefficient." He concludes that "the creative act is not performed by the artist alone; the spectator brings the work in contact with the external world by deciphering and interpreting its inner qualification and thus adds his contribution to the creative act" (78). Similarly, throughout DeLillo's oeuvre art functions less as object than as transaction, a mutually transformative process whereby the spectator enters into dialectical engagement with a piece, projecting his or her own experiences, desires, anxieties, and fantasies onto the canvas or screen, metamorphosing the artwork into what he or she needs it to be. This dynamic informs all of DeLillo's art stalker stories, beginning with "Baader-Meinhof."

From the perspective of the female spectator in "Baader-Meinhof," the "art coefficient" of Richter's paintings is keyed to forgiveness, specifically the capacity to forgive acts of terror. By comparing her museum visit with "keeping watch over the body of a relative or a friend" (BM 105), she acknowledges a sense of empathetic kinship with the Baader-Meinhof figures. Her impulse to mourn their deaths is most evident in her response to *Beerdigung* (*Funeral*), the final canvas in the sequence. "The painting of the coffins had something else that wasn't easy to find. She hadn't found it until the second day, yesterday, and it was striking once she'd found it, and inescapable now—an object at the top of the painting, just left of center, a tree perhaps, in the rough shape of a cross" (BM 108).

Curator and critic Robert Storr also calls attention to *Funeral*'s cross in his catalog for *October 18, 1977*. He concedes that many viewers are likely to resist the religious connotations of such a gesture, yet he observes, "it is hard not to acknowledge the deliberateness of what Richter has done and recognize his addition to *Funeral* as a discrete benediction at the end of a modern-day passion play which, in his scrupulous and agonizing rendition, offers no other consolation" (110). The woman's conjectures are perfectly compatible with Storr's commentary when she muses, "It was a cross. She saw it as a cross and it made her feel, right or wrong, that there was an element of forgiveness in the picture, that the two men and the woman, terrorists, and Ulrike before them, terrorist, were not beyond forgiveness" (BM 109). In her personal and private communion with Richter's series, she consistently labels the RAF members as "terrorists"; nevertheless, moved by their ghostly images, she is also inclined, rightly or wrongly, to extend them forgiveness for their crimes.

An aura of collaboratively conferred benediction might have prevailed in the story were it not for the intrusion of a countervailing perspective interjected by the male museum visitor. Most art theory (including Duchamp's "The Creative Act") presupposes an ideal interface between the

FIGURE 7.2 Funeral *(1988) by Gerhard Richter. Oil on canvas.* © *Gerhard Richter,* courtesy Atelier Richter, Cologne, Germany.

solitary artist and the fully engaged spectator, an abstraction that rarely matches up with the material facts. What such theories fail to account for are the real institutional conditions in which art is usually encountered, public conditions where any number of extraneous factors and contingent influences can disrupt, divert, compromise, or otherwise short-circuit the pure communication between artist and spectator. Christian Heath and Dirk vom Lehn have attempted to redress the undervaluation of context in the critical hermeneutics of art. They assert, "Theories of the perception and experience of art and artifacts largely rely upon an imaginary situation in which an individual views a single artwork alone, independently of the circumstances of viewing. Both the viewer and the artwork are removed from the context, the situation in which they encounter an exhibit" (46). By contrast, Heath and vom Lehn observe that, "in visiting museums and galleries, the very presence and conduct of others, whether they are people one is with, or others who just happen to be in the same space, may be consequential not only to the ways in which one navigates exhibitions but also to how one examines a work of art or artifact" (46). They contend that social interaction "is of profound relevance to the ways in which an aesthetic experience is 'created.' Underlying these concerns is an interest in revealing the ways in which the participants' bodies, and in particular their bodily and spoken conduct, feature in the perception and experience of exhibits in museums and galleries" (46). The "bodily and spoken conduct" of the male spectator completely rewires the artistic circuitry of "Baader-Meinhof."

The man initiates contact by asking, "Why do you think he did it this way?" (BM 105) This opening gambit could indicate genuine curiosity, but as the conversation unfolds his skepticism and distaste for the material soon become evident. He eventually admits that he is utterly unmoved by the paintings and has only come to the museum to kill time before an afternoon job interview. He takes issue with the woman's apologist defense of the terrorists, mocking her suggestion that they may have been killed by "the state" and denouncing the RAF's entire enterprise: "They were terrorists, weren't they? When they're not killing other people, they're killing themselves" (BM 106–07). The man persistently attempts to wedge himself and his derisive perspective between the woman and her sense of sanctified connection to the Baader-Meinhof images. Because the story is told in third person but exclusively from her perspective, the reader has no direct access to his inner motives. His manner may seem abrasive, but nothing that he does or says in the opening scene is overtly threatening. Nevertheless, the pall cast by *October 18, 1977*, makes the attentive reader wary that DeLillo is preparing the stage for a similar date with terror and death. Asked what the paintings make her feel, she replies, "I think I feel helpless. These paintings make me feel how helpless a person can be" (BM 109). She is hypersensitive to the figures' helplessness, but she seems oblivious to her own potential vulnerability. As Linda Kauffman rightly notes, "The contrast between the portentous paintings and the mundane (if perverse) boy-meets-girl story seems incongruous. But the paintings are an objective correlative for blindness and insight: she studies the canvasses, but is blind to the man's motives; he is blind to the paintings, but shrewdly sizes her up" (359).

Falling Man

Although 9/11 is never named, DeLillo makes several veiled allusions to it in "Baader-Meinhof." The story first appeared in the April 1, 2002, edition of the *New Yorker*, mere months after the attacks of September 11, 2001, and demands consideration within a post-9/11 context.[5] As DeLillo's first published work of fiction after 9/11, "Baader-Meinhof" still gropes for purchase on how to address terrorism through art. The female spectator recognizes that Richter is grappling with that very problem through his series on the Baader-Meinhof terrorists. She tells the man, "What they did had meaning. It was wrong but it wasn't blind and empty. I think the painter's searching for this. And how did it end the way it did? I think he's asking this" (BM 110). The search for meaning behind terrorist acts can be easily misconstrued as justifying those acts or sympathizing with the terrorists. The male spectator implies at times that the woman is beginning to fall down this slippery slope. Robert Storr notes that Richter himself has been accused of glorifying the Baader-Meinhof gang. However, in the catalog for

Richter's career retrospective, Storr astutely argues, "Richter's aim was more complex than hagiography and by far harder to achieve." Storr contends that Richter's ambivalent agenda was to mourn, but also "he wanted to give a human face to the victims of ideology who, for ideology's sake, created victims of their own, and to free the suffering they experienced and caused from reductive explanations of their motives and actions, and from political generalizations and rigid antagonisms that triggered the events in the first place" (Forty Years 77). DeLillo is inspired by Richter's example to create art that remembers, interrogates, and mourns, and to do so in ways that avoid hagiography or sloganeering. "Baader-Meinhof" represents his first fictional attempt at processing 9/11, but his efforts in that respect are still preliminary and tenuous. Although DeLillo's essay "In the Ruins of the Future" challenged post-9/11 writers to produce "counternarratives" that dared "to take the shock and horror as it is" (IRF 39), he was not yet fully prepared to do that himself in 2002. But DeLillo does begin to pose troubling questions raised by terrorism at home, and he establishes his specialized interest in using art as a mirror or projection screen for both artists and spectators to mediate terrors great and small. He builds upon these nascent efforts in his most fully developed response to 9/11, the novel Falling Man.[6]

Several details carry over from "Baader-Meinhof" to Falling Man. For instance, one of DeLillo's characters, the art dealer Martin Ridnour (an alias for Ernst Hechinger), was once a member of Kommune 1, a forerunner of the RAF. His prior affiliation with the German radical movement leads him to sympathize with the 9/11 attackers: "He thinks these people, these jihadists, he thinks they have something in common with the radicals of the sixties and seventies. He thinks they're all part of the same classical pattern. They have their theorists. They have their visions of world brotherhood" (FM 147). DeLillo again ascribes prescience to German movements of the 1960s and 1970s in anticipating terrorist dilemmas of the new millennium. He also follows Richter's genre-mixing lead by making central use of multiple media for his own novelistic response to terrorism. The book's title refers simultaneously to three distinct sources, each representing a frame of reference progressively further removed from Ground Zero: (1) an anonymous jumper from the south tower, whom Keith Neudecker sees falling past his office window; (2) the notorious "Falling Man" photo by Richard Drew, capturing the harrowing image of one of the jumpers plummeting headlong to his death; and (3) the performance artist known as Falling Man (posthumously identified as David Janiak), a character invented by DeLillo, who appears unannounced at various sites around the city and reenacts the "Falling Man" photographic pose while suspended from a harness. Each of these falling men summons up the terror of 9/11, and yet each denies full access to the story, taking his testimony with him to his death. Some crucial missing essence of the experience seems to defy apprehension. But art offers a potential portal into that experience, as DeLillo asserts in "In the Ruins of the Future": "The writer tries to give memory, tenderness and meaning to all that howling space" (IRF 39). The still life paintings of Giorgio Morandi in particular offer some purchase on 9/11 for Lianne Glenn, Keith's estranged wife, who develops perceptual strategies first tested by the female spectator in "Baader-Meinhof."

The woman in "Baader-Meinhof" reads retrospectively like a preliminary sketch of Lianne. Julia Apitzsch goes so far as to label the story "an intertext for the novel" (105). Both female leads are employed irregularly in the book publishing trade. Both are troubled by failing marriages, and both are haunted by images of death. Both even have brushes with art stalkers, or at least men who interfere with their aesthetic experiences at an art venue. Lianne's experience takes place at a Chelsea gallery where she has gone to view a Giorgio Morandi exhibition.[7] "A man came in. He was interested in looking at her before he looked at the paintings. Maybe he expected certain freedoms to be in effect because they were like-minded people in a rundown building, here to look at art" (FM 210). No interaction develops between Lianne and the anonymous male creeper; nevertheless, as in "Baader-Meinhof," the man's intrusive presence is enough to break the spell of the woman's artistic communion: "She went back to the main room but could not look at the work the same way with the man there, watching her or not. He wasn't watching her but he was there" (FM 210). Not only are Lianne

FIGURE 7.3 Still Life (Natura morta) (1956) by Giorgio Morandi. Oil on canvas. Private collection. © 2018 Artist Rights Society (ARS), New York / SIAE, Rome. Photo Sergio Anelli, courtesy Mondadori Portfolio.

and her predecessor in "Baader-Meinhof" both art lovers but both are also drawn repeatedly to images that seem to address their innermost personal demons and extend the promise of exorcism. In fact, both find their deepest concerns already mirrored in the artworks that move them, setting up a symbiotic fantasy of identification where the viewer supplies the missing value in the artwork and the artwork addresses a "spectator coefficient" within the viewer.

This kind of artistic exchange in *Falling Man* is best captured through Lianne's repeated encounters with Morandi. The painter's work has long been a part of her life through her mother:

> What she loved most were the two still lifes on the north wall, by Giorgio Morandi, a painter her mother had studied and written about. These were groupings of bottles, jugs, biscuit tins, that was all, but there was something in the brushstrokes that held a mystery she could not name, or in the irregular edges of vases and jars, some reconnoiter inward, human and obscure, away from the very light and color of the paintings. *Natura morta.* The Italian term for still life seemed stronger than it had to be, somewhat ominous, even, but these were matters she hadn't talked about with her mother. Let the latent meanings turn and bend in the wind, free from authoritative comment. (*FM* 12)

The ekphrastic passage above communicates a sense of familiarity, but also traces the outline around a mysterious lacuna at the heart of the piece that resists interpolation. Immediately following the September 11 attacks, everything seems to offer implied commentary upon terror. Viewed within this context, Morandi's lacuna becomes filled with 9/11. Martin Ridnour muses, "I keep seeing the towers in this still life" (*FM* 49). Guided by this prompt, the familiar paintings gradually become defamiliarized for Lianne: "Two of the taller items were dark and somber, with smoky marks and smudges, and one of them was partly concealed by a long-necked bottle. The bottle was a bottle, white. The two dark objects, too obscure to name, were the things that Martin was referring to" (*FM* 49). Ultimately she admits to herself, "She saw what he saw. She saw the towers" (*FM* 49). Three years later, after her mother's death, Lianne pursues Morandi to the Chelsea Gallery. There her recent loss colors her perspective, and she refashions Morandi's still life paintings accordingly: "She could not stop looking. There was something hidden in the painting. Nina's living room was there, memory and motion. The objects in the painting faded into the figures behind them, the woman smoking in the chair, the standing man" (*FM* 210). After 9/11 the bottles reminded Lianne of the towers, but after her mother's death each Morandi memento reminds her of a different mori: "All the paintings and drawings carried the same title, *Natura Morta.* Even this, the term for still life, yielded her mother's last days" (*FM* 211). DeLillo's choice of Morandi is appropriate, with his simple bottles, jugs, vases, and biscuit tins, because the imagery consists of containers, vessels that can be emptied and replenished whenever and with whatever the occasion requires. On a meta-artistic level, too, the paintings contain empty spaces which Lianne as spectator fills with projections of the deaths, losses, anxieties, and regrets that she brings with her to the viewing experience.

"Baader-Meinhof" 2

Art contains death in other senses as well, irrespective of subjective projections brought to bear by the spectator. *Et in MoMA ego.* The Italian term *"natura morta"* elegantly communicates a central truth, not just about still life painting but about all figurative art: "dead nature," a thing modeled after the living, transferred from the organic to the inorganic state of dead matter. The woman in "Baader-Meinhof" compares the museum to a mortuary where she is visiting old friends, but then all museums function as mausoleums for dead art, whether or not death is the overt subject matter of a given artwork. Theodor Adorno asserts, "Museum and mausoleum are connected by more than phonetic association. Museums are like the family sepulchres of works of art" (175). DeLillo has long been intrigued by art in multiple media as the crossroads where life and death—or more pointedly, sex and death—converge. Actually, the road metaphor can be misleading since it suggests that sex and death are divergent paths to begin with; whereas in DeLillo they are more often configured as a continuous loop, where laps through one state invariably lead back through the other.

While Richter's morbid images lead the woman in "Baader-Meinhof" to contemplate mortality, the gaze of her scopophilic male counterpart moves sexward instead of deathward. It is worth noting that sex and death were inextricably intertwined in popular representations of the Baader-Meinhof gang. A disproportionately high number of the group's militants were women (the German press often called them *"Terrormädchen"* [terrorist girls]), and an atmosphere of free love between members was fostered as an extension of their larger campaign against bourgeois values. Two of the leaders in particular, Andreas Baader and Gudrun Ensslin, have often been compared to the cinematic anti-heroes Bonnie and Clyde, as young, sexy, magnetically attractive killers.[8] The art stalker in "Baader-Meinhof" may not know the historical links between sex and violence in the RAF, but DeLillo assuredly does and draws upon them in depicting the museum as a passageway through Thanatos en route to Eros and back again. After an opening scene steeped in art and death, the action shifts to the livelier setting of a snack bar, followed by the intimate setting of the woman's nearby apartment. Even though the narrative trajectory leads nominally "back to her place," the movement away from the museum signifies a shift away from comfort and control, out into the surrounding world where she is less at ease and more vulnerable. There the man soon presses the plot sexward, announcing that he has canceled his interview so that he can spend the afternoon with her. "Tell me what you want. . . . Because I sense you're not ready and I don't want to do something too soon. But, you know, we're here" (BM 114). His matter-of-fact manner belies an unmistakably coercive agenda: he regards her invitation to the apartment as implied consent, and one way or the other he does not plan on leaving until he has achieved the sexual release to which he feels entitled. She tells him unequivocally: "I want you to leave, please" (BM 114). Undeterred, he confesses to sizing her up from the start, measuring her wounded helplessness: "She's like someone convalescing. Even in the museum, this is what I thought. All right. Fine. But now we're here" (BM 115). While the man makes his way to the bed, the woman escapes into the bathroom, listening intently at the door to the sound of him undoing his belt and zipper. "When he was finished, there was a long pause, then some rustling and shifting" (BM 117). DeLillo does not spell out precisely what he was finished doing, but the implication is that he masturbated in her bed. Afterward, he leans against the bathroom door and says, "Forgive me. . . . I'm so sorry. Please. I don't know what to say" (BM 117). Then he leaves.

The apartment scene is deeply disturbing, but it also defies expectations and resists clear comprehension in ways that resonate with Richter. To borrow the man's opening gambit at the museum, "Why do you think he did it this way?" (BM 105) The semiotic signs DeLillo plants for the reader instill an expectation of rape and murder. Needless to say, it is a relief that the story stops short of this vile scenario. But it is difficult to determine what to make of the alternate route the story follows instead. Were pursuit, territorial violation, and psychological terror the full measure of the man's intentions all along? Or does his masturbation represent an unplanned interruptus, an impromptu departure from the usual script? His subsequent plea for forgiveness is even more maddening. Can it possibly be understood as sincere, the unlikely onset of post-climactic scruples? If not, is it merely an attempt to squirm out of criminal culpability after the fact? In fact, all of the most contentious questions are left unanswered. DeLillo once compared his approach to scene construction with painting:

I try to examine psychological states by looking at people in rooms, objects in rooms. It's a way of saying we can know something important about a character by the way he sees himself in relation to objects. People in rooms have always seemed important to me. I don't know why or ask myself why, but sometimes I feel I'm *painting* a character in a room, and the most important thing I can do is set him up in relation to objects, shadows, angles. (LeClair 14, emphasis in original)

The way DeLillo chooses to position the characters and objects in relation to one another in the apartment scene conceals psychological states as much as it reveals them. By choosing to place the woman behind the bathroom door during the scene's climax, DeLillo provides her with some flimsy protection, but he also partitions off her perception of what actually takes place. Consider the true depth of our mutual ignorance: neither the woman nor the reader can say with any certainty what—*if anything*—the man actually did while she was in the bathroom. By erecting such fundamental perceptual barriers and occluding the view of his subjects, DeLillo employs literary techniques comparable to Richter's distortion effects in *October 18, 1977*.

Point Omega

In *Point Omega* DeLillo re-envisions the art stalker theme from the man's perspective. This time obsessive art lover and creepy museum lurker are one and the same. The scene is once again at MoMA, and the artwork is Douglas Gordon's *24 Hour Psycho*, a video installation which ran from June to September 2006. Again DeLillo was inspired by a work inspired by another work, in this case Gordon's manipulation of Alfred Hitchcock's iconic film *Psycho*. Gordon projects the film on a translucent screen at the speed of two frames per second, as opposed to the standard twenty-four frames per second, slowing the total running time down to approximately a full day. Ken Johnson of the *New York Times* described re-viewing the familiar film in such a defamiliarized way:

> Shown on a see-through screen in a dark, empty room, the blurry, pixilated video progresses at a jerky snail's pace, so slowly that few viewers will be able to tolerate it for very long. But you don't have to watch for long to get the idea and to begin meditating: How does film time relate to real time? What is real time, anyway? If I watch this thing long enough, will it reprogram my brain? (Johnson)

The answer to that last question, according to *Point Omega*, is "Yes." DeLillo's first treatments of the art stalker theme emphasize what the spectator brings to the artistic transaction and how her perspective reshapes the artwork under examination. *Point Omega* reverses the focus, examining how art can reprogram the spectator, in this case transforming a virtual stalker into a real one.

The prologue and epilogue take place on the final two days of the exhibition and are told from the perspective of a male spectator who comes back for six consecutive days to view *24 Hour Psycho*. These sections are labeled "Anonymous" and "Anonymous 2," not because the man's identity is unknown (his name is later disclosed as most likely Dennis), but because his identity is in the process of being erased and reprogrammed; he is a tabula becoming steadily reinscribed by the images on screen. DeLillo never invokes Jacques Lacan by name, but his depiction of Dennis's encounter with *24 Hour Psycho* effectively replicates the mirror stage of ego formation. As discussed in the first chapter, Lacan posits this key experience of infantile development as the stage where the child sees its image reflected in a mirror, or in the person of its mother, and is so enthralled by this coherent external image that the child models an internal sense of "I" which emulates the idealized imago. From the first page of *Point Omega*, Dennis is devoted to this kind of exercise in identification, mirroring the gestures on screen: "The man standing alone moved a hand toward his face, repeating, ever so slowly, the action of a figure on the screen" (*PO* 3). The man is conscious enough of his surroundings to register the presence of others, but unlike the woman in "Baader-Meinhof," he is able to shut out the corrupting influence of fickle passersby (at least until the epilogue) and maintain a privileged sense of connection with the artwork. He even compares his encounter with the artistic imago to his (dead) mother's gaze:

> This was the ideal world as he might have drawn it in his mind. He had no idea what he looked like to others. He wasn't sure what he looked like to himself. He looked like what his mother saw when she looked at him. But his mother had passed on. This raised a question for advanced students. What was left of him for others to see? (*PO* 8)

Frames of reference proliferate here even more than in "Baader-Meinhof," but one perceptual matrix subsumes all others, that between mother and child. Now that Dennis's constitutive gaze with his dead mother is broken, he seeks to establish a new identification fantasy drawn from *24 Hour Psycho*.

As with "Baader-Meinhof," DeLillo adopts themes and techniques from his artistic sources and reflects them in his fiction. *Point Omega* functions on the whole as a resilvered mirror of Hitchcock's *Psycho*. DeLillo's Dennis shares a number of disturbing affinities with Hitchcock's Norman Bates, the unassuming motel clerk ultimately exposed as a schizoid killer and the most famous psychosexual stalker in cinematic history. By all appearances, both are damaged sons of dead mothers; both pathologize their identification fantasies; both are voyeurs driven by strong scopophilic desire; both battle unresolved difficulties in forming and transferring libidinal attachments; and both stalk their female prey and lash out with violence, tellingly selecting phallic knives for their weapons.

Well, maybe. Actually, unlike Hitchcock who solves his mysteries, exhumes his bodies, quarantines his killer, and explains Norman's psychological motives and lethal methods, DeLillo hints at much but confirms little. What we do know from the dominant middle section of the novel is that filmmaker

FIGURE 7.4 *Norman Bates (played by Anthony Perkins) in Alfred Hitchcock's* Psycho *(Paramount Pictures, 1960).*

Jim Finley and war theorist Richard Elster visited the Gordon exhibition at MoMA on September 3, 2006, the day before it closed. Elster recommended *24 Hour Psycho* to his daughter, Jessie, who presumably checked it out the following day. In the early fall the daughter arrives in the desert to visit her father. Her mother recommended that she get out of the city for a while to avoid a recently estranged boyfriend, Dennis (if the mother remembers the name correctly), who had begun harassing her. Jessie soon goes missing in the desert, and by the end of the novel she has still not been found. Finley and Elster suspect she is the victim of the stalker ex-boyfriend Dennis. This theory is lent possible credence when police investigators discover a knife in the desert that might have been used as a weapon. Meanwhile, the epilogue returns to MoMA on September 4, the last day of the exhibition. There the male spectator meets a woman who fits the profile of Jessie, although they fail to exchange names. They do strike up a conversation, however, and he follows her out onto the street, where they exchange phone numbers to arrange a future rendezvous. Is the man at the museum Dennis? Is the woman Jessie? Was Jessie abducted at knifepoint and murdered by Dennis? As in "Baader-Meinhof," DeLillo raises fundamental questions about his art stalker and victim but declines to answer them.[9]

Point Omega also displays DeLillo's deep dialectical engagement with *24 Hour Psycho*. Gordon's manipulation of Hitchcock's film consciously drains the thriller of its thrills. The video installation diverts attention away from pulse-racing plot twists and psychoanalytic criminology and refocuses it with pulse-slowing calcification on the ravages of time.

At two frames per second, the moving images of Hitchcock's film have all but ceased to move. The effect is of Eros grinding down toward Thanatos, approaching the omega point. DeLillo takes his title from Pierre Teilhard de Chardin, the controversial French Jesuit who proposed the evolutionary development of humans toward ever greater complexity and heightened consciousness, ultimately approaching the Omega Point, his term for supreme transcendence of the cosmos. Richard Elster embroiders upon these theories in his own predictions for humanity's future: "Because now comes the introversion. Father Teilhard knew this, the omega point. A leap out of our biology. Ask yourself this question. Do we have to be human forever? Consciousness is exhausted. Back now to inorganic matter. This is what we want. We want to be stones in a field" (*PO* 53). David Cowart is spot on when he observes, "These formulations owe more to the Freud of *Jenseits der Lustprinzip* (*Beyond the Pleasure Principle*) than to the Teilhard of *Le phénomène humain* (*The Phenomenon of Man*)" (47–48). That is to say, Elster's prognostications sound less like Teilhard's omega point and more like Freud's death drive, that primal human urge to return to the prior condition of inorganic matter. In *Beyond the Pleasure Principle*, Freud posits compulsions to repeat and return that are even more fundamental than the pursuit of pleasure. These primal drives serve as animating forces behind DeLillo's art stalker narratives.

Elster's appropriation of Teilhard de Chardin, Gordon's appropriation of Hitchcock, and DeLillo's appropriations of them all lead asymptotically toward death. However, the culminating satisfaction of a concrete ending, the final destination of death achieved, remains tantalizingly out of reach. Elster is dying, and with Jessie's disappearance seems to wish he were dead, but he's not dead yet. Jessie may well have been murdered, but her body has not been found and her precise fate remains uncertain. Gordon's rendition of *Psycho* strangles it down to near stillness, but it still manages to limp through its paces on a 24-hour loop. DeLillo's decision to close the novel on the final day of the exhibition reminds us that the end of this particular loop is immanent, but the final page ends before the final frame. Indeed, the pending consummation of one deathly loop promises to spawn yet another. After following Jessie out into the street, Dennis returns to the museum to resume his vigil during MoMA's final hour of *24 Hour Psycho*. "The man separates himself from the wall and waits to be assimilated, pore by pore, to dissolve into the figure of Norman Bates" (*PO* 116). This total immersion fantasy marks a crucial turning point in Dennis's identification with Norman Bates. The circumstantial evidence suggests that Dennis is now prepared to assume the identity of the virtual stalker and carry out his mission in the real world beyond the museum. The novel thus ends poised on a pivot between the omega point of death-based art and alpha point of art-based death.

"Baader-Meinhof" 3

As a senior at Fordham University in 1958, Don DeLillo was required to take a course sequence called "Alpha and Omega" as part of the core curriculum.[10] According to the catalog description, this sequence was designed as an "integrating course, aimed to assist the mature senior in forming a unitary view of all reality. God as efficient, exemplary and final cause of the created universe. God's special creation, elevation and providential care of man. . . . God's nature, attributes and personality as revealed in His natural and supernatural creations. God, ALPHA and OMEGA" (Fordham 112–13). The courses place special emphasis upon God as creator, God's proprietary autonomy over his creations, and God's reflected genius discernible within his creations. Such a "unitary view of all reality" grows out of the Ignatian principle of finding God in all things. But it also faithfully characterizes a Western, Christian understanding of artistic creation and reception that predominated until the nineteenth century. According to this view, the artist is master of his material and reflects his genius in the work of art. It falls to the spectator to appreciate the beauty and truth of the creation by discerning the embedded genius of the creator.

Very different assumptions about the creation, reception, and function of art adhere in DeLillo's work, where genius is replaced by confusion, mastery replaced by uncertainty, passive audience appreciation replaced by active reconstitution, and a unitary view replaced by fragmented and shifting perspectives. Nonetheless, reflection remains a core principle for the Jesuit-educated DeLillo. From his very first novel *Americana*, he acknowledges art's capacity to function as a mirror of its creator. Remember filmmaker-protagonist David Bell's self-reflexive manifesto:

> What I'm doing is kind of hard to talk about. It's a sort of first-person thing but without me in it in any physical sense, except fleetingly, not exactly in the Hitchcock manner but brief personal appearance nonetheless, my mirror image at any rate. . . . I mean you can start with nothing but your own mirror reality and end with an approximation of art. (*A* 263)

DeLillo's more recent fiction studies this mirror principle from the other side of the looking glass, examining strategies employed by spectators, either to conceptualize art as an external reflective surface for their internal preoccupations or to reconfigure their inner makeup to conform more perfectly to the ideal images depicted on canvas or screen. But these mirroring dynamics do not pertain exclusively to a spectator's isolated interaction with an artwork. Beginning with "Baader-Meinhof," DeLillo's art stalker stories investigate the consequences when one spectator begins to regard another person as his projection screen or mirror reflection.

The disturbing encounter at the woman's apartment radically alters her perspective. "She saw everything twice now. She was where she wanted to be, and alone, but nothing was the same. Bastard. Nearly everything in the room had a double effect—what it was and the association it carried in her mind" (BM 117). In part this is DeLillo's microcosmic translation of the pervasive post-9/11 syndrome where everything seemed divided into "before" and "after," and everything seemed coated with the residue of violent destruction and traumatic violation. One might expect that, given this unsettling experience, the woman would not want to return to the museum, another space sure to be haunted by this spectral "double effect." Nevertheless, she does compulsively gravitate back to MoMA, where she finds not the man's ghost but the man himself: "When she went back to the museum the next morning he was alone in the gallery, seated on the bench in the middle of the room, his back to the entranceway, and he was looking at the last painting in the cycle, the largest by far and maybe most breathtaking, the one with the coffins and the cross, called *Funeral*" (BM 118). Any number of motives might have prompted his return. His reappearance at the Richter exhibition may constitute a calculated escalation in his stalking of the woman. Or, assuming that she would not dare return, he may be positioning himself to stake out his next prey. DeLillo's decision to place him in front of *Funeral*, the very painting that had inspired the woman's instincts for empathy and forgiveness the day before, is particularly provocative. Kauffman enumerates several thorny questions raised by this concluding image:

> The ending makes us reevaluate the beginning, when the heroine was still innocent—or blind. She wants to see an element of forgiveness in Richter's paintings, but, by the end, forgiveness seems preposterous. What are we to make of her harsh transformation? Are we to conclude that forgiveness is fine in the abstract, but impossible once one's territory has been invaded? Or that, such noble sentiments are only possible in art, not in life? Or that they only apply to those long dead? (361)

Kauffman is attuned to the post-9/11 resonance of the scene, articulating the difficulty, and maybe the foolishness, of answering unprovoked terror with unconditional clemency. However, Kauffman also perceives this scene as a contrast in blindness and sight, a perception worth considering further. If the woman can see things by the end that she was blind to at the start, could the same be true of the man? Among the possibilities DeLillo invites is that the man returns to MoMA, not to resume stalking, but to look more carefully at the Baader-Meinhof paintings. The day before, he expressed mild curiosity for Richter's art, and subdued scorn for the RAF terrorists. But in the interim he has committed acts that can be classified as "domestic terrorism" of a sort. Does *October 18, 1977*, signify differently "after" than it did "before"? Might he now see himself mirrored in these images?

On the harsher end of the interpretive spectrum, he could be attracted by a deepening sense of kinship with the terrorists; on the kinder end, his plea to be forgiven may have been sincere, leading him back to the museum in search of the same absolution the woman first gleaned from Richter's images.

Ultimately, the female spectator ends "Baader-Meinhof" in a position to see both Richter's paintings and the male spectator from a parallax view because of DeLillo's painterly repositioning of his figures in the room. The story began with the art stalker standing behind the woman, gazing at her as she gazed at Richter's paintings. In the closing scene, however, DeLillo places her behind him. This would seem to be the more advantageous position, since she can now scope out the scene fully, monitoring his actions before calculating her next move. As Karin Crawford notes, "She is in a position to determine the ending: she is standing in the doorway and can either enter the exhibition hall or leave. She is on the threshold of regaining her subjectivity (either in confronting the man or in leaving)" (228). DeLillo's reconfiguration also sets up an inversion that potentially alters the stakes of the final scene. The woman ends up occupying an identical vantage point to the one initially occupied by the man, and vice versa. He sees from her perspective, and she sees from his. This may sound like a situation conducive to communication. However, context is everything, and given all that has transpired between them, it is, to use Kauffman's word, fairly preposterous to imagine that the ensuing scene would end well. But there is no ensuing scene; the story ends there, and here lies the salient point. DeLillo cranks up the potential energy of the scene, primed for either confrontation or reconciliation, but he does not release it into the kinetic momentum of narrative. He brings the story full circle back to the museum, rearranging his figures into new patterns; but then he suspends all animation, replacing the dynamics of plot and character with an arresting image, an ekphrastic *natura morta*, where the man and woman end up as fixed and inscrutable as the Richter canvases that surround them.

"The Starveling"

The last story in *The Angel Esmeralda* returns to the art stalker theme, borrowing a number of elements from previous treatments. But DeLillo departs from his previous prototypes in important ways, pointing tentatively toward a potential exit from the perpetual cycle of repetition. The protagonist of "The Starveling," Leo Zhelezniak, is the latest in a long line of DeLillo characters obsessed with films. Leo has kept to a strict schedule for years, attending multiple film screenings each day at various venues scattered across the city. As with all of the primary characters in the art stalker stories, Leo's human relationships suffer because of his artistic obsessions. Years ago he broke up with his wife Flory, although they amicably share an apartment now and have a better relationship as a divorced couple than they ever had while married. Unlike the previous art stalker stories, where DeLillo limited access to only one privileged perspective, in "The Starveling" he gives voice to both Leo and Flory's thoughts. One might expect his ex-wife to be resentful of his cinematic fixations, but she actually finds much to admire in Leo's rigorous discipline. "He was an ascetic," according to one of her theories. "She found something saintly and crazed in his undertaking, an element of self-denial, an element of penance. Sit in the dark, revere the images" (S 187). However, Flory also suspects that Leo's obsession is symptomatic of some old and deep wound, and that he goes to the movies seeking a cure for this formative trauma: "Or he was a man escaping his past. He needed to dream away a grim memory of childhood, some misadventure of adolescence. Movies are waking dreams—daydreams, she said, protection against the recoil of that early curse, that bane" (S 187).

Flory is on the right track, but Leo's pathology stems more from something that has failed to happen, a beast in the jungle that has yet to pounce. Leo's perception of this central lack is thrown into sharp relief by his growing obsession for a fellow obsessive, a female spectator who likewise attends multiple movies each day. Drawn to this gaunt doppelganger, Leo begins stalking her, first following her out of the theater, later shadowing her from one venue to the next, and eventually going so far as to track her all the way to her neighborhood in the Bronx. The woman apparently never notices him, or anyone else for that matter, so withdrawn is she into the hermetically sealed solipsism of her own private world (or so Leo supposes). Because of her extremely thin frame, he suspects she is anorexic, but he coins an even more evocative term for her condition and her identity: the Starveling. As he conceives her, she is so devoted to film, to the uncompromising discipline of her devotion, that she cannot even be bothered to eat. Her condition is not medical so much as spiritual, existential; like Kafka's hunger artist, her only appetite is for starvation, since the world fails miserably to provide her with whatever ineffable sustenance she needs to fill her inner void. Or so Leo supposes. Once again, DeLillo's arch-perceiver sees in objects and in others whatever he needs them to be, which generally comes down to exorcizing his personal demons onto another and mirroring his narcissistic fantasies. In the initial stages of his obsession, he simply projects his own traits outward: "He thought she was a person who lived within herself, remote, elusive, whatever else. . . . She had no friends, one friend. This is how he chose to define her, for now, in the early stages" (S 196). When he presumes to name her the Starveling, he defines her primarily as empty inside, depleted, hollow—in short, he treats her as his vessel, like one of Morandi's bottles, ready to be filled by whatever elixirs he concocts. Paradoxically, what he fills her with is emptiness. He is the real "starveling," and he projects his sense of incompleteness and spiritual hunger onto her.

He regards her by stages as his kindred spirit, secret sharer, and soul mate—his better half. This fantasy leads him to recognize what he has really been searching for all these years at the movies: the missing half of his life. Leo muses,

> It was something he'd never tried to penetrate until now, the crux of being who he was and understanding why he needed this. He sensed it in her, knew it was there, the same half life. They had no other self. They had no fake self, no veneer. They could only be the one embedded thing they were, stripped of the faces that come naturally to others. They were bare-faced, bare-souled, and maybe this is why they were here, to be safe. The world was up there, framed, on the screen, edited and corrected and bound tight, and they were here, where they belonged, in the isolated dark, being what they were, being safe. (S 206)

Leo laments, but also boasts, that he and the female spectator lead half-lives. This shared condition is a source of pain that permanently alienates them from most people; but it is also a point of pride in that each remains genuine, "bare-faced, bare-souled," and has never stooped, in the words of J. Alfred Prufrock, "To prepare a face to meet the faces that you meet" (Eliot 27). Instead they retreat to the larger-than-life fantasy world of the movies, a regression into a dark sanctuary safe from the real world's glaring duplicity. Like twins joined in the womb, Leo fancies that he and the woman might fill in the missing parts of each other's incomplete lives.

Much as he tries to merge his life completely and harmoniously with hers, as Dennis attempts to do with Norman Bates, Leo can never square his perspective as perfectly as he wants with that of the Starveling. He tries sitting directly behind her in the cinema, replicating the sightlines first established in "Baader-Meinhof," in hopes of seeing through her eyes. But he aborts the effort when their perceptual wavelengths prove ineluctably out of sync: "Their bodies were aligned, eyes aligned, his and hers. But the movie was hers, her film, her theater, and he wasn't prepared for the confusion. The movie seemed stillborn" (S 198). He then tries to achieve synthesis through purely imaginative channels, attempting to conjure up a vision of her: "He closed his eyes for a time. He tried to see her standing naked in body profile before a mirror" (S 199). This exercise emphasizes most emphatically his efforts to co-opt her as mirror-double. His salacious gaze at her naked body hints at the sexual menace of a stalker. However, the primary function of her nudity here seems to emphasize her physical diminishment and her unadorned authenticity. Most telling is the fact that, even in his fantasy, he only views her mediated reflection, not her actual body. For that matter, he does not view her head-on but only in profile, like the image of the deceased Ulrike Meinhof that opens "Baader-Meinhof." He sees a view of her that she could never see herself, but this perspective also effectively deflects her gaze and withholds direct access to her identity.

Finally, frustrated by these half-measures, Leo recklessly barges in on her in the women's restroom of a movie theater. The echoes of "Baader-Meinhof" ring clearly, but there the bathroom provided a protective barrier between the art stalker and his prey, whereas in "The Starveling" it serves as the site for direct confrontation. The tenor of these scenes is radically different as well. In the former, DeLillo built tension on the woman's part and suspense on the reader's part because the stalker was an unknown quantity; we were given no access to his inner thoughts or true motives, and the clues planted from the start all point toward terror and death. In the latter story, Leo is humanized by our privileged access to his thoughts and his sympathetic portrayal by Flory. His stalking behavior is unconditionally wrong, but he comes across more as a social misfit than a full-blown sociopath. Accordingly, the bathroom scene in "The Starveling" plays more as farce than tragedy. Leo's excuses are lame, his speech rambling, his efforts to bond with her pathetically misjudged, and his overall demeanor that of a delusional loser. He fails to solicit a single word of response from the flabbergasted woman, who takes advantage of another patron's arrival in the restroom to dash out the door.

Exit?

"The Starveling" might well have concluded here on a note of abject starvation. However, in the end Leo receives unexpected sustenance from the last place he thought to seek it: Home. DeLillo experiments for once with sending his stalker home at the end instead of back to the museum, and this simple mutation yields remarkable results. Leo always trudges home at the close of a long day, mounting each step to Flory's apartment as wearily as Sisyphus approaching the summit with his boulder. The night after the bathroom fiasco, he opens the apartment door to find Flory performing her workout regimen in the flickering fluorescent light of the kitchen. This is the sort of domestic sight he has witnessed on countless nights and always blindly dismissed. From the story's beginning we are informed, "It was a life that had slowly grown around them, unfailingly familiar, and there was nothing much to see that had not been seen in previous hours, days, weeks, and months" (S 183–84). But for some reason on this particular evening he sees something in Flory's quotidian image that he has failed to see before, and the sight staggers him with all the power of an epiphany, the beast pounced at last:

> He didn't move a muscle, just sat and watched. It seemed the simplest thing, a person standing in a room, a matter of stillness and balance. But as time passed the position she held began to assume a meaning, even a history, although not one he could interpret. Bare feet together,

legs lightly touching at knees and thighs, the raised arms permitting a fraction of an inch of open space on either side of her head. The way the hands were entwined, the stretched body, a symmetry, a discipline that made him believe he was seeing something in her that he'd never recognized, a truth or depth that showed him who she was. He lost all sense of time, determined to remain dead still for as long as she did, watching steadily, breathing evenly, never lapsing.

If he blinked an eye, she would disappear. (S 211)

The blindness/sight imagery Kauffman locates in "Baader-Meinhof" is at play once again here, as Leo's eyes are finally opened to the beauty, discipline, symmetry, and strength of the woman he has been more or less ignoring for years while escaping to the movies. Instead of stopping at the threshold of some major perceptual breakthrough or life-altering experience, this time DeLillo gives his protagonist and his readers a glimpse of what might lie on the other side. After years of seeking transcendence, transformation, completion, or safety in art, Leo seems suddenly prepared to recognize that what and who he was looking for was waiting at home all along.

Before dismissing this conclusion as a hackneyed and sentimental happy ending, one must acknowledge how precariously Leo's epiphany hangs in the balance of the last line: "If he blinked, she would disappear" (S 211). Viewed in concert with the flickering fluorescent light illuminating the scene, this closing remark begs comparison with something Leo was told many years earlier in a college philosophy class: "*All human existence is a trick of the light*" (S 195, emphasis in original). The story's closing revelation links back to Leo's earlier interrogation of that philosophy lesson: "Was it about the universe and our remote and fleeting place as earthlings? Or was it something much more intimate, people in rooms, what we see and what we miss, how we pass through each other, year by year, second by second?" (S 195) By the end of the story, Leo has learned to recognize something intimate that he had missed for years. However, just because he sees it in a flash of clarity does not guarantee that he will continue to see it, that this insight will remain permanently imprinted on his consciousness and alter his behavior henceforward. In fact, given years of blindness, neglect, and retreat, it seems more likely that he will forget this lesson just as quickly as he learned it. But at the story's conclusion he is clinging to this freshly minted perception for as long as he can. "All human existence is a trick of the light" suggests a perception-based philosophy like that of Bishop Berkeley, who asserted "*esse est percipi*" (to be is to be perceived). From this ontological viewpoint, Leo stands to lose the incandescent being before him the instant he ceases to perceive her in the proper light. Furthermore, if human existence is merely an ephemeral trick of light, then is humanity really so fundamentally different than the flickering make-believe of the movies? Tempting as it is to read the story's conclusion as a deep and lasting transformative experience where Leo finally chooses Flory over the Starveling, reality over fantasy, and life over art, one must also recognize an equally valid interpretation in which Leo merely learns to view Flory in the same way he views the movies: captivating images capable of delivering powerful virtual experiences, but ultimately destined to dissolve once the lights change, replaced by the next magical but fleeting chimera.

* * *

All of DeLillo's stories on this theme feature characters pursuing something they lack, namely an acceptable way of seeing and being in the world. They turn to art in pursuit of elusive remedies that will heal what is damaged or restore what is missing. Art offers the allure of total communion, lasting catharsis, complete integration, and perfect harmony—in short, all that the cruel and broken outer world fails to provide. However, DeLillo dispels this idyllic fantasy in these stories, uncovering the confusion, duplicity, and menace lurking within the supposed sanctuary. When one enters an art venue, one does not exit the world of others or the inner turmoil of the self. "Baader-Meinhof" establishes the rules of this game, and DeLillo plays out variations in *Falling Man*, *Point Omega*, and "The Starveling." The latter work offers a potential exit strategy, but whether this strategy is tenable or sustainable remains profoundly uncertain. Rather, Leo is a blink away from resuming the pattern of his art stalker predecessors, revolving to and fro like

FIGURE 7.5 Confrontation 1 *(1988) by Gerhard Richter. Oil on canvas.* © *Gerhard Richter, courtesy Atelier Richter, Cologne, Germany.*

Dante's damned, pausing occasionally for placid moments of lucidity before resuming their doomed wanderings. Their revolutions invariably intersect the paths of other wanderers, colliding suddenly then separating again, in a desolate pattern of catch and release.

Museums, galleries, and cinemas bring strangers together and invite them into intensely intimate experiences with artworks, and potentially with one another. It deserves emphasizing that, present evidence to the contrary, these encounters are often entirely positive and benign, in real life and in DeLillo's earlier work. But in his later work DeLillo becomes increasingly fascinated by artistic experiences that take a darker, pathological turn. This is not just a matter of inventing aberrational scenarios in which a sicko is let loose among the otherwise enlightened clientele and noble artwork of a venerable cultural institution. Rather, DeLillo considers ways in which artworks and art venues can subvert the higher impulses traditionally attributed to them. Artistic reception involves separation and distance; a canvas or movie screen cannot be regarded clearly if one gets too close. Art venues also facilitate a kind of aesthetic promiscuity, encouraging spectators to shuttle from one intensely intimate experience to the next. Thus, DeLillo characterizes the spectator's transaction with art as a fervent but fleeting exchange across an unbridgeable divide, and this same dynamic informs and undermines the human relationships he depicts among spectators gathered in the shadows of art.

8

Literary triangulation

DeLillo
/   \
O'Hara   Oates

First published in November 2009 in *The New Yorker* and reissued in *The Angel Esmeralda* (2011), "Midnight in Dostoevsky" is a remarkable variation on the "art stalker" theme analyzed in the previous chapter. The two main characters, narrator Robby and his best friend Todd, follow a man around the streets of their small college town. However, there is no sinister threat of sexual assault or murder as in the story's creepier cousins "Baader-Meinhof," *Point Omega*, and "The Starveling." These curious freshmen are simply engaged in a competitive game of fiction-making, challenging each other to imagine their ways into the life of an old man in a hooded coat who keeps crossing their path. Taken at face value this seems much ado about nothing. To understand the disturbing impact on Robby by story's end one must first appreciate "Midnight in Dostoevsky" as a richly complex exercise in *literary triangulation*.

I use the term "triangulation" here to describe a form of deflection and sublimation where one character (in this case Robby) works through his feelings toward another character (Todd) by redirecting them through a third figure (the Hooded Man). The intratextual dynamics of literary triangulation within "Midnight in Dostoevsky" are reiterated through intertextual triangulation between the story and other artworks. DeLillo's story takes its title from a line in Frank O'Hara's "Meditations in an Emergency," a cri de coeur written after the poet's breakup with his lover. David Cowart alertly recognizes the connection to O'Hara's poem, which features a witty analysis of homosexual identity and intimations of the martyrdom 1950s gays underwent daily at the hands of the straight world, suggest[ing] a current of unacknowledged homosexual anxiety in the relationship between Robby, the evidently heterosexual narrator of DeLillo's story, and the friend with whom he finds himself violently at odds in the end. (31)

I agree with Cowart's identification of a gay subtext and want to draw it to the surface in this chapter. My method constitutes a kind of critical triangulation, juxtaposing "Midnight in Dostoevsky" with the O'Hara source poem (and the art of Francisco de Zurbarán to which O'Hara alludes) and with "Three Girls" by Joyce Carol Oates. I doubt DeLillo was directly influenced by this story in the way he was irrefutably influenced by "Meditations in an Emergency." Nevertheless, my selection of "Three Girls" as the third leg of the triangle is not arbitrary. Oates incorporates a number of the same elements in her 2004 story that DeLillo later uses, but she treats them in a less disguised manner, exposing the homoeroticism which DeLillo keeps cloaked. Reconsidered in triangulation with the outed works of O'Hara and Oates, the closeted "Midnight in Dostoevsky" emerges as a story of repressed homoerotic desire refracted through the prism of artistic collaboration.

The walking dead

"Midnight in Dostoevsky" is set against a backdrop of wintry desolation in a small town. Aside from their classes, young undergrads Robby and Todd chiefly occupy themselves as flâneurs exploring their new surroundings. The story opens: "We were two somber boys hunched in our coats, grim winter settling in. The college was at the edge of a small town way upstate, barely a town, maybe a hamlet, we said, or just a whistle-stop, and we took walks all the time, getting out, going nowhere, low skies and bare trees, hardly a soul to be seen" (MD 119). The first word of the story is "We," and from the start the first-person plural voice vies with first-person singular for predominance. Like many college freshmen, Robby seeks community and struggles to adapt to his new circumstances. He wants to belong but often feels alien, misunderstood, and isolated, a stranger in a strange land. That land is frequently figured in the story as a deathscape.

Robby describes the town as if it were populated by the walking dead: "This was how we spoke of the local people: they were souls, they were transient spirits, a face in the window of a passing car, runny with reflected light, or a long street with a shovel jutting from a snowbank, no one in sight" (MD 119). Later when Todd goes home for winter break and Robby remains behind on campus, he walks the now familiar streets alone: "In snowfall, the town looked ghosted over, dead still at times. . . . I began to feel intimate with these streets. I was myself here, able to see things singly and plainly, away from the only life I'd known, the city, stacked and layered, a thousand meanings a minute" (MD 135). Becoming acclimated to his new surroundings may sound like a freshman orientation success story. Then again, only the dead feel at home in death. His relationship with Todd represents a possible life-saving antidote to the death that threatens to engulf him. But that relationship is itself fraught with ambivalence, anxiety, and potentially fatal consequences. "*Consider the origins of the word*," Robby stresses early on, italicizing the mantra for emphasis (MD 121). It is surely no coincidence that the etymological origin of Todd is *Tod*, German for Death.

As if wandering this necropolis accompanied by a partner named after death were not enough, Robby also pursues a third figure shrouded with deadly associations. "This was the day we saw the man in the hooded coat. We argued about the coat—loden coat, anorak, parka. It was our routine; we were ever ready to find a matter to contest" (MD 119). In a story so saturated with morbid references, there is no escaping the hooded man's resemblance to a shabby Grim Reaper. Robby tells the story as if he and Todd are literary detectives on the trail of the hooded man. However, the Grim Reaper connotations force the reader to wonder precisely who is following whom. Perhaps this is a stalker story after all, where the predator will become the prey. In a seemingly throwaway observation, we learn this about Robby and Todd: "We both played chess. We both believed in God" (MD 126). Whether intentional or not, this reference conjures up for me the famous scene of the Knight playing chess for his soul with hooded Death in Ingmar Bergman's *The Seventh Seal*.[1]

White versus Black, Life versus Death. The same tension animates "Midnight in Dostoevsky." In the midst of so much death imagery, the story is also enlivened with the spirit of playful imagination, competitive language games, and the life-giving power of creative fiction. The "transient spirits" who inhabit this region resemble the walking dead. But in another sense they are like ideal forms that have not yet been fleshed out and given substance, the unborn, characters in search of an author. Cue our co-creators Robby and Todd. They play chess and believe in God; but they also play God: "This was why the man had been born, to end up in this town wearing this coat" (MD 119). As far as Robby is concerned, this man exists for the purposes of their creative exercises: he is whomever they make him out to be. As they debate the particulars of his wardrobe, name, nationality, and background, these fiction-making demiurges collaboratively create the Hooded Man into being through language.

Another crucial figure in the story with respect to the relationship of language and reality is the Logic professor Ilgauskas. Again assuming the

FIGURE 8.1 *Death (Bengt Ekerot) plays chess with the Knight (Max von Sydow) in Ingmar Bergman's* The Seventh Seal *(AB Svensk Filmindustri, 1957).*

plural voice, Robby declares, "We were fascinated by Ilgauskas. He seemed in a trance state. . . . We'd decided, some of us, that he was suffering from a neurological condition. He was not bored but simply unbound, speaking freely and erratically out of a kind of stricken insight" (MD 123). The reader mostly experiences this genius second-hand through Robby's reverent impressions, with only scattered fragments of lectures reproduced in the narrative. But those snatches of stricken insight—"causal nexus" (MD 122); "atomic fact" (MD 123); "*F* and not-*F*" (MD 123); "Logic ends where the world ends" (MD 131)—make it clear that Ilgaukas is modeled after Ludwig Wittgenstein, the twentieth century's most influential Logic philosopher.[2]

Several DeLillo works draw upon Wittgenstein. Asked by Tom LeClair about allusions to the philosopher in *End Zone*, DeLillo replied, "I've read parts of the *Tractatus*, but I have no formal training in mathematical logic and I couldn't say a thing about the technical aspects of the book. I like the way he uses language. Even in translation, it's very evocative. It's like reading Martian" (10). DeLillo was being deflective and self-deprecating. His early novels display more than passing familiarity with Wittgenstein's core concepts. In *Tractatus Logico-Philosophicus* Wittgenstein tests the limits of language's capacity to express reality. Beyond those limits lies the ineffable, and, as Wittgenstein famously concluded the *Tractatus*: "What we cannot speak about we must pass over in silence" (Wittgenstein 74). Both Wittgenstein's philosophy and DeLillo's fiction oscillate between the poles of language and silence. One hears direct echoes of Wittgenstein in the central Logos College of *End Zone*, where an entire course is offered on "the untellable," and in the Logicon project of *Ratner's Star*. Wittgenstein also provides a philosophical basis for the compulsion so many DeLillo characters feel toward ascetic withdrawal into silence. Peter Boxall asserts that, particularly in DeLillo's early novels, "as language reaches for a mode or form of expression that can take it beyond its functional properties, towards a Wittgensteinian space in which language and the world might be remade, it collapses back insistently into vacuousness and emptiness, into a simple, repetitive, infantile renaming of what is already here" (43). Boxall characterizes the affinity in genealogical terms as the "Wittgensteinian poetics that stretches from the *Tractatus*, through Kafka and Beckett to DeLillo" (68).

That affinity is renewed and extended in "Midnight in Dostoevsky" through the character Ilgauskas. The Logic professor shares Wittgenstein's preoccupation with language and its expressive limits, which accounts in part for his appeal to the budding fiction-maker Robby. DeLillo also endows Ilgauskas with the peculiar aura surrounding the iconoclastic Wittgenstein, consisting in equal measures of genius and madness, rising to heights of lucid inspiration then withdrawing into hermetic introversion. White and black, life and death, language and silence. Ilgauskas is also visibly ill, suggesting that the specter of an untimely death may loom over him as it did Wittgenstein. Although the death certificate listed cancer as the cause of his death, the romantic myth of Wittgenstein suggests that he died of a metaphysical illness. It is tempting to typecast Wittgenstein as the Greta Garbo of philosophy, an alluring but delicate creature ill-equipped to survive in this harsh, sordid world. He was certainly tortured in terms of his personal relationships, as were so many homosexuals and bisexuals of his era, and one wonders if a similar unspoken identification is part of Ilgauskas's magnetic attraction for Robby. Finally, like Wittgenstein, Ilgauskas is a mesmerizing if erratic teacher. He is the center of a circle of acolytes, but he is no megalomaniac. Rather, he urges his pupils to look inward and rigorously interrogate themselves. The impressionable Robby struggles with this, inclined as he is toward hero worship. But he also struggles because there are hidden corners of his inner self where he prefers not to shine a light.

> Did we see dysfunction and call it an inspired form of intellect? We didn't want to like him, only to believe in him. We tendered our deepest trust to the stark nature of his methodology. Of course there was no methodology. There was only Ilgauskas. He challenged our reason for being, what we thought, how we lived, the truth or falsity of what we believed to be true or false. Isn't this what great teachers do, the Zen masters and Brahman scholars? (MD 131–32)

And what are Robby's deepest thoughts, his reasons for being? What is true and what is false in how he lives his life? "What we cannot speak about we must pass over in silence" (74). If Robby is silent on these subjects, however, DeLillo is subtly more forthcoming, dropping clues about what was termed in doomed Wittgenstein's day as "the love that dare not speak its name."

An important intertextual hint comes when Robby's classmate Jenna unexpectedly runs into Ilgauskas at a local diner. Intimidated by a personal encounter with His Eminence, she engages in small talk by asking what he has been reading. She reports to Robby:

> "He said he was reading Dostoevsky. I'll tell you exactly what he said. He said, 'Dostoevsky day and night.'"
> "Fantastic."
> "And I told him my coincidence, that I'd been reading a lot of poetry and I'd read a poem just a couple of days earlier with a phrase I recalled. 'Like midnight in Dostoevsky.'" (MD 134)

As a young man with a literary bent, Robby is elated to learn of his hero's passion for Dostoevsky. Not that he has much familiarity with Dostoevsky at this point. For that matter, he seems utterly clueless about the source of Jenna's poetry quotation. DeLillo knows the source well, however, appropriating it deliberately and strategically. Frank O'Hara's "Meditations in an Emergency" provides the spit in the lock to open the secret doors of DeLillo's story.

Meditations and martyrdom

Frank O'Hara was the prototypical New York poet and one of the leading figures of the New York School. He had a foot firmly planted in both the literary and artistic avant-garde of the city, contributing frequently to poetry magazines and readings while also posing for his many painter friends and holding down a day job at the Museum of Modern Art.[3] No poet better captures the urbane wit, sassy camp, experimental innovation, and boundless energy of 1950s New York. However, O'Hara was actually twenty-five years old before he moved to the city. He was born in Baltimore in 1926 (only ten years DeLillo's senior), raised in Grafton, Massachusetts, stationed in the Pacific as a Navy seaman during the Second World War, and educated at Harvard and the University of Michigan before moving to New York in 1951. Nevertheless, as Brad Gooch notes in his splendid biography *City Poet: The Life and Times of Frank O'Hara*, "In the bohemian artworld of 1950s Manhattan where O'Hara was such a leading player and a prime creative force, one of the unspoken rules was that people did not need to have come from anywhere special. . . . Self-creating was part of the ethos of the times" (13). DeLillo is doubtlessly drawn as much to O'Hara's protean spirit of reinvention as to his time-capsule paeans to the New York of his youth.

Gooch depicts O'Hara's artistic evolution as taking place hand in glove with his sexual awakening:

> The solitary times that O'Hara spent in his attic, or in the hay bins at Tower Hill farm, were not only artistic epiphanies in the footsteps of Stephen Dedalus. They were also sexual epiphanies, seeking the truth of his sexual identity, in his case a homosexual identity, which was becoming quite obvious to this sensitive adolescent while he was still living at home in Grafton, and which could only have been circumspectly expressed in a small American town in the 1940s, especially within the restrictive rulings of the Catholic Church. (50)

Though far from tolerant or accepting by today's standards, 1950s New York was much more progressive and less restrictive in its sexual mores than anything O'Hara had previously experienced. "Soon after his arrival in the city," according to Gooch, "he set up a pattern of episodic promiscuity that characterized his sexual life over the next five years, and these episodes fed his conversation and poetry as much as, if not more than, his sexuality" (195). To paint the picture in broad strokes, O'Hara's move from the provinces to the city fostered a mutual blossoming of both his sexuality and his art. One might expect even greater openness and acceptance in DeLillo's twenty-first-century story, but the opposite is true. It is as if Robbie's geographical relocation from the city to upstate is accompanied by a temporal transplant back to a more repressive era, where both his artistic and sexual impulses are stifled. O'Hara first published "Meditations in an Emergency" in *Poetry* magazine in November 1954, when eighteen-year-old Don DeLillo was a freshman at Fordham. The poet is credited in the title as the wellspring of "Midnight in Dostoevsky," and indeed the story feels much more like it is set in the 1950s of DeLillo's undergraduate years than in the twenty-first century, despite all the contemporary references to laptops, cell phones, elliptical machines, and hand-held devices.

DeLillo establishes the connection between art and sex obliquely, through triangulation, by pointing the reader outside the story to O'Hara's more explicit poetry. The inspiration for "Meditations in an Emergency" was O'Hara's breakup with Larry Rivers, a painter with whom he had collaborated and his on-and-off lover. After their split in the summer of 1954, O'Hara retreated to the country to lick his wounds, and it was during this self-imposed exile that he wrote "Meditations in an Emergency."[4] Viewed from this vantage point, the poem reads in part like an anti-pastoral. Surrounded by bucolic nature, O'Hara longs to return to the city where he left his heart behind. As he puts it in the prose poem: "One need never leave the confines of New York to get all the greenery one wishes—I can't even enjoy a blade of grass unless I know there's a subway handy, or a record store or some other sign that people do not totally *regret* life" (38, emphasis in original).

The breakup with Rivers prompted the "emergency" of the title, and from the start the poem is a meditation upon various possible responses: "Am I to become profligate as if I were a blonde? Or religious as if I were French?" (38) Having been burned again by love, the poet considers two opposite alternatives, promiscuity or chastity. Get thee to a nunnery, either the brothel or the convent variety. "Each time my heart is broken it makes me feel more adventurous (and how the same names keep recurring on that interminable list!), but one of these days there'll be nothing left with which to venture forth" (38). The tone of the poem caroms wildly across the emotional register; from bitchy jabs at his ex-lover ("Why don't you get rid of someone else for a change?" [38]) to sarcastic self-mockery ("I am the least difficult of men. All I want is boundless love" [38]); from Wildean aphorisms ("It is easy to be beautiful; it is difficult to appear so" [39]) to wounded regret ("yes, there, even in the heart, where the filth is pumped in and slanders and pollutes and determines" [39]); from melodramatic recrimination ("Destroy yourself, if you don't know!" [39]) to fuck-you determination ("I'll be back, I'll re-emerge, defeated, from the valley" [40]). This is less Wordsworthian emotion recollected in tranquility than storm-chaser footage of an emotional tornado.

While the poet's heartrate spikes and plunges, he never loses cerebral control over the poem. The situation may be an emergency, but it is also a meditation. The poet is detached enough to cast a cold eye and maintain a critical perspective on his experience. This meditative stance enables him to recognize useful antecedents, forge unexpected connections, and thus transform a deeply personal breakup into an aesthetically rich work of art. Consider, for instance, the closing verse paragraph, which heralds O'Hara's return to New York with eclectic imagery ranging from Greek mythology (Orpheus and Eurydice), the Bible ("Yea, though I walk through the shadow of the valley of death, I will fear no evil" [Psalms 23:4]), to graphic sex (blow job? hand job?): "I've got to get out of here. I choose a piece of shawl and my dirtiest suntans. I'll be back, I'll re-emerge, defeated, from the valley; you don't want me to go where you go, so I go where you don't want me to. It's only afternoon, there's a lot ahead. There won't be any mail downstairs. Turning, I spit in the lock and the knob turns" (40). The poem closes with an opening door and the poet crossing the threshold into whatever or whoever comes next.

Perhaps the best example of O'Hara's allusive ingenuity comes midway through the poem in the line DeLillo co-opts for his title: "St. Serapion, I wrap myself in the robes of your whiteness which is *like midnight in Dostoevsky*"

(39, emphasis added). There is a lot to unpack here and two distinct lines of inquiry. First, what is O'Hara doing with these allusive images? Second, why and how does DeLillo use O'Hara's imagery for his own purposes? In other words, what is DeLillo's triangulation approach intended to divulge, indirectly via an O'Hara bankshot, that Robby withholds or represses from "Midnight in Dostoevsky"?

Saint Serapion was a twelfth-century friar in the Mercedarian Order, an order devoted to ransoming Christian captives during the Crusades. According to Jeannine Baticle, pirates murdered him in a particularly brutal way: "Serapion was bound by the hands and feet to two poles, and was then beaten, dismembered, and disemboweled. Finally, his neck was partly severed, leaving his head to dangle" (102). His martyrdom is most famously captured by Francisco de Zurbarán in his 1628 painting *Saint Serapion*. This powerful piece hangs in the Wadsworth Atheneum in Hartford, Connecticut, where O'Hara must have seen it. His reference to Serapion in "Meditations in an Emergency" unmistakably refers to Zurbarán's rendition. The ostensible subject is martyrdom, but the painting's most striking feature is its ornate fabric, the intricate folds, crinkles, nuanced coloration, and interplay of shadow and light in Serapion's massive garments. O'Hara uses the plural "robes" in his description, which shows his careful eye for detail. Close inspection reveals that there are in fact two components of the saint's habit on display: the massive white cape on top, and a humbler robe underneath. Serapion's slumped, unresponsive demeanor suggests that he has endured torture and may already be dead, yet the gruesome evidence of his suffering has literally been covered up, cloaked in a dissembling whiteness which hides untellable cruelties.

Zurbarán's painting is a masterful exercise in the art of *concealment*. This was surely one of O'Hara's chief attractions to the painting. Comparing his suffering to that of a Christian martyr sounds outlandishly exaggerated, though in time it would seem less so, after O'Hara's excruciating death on Fire Island when he was only forty years old.[5] In any case, like Zurbarán, O'Hara takes meticulous care in "Meditations" to conceal the worst wounds, masking his pain in self-mockery, catty swipes, erudite cross-references, and any number of rhetorical diversionary maneuvers. Noting the relevance of Zurbarán to both O'Hara's poem and DeLillo's story, David Cowart observes,

This painting . . . offers a remarkable picture of martyrdom: the saint is unconscious, in repose, the ropes around his wrists not immediately noticed by the viewer. But the saint's robe, of a startling whiteness, belies the violence to which he has been or will be subjected. Like midnight, such whiteness makes seeing difficult; like Dostoevsky's midnight, the image cloaks a universe of existential, solitary suffering. (31)

FIGURE 8.2 Saint Serapion *(1628) by Francisco de Zurbarán. Oil on canvas. Wadsworth Atheneum, Hartford, Connecticut.*

Cowart touches upon the enigma at the heart of O'Hara's allusion: Why compare the startlingly white garment in Zurbarán's painting to black midnight? Cowart may be right that the Dostoevsky comparison signals an existential darkness beneath the deceptive cloak of tranquility and purity. But O'Hara was a Russophile, and I suspect he had a more specific light/dark paradox in mind. Dostoevsky's hometown of St. Petersburg is the northernmost major metropolis in the world, and from May through July the sun never sets there, a phenomenon known as the "White Nights." Dostoevsky wrote a short story about unrequited love called "White Nights" which is set during this topsy-turvy time of year. O'Hara posits an ingenious link between the dark depravity concealed within both Serapion's white robes and Dostoevsky's "White Nights."

Robby's relationship with Todd bears the markers of unrequited love, but his homoerotic desire is thoroughly repressed and cloaked in a wintry pall. As is so often the case in DeLillo's fiction, he subtly guides readers to uncover hidden facets of his characters to which the characters themselves are oblivious. By 1954 O'Hara was already out as a gay man. He declares in "Meditations," "Now there is only one man I love to kiss when he is unshaven" (39). He also coyly mocks the alternative: "Heterosexuality! you are inexorably approaching. (How discourage her?)" (39). Yet in DeLillo's 2009 story, the sexually ambivalent Robby is incapable of expressing or acknowledging (even to himself) his true feelings for Todd. Instead he sublimates them through artistic collaboration in their coauthored fantasies about the Hooded Man.

Given DeLillo's lifelong love of art and his regular patronage of New York museums and galleries, he may well have direct familiarity with Zurbarán, rather than depending exclusively upon O'Hara's second-hand reference. The first major career retrospective of Zurbarán was held in 1987 at The Metropolitan Museum of Art. The *New York Times* regarded this event as significant enough to publish two separate reviews, and both critics devoted significant space to commenting upon the celebrated *Saint Serapion*.[6] If DeLillo visited this exhibition, other paintings would likely have made a strong impression, too. Zurbarán frequently depicted saints, monks, friars, and priests as subjects in his paintings. The most distinguishing physical feature of the man Robby and Todd trail is his hooded garment. The two literary sleuths debate the proper terminology for this garb, parsing the relative merits of parka, loden coat, duffel coat, and anorak. Robby and Todd would have been in semantic heaven wandering the galleries of the Zurbarán exhibit, surrounded by capes, cowls, tunics, habits, and scapulars. "*Consider the origin of the word*" (MD 121, emphasis in original). DeLillo points outside his story to O'Hara's poem, and O'Hara points outside his poem to Zurbarán's painting. Having followed O'Hara's breadcrumbs back to *Saint Serapion* and invoked it for his portrait of Robby, DeLillo may well have absorbed other influences from Zurbarán in his depiction of the Hooded Man.

The excellent catalogue from The Met exhibition featured another Zurbarán masterpiece on its cover, the National Gallery of London's *Saint Francis in Meditation*. Could this image be yet another intertextual influence for DeLillo's portrait of the Hooded Man? As the title of the canvas indicates, Saint Francis is captured in a moment of intense meditation. He clutches a skull and gazes darkly up to heaven, suggesting that the subject of his meditation is death. Jeannine Baticle provides a perceptive gloss on this painting in the catalogue:

> The figure of Saint Francis, which is life-size and shown close up, occupies most of the otherwise bare pictorial space. This "cinematographic" disposition, unusual for the seventeenth century, creates a striking, almost

FIGURE 8.3 Saint Francis in Meditation *(c. 1635–40) by Francisco de Zurbarán. Oil on canvas. The National Gallery, London, England.*

intolerable, image of the saint and makes us participate intimately in his mystical ecstasy. This way of focusing attention on a figure by isolating it is in keeping with Counter-Reformation aesthetics as defined by such theologians as Ignatius of Loyola and Cardinal Federico Borromeo, who prescribed directness and realism in the representation of religious subjects. Here, rather than producing an image of the Divine by idealizing the model's features, Zurbarán evokes the Divine in his rendering of the intensity of Saint Francis's ecstatic expression as he meditates on the vision of death; one can almost hear his halting breath. (272)

There are several features of *Saint Francis in Meditation* ideally suited to DeLillo's interests, from its anachronistically cinematic quality and its Ignatian exercise in intense empathy to its searing focus on death and its aesthetic contrast between light and shadow, between mysterious revelation and hooded concealment. Furthermore, the serendipitous connection with O'Hara's "Meditations" would not have escaped DeLillo's attention. In this case, the Francis doing the meditating is not Frank contemplating a breakup but Saint Francis contemplating death. Both scenarios resonate deeply with Robby's attraction toward both Todd and *Tod* (Death) in "Midnight in Dostoevsky."

Game over

Inside class the most important figure in Robby's life is Ilgauskas, and outside of class it is Todd. Everyone else has abandoned him. Robby meditates upon his acute isolation as one of "The Left Behind" during winter break. His dysfunctional family provides no solace. His father is away on business in China and his mother is adrift with her ex-boyfriend. The only other person at school who pays him any attention is his classmate Jenna, but she announces that she is moving to Idaho and so will not be returning to school. Ilgauskas and Todd are all he has. Ilgauskas is impenetrably remote, but after Jenna's revelation from the diner Robby now knows a triangular method for communing indirectly with his unapproachable professor through Dostoevsky. He spends countless hours during the break holed up in the library reading the Russian author. The combination of solitude, harsh weather, intense concentration, devotion, and desperation provide the necessary conditions for mystic visions. An epiphany finally arrives: "It came from nowhere, from the night, fully formed, extending in several directions, and when I opened my eyes in the morning it was all around me, filling the room" (MD 136).

After winter break Robby shares his breakthrough with his collaborator: "I told Todd about the idea I'd had, the revelation in the icy night. I knew who the man was, I said. Everything fit, every element, the man's origins, his family ties, his presence in this town" (MD 137). Robby's revelation is that the Hooded Man is named Ilgauskas—because he is the father of the Logic professor. Todd is skeptical at first, but Robby will not be moved: "The point is that it all fits together. It's a formulation, it's artful, it's structured" (MD 138). This solution is ideal from Robby's perspective because it binds together the most important people and pursuits in his life. "This was my crystalline link, the old man to Ilgauskas to Dostoevsky to Russia. I thought about it all the time. Todd said it would become my life's work. I would spend my life in a thought bubble, purifying the link" (MD 141). Typical of his deep denial and repression, Robby neglects to mention the most important link, namely Todd. The more they commit themselves to co-creating a fictional identity for the Hooded Man, the closer it will bring them to Ilgauskas and—gradually, unconsciously, inevitably—the closer it will bring Robby and Todd together.

At first the plan unfolds successfully. Robby and Todd comb the streets, pursuing the Hooded Man and refining him into fuller existence. "We weren't sure why we were doing this. But we tried to be scrupulous, adding new elements every day, making adjustments and refinements, and all the while scanning the streets, trying to induce an appearance through joint force of will" (MD 140). There is an element of obsession fueling their search, a trademark theme in DeLillo's fiction. They treat the hunt like a highly competitive game, motivating each other to create ever more convincing details and challenging every false move in a quest for perfection. In the LeClair interview DeLillo characterized his early work as "books of games, books in which fiction itself is a sort of game" (5). He elaborated, "Games provide a frame in which we can try to be perfect. Within sixty-minute limits or one-hundred-yard limits or the limits of a game board, we can look for perfect moments or perfect structures" (6). But he added an important caveat: "In my fiction I think this search sometimes turns out to be a cruel delusion" (6).

The cruel delusion of "Midnight in Dostoevsky" is exposed at story's end during the boys' final encounter with the Hooded Man. They had not seen the man for some time, leading Robby to fear that he might have died. They are heartened, therefore, when they eventually spot him again. Robby's relief quickly turns to horror, however, when Todd radically violates the rules of the game: "I think we need to take the next step. . . . I think we need to talk to him" (MD 143). Robby balks:

"That's crazy."

"It's completely reasonable,' he said.

"We do that, we kill the idea, we kill everything we've done. We can't talk to him."

"We'll ask a few questions, that's all. Quiet, low key. Find out a few things."

"It's never been a matter of literal answers." (MD 143)

Robby had thought he and Todd were working together in perfect synchronicity on a shared vision. Then suddenly they are pitted against one another in an irreconcilable conflict between the literalist and the fabulist. Apparently Todd was only temporarily satisfying his desire to know the old man through this fictional prelude, all the while planning to replace fiction with fact by actually meeting the man. Robby is appalled by this desecration. Talking to the Hooded Man would be like Stephen Dedalus talking to the Bird Girl. Why break the magic spell, why denigrate pure idealism only to exalt sullied, inferior reality? Todd insists, "All we're doing is searching out the parallel life," he said. "It doesn't affect what we've been saying all this time." Robby will hear none of it: "It affects everything. It's a violation. It's crazy" (MD 144).

Their artistic differences rapidly escalate into a fight. A shove leads to a grapple leads to a punch: "I wanted to wrestle him down and pound his head into the asphalt" (MD 145). This is no longer a game; it's a battle for something. Something Robby cannot admit. He is too emotionally immature and psychologically repressed to confront the true source of his turmoil, so he lashes out with dumb brute male violence. He does, however, poignantly register his sense of detachment and loss as Todd runs away:

> I saw my lost glove lying in the middle of the street. Then Todd running, bareheaded, trying to skirt areas of frozen snow. The scene empty everywhere around him. I couldn't make sense of it. I felt completely detached. His breath visible, streams of trailing vapor. I wondered what it was that had caused this thing to happen. He only wanted to talk to the man. (MD 145)

Robby may be naïve, but the reader should not be. We know how to interpret the imagery of that lost glove because DeLillo has taught us through literary triangulation. By juxtaposing "Midnight in Dostoevsky" with "Meditations in an Emergency," we can recognize this story as a tale of unrequited love and this conclusion as an emotional emergency triggered by Robby's devastating breakup with Todd.

Three girls and two boys

Joyce Carol Oates is two years younger than Don DeLillo, but she heard her calling earlier. She published her first novel in 1964, seven years before he debuted with *Americana*. Oates was already well established when she wrote one of the earliest rave reviews of *Americana* in the *Detroit Sunday News*, calling it "a robust and intellectually exciting work" and proclaiming that "DeLillo is a man of frightening perception." She concluded with high praise: "DeLillo is to be congratulated for having accomplished one of the most compelling and sophisticated of 'first novels' that I have ever read" (*Uncensored* 340). If DeLillo has an opinion of Oates's work he has kept it to himself, or at least never committed it to print. I am not attempting to prove that Oates has exerted a direct influence on DeLillo. There are no explicit allusions to "Three Girls" in "Midnight in Dostoevsky." Rather, I am following DeLillo's lead by proposing my own triangulation, juxtaposing Oates's three girls alongside DeLillo's two boys to show how each story can be used instructively to illuminate the other.

First published in her 2004 collection *I Am No One You Know* and frequently anthologized since then, "Three Girls" shares a number of affinities with DeLillo's 2009 story. Oates features two intimate college friends who share a deep love of literature. She sets her story in New York on a wintry night in 1956, which just happens to be the year Oates herself became a college freshman. Both stories are told by a first-person narrator who often assumes the plural "we" voice. Both are told in retrospect from some unidentified future vantage point, a time when presumably the narrators appreciate the significance of their respective encounters more clearly than they did at the time. Each story is animated by sexual tension between the two college friends. Oates confronts this issue far more transparently than DeLillo, however. The homoeroticism is almost completely snowed under in "Midnight in Dostoevsky," but Oates digs it out and puts it on display in "Three Girls." Finally, both stories feature exemplary uses of literary triangulation, developing the relationships between the two main characters through their focus on a third figure. In DeLillo this role is of course played by the anonymous Hooded Man; in Oates the subject is a major celebrity incognito: Marilyn Monroe.

For all these similarities, the tone of Oates's story differs sharply from "Midnight in Dostoevsky." Robby depicts his upstate exile as if he is wandering the land of the dead. How different from the prevailing tone of "Three Girls," where the unnamed narrator strolls through the blissful sanctuary of a fairy-tale kingdom: "In Strand Used Books on Broadway and Twelfth one snowy March early evening in 1956 when the streetlights on Broadway glimmered with a strange sepia glow, we were two NYU girl-poets drifting through the warehouse of treasures as through an enchanted forest. . . . Enchanted by books. Enchanted by the Strand" (271). The girl-poets (to use the narrator's own preferred term) are euphoric from their love of literature—and of each other. The story leaves no doubt that the worshipful narrator is infatuated with her friend, and signs suggest that this love is requited. "We were enchanted with the Strand and with each other in the Strand" (272). Oates's narrator is honest with herself (at least in retrospect), far more than Robby ever could be, about her desires during "these romantic evenings at the Strand" (272). Until this snowy evening in March 1956, however, she had never found the courage to declare her devotion: "In an agony of unspoken young love I watched you" (272). She reflects, "I adored and feared you knowing you'd break my heart, my heart that had never before been broken because never before so exposed" (273).

The catalyst that finally precipitates an open expression of love is Marilyn Monroe. The friend leads the narrator to the modern poetry section of the store where, to their amazement, they discover Marilyn Monroe, disguised in men's clothing, poring over poetry books. As in her most famous story "Where Are You Going, Where Have You Been?" Oates shows her special talent here for capturing the narrator's occluded perceptions, shifting from confusion to curiosity to suspicion to revelation:

Someone we knew? An older, good-looking student from one of our classes? *A girl-poet like ourselves?* I was about to nudge you in the ribs in bafflement when the blond women turned, taking down another book from the shelf (e. e. cummings' *Tulips and Chimneys*—always I would remember that title!), and I saw that she was Marilyn Monroe.

Marilyn Monroe. In the Strand. Just like us. And she seemed to be alone.

Marilyn Monroe, alone! (273, emphasis in original)

Ironically, it would have been difficult in 1956 to find two girls less inclined to revere the Hollywood star. These self-professed "girl-poets" are far more impressed by their literary heroes (including Ilgauskas's beloved Dostoevsky): "We were admiring though confused by the poetry of Yeats, we were yet more confused by the lauded worth of Pound, enthusiastically drawn to the bold metaphors of Kafka (that cockroach!) and Dostoevsky (sexy murderer Raskolnikov and the Underground Man were our rebel heroes) and Sartre ('Hell is other people'—we knew this)" (272). They regard themselves as protégés of those great writers, and they reject the facile, limiting, misogynist expectations for women in the 1950s: "Admittedly we were American middle class, and Caucasian, and female (Yet we were not 'conventional' females. In fact, we shared male contempt for the merely 'conventional' female.)" (272). Sex symbol Marilyn Monroe did not conform to the conservative housewife gender role in which most women of the Eisenhower era were cast. Nevertheless, in a more fundamental sense the girl-poets see her as contemptible for catering to male objectifications of women. They regard her as the epitome of the brainless sex toy men wanted women to be, and they denounce her as cynically (or just stupidly) complicit in her own exploitation. As the narrator puts it, "All that was makeup, fake, cartoon sexiness subtle as a kick in the groin. All that was vulgar and infantile" (278). In short, they considered Marilyn Monroe to be a sell-out and the antithesis of all the countercultural values they held dear. But this is *not* the person the girls encounter at the Strand. The bookworm poring through the stacks is a genuinely unconventional 1950s woman. As the title "Three Girls" intimates, the girl-poets immediately recognize her as one of their own:

Here was the surprise: this woman was / was not Marilyn Monroe. For this woman was an individual wholly absorbed in selecting, leafing through, pausing to read books. You could see that this individual was a *reader*. One of those who *reads*. With concentration, with passion. With her very soul. And it was poetry she was reading, her lips pursed, silently shaping the words. Absent-mindedly she wiped her nose on the edge of her hand, so intent was she on what she was reading. For when you truly read poetry, poetry reads *you*. (273–74, emphasis in original)

All lovers of literature will see their reflection in that description. Indeed, Robby makes a like-minded observation in the library while devouring

Dostoevsky: "I placed the book on the table and opened it and then leaned down into the splayed pages, reading and breathing. We seemed to assimilate each other, the characters and I, and when I raised my head I had to tell myself where I was" (MD 135). As Oates's narrator assimilates this new image of Marilyn Monroe, she discovers more in common with the young woman than a shared love of books.

When I teach "Three Girls," I always ask my students why they think Marilyn Monroe has remained such an enduring icon. Almost none of them have seen any of her movies, but they all have vivid associations with her image. I am particularly interested in Marilyn Monroe's legendary status within the gay community. She has been commemorated in art by Andy Warhol and in song by Elton John, and one expects to see at least one Marilyn at every drag show worth its rhinestones. She might seem an unlikely candidate for such distinction, given that she was notorious for sexual relations with the most famous men of her era: President Kennedy (and maybe his brother Robert, too), Joe DiMaggio, Arthur Miller. She was heterosexuality incarnate, the prototype of the profligate blonde O'Hara invokes at the opening of "Meditations in an Emergency." But she was also sensitive, misunderstood, easily wounded, and increasingly desperate, a martyr to the suffocating gender expectations of her times if ever there was one. Norma Jean Baker was banished and gradually eradicated by her "Marilyn Monroe" persona (Latin for *mask*).[7] She was exploited to feed prurient appetites and ultimately hounded into an early grave by the unrelenting pressure. Countless closeted homosexuals have related personally to the saga of Marilyn Monroe, so fabulous on the outside but so insecure on the inside, having to pretend to be something she was not because the world was not ready or willing to accept who she really was. Her low-cut, up-drafted white dress hid wounds as fatal as Serapion's, and beneath her platinum blonde hair lurked a mind which was troubled and dark—like midnight in Dostoevsky.

The two girl-poets identify with the person they glimpse behind the third girl's mask. In hindsight the narrator understands that Norma Jean Baker was killed by Marilyn Monroe, or at least killed by the historical, patriarchal, consumerist forces which created and perpetuated her false image. The Strand may be a magical, idyllic, safe space for the narrator and her friend, but Marilyn Monroe could never be safe. Even in Arcadia, the Grim Reaper lies in wait: "To enter history is to be abducted spiritually, with no way back. . . . 'Marilyn Monroe' has entered history, and you have not. She will endure, though the young woman with the blond braid will die. *And even should she wish to die, 'Marilyn Monroe' cannot*" (276–77, emphasis in original). That last observation is particularly damning, given the knowledge that she overdosed six years later. Of course, as Elton John and Bernie Taupin eulogized in their song "Candle in the Wind," the legend of Marilyn continues to burn long after Norma Jean's flame was extinguished.

FIGURE 8.4 *Marilyn Monroe, whose character is known merely as "The Girl," standing over a subway vent in Billy Wilder's* The Seven Year Itch *(20th Century Fox, 1955).*

On this memorable 1956 evening at the Strand, however, Death had not yet come to collect his most prized Maiden. This was a night for literature, life, and love. Giddy in the afterglow of the luminous experience, the narrator ends the story by revealing what made this evening most unforgettable: "That snowy early evening in March at Strand Used Books. That magical evening of Marilyn Monroe, when I kissed you for the first time" (280). It is a perfectly tender, intimate, unexpected, exhilarating conclusion—the exact opposite of the violent rupture which closes "Midnight in Dostoevsky." Oates delivers the affectionate ending that Robby might have hoped for had he allowed himself to admit his attraction to Todd. So he opts for a punch instead of a kiss. Oates's narrator was a major step ahead of Robby in confronting her true feelings, but she may never have acted upon them had it not been for the encounter with Marilyn Monroe. It is not just that the euphoria of the experience allowed her inhibitions to temporarily dissipate. She also seems to have learned some important lessons from the experience and applied them to her own situation. Recognizing the blatant dishonesty of the "Marilyn Monroe" persona, she was able to recognize her own mendacity and finally to rip away her own mask, even at the risk of rejection and heartbreak. We are not told the immediate results. Oates strategically chooses to end the story on the fairy-tale first kiss. Describing it as "the first time," however, unmistakably hints that it was not their last kiss.

This ending might be counted as unequivocally happy were it not for a revealing aside Oates places midway through the story. Listing the traits that distinguished these best friends back in 1956, the narrator lets her own mask slip for a moment to reveal the very different paths the two later followed as adults:

> I was the more pushy of the two of us, a tall gawky Rima the Bird Girl with springy carroty-red hair like an exotic bird's crest, while you were petite and dark haired and attractive with long-lashed Semitic sloe eyes, you the wily gymnast and I the aggressive basketball player, you the "experimental" poet and I drawn to "forms," our contrary talents bred in our bones. Which of us would marry, have babies, disappear into "real" life, and which of us would persevere into her thirties before starting to be published and becoming, in time, a "real" poet—could anyone have predicted, this snowy March evening in 1956? (274–75)

This is a metafictional masterstroke. The passage discloses the postlapsarian repercussions after the fall from paradise at the Strand. One girl remained faithful to art into adulthood; the other sold out and conformed to the expectations of conventional womanhood they had both abhorred back in 1956. You might say that one became Klara Sax and the other became Klara Bronzini.

Which one is the narrator? The answer may not be as obvious as it seems. The easy assumption—too easy, I think—is that the narrator is the one who remained true to literature. But we are told that this woman became a poet, not a writer of prose like the piece we are reading. Could it be the other woman, the eventual "sell-out," who is recounting this story? I find this to be a much more compelling interpretation. It would explain why the narrator is so enchanted, seeing everything through the sepia-tinted lens of nostalgia. She presents a romanticized fairy tale too good to be true, from a bygone time and place so different than the bland, conformist, fallen world she has occupied since her acquiescence to conventionality. She married, had babies, surrendered to the "real" world of adult responsibilities—and in the process adopted a mask just as falsifying and stultifying as that worn by "Marilyn Monroe," with whom she can now identify all too well.

Birth and death ▲ gloves and games

At one point the narrator of "Three Girls" describes herself and her friend in terms equally apt for Robby and Todd: "We were mature for our ages, and we were immature. We were intellectually sophisticated, and emotionally unpredictable. We revered something we called *art*, were disdainful of something we called *life*" (278, emphasis in original). One of the friends remained committed to art, while the other turned away from art toward a conventional life which reads like a form of death. It would be nice to hope that art and life are not mutually exclusive, that artistic creation can in fact be a life-giving and life-enhancing activity not requiring a misanthropic rejection of life. "Midnight in Dostoevsky" tests this proposition. For all the references to their college town as a land of the dead, and for all the associations of the Hooded Man with the Grim Reaper, there is competing dimension of the story pulsing with life.

"This was why the man had been born, to end up in this town wearing this coat" (MD 119). Because Robby is unable to express his strongest feelings directly to Todd, he redirects that energy toward their collaborative creation. The Hooded Man as such is a fiction, but Robby comes to regard him as more than that—as his imaginary offspring with Todd. Here DeLillo plays with birth imagery as he did with Nick and Klara in *Underworld*, but the context is radically different with Robby and Todd. The two boys make the Hooded Man together, they sustain him with the invented details of a plausible life, and they fret over his upkeep like worrying parents. "We shared a vision of the man in his bed, at night, mind roaming back—the village, the hills, the family dead. We walked the same streets every day, obsessively, and we spoke in subdued tones even when we disagreed. It was part of the dialectic, our looks of thoughtful disapproval" (MD 141). For the reader attuned to late DeLillo's understated humor, there is something quite ludicrous about this situation. The emotionally stunted and sexually deprived Robby imagines his way into parenthood and domestic partnership with a boy he can't even admit he likes—a boy named after Death, with whom he conceives an offspring in the form of an old man who looks like the Grim Reaper. How utterly pathetic and doomed. It reminds me of Beckett's tragicomic image from *Waiting for Godot*: "Astride of a grave and a difficult birth. Down in the hole, lingeringly, the gravedigger puts on the forceps" (84). Or as Beckett puts it in the opening line of *A Piece of Monologue*, "Birth was the death of him" (425). This is all deadly serious for Robby, however. When Todd recklessly suggests that they dispense with the fiction of the Hooded Man in favor of confronting the real person, Robby feels betrayed. Todd's act of abandonment amounts to both a personal rejection and an abdication of parental responsibility tantamount to abortion: "We do that, we kill the idea, we kill everything we've done" (MD 143). This is a matter of life and death. Robby chooses life, but his partner chooses death.

DeLillo's conclusion is as sad as Oates's ending is happy—which is to say: not as much as it might seem at first. Robby is confused, dejected, and still deeply repressed by the end; no nostalgic first kisses here. The sadness of the protagonist is offset for the reader, however, by the perfectly proportioned and deftly handled aesthetic experience DeLillo crafts over the course of the story. Take, for instance, the highly evocative final tableau. Todd retreats from Robby and runs toward the old man. Our jilted narrator can only watch him recede into the distance and meditate upon his emergency. The image evokes not only O'Hara but also Orpheus watching Eurydice retreat to the Underworld. And positioned perfectly between the two separated friends DeLillo places an emblematic lost glove lying in the street. In a work fertile with pregnant allusions, possible antecedents abound for that solitary glove. One thinks of the glove Eva Marie Saint accidentally dropped in *On the Waterfront*, prompting the resourceful Marlon Brando to use it as an improvisational prop to communicate Joey's fumbling affection for Edie. Or one recalls the crucial lost glove that Angie Dickinson's character dropped in The Met, leading directly to her seduction by an "art stalker" and then murder by a psychotic transvestite in Brian De Palma's *Dressed to Kill*.[8] But the image I keep circling back to is the lonely one-gloved woman in Edward Hopper's painting *Automat*.

FIGURE 8.5 Automat *(1927) by Edward Hopper. Oil on canvas. Des Moines Art Center Permanent Collections, purchased with funds from the Edmundson Art Foundation, Inc., 1958.2. © 2018 Heirs of Josephine Hopper / Licensed by VAGA at Artist Rights Society (ARS), NY.*

The medium, setting, time period, and gender differ from DeLillo's story, but the mood feels entirely compatible. In his essay "The Pleasures of Sadness," Alain de Botton sensitively describes Hopper's painting and the response it inspires:

> In *Automat* 1927, a woman sits alone drinking a cup of coffee. It is late and, to judge by her hat and coat, cold outside. The room seems large, brightly lit and empty. . . . The woman looks self-conscious and slightly afraid, unused to being alone in a public place. Something appears to have gone wrong. She unwittingly invites the viewer to imagine stories for her, stories of betrayal and loss. (de Botton)

One suspects that the lost glove quietly testifies to that betrayal and loss. Details like this draw the viewer in and invite imaginative speculation. That was the experience Robby and Todd had looking at the wandering old man in the hooded coat; it is what de Botton feels when looking at the woman in the automat; and it is what the reader experiences in viewing Robby at the end of DeLillo's story. "*Automat* is a picture of sadness," de Botton admits, but he hastens to add

> yet it is not a sad picture. It has the power of a great melancholy piece of music. . . . Hopper invites us to feel empathy with the woman in her isolation. She seems dignified and generous, only perhaps a little too trusting, a little naïve—as if she has knocked against a hard corner of the world. The artist puts us on her side, the side of the outsider against the insiders. (de Botton)

So true of Hopper, and equally true of DeLillo.

"I couldn't make sense of it," admits Robby in the final paragraph (MD 145). Maybe he cannot, but DeLillo invites the engaged reader to try and do just that. The author challenges us to a game analogous to the one Robby and Todd play in "Midnight in Dostoevsky." Starting from the conclusion and working backwards, fill in the gaps and darken the white spaces. Follow the clues. Trace the connections. Reconstruct the life out of intertextual shreds and patches, empathy and intuition. Calculate the sine, cosine, and tangent of DeLillo's triangulations with Wittgenstein, O'Hara, and Zurbarán. Reciprocate with triangulations of your own (suggestions: Bergman, Oates, and Hopper). Develop and purify crystalline links. *Game On.*

9

A miniature star

Remains and returns in the metafiction of *Zero K*

"This is what long journeys are for. To see what's back behind you, lengthen the view, find the patterns, know the people, consider the significance of one matter or another and then curse yourself or bless yourself or tell yourself ... that you'll have a chance to do it all over again, with variations" (*ZK* 229–30). This rumination comes late in *Zero K* from the narrator Jeff Lockhart. He is referring to the return journey with his father Ross to the cryonics facility known as the Convergence. However, this observation might just as well be applied to the long and extraordinary writing career of Don DeLillo. His work has progressed steadily forward while continuously reflecting back, a journey consisting of signature patterns repeated with resourceful variations. His 2017 novel reads like a self-reflexive culmination, a retrospective of his preoccupations for the last half century, from A(*mericana*) to Z(*ero K*). The novel is not just about cryonics, it is itself an exercise in literary cryonics—a metafictional reanimation of previous characters, tropes, and themes. *Zero K* is also the apotheosis of DeLillo's autological approach, mirroring the creative process within his work by embedding an author-figure responsible for part of its creation.

Literary metempsychosis

Cryonics and fiction have a lot in common. Both of these elegant systems attempt to erect a bulwark against mortality. They provide safe havens of order, meaning, symmetry, and consolation. They make leaps of faith by preserving a past with the capacity for resurrection in the future. Ross justifies the Convergence in just those terms to his skeptical son Jeff:

> "Faith-based technology. That's what it is. Another god. Not so different, it turns out, from some of the earlier ones. Except that it's real, it's true, it delivers."
> "Life after death."
> "Eventually, yes."
> "The Convergence."
> "Yes."
> "There's a meaning in mathematics."
> "There's a meaning, in biology. There's a meaning in physiology. Let it rest," he said. (*ZK* 9)

Like so many names in *Zero K* and throughout the DeLillo canon, "the Convergence" is pregnant with significance. As Ross and Jeff point out, the term has discipline-specific meanings in various fields. DeLillo had already wrestled with mathematical convergence in his early underrated masterpiece *Ratner's Star*, where Chapter Six is titled "Convergence Inward." He also alluded to biological/cosmological convergence in his late novel *Point Omega*, which draws its title and inspiration from *The Phenomenon of Man* by Father Pierre Teilhard de Chardin. *Zero K* actually incorporates more of Teilhard's philosophy, and does so more faithfully, than did *Point Omega*. Teilhard asserted, "Like the meridians as they approach the poles, science, philosophy and religion are bound to converge as they draw nearer to the whole. I say 'converge' advisedly, but without merging, and without ceasing to the very end to assail the real from different angles and on different planes" (30). Teilhard believed that human evolution was directed toward a supreme culmination which he termed the Omega Point: "Space-time is necessarily *of a convergent nature*. Accordingly its enormous layers, followed in the right direction, must somewhere ahead become involuted to a point which we might call *Omega*, which fuses and consumes them integrally in itself" (259, emphasis in original). In "The Ultimate Earth," the final chapter of *The Phenomenon of Man*, Teilhard refers to Omega as the "point of convergence—at the 'end of the world'" (272). He makes eschatological reference several times to "the end of the world," as does DeLillo in *Zero K*. The opening line of the novel is "*Everybody wants to own the end of the world*" (*ZK* 3, emphasis in original). The end is in sight from the beginning, but with an eye toward reimagining the end of the old world as the beginning of a brave new world.[1] The beginning is in sight from the end, too, metafictionally speaking. One half expects DeLillo to write "Everybody wants to own the end of the *dull and lurid* world," so persistently does he circle back to his earlier formulations about endings over the course of *Zero K*.[2]

The Convergence is a speculative investment by billionaires to outsmart and outspend Death, an attempt to "own the end of the world" by constructing what reviewer Mark Medley calls "an ark for the 1 percent" (Medley). Jeff rejects the project on that level, but he gradually becomes enthralled by the end-times implications of the Convergence. Near the close of the novel he reflects, "Then I thought of the Convergence, the name itself, the word itself. Two distinct forces approaching a point of intersection. The merger, breath to breath, of end and beginning . . . when the forces of death and life join" (*ZK* 255). This description acknowledges that, for all its futuristic aspirations, the Convergence is also deeply connected to the past, and not just the individual or the recent past. In the words of Bing Jackmin in DeLillo's *End Zone*, the Convergence "harks back" (*EZ* 36). Ross compares those preparing for cryopreservation in the hospice wing of the Convergence to medieval pilgrims: "There's a reverence, a state of astonishment. They're together in this. Something far larger than they'd ever imagined. They feel a common mission, a destination. And I find myself trying to imagine such a place centuries back. A lodging, a shelter for travelers. For pilgrims" (*ZK* 9). A man whom Jeff nicknames "the Monk" works with these dying patients and compares them to Knights Templar or figures from a Bruegel painting: "He talked about advanced equipment, trained staff. Still, it made him think of twelfth-century Jerusalem, he said, where an order of knights cared for the pilgrims. He imagined at times that he was walking among lepers and plague victims, seeing gaunt faces from old Flemish paintings" (*ZK* 42). At a meeting with potential donors and clients, a Convergence spokesperson at first contrasts their private, clinically controlled project with "great human spectacles, the white-clad faithful in Mecca, the hadj, mass devotion, millions, year after year, and Hindus gathered on the banks of the Ganges, millions, tens of millions, a festival of immortality" (*ZK* 63). However, in a more pensive mood she wonders, "But is there a link to older beliefs and practices? Are we a radical technology that simply renews and extends those swarming traditions of everlasting life?" (*ZK* 64) DeLillo locates the Convergence at the juncture where the ultra-modern and futuristic intersect with the pre-modern and primitive, a nexus best described, to borrow another term from Bing Jackmin, as "Hyperatavistic" (*EZ* 63).

Not only does the Convergence hark back to previous eras and primal human impulses, but *Zero K* also harks back metafictionally to the author's previous works. DeLillo the Interviewee sometimes claims to have forgotten specific details about his earlier books—but DeLillo the Writer remembers. In a revealing 2016 interview with British poet Kate Tempest, he described his writing process as transferring his subject through his fingertips into his Olympia typewriter and onto the printed page. Channeling one reality or consciousness into another involves communion of the work in progress with the works already completed. "At this point in my writing life there's a line that goes backwards to when I started and to other periods, and it all seems to be contained in the moment in which I'm now working somehow, it's all compressed within that" (Tempest). This observation recalls novelist Bill Gray's intimation in *Mao II*: "As many books as a writer has published, those are the books he keeps on writing plus the one in his typewriter. Old books haunt the blood" (*M* 73). With these descriptions in mind, it's tempting to think of DeLillo's typewriter as his time machine, a vehicle for mentally traveling back to prior works, or teleporting earlier characters and circumstances into the future. What he is really talking about, however, is an ancient concept with a substantial philosophical and literary tradition: *Metempsychosis*.

The crowning achievement in literary metempsychosis remains James Joyce's *Ulysses*, a novel DeLillo has credited numerous times as one of his seminal influences. The term is introduced casually over breakfast when Molly finds it in a book and asks Bloom what it means:

—"Metempsychosis?"

—"Yes. Who's he when he's at home?"

—"Metempsychosis, he said, frowning. It's Greek: from the Greek. That means the transmigration of souls."

—"O, rocks! She said. Tell us in plain words." (52)

Bloom chuckles to himself at her mispronunciation ("Met him pike hoses") and fumbles to explain the concept to her clearly: "'Some people believe,' he said, 'that we go on living in another body after death, that we lived before. They call it reincarnation. That we all lived before on the earth thousands of years ago or some other planet. They say we have forgotten it. Some say they remember their past lives'" (53). Metempsychosis becomes one of the cornerstones of Joyce's structuring principle in *Ulysses*. Bloom, Molly, and Stephen are discrete and fully realized characters, but they also simultaneously function as hosts for the reincarnations of Odysseus, Penelope, and Telemachus, and countless other transmigrated souls, over the course of the novel.

DeLillo adopts this strategy of literary metempsychosis in multiple works. The archaeologist and epigrapher Owen Brademas references the term in *The Names* in an effort to explain his instinctive familiarity with Greece:

I realize finally what the secret is. All these months I've wondered what it was I couldn't quite identify in my feelings about this place. The deep-reaching quality of things. . . . Then I realized. These are all things I seem to *remember*. But where do I remember them from? . . . I feel I've known the particular clarity of this air and water, I've climbed these stony paths into the hills. It's eerie, this sense. Metempsychosis. It's what I've been feeling all along. But I didn't know it until now. (*N* 112–13, emphasis in original)

Later he reiterates this sense of unknown predecessors channeling through him: "Is it someone else's memories we sometimes have? The laws of physics don't distinguish between past and future. We are always in contact. There is random interaction. The patterns repeat. Worlds, star clusters, even memories perhaps" (N 133). Metempsychosis is one useful way to account for the uncanny metafictional aura that surrounds so many DeLillo characters like Owen who seem on the verge of *realizing that they are characters in a Don DeLillo novel*—connected, contained, and compressed alongside all the others who have rolled through the platen of that Olympia typewriter. Many of them return for veiled cameos and a final curtain call in *Zero K*. "Here Comes Everybody," as Joyce would put it in *Finnegans Wake*. Or, to adapt Yeats's great culminating poem, one might think of *Zero K* as DeLillo's "Circus Animals' Convergence."

Artis Martineau and Jeff Lockhart directly introduce the metempsychosis theme early in *Zero K*. Artis is Ross's second wife, the woman he married after walking out on Jeff and his mother Madeline. Artis has long suffered from multiple sclerosis, and with Ross's support she decides to be cryopreserved when she dies. Jeff goes to the Convergence for the first time to say goodbye to his dying stepmother. She has a host of unanswered questions about what will happen to her after she dies, and so does he. This leads to an exchange that reads in part like a pastiche of Molly and Bloom in *Ulysses*:

> "Ross and I have a running joke. Who will I be at the reawakening? Will my soul have left my body and migrated to another body somewhere? What's the word I'm looking for? Or will I wake up thinking I'm a fruit bat in the Philippines? Hungry for insects?"
> "And the real Artis. Where is she?"
> "Drifting into the body of a baby boy. The son of local sheepherders."
> "The word is *metempsychosis*."
> "Thank you." (*ZK* 48, emphasis in original)

Like Joyce before him, DeLillo explicitly invokes metempsychosis to alert the reader to its relevance within the novel. And as with Joyce, familiarity with the author's entire body of work is necessary to appreciate the finer points of DeLillo's self-reflexive use of this technique.

For example, late in *Zero K* one of the two chief architects of the Convergence (dubbed "the Stenmark twins" by Jeff) offers this tantalizing quotation for his audience's consideration:

> "Saint Augustine. Let me tell you what he said. Goes like this."
> He paused and closed his eyes, giving the impression that his words belong to darkness, coming to us out of the centuries.
> "And never can a man be more disastrously in death than when death itself shall be deathless."
> I thought *what*. (*ZK* 240, emphasis in original)

When I first read this passage, I didn't think *what* but *where*. Like Owen in *The Names*, I had an uncanny sense of familiarity, certain that I had encountered this quotation from Augustine before, but unsure where. Many of DeLillo's devoted readers must have had a similar sense of déjà vu. Then it hit me:

To: Tech Unit B
From: St. Augustine

And never can a man be more disastrously in death than when death itself shall be deathless.

    Nobody knew who sent these memos. . . . No one had ever seen these particular memos delivered; they simply appeared, either in the morning or the early afternoon. This was the first of the St. Augustines. Previous memos had borne messages from Zwingli, Lévi-Strauss, Rilke, Chekhov, Tillich, William Blake, Charles Olson and a Kiowa chief named Satanta. Naturally the person responsible for these messages became known as the Mad Memo-Writer. I never referred to him that way because it was much too obvious a name. I called him Trotsky. (*A* 21)

DeLillo recycles verbatim a quote from St. Augustine that he already used in his first novel *Americana*, attributed there to Trotsky (eventually revealed as Ted Warburton). Why would DeLillo recycle this quotation in *Zero K*? It's certainly not because he ran out of original ideas, or that he forgot he had already quoted this passage once before. Although Augustine's words remain unchanged, their meaning is very different in the context of these respective novels. I am reminded of the serious premise on which Jorge Luis Borges erects his comic story "Pierre Menard, Author of the *Quixote*," where *Don Quixote*, written by Miguel de Cervantes in seventeenth-century Spain, is fundamentally different than when it is reconceived word for word by Pierre Menard in twentieth-century France. Similarly, when Augustine is cited by Ted Warburton in *Americana*, his observation serves as a critique of the lethal drudgery of the modern office, a superficial, mundane, ludicrous death-in-life existence. Cited by a Stenmark twin in *Zero K*, Augustine presents a challenge and obstacle to overcome: the disaster of deathless death supplanted by the triumph of deathless life. The more salient point, however, isn't the specific content or interpretation of the passage so much as its uncanny reappearance forty-five years later, as if the reincarnated Ted Warburton (whose death is reported in *Americana*) has sent a memo across space and time addressed to Jeff Lockhart and to the reader: *A* to *Z*; Beginning to End. DeLillo's first novel is not some distant bygone memory in his latest novel. Through literary metempsychosis the poles of his career are joined. The 1971 novel returns to exert a palpable, reanimated presence in the 2016 novel.

Another striking instance of literary metempsychosis in *Zero K* comes in the form of self-immolation. As Jeff wanders the desolate hallways of the Convergence, he occasionally comes upon screens where scenes of natural or man-made catastrophes are projected. In one such film he encounters "three men seated cross-legged on mats with nothing but sky behind them. They wore loose-fitting garments, unmatched, and sat with heads bowed, two of them, the other looking straight ahead" (*ZK* 61). As Jeff watches in horrified fascination, the three men douse themselves with flammable liquid and set themselves on fire. The original inspiration for this gesture is Thích Quảng Đức, the Buddhist monk who set himself on fire in a crowded Saigon street in 1963 to protest his group's persecution at the hands of the South Vietnamese government. This extraordinary form of defiance made an indelible impression on Don DeLillo, who incorporated self-immolation into two novels prior to *Zero K*. In *Players* Jack Laws goes out to a landfill and commits suicide by setting himself on fire. There is nothing noble or principled in Jack's death, however. His self-immolation is a capricious corruption of Thích Quảng Đức's death. By comparison, what does Jack have to protest or to be so miserable about, this affluent, comfortable, bored Manhattanite on vacation in Maine? In *Cosmopolis*, begun before and completed after the September 11th attacks, the urgency and gravity of self-immolation is restored. Eric Packer witnesses a protester set himself on fire. Capturing the mood of the crowd in the immediate wake of this spectacle, Eric thinks, "They wanted him to be young and driven by conviction. Eric believed even the police wanted this. No one wanted a deranged man. It dishonored their action, their risk, all the work they'd done together. He was not a transient in a narrow room who suffers episodes of this or that, hearing voices in his head." Instead, "Eric wanted to imagine the man's pain, his choice, the abysmal will he'd had to summon" (*C* 98). Again, context is everything. It is impossible to read this scene so soon after 9/11 and not interpret it as a comment upon the suicide bombers of Al-Qaeda and their sacrificial rationalizations for inflicting fiery death upon themselves and their victims.

The self-immolations in *Zero K* unmistakably hark back to these antecedents. On one level, it seems as if Thích Quảng Đức, Jack Laws from *Players*, and the street protester from *Cosmopolis* have all transmigrated from the past into the present novel. To express it in the terms DeLillo used with Kate Tempest, they have traveled that line still connecting the past and present work to be contained and compressed in *Zero K*. But there are also important differences in how DeLillo uses these resurrected figures the second time around, crucial variations in the pattern. Importantly, neither Jeff Lockhart nor the reader knows anything about the men who burn themselves to death in *Zero K*. They are flat, aestheticized images on screen with no humanizing backstory or political message. They are a triptych of death by fire. Their choreographed spectacle functions as a single wave in the tidal flow of catastrophic images washing across the screen. Furthermore, self-immolation necessarily accrues new layers of meaning when screened in a cryonics facility. Burning oneself to death, be it for a cause or for mere spectacle, seems doubly inflammatory juxtaposed against a warehouse of frozen humans attempting to live forever. By burning effigies of earlier self-immolations, DeLillo throws in sharp relief the Convergence's coldly clinical approach to life, death, and the end of the world.

Ratner's Star

DeLillo's most extensive previous experiment with literary metempsychosis, and the novel which exerts the strongest gravitational pull on *Zero K*, is *Ratner's Star*. In his *Paris Review* interview DeLillo commented, "Somebody said that *Ratner's Star* is the monster at the center of my work. But maybe it's in orbit around the other books. I think the other books constitute a single compact unit and that *Ratner's Star* swings in orbit around this unit at a very great distance" (Begley 95–96). To extend that metaphor, one might visualize *Zero K* as a satellite circling *Ratner's Star* in its orbit around the rest of the canon. *Ratner's Star* is an audaciously elaborate feat, channeling Lewis Carroll's Alice books and key figures and concepts from the history of mathematics. DeLillo was unusually forthcoming about his intentions and methodology in the classic 1982 interview with Tom LeClair. He candidly divulged,

> In *Ratner's Star* I tried to weave this secret life of mankind into the action of the book in the form of a history of mathematics, a cult history, the names of the leaders kept secret until the second half of the book, the mirror image, when the names appear in reverse order. This purest of sciences brings out a religious feeling in people. Numbers in particular have always had a mystical appeal. Numbers work in such surprising ways it's hard not to feel a sense of mystery and wonder. (11)

DeLillo also told LeClair that one figure above all others presided over the novel's "secret life of mankind" and "cult history" of mathematics: "There is also a kind of guiding spirit. This is Pythagoras. The mathematician-mystic. The whole book is informed by this link or opposition, however you see it, and the characters keep bouncing between science and superstition" (11). As LeClair explains in his book *In the Loop: Don DeLillo and the Systems Novel*, "For DeLillo, Pythagoras is the crucial meeting point of concrete experience and abstract speculation, precision and mystery, rationality and irrationality, science and religion" (126). Pythagoras' chief legacy today is as namesake for the Pythagorean Theorem. More significant for DeLillo's purposes, however, is Pythagoras' legendary status as the first Western proponent of metempsychosis. In Porphyry's *Life of Pythagoras*, the third-century Neoplatonist described these teachings: "He taught that the soul was immortal and that after death it transmigrated into other animated bodies. After certain specified periods, the same events occur again; that nothing was entirely new; that all animated beings were kin, and should be considered as belonging to one great family. Pythagoras was the first one to introduce these teachings into Greece" (5).

Not only is Pythagoras the guiding spirit of *Ratner's Star*, but metempsychosis is the guiding principle behind the novel's construction. Mark Osteen describes it this way in *American Magic and Dread: Don DeLillo's Dialogue with Culture*:

> The Pythagoreans combined a highly developed understanding of geometry with a set of sophisticated spiritual practices and beliefs. One of these was the doctrine of metempsychosis or transmigration of souls, which is metaphorically displayed throughout *Ratner's Star*: in its intertextual relations to previous texts; in its reincarnation of figures from the history of science; and in its speculative philosophy of history, in which things turn inside out and repeat themselves as on a giant wheel. (67)

Osteen points out numerous instances of literary metempsychosis in *Ratner's Star*, identifying correspondences between characters and scenes in the novel and their precursors in Carroll's *Alice's Adventures in Wonderland* and *Through the Looking-Glass*. LeClair includes a remarkably detailed schema in his book (*Loop* 125) classifying the period, reference, concept, and primary mathematician associated with each chapter in Part One of *Ratner's Star*, with the same catalogue followed in reverse/mirror order in Part Two.

Needless to say, critics sometimes read too much into the works they study. We are occasionally guilty of overzealousness, imagining puzzles and fantasizing codes as a pretense for proving our own cleverness in solving those brain-teasers. But to be fair, certain artists *do* intentionally embed puzzles and codes in their work. James Joyce was one. The famous "Gilbert Schema," an answer key of correspondences Joyce gave critic Stuart Gilbert, stands as a testament to the carefully devised, subtly planted, and artfully concealed referents planted throughout *Ulysses* (Gilbert 30). The "LeClair Schema," to coin a phrase, bears a strong family resemblance to the Gilbert Schema, and one strongly suspects that this Rosetta Stone for *Ratner's Star* was likewise cribbed by the critic directly from the novelist, or at least vetted for accuracy. Like his literary hero, DeLillo is one of those artists who occasionally inserts codes and challenges readers (or more accurately *re-readers*) to decode them. A major key to decoding *Zero K* is *Ratner's Star*.

Both are works of science fiction set in the near future. Both begin with the protagonist's arrival at a surreal science facility located in a remote hinterland. Jeff Lockhart arrives at the Convergence, a subterranean complex of buildings somewhere in the vicinity of Chelyabinsk. His counterpart in *Ratner's Star*, the fourteen-year-old math prodigy Billy Twillig, arrives at a cycloid-shaped structure in the desert, home to Field Experiment Number One. The Convergence is devoted to cold-storage preservation of recently deceased humans in cryonic pods until such time in the technologically advanced future when they can be reanimated in enhanced condition. Field Experiment Number One is also built upon a foundation of faith in a brighter future through science. Administrator Byron Dine explains to Billy that "we're trying to create a sense of planetary community. One people et cetera" (*RS* 20). Field Experiment Number One is rooted in positivism and progressive human development: "'Knowledge,' Dyne said. 'Study the planet. Observe the solar system. Listen to the universe. Know thyself. . . . Outer and inner space. Each bends into the other'" (*RS* 21). Eccentric geniuses from a variety of disciplines fuel the work of both projects. Some thirty Nobel laureates ply their diverse talents at Field Experiment Number One with a shared utopian vision. At the Convergence, Ross brags, "What's happening in this community is not just a creation of medical science. There are social theorists involved, and biologists, and futurists, and geneticists, and climatologists, and neuroscientists, and psychologists, and ethicists, if that's the right word. . . . All the vital minds" (*ZK* 33).

For all the optimism, intelligence, ingenuity, and capital concentrated in these utopian projects, *Ratner's Star* and *Zero K* are saturated with anxiety. Both novels are highly attuned and deeply responsive to contemporary as well as timeless threats to Earth's future.[3] One typically thinks of cryonics as a last-ditch effort by someone with a terminal illness to forestall death until a cure is found, and that motive is certainly at work in *Zero K*. But the larger fear driving the Convergence is that the entire planet is facing apocalypse. One cause is the rise of terrorism and war, a wildfire of hate and violence that threatens to consume the world. Another cause is climate change, with rapidly accelerating effects of global warming threatening to render Earth uninhabitable in the foreseeable future. DeLillo is often credited for his prescience in predicting the next catastrophe looming on the horizon, and in *Zero K* he once again sounds like a weatherman who knows which way the wind blows. Finally, there are the age-old vulnerabilities of a planet orbiting a burning star in a universe beset by massive hurtling objects. As Convergence representatives stress,

> The sun is an unknown entity. They spoke of solar systems, flares and superflares, coronal mass ejections. The man tried to find adequate metaphors. He cranked his hand in odd synchrony with his references to earth orbit. I watched the woman, bowed down, silent for a time in the setting of billions of years, our vulnerable earth, the comets, asteroids, random strikes, the past extinctions, the current loss of species.
>
> "Catastrophe is our bedtime story." (*ZK* 65–66)

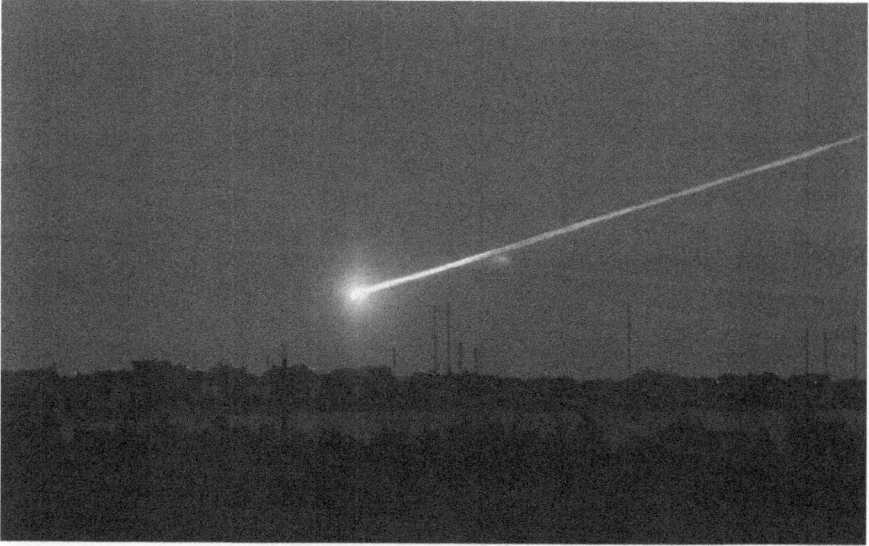

FIGURE 9.1 *Anonymous footage of Chelyabinsk meteor. "Meteor Hits Russia Feb 15, 2013 – Event Archive." YouTube. https://www.youtube.com/watch?v=dpmXyJrs7iU. Posted by Tuvix72 on February 18, 2013.*

Part One of *Zero K* is titled "In the Time of Chelyabinsk." This is not merely a GPS indicator. The title invokes the meteor which penetrated the earth's atmosphere on February 15, 2013, and exploded in a fireball above Chelyabinsk. This meteor was notable for several reasons: its enormous size and blinding brilliance; its close proximity to landfall before explosion; its capture on video and subsequent viral dissemination on the internet; and, perhaps most disturbing of all, its completely unpredicted, undetected, and undefended penetration until it was already burning a path through the atmosphere. "In the Time of Chelyabinsk" is less a time and place than a condition of perpetual existential crisis for the entire planet.

Watch the videos of the Chelyabinsk meteor.[4] One reason this footage is so unsettling is that it forces the viewer to visualize what a meteor which *doesn't* miss will look like. Perhaps this blazing sight is what the dinosaurs witnessed just before the meteor struck which incinerated some and initiated an impact winter that killed off the rest. "Some say the world will end in fire, / Some say in ice," as Robert Frost famously put it (268). Neither option sounds appealing, but one or both are headed this way. Just as the Chelyabinsk videos seem to look back into the planet's primeval past, they seem simultaneously to offer glimpses of alternate modern history and provide foreshadows of future catastrophes. Anyone who lived through the second half of the twentieth century will likely shiver while watching videos of a fiery projectile speeding across Russian airspace and detonating above the former Soviet Union. This is the stuff that a million Cold War nightmares were made on. Again there is an eerie sense of déjà vu, of reliving a past event that never happened. Or maybe it just hasn't happened yet. The Chelyabinsk meteor marks the flashpoint where global anxieties from the past, present, and future converge.

The notion that premonitions about coming disasters are actually memories of past catastrophes is given literal credence in *Ratner's Star*. At a dig in Sangkan Ho, archaeologist Maurice Xavier Wu uncovers evidence of an advanced civilization in Earth's distant past:

> Man more advanced the deeper we dig. This revolutionary thesis was beginning to develop urgency. He'd seen evidence of it in the field over the past several months. . . . But the notion itself—that at a certain layer of soil the signs of man's increasing primitivism cease abruptly, to be replaced by a totally converse series of findings—this idea had been too radical to take firm hold in his mind until recently, when . . . he'd felt the first trifling stir of implication. (*RS* 321)

The implications come into focus when Wu combines his discoveries from Sangkan Ho with other mysterious revelations: "Some time back some experts in reactor engineering were having trouble explaining the details of what they believed to be a spontaneous nuclear reaction in a uranium deposit over a billion years ago" (*RS* 404). His inescapable conjecture is that an advanced human civilization inhabited the earth over a billion years ago, developed nuclear capabilities, and eventually extinguished all humanity through massive nuclear explosions. Wu confronts "the possibility that our original evolutionary thrust was followed by a period of degeneration that might have been connected to radiation diseases and such. Then, at a crude toolmaking level, things swung upward once again, taking us to the point we now occupy" (*RS* 404). "The point we now occupy" in that 1976 Cold War novel was the point at which the United States and the Soviet Union were poised to wipe out mankind (again) in a nuclear holocaust. Incidentally, the Sangkan Ho valley is surely not an arbitrarily chosen site for Wu's discovery. Observe the telltale Jesuitical middle name of Maurice Xavier Wu. As DeLillo doubtlessly knows, Father Pierre Teilhard de Chardin worked the Sangkan Ho valley as a paleontologist in the 1920s and was instrumental in classifying the *Homo erectus* fossils found there dubbed "Peking Man." DeLillo subtly but sharply registers his skepticism toward Teilhard's theories of human evolutionary progress by reimagining Peking Man as proto-Robert Oppenheimer.

Moholean relativity

In *Ratner's Star* DeLillo places the past, present, and future in direct communication via an ingenious variation on metempsychosis: Moholean relativity. Billy Twillig has been summoned to Field Experiment Number One to decode a signal seemingly emanating from the vicinity of Ratner's Star. This signal appears to confirm the existence of extraterrestrial life. It is presumed that, if the message from the "artificial radio source extant" (yes, ARSE) can be deciphered, it will be of vital importance to all Earthlings and to the future of our planet. After many false hypotheses, Billy eventually decodes the message as indicating a time, specifically the time at which an unpredicted solar eclipse will take place. By pinpointing this surprise event the ARS extant draws attention to the limits of science, reason, and human intelligence. The unexpected solar eclipse, like the unexpected Chelyabinsk meteor, reminds humans of our essential ignorance of the universe and our vulnerability to grand forces beyond our understanding or control. What proves even more interesting than the message is its source and mode of transmission. Late in the novel scientists discover that the signal was sent by the extinct civilization of humans from billions of years ago; a message addressed to Earth from Earth. "We've reconstructed the ARS extant and it turns out to be us" (*RS* 405). These ancient Earthlings transmitted their interstellar "message in a bottle" to future inhabitants of the planet by beaming it into a mohole.

Orang Mohole introduces himself to Billy as the "acknowledged kingpin of alternative physics" (*RS* 178). His notoriety hinges on his proposed extensions and corrections to Einstein's theory of relativity: "I developed a theory, listen to this, about a strange kind of mechanism at work in the universe. This is the value-dark dimension, or mohole totality, and it's the core idea of a unique system of relativity. This is Moholean relativity, just beginning to attract attention, very controversial, named by me after myself" (*RS* 180). The distinguishing phenomenon of Moholean relativity is the mohole:

> A mohole traps electromagnetic information, among other things, and then either releases it or doesn't. It's as though the mohole were a surface that absorbs light and sound and then reflects either or both to another part of the universe. But it's not a surface and it doesn't absorb. It's a mohole. It's part of a theoretical dimension lacking spatial extent and devoid of time value. Value-dark in other words. (*RS* 181)

A mohole functions much like a black hole. However, instead of sucking in matter, light, and energy which can never escape, a mohole is capable of retaining what it ingests and expelling it at any other point in the space-time continuum. This is precisely what happens with the so-called

Ratner's Star message. Ancient Earthlings mastered quantum mechanics to such an extent that they were able to send a message postdated a billion years into the future by inserting it in a Moholean mailbox. By the end of the novel chemist Walter X. Mainwaring announces another amazing discovery:

> What they've apparently discovered is that we are in the mohole, if that's the way to phrase it. This solar system appears to be what we call mohole-intense. We are part of the value-dark dimension. . . . Everything around us on out at least to the most distant planet and right in to the sun itself, our sun, we ourselves, all of us, people, matter, energy, we're part of a mohole, we're in it, we're mohole-intense. (*RS* 410)

What I find so marvelous about DeLillo's invention of Moholean relativity in *Ratner's Star*, much like his appropriation of cryonics in *Zero K*, is how perfectly these concepts double as meta-commentary on the nature of fiction. To be in a mohole is to become unstuck in time and space (cf. Billy Twillig's forerunner Billy Pilgrim in Kurt Vonnegut's *Slaughterhouse-Five*). To be in a mohole is also to become capable of being projected to any time or place in the future. Isn't that exactly the condition that prevails in all fiction? *To be in a novel is to be in a mohole.* Billy Twillig was created in the 1970s; that's when Don DeLillo banged him out on his typewriter and beamed him out into the world. But a reader of the novel doesn't "receive the signal" until he or she opens *Ratner's Star* and begins to read it, maybe decades later, eventually long after DeLillo himself has ceased to exist. It's why we as literary critics are trained to use present tense verbs; because the action within literature is always present, always unfolding for the reader right now, regardless of when the text was written. The whole world of a novel—*Zero K* or any novel—remains frozen in space and time, awaiting reanimation by a reader in the future. *To be in a novel is to be cryopreserved in its pages.* In essence, all literature is bound by the laws of Moholean relativity, not just *Ratner's Star*; and all novels serve as cryonic pods for preserving characters, not just *Zero K*.

Inner stars

Each DeLillo novel constitutes a self-contained world, but these worlds also exist in a larger canonical cosmos in which they are all related and through which transmigrations take place. The character most attuned to these cosmic connections in *Ratner's Star* is the eponymous Shazar Lazarus Ratner, a literary soul reincarnated in *Zero K* as Ben-Ezra. Each of these characters is strategically positioned by DeLillo at the midpoint of their respective novels, signaling their central importance. Ratner established his reputation as an astronomer studying the sun and stars, earning the distinction of having a star (and a novel) named after him. But he eventually drifted away from astronomy toward cosmology and finally Kabbalah. By the time Billy meets him Ratner is gravely ill, enclosed in a biomembrane and attended by a team of physicians. Billy is creeped out by the encounter, feeling as if he is conversing with a dead man. DeLillo gives Ratner the name "Lazarus" to locate his position on the liminal threshold between life and death. Indeed, Shazar Lazarus Ratner (SLR) would have made as ardent a client for the Convergence as Ross Lockhart (née Satterswaite) (RLS) eventually does.

Ratner's philosophy and eschatology connect outer space with inner space, physics with metaphysics, in repeating cycles of convergence inward and expansion outward. Ratner believes that the origin and ultimate fate of each individual is bound up with that of the sun. We come from our star. The planet and everything upon it derives life and its very matter from the sun, and we will eventually return to the sun and die with it. He instructs Billy,

> I decided to study the sun. . . . I thought ahead to the helium flash. The final expansion. Having come from the stars, we are returned. The sun within us, the source of all mystical bursts, is perfectly counterbalanced by the physical sun that presses outward, swallowing up the orbits of the nearest planets. . . . From that great unstable period, the sun collapses drastically. It becomes the same size as the former earth. Now we're right inside it, mongrelized with three other planets, compacted down to a whiff of gas. The sun proceeds to cool, white dwarf, red dwarf, black dwarf, a dead star, dark black. No energy, no light, no heat, no twinkle. The end. (*RS* 223)

Star dust thou art, and unto star dust shalt thou return. Long before *Zero K*, DeLillo articulates an elegant cosmic account of "the end of the world" through Shazar Lazarus Ratner. According to this astronomer turned mystic, the world will end first in fire and then in ice.

Ratner provides an eloquent account of the birth and death of our world. His counterpart in *Zero K*, the "crackpot sage" Ben-Ezra (*ZK* 131), enlarges the cosmic frame of reference to incorporate multiverses without end. Jeff Lockhart encounters Ben-Ezra in a walled garden within the Convergence facility. The setting unmistakably alludes to Borges's "The Garden of Forking Paths." Like Stephen Albert in Borges's metafictional labyrinth, Ben-Ezra posits the existence of multiple dimensions in time and space with alternate realities. Jeff reports,

> He talked, I listened, the subject beginning to approach new magnitudes.
>
> The universe, what it was, what it is, where it's going.
>
> The expanding, accelerating, infinitely evolving universe, so filled with life, with worlds upon never-ending worlds, he said.

The universe, the multiverse, so many cosmic infinities that the idea of repeatability becomes unavoidable.

The idea of two individuals sitting on a bench in a desert garden having the conversation we are having, you and I, word for word, except that they are different individuals, in a different garden, millions of light-years from here—this is an inescapable fact. (*ZK* 130)

Call it literary metempsychosis or call it Moholean relativity, this concept of characters and scenarios replicating ad infinitum across time and space is thematically and structurally central to both *Ratner's Star* and *Zero K*. A reader need not advance millions of light years into the future to find examples of such transmigrations. One can simply read the writings of Don DeLillo.

DeLillo tips his hand by having by having Ben-Ezra quote from Thomas Browne's *Urn Burial*: "It is the heaviest stone that melancholy can throw at a man to tell him that he is at the end of his nature, or that there is no further state to come" (*ZK* 131). Browne wrote his treatise in response to the discovery of dozens of ancient Roman burial urns in Norfolk. He used this occasion to reflect upon the Ozymandias-like desire of humans to monumentalize themselves in an effort to live forever. Although Browne is critical of such vanity, his book *Urn Burial* effectively serves as his own literary urn, a relic which has allowed his words and ideas to outlive him by

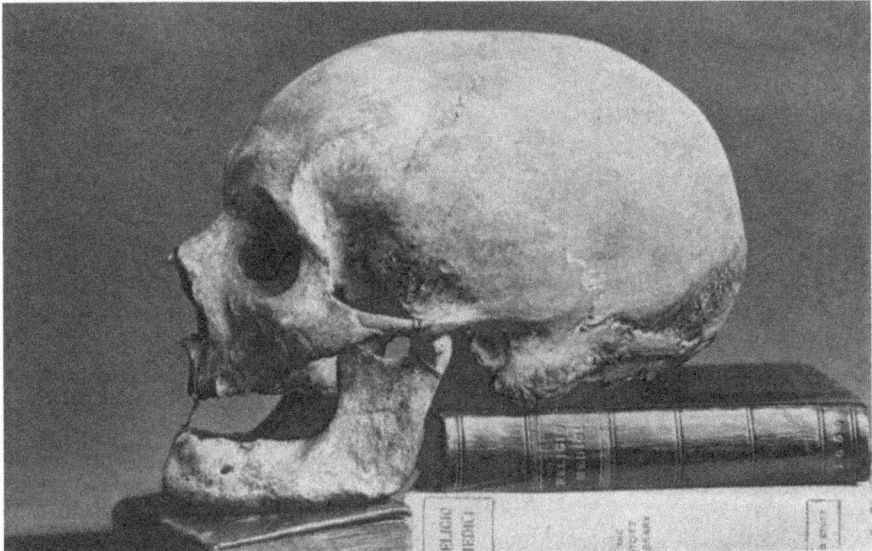

FIGURE 9.2 *Thomas Browne's skull, resting on volumes of his book* Religio Medici. *Used as frontispiece for* The Works of Sir Thomas Browne *(1904).*

several centuries. One writer inspired to reincarnate Browne was Jorge Luis Borges. At the close of "Tlön, Uqbar, Orbis Tertius," his mind-bending story about simulated reality overtaking the real world, the narrator announces that he is retiring to complete a translation of Browne's *Urn Burial.*[5] Browne, like Borges and DeLillo, was also fascinated with metempsychosis. He asserts in *Religio Medici,*

> To see our selves againe wee neede not looke for *Platoes* yeare, every man is not onely himselfe; there have beene many *Diogenes,* and as many *Tymons,* though but few of that name; men are lived over againe; the world is now as it was in ages past; there was none then, but there hath been some one since that parallels him, and is, as it were, his revived self. (16)[6]

Jeff's conversation with Ben-Ezra at once mirrors Yu Tsun's conversation with Stephen Albert in "The Garden of Forking Paths," Borges's intertextual conversation with Browne, Billy's conversation with Ratner, and *Zero K*'s metempsychotic reincarnation of *Ratner's Star.*

Browne's most sublime observation in *Urn Burial* is his assertion of humanity's shared birthright as children of the sun: "Life is a pure flame, and we live by an invisible Sun within us" (169). DeLillo may have this luminous passage in mind when Jeff sees his stepmother's cryopreserved body. Despite being frozen, she appears to be incandescent: "Her body seemed lit from within. She stood erect, on her toes, shaved head tilted upward, eyes closed, breasts firm. It was an idealized human, encased, but it was also Artis" (*ZK* 258). This glowing imagery fits hand in glove with Ratner's resplendent cosmic vision:

> "*We come from the stars,*" Ratner said. "Our chemicals, our atoms, these were first made in the centers of old stars that exploded and spread their remains across the sky eventually to come together as the sun we know and the planet we inhabit. . . . Atoms from these stars are in our bones and nervous systems. *We're stellar cinders,* you and me. We come from the beginning or near the beginning. In our brain is the echo of the little bang. This is science, poeticized here and there, and this you can compare with the kabbalistic belief that every person has a sun inside him, a radiant burst of energy." (*RS* 218, emphasis added)

We are made of stars, and the proof is that a miniature star still radiates within us. The idea that the creator's stamp is emblazoned as an authenticating mark within the created (cf. the Jesuit motto "find God in all things") is common to each of DeLillo's embedded narratives. Jeff echoes Ratner's awe when he sees Artis's shining form: "It was a beautiful sight. It was the human body as a model of creation. I believed this" (*ZK* 258). Jeff believes not only that the human body is a beautiful creation but also that, embedded within the human body, lies a semblance of its creator, a reflection of the creative fire in which it was forged—a model of its own creation.

Anagrams

An equally important tenet of Ratner's philosophy is that creation is fundamentally recombinational, both on the macrocosmic and microcosmic levels. The Little Bang of each human life is a recombination of preexisting elements, just as the Earth is a variant siphoned off the Sun, and the Sun is a reconfiguration of previous stars and interstellar gases dating back to the Big Bang. The antecedents of these recombinations remain embedded within, and these miniature stars are discernible to those who know how to read the signs. "'There is always something secret to be discovered,' Ratner said. 'A hidden essence. A truth beneath the truth'" (*RS* 221). Ratner once believed that science was the key to unlocking these truths, but later he turned to Kabbalah for the combination codes: "*If you know the right combination of letters, you can make anything*. This is the secret power of the alphabet. Meaningless sounds, abstract symbols, they have the power of creation. This is why the various parts of the mystical writings are not in proper order. Knowing the order, you could make your own world from just reading the writings" (*RS* 222, emphasis added). Summing up this recombinational credo most succinctly, Ratner declares, "*Creation depends on an anagram*" (*RS* 223, emphasis added).

Literature draws upon the material world but rearranges the pieces into different patterns to create alternate fictional realities. This is what John Barth had in mind when he declared, "The storytellers' trade is the manufacture of universes" (17). The quintessence of this process is the anagram, alphabetical alchemy which transforms one name into another. From the beginning of his career DeLillo has been drawn to the coded creative power of anagrams. When David Bell consulted Ted Warburton to interpret the Saint Augustine passage in *Americana*, the office elder demurred, "I'm the kind of man who likes to rest his wits with anagrams. Theology is a bit out of my line" (*A* 99). The last secret memo he sent before he died was signed with the alias Otto Durer Obenwahr. No one in the office understood this obscure reference, but at novel's end David Bell solves the puzzle: "It made me think of Warburton for a moment, his final memo, and I began to juggle the alphabet, to fit it together finally, three names from two, anagrammatized, a last jest from corporate exile" (*A* 375). David belatedly recognizes that "Otto Durer Obenwahr" is an exact anagram of "Theodore Warburton." In *The Names* the epigrapher Owen Brademas is fascinated by the alphabet and its infinite variety of possible recombinations. At one point Owen travels the Zarqa-Azraq road on his way to a job at Qasr Hallabat, where workers are attempting to reassemble the scrambled stone inscriptions from different languages and historical periods. The narrator James Axton observes,

> And all of this, the castle, the stones, the inscriptions, is situated midway between Zarqa and Azraq. To Owen, to someone with Owen's bent for spotting such things, these names are seen at once to be anagrams.... How strange, he wanted to say, that the place he was looking for, this evocative botched ruin, lay between perfect twin pillars—place-names with the same set of letters, rearranged. And it was precisely a rearrangement, a reordering, that was in progress at Qasr Hallabat. (*N* 77)

Like his characters, DeLillo is acutely attuned to the letters in names and the encrypted mysteries they contain. In a 2016 promotional interview for *Zero K*, DeLillo referred to the revelatory importance of letters in *White Noise*, *Point Omega*, and other novels:

> And there was something in that name—JA for Jack and GLA for Gladney—which felt important. I've done the same thing in other books. I'm always very conscious of the patterns of letters in a name. Ross Lockhart isn't a great example, but it's RO and then LO. So it's a thing that I do. A character takes shape because of that confluence of letters. (Brooks)

An entire novel can also take shape because of the confluence of its letters, as DeLillo intimated in another *Zero K* interview:

> Let me tell you one thing that comes to mind about "Ratner's Star." It's that the words in the title sort of sum up the book it is. You have the second word, star, S-T-A-R, and then you have Ratner's, R-A-T with an S at the end, so that one set of letters in the title mirrors another set of letters. Same four letters are in both words. (Kellogg)

DeLillo's multiple references in 2016 interviews to letters in the names of characters and in the titles of novels is no coincidence. I think he is dropping clues, consciously or unconsciously, to his continued use of anagrammatical word games in *Zero K*. The allusion above to *Ratner's Star* is especially tantalizing. We have already considered Ratner's belief, echoing Kabbalist mystics and Thomas Browne, that every human has a miniature star embedded within. Now DeLillo draws attention to the fact that the title itself is an incarnation of this very concept: both "Ratner's" and "Star" contain the letters S-T-A-R. Stars remain deeply embedded in *Zero K* as well. The Convergence is modeled in part after an actual cryonics facility in

Arizona called the Alcor Life Extension Foundation. DeLillo must be aware that Alcor takes its name from a star. Founders Fred and Linda Chamberlain explain:

> Alcor, a companion star of Mizar in the "Big Dipper's" handle, is approximately fifth magnitude, barely within the threshold of human vision. Additionally, it is quite close to Mizar from an angular standpoint, and dimmer. Only with excellent eyesight can one tell there are two stars rather than just one. For thousands of years, people in the Middle East have used Alcor as a critical test of visual sensitivity and focus. If you could see Alcor, you had excellent vision indeed. In the early days of cryonics itself, few people could see the need for a rescue team, or even the need for cryonics itself. Symbolically, then, Alcor would be a "test" of vision as regards life extension. (8)

Assuming DeLillo did some homework he would also know that the first time Alcor successfully brought a dead mammal back to life was in July 1984; the animal was a shepherd dog named (what else?) *Star* (Perry 6). So the name and conceptual resonance of "Star" already came "pre-installed" as it were in the Convergence before DeLillo started adding layers of signification from *Ratner's Star*. But the deepest encryption level of the stars-within-stars motif in *Zero K* comes by way of anagram.

All of the narrator-protagonist's family members contain S-T-A-R within their names: Jeff's father RosS LockhART, his mother MAdeline SiebeRT, and his stepmother ARTiS Martineau. "Jeff Lockhart" is the sole exception—but only because his father changed his name. Ross was born Nicholas Satterswaite. When Jeff discovered this as a teenager, it unlocked mysteries about his father and shed light on his own obscured identity: "But this was my father's design, not mine. The name Lockhart was all wrong for me. Too tight, too clenched. The solid and decisive Lockhart, the firm closure of Lockhart. The name excluded me" (*ZK* 82–83). The legacy from which Jeff Lockhart feels excluded is his birthright of an embedded S-T-A-R as Jeff SATteRswaite.

The name that cinches the cryptic significance of anagram in *Zero K* is "Artis Martineau." DeLillo draws immediate attention to her name through its sheer strangeness. "Artis"? Other than perhaps the great basketball center Artis Gilmore, most readers will never have heard of anyone named Artis. "Martineau" is uncommon, too, though it is noteworthy for being recycled; DeLillo used it before for Scott Martineau in *The Names*. But the name "Artis Martineau" invites several other connotations. Not only does it contain the word "star," but it also contains the word "art" in both the first and last name. In its Latin form the name echoes *ars gratia artis*— "art for art's sake." "Artis" needs only to borrow a T from Martineau to become "Artist," a pointer to the metafictional mise en abyme function this

FIGURE 9.3 *Up to four whole-body patients are contained in a Dewar like the one above at Alcor. Courtesy of Alcor Life Extension Foundation.*

character ultimately serves. Artis Martineau performs a pivotal role not only in the plot of *Zero K* but also in its structure. Part One is divided from Part Two by a brief but startling section which ostensibly captures the thoughts of a frozen woman in a pod. The "ARTIS MARTINEAU" section is distinct from Parts One and Two not only in its language and perspective but also in its use of all capital letters for the title. This epigraphic strategy invites consideration of the letters that make up the name, the patterns they form and the possible recombinations of those letters. Given DeLillo's belief that "A character takes shape because of that confluence of letters" (Brooks), and given his career-spanning incorporation of anagrams and coded language games in his fiction, and given his special interest in the word S-T-A-R and the cosmological significance expressed by Ratner of the stars embedded within us all—given all that, surely it is no coincidence that ARTIS MARTINEAU is a perfect anagram for *A MINIATURE STAR*.

10

A portrait of the ARTIS

Jeff Lockhart as embedded author in *Zero K*

Within the fictional universe of *Zero K*, internal evidence suggests that Jeff Lockhart is the author of the "ARTIS MARTINEAU" section.[1] Jeff employs fiction to reanimate the frozen Artis, imagining his way into her experience, assuming her perspective, and ventriloquizing her voice. He is drawn to authorship for many of the same reasons as DeLillo's previous embedded creators—reasons that may have attracted DeLillo himself to the profession. He confided to Kevin Connolly, "I think fiction can be a refuge and a consolation. . . . Beyond that, fiction offers patterns and symmetry that we don't find in the experience of ordinary living. Stories are consoling, fiction is one of the consolation prizes for having lived in the world" (31). DeLillo acknowledges that these patterns and symmetries impose an order which does not otherwise pertain in lived experience. The characters drawn to fiction in DeLillo's works are often those stunted since youth by chaos, disruption, and powerlessness. They turn to fiction as refuge, consolation, and antidote. As the one-eyed scientist Celeste Dessau ruefully observes in *Ratner's Star*, "Symmetry is a powerful analgesic" (*RS* 115). Fiction not only provides a means for imposing order on external reality; it also offers an opportunity for inventing a stable identity, recomposing a new anagrammatized self. DeLillo told LeClair,

> I think after a while a writer can begin to know himself through his language. He sees someone or something reflected back at him from these constructions. Over the years it's possible for a writer to shape himself as

a human being through the language he uses. I think written language,
fiction, goes that deep. He not only sees himself but begins to make
himself or remake himself. (6–7)

It is important to recognize that this process rarely involves straightforward
self-examination in DeLillo. The creator instead uses various strategies—
deflection, projection, misprision, triangulation, metempsychosis—to probe
the self in the guise of the other. DeLillo minted a fresh metaphor to describe
this alchemy in his 2016 interview with Kate Tempest: "In a curious way
we could think of a novel as a kind of *camouflage*. It's a way in which a
writer can explore his feelings about people without being specific either
about himself or certain individuals" (Tempest, emphasis added). The reader
is given a wealth of background information and psychological data to
see through Jeff Lockhart's camouflage. A portrait of the artist of ARTIS
MARTINEAU emerges, painted in the primary colors of loss, anxiety, and
fantasy.

Like that other embedded author Nick Shay, creator of "The Martiniad"
saga in *Underworld*, Jeff's world was turned upside down when his father
abandoned the family:

> He left when I was thirteen. I was doing my trigonometry homework
> when he told me. He sat across the small desk where my ever-sharpened
> pencils jutted from an old marmalade jar. I kept doing my homework
> while he spoke. I examined the formulas on the page and wrote in my
> notebook, over and over: *sine cosine tangent.*
>   Why did my father leave my mother?
>   Neither ever said. (*ZK* 14, emphasis in original)

The other major catastrophe in his life prior to the action of *Zero K* was
the death of his mother, Madeline. Her name seems DeLillo's tip of the cap
to Proust's madeleine, that most famous spur to memory in *À la recherché
du temps perdu*. Just as all of Jeff's memories of Ross lead back to that
moment of abandonment at the homework desk, all memories of Madeline
lead back to Jeff's vigil over her deathbed: "When my mother died, at home,
I was seated next to the bed and there was a friend of hers, a woman with
a cane, standing in the doorway. That's how I would picture the moment,
narrowed, now and always, to the woman in the bed, the woman, in the
doorway, the bed itself, the metal cane" (*ZK* 9). In Part One of *Zero K*
Jeff is forced to confront another traumatic death in his inner circle, that
of his stepmother Artis. And in Part Two he is faced with the loss of his
father a second time, this time when he volunteers to be euthanized in the
Convergence's clandestine "Zero K" unit.

Gathered with Ross to say goodbye to Artis, Jeff reflects, "Three of us.
I realized we hadn't been in the same room for many months. We three.

Now, unimaginably, we are here, another kind of convergence, the day before they come and take her" (*ZK* 49). One of the persistent indications of Jeff's pattern-making propensity is his obsession with configurations of three. He always conceives of relationships in triads. Before Ross walked out, Jeff enjoyed the childish fantasy of the family as a single cohesive whole. After his father's abandonment, Jeff's family is divided into a triangulation of competing interests, pressures, and dependencies. It is no coincidence that teenager Jeff is working on trigonometry when Ross announced that he was leaving. DeLillo highlighted this detail when he published an excerpt of *Zero K* in the *New Yorker* magazine and titled it "Sine Cosine Tangent."[2] Jeff invests mystical significance in the triad, comparable to the Pythagorean veneration of the holy *tetraktys*. Late in *Zero K* Jeff revisits his personal Ground Zero yet again: "He had walked out the door, rejecting his wife and son while the kid was doing his homework. *Sine cosine tangent.* These were the mystical words I would associate with the episode from that point on" (*ZK* 234, emphasis in original).

Jeff goes on to replicate these trigonometric dynamics in subsequent relationships. In Part Two he has a brief relationship with Emma Breslow. She has recently split with her husband and shares joint custody of Stak, the son they adopted from a Ukrainian orphanage. This triad bears an uncanny resemblance to the "We Three" of Ross-Artis-Jeff:

Ross	→	Parent, Ex-Spouse	→	Emma
Artis	→	New Lover, Surrogate Parent	→	Adult Jeff
Young Jeff	→	Abandoned/Surrogate Son	→	Stak

It goes without saying that this later relationship does not last. By novel's end, Emma and Jeff have drifted apart, and Stak has run away from home, possibly to meet his demise as a rebel fighter in his war-torn native country. All of Jeff's relationships are foredoomed by design, like triangles whose legs don't fit together or support each other properly and so collapse. He looks at the world through fractured tri-focal lenses and replicates iterations of his broken family. Nevertheless, for present purposes it is important to recognize that this proclivity for imposing patterns as a way of structuring and understanding experience is a predisposition which will eventually guide Jeff toward fiction-making. It may not make him a great boyfriend or son, but it can lead him to become a certain kind of compulsive, introverted writer.

Jeff is idiosyncratic to be sure, but in comparison to the eccentrics inhabiting *Zero K* he often comes across as the voice of reason. He is perceptive enough to see through the shams of the Convergence, even if he proves less self-aware at recognizing his own delusions. After visiting Artis and politely listening to her optimistic hopes for life after death, he thinks to himself, "She would die, chemically prompted, in a subzero vault, in a highly precise medical procedure guided by mass delusion, by superstition and arrogance and self-deception." He adds, "I felt a surge of anger. I hadn't known until now the depth of my objections to what was happening here" (ZK 50). Jeff serves as chief spokesman for DeLillo's own skepticism and at times downright denunciation of the utopian pipe dreams peddled at the Convergence. Mannequins, mannequin body parts, and even cryopreserved human bodies are scattered about the facility as objects of art. "This was art that belongs to the afterlife. It was art that accompanies last things, simple, dreamlike and delirious. You're dead, it said" (ZK 119). Jeff recognizes the fascist tendency behind such art. Aestheticization and objectification are stepping stones toward subjugation, where "utilitarian become[s] totalitarian" (ZK 147). He reflects, "I wondered if I was looking at the controlled future, men and women being subordinated, willingly or not, to some form of centralized command. Mannequinized lives" (ZK 146). The Convergence promises to make humans immortal, but at the price of their humanity: "Die a human, be reborn an isometric drone" (ZK 147).

DeLillo has been consistently critical of autocracy throughout his career, and he returns to this theme again in Zero K. One hears reverberations from Mao II and the novelist Bill Gray's rousing championship of the unruly "democratic shout" against the obedient homogeneity of totalitarianism: "The experience of my own consciousness tells me how autocracy fails, how total control wrecks the spirit, how my characters deny my efforts to own them completely, how I need internal dissent, self-argument, how the world squashes me the minute I think it's mine" (M 159). So much for owning the end of the world. Jeff rejects the ethos of the Convergence, and so does DeLillo. It is telling that he titles the novel Zero K. We are reminded that "zero K" is shorthand for absolute zero on the Kelvin scale (-273.15 °C). However, Jeff learns that the cryostorage pods actually never approach this temperature. "The term, then, was pure drama, another stray trace of the Stenmark twins" (ZK 143). The Zero K unit Ross enlists in to die prematurely, and indeed the entire novel, is named after a completely bogus claim, exposing the pervasive mendacity of the Convergence's immortality scheme.

Not all of Jeff's objections to the Convergence are based on high-minded principles, however. His deepest indictments are long-standing and personal. He holds back when discussing cryonics with his dying stepmother, but his anger bursts the dam when Ross announces that he plans to join Artis. Jeff is dumbfounded for a moment, but then he unloads on Ross. For all its scientific pretensions, the Convergence is no better in Jeff's mind than a crazy death cult. This is not some new-age NASA launching a moonshot into immortality; this is a glorified version of Jonestown, Heaven's Gate, or the Branch Davidians. He charges, "I think you've been brainwashed. You're a victim of these surroundings. You're a member of a cult. Don't you see it? Simple old-fashioned fanaticism. One question. Where is the charismatic leader?" (*ZK* 113) It's as if Jeff has read DeLillo's *Mao II* and is on the lookout for Sun Myung Moon to preside over this mass wedding with death. Ross practically speaks of it in those terms in defending his decision: "Try to understand that she and I share a life. The decision I made only deepens the bond. . . . We want to be together'" (*ZK* 114). Ross regards his decision as an act of fidelity and love. But this explanation only further infuriates Jeff. He shifts tactics, pressing Ross on the illegality of this act:

> "Those in authority here. They will carry out your wishes."
> "We don't need to get into that."
> "They will do this for you. Because it's you. Simple injection, serious criminal act."
> "Let it go," he said. . . .
> "Is it outright murder? Is it a form of assisted suicide that's horribly premature? Or is it a metaphysical crime that needs to be analyzed by philosophers?"
> He said, "Enough."
> "Die a while, then live forever." (*ZK* 114)

Jeff finally gets his father so upset that Ross strikes his son just to shut him up.

Jeff marshals every logical argument he can think of to talk his father out of this decision. At bottom, however, his objections are not intellectual but visceral. The subtext to all of his arguments reads something like this: "You walked out on my mother and me, but you're willing to kill yourself to be with your other wife. You abandoned me once when I was thirteen, and now you're going to abandon me again. I'm not enough to live for or stay for. *I was never good enough for you.*" Even as a thirty-four-year-old adult, Jeff harbors deep within—cryopreserved at his core—the abandoned boy he once was.

These deep-rooted anxieties lie behind his peculiar habit of "doubling the dark." As he confides to Artis,

> "Sometimes in a dark room," I said, "I will shut my eyes. I walk into the room and shut my eyes. Or, in the bedroom, I wait until I approach the lamp that sits on the bureau next to the bed. Then I shut my eyes. Is this a surrender to the dark? I don't know what this is. Is this an accommodation? Let the dark dictate the terms of the situation? What is this? Sounds like something a weird kid does. The kid I used to be. But I do it even now. I walk into a dark room and maybe wait a moment and stand in the doorway and then shut my eyes. Am I testing myself by doubling the dark?" (*ZK* 18)

The scared kid Jeff used to be never entirely goes away; he lingers within, Jeff's dark double. This boyhood double is reanimated at times of agitation. Eyes closed, Jeff channels his damaged inner child again near the end of the novel:

> The emptiness, the hush of the long hall, the painted doors and walls, the knowledge that I was a lone figure, motionless, stranded in a setting that seemed designed for such circumstances—*this was beginning to resemble a children's story.*
>
> I open my eyes. Nothing happens. *A boy's adventures in the void.* (ZK 235, emphasis added).

This condition does indeed resemble a scary children's story, and Jeff self-reflexively recognizes himself as the child-protagonist. His story also echoes other existential parables of alienation. His "adventures in the void" read like *Josef K. in Wonderland.* Jeff is drawn to a certain kind of fiction, an artistic medium for giving shape, pattern, and voice to his confusion. This is the world one enters in Kafka or Beckett—or "ARTIS MARTINEAU."

Jeff exhibits a number of writerly traits from an early age. He is fascinated with arcane words, precise definitions, and deft turns of phrase. He challenges himself by reading impenetrably dense European novels. Into adulthood he continues to invent names and imagine backstories for people he encounters. Even though the narrator-protagonist drifts aimlessly from one obscure job to the next, DeLillo makes it clear that Jeff has all the makings of a writer. In some respects he inherits these traits from his father. For all the tense ambivalence in their relationship, Jeff can certainly appreciate the bold move his father made to invent a new identity as "Ross Lockhart": "It was an incentive, an inducement. It would motivate him to work harder, think more clearly, begin to see himself differently. In time he would become the man he'd only glimpsed when *Ross Lockhart* was a series of alphabetic strokes on a sheet of paper" (ZK 81, emphasis in original). That link between writing a new name on paper and extending a new identity into the world holds a powerful attraction to Jeff: "I understood the lure of an invented name, people emerging from shadow selves into iridescent fictions" (ZK 82).

Jeff is a chip off the writer's block, too, as the fictional progeny of Don DeLillo. In the Tempest interview DeLillo identifies closely with Jeff Lockhart:

> What I notice mainly in Manhattan: people and traffic. And what can one make of that? "This isn't the stuff of fiction." Well, it can be. In the novel *Zero K* the young narrator does describe such things. He has a kind of, I suppose, highly sensitive apparatus of perception, and he sees

these things quite clearly. I don't know what he makes of them ultimately except they're worth writing down, they're worth thinking about, worth noticing, worth writing down. And that's pretty much what my experience was in the last few years in Manhattan and still is. (Tempest)

Notice the slippage between the author's perspective and the character's, so much so that it is hard to distinguish when DeLillo is referring to himself and when to Jeff. They see the city through the same eyes, notice the same details, *and write it down.* Perhaps it is no coincidence that the seventy-nine-year-old author of *Zero K* chose to make Jeff Lockhart thirty-four years old—DeLillo's age when he completed his first novel *Americana.* This is not to suggest that *Zero K* is autobiographical or that Jeff Lockhart=Don DeLillo. What I am suggesting is that *Zero K*—like Joyce's *A Portrait* and *Ulysses* and like DeLillo's *Underworld*—is *autological.* Margaret McBride's explanation of the term as it pertains to Joyce is worth recalling: "But there is another way to approach the issue of Stephen's authorship of *Ulysses,* one that sees the novel not as autobiographical but as *autological,* as a sophisticated, self-reflexive system dramatizing its own conception and development" (30, emphasis in original). The "all-pervasive *metafictional* dimension" (30, emphasis in original) which McBride identifies in *Ulysses* applies specifically to Jeff Lockhart's authorship of the "ARTIS MARTINEAU" section of *Zero K.*

"ARTIS MARTINEAU" by Jeff Lockhart

Near the end of *Zero K* Jeff more or less confesses to being the intelligent designer behind the internal monologue placed between Parts One and Two of the novel:

I think of Artis in the capsule and try to imagine, against my firm belief, that she is able to experience a minimal consciousness. I think of her in a state of virgin solitude. No stimulus, no human activity to incite response, barest trace of memory. Then I try to imagine an inner monologue, hers, self-generated, possibly nonstop, the open prose of a third-person voice that is also her voice, a form of chant in a single low tone. (*ZK* 272)

On one hand, he concedes that he does not really believe she has conscious thoughts in her current state. On the other hand, his authorial instincts lead him to imagine what those thoughts would be if she did have them. Jeff's resulting speculations are presented as "ARTIS MARTINEAU," an embedded fiction that reveals as much about its deviser as about its subject.

Although Jeff is suspicious from the start about cryonics, he is eager to engage with the ontological questions it raises. When he visits Artis at the Convergence facility, he interrogates her with a flurry of questions:

> Do you think about the future? What will it be like to come back? The same body, yes, or an enhanced body, but what about the mind? Is consciousness unaltered? Are you the same person? You die as someone with a certain name and with all the history and memory and mystery gathered in that person and that name. But do you wake up with all of that intact? Is it simply a long night's sleep? (*ZK* 48)

These questions concerning the continuity of memory and identity provide the skeletal framework for "ARTIS MARTINUEAU," one which is fleshed out by details he gathers along the way about cryonics. For example, he attends a lecture by a Convergence official preparing participants for what comes after death. She blithely reassures them,

> It will not be total darkness and utter silence. You know this. You've been instructed. First you will undergo the biomedical redaction, only a few hours from now. The brain-edit. In time you will re-encounter yourself. Memory, identity, self, on another level. This is the main thrust of our nanotechnology. Are you legally dead, or illegally so, or neither of these? Do you care? You will have a phantom life within the braincase. Floating thought. A passive sort of mental grasp. Ping ping ping. Like a newborn machine. (*ZK* 238)

Jeff incorporates these details to sinister effect in his depiction of Artis's mental state in the pod. A "brain-edit" that results in "phantom life within the braincase" sounds disturbingly reminiscent of the lobotomies performed in *One Flew over the Cuckoo's Nest*. And rebirth as a "newborn machine" sounds much closer to the nightmarish dystopia of *The Matrix* films than to de Chardin's aspirations for evolutionary perfection at the Omega Point. Jeff channels his most pressing existential questions and his worst fears about cryonics into "ARTIS MARTINEAU."

"But am I who I was" (*ZK* 157 [x 2], 160, 161, 162). This "question" begins and ends the internal monologue and appears five times in just six pages. Despite including four dozen questions, the utterances in "ARTIS MARTINEAU" all end in periods, not question marks. Why would Jeff do it this way? His strategy emphasizes the inscrutability of the questions being posed. Only the dead can truly know about any life after death, and they aren't around to tell us. But what if the dead don't understand what is happening to them any better than the living? Fiction affords Jeff an opportunity to leap the barrier of unknowability and gain imaginary access to death's sealed vaults. Even in art, however, he is denied access to the answers he seeks. This Lady Lazarus has no wisdom to impart to the living. Instead she floats on a black sea of aborted questions. In Jeff's vision of the afterlife or the inter-life—"no longer and not yet," to use DeLillo's favorite line from Hermann Broch[3]—the dead remain shrouded in ignorance of their own condition. Jeff's Artis is even more disoriented in death than she was in life. Pure oblivion would be a blessing, but instead she is cursed with a trickle of consciousness sufficient to apprehend but not comprehend her mental anguish. Jeff's alternative vision of life in the pod offers a damning rebuttal to the lavishly fraudulent claims of the Convergence charlatans.

One of the most prominent features of "ARTIS MARTINEAU," and one of its sharpest instruments of torture, is repetition. "I hear words that are saying things to me again and again. Same words all the time going away and coming back" (*ZK* 157). The section is only six pages long, but, as Samuel Johnson said of *Paradise Lost*, "None ever wished it longer than it is" (290). Over the course of "ARTIS MARTINEAU" the following sentences and phrases are repeated multiple times:

"But am I who I was" [5 times]
"I think I am someone" [3 times]
"Am I just words" [3 times]
"Where is here" [3 times]
"Here and now" [3 times]
"Do I need to wait" [3 times]
"Same words all the time" [2 times]
"I listen to what I hear" [2 times]
"I try to know who I am" [2 times]

Add to this list the following six-sentence sequence, which appears twice in its entirety:

Am I someone or is it just the words themselves that make me think I'm someone.
Why can't I know more. Why just this and nothing else. Or do I need to wait.
Are the words themselves all there is. Am I just words. (*ZK* 158, 160)

Identity propositions keep metastasizing: "I am" (or "I'm) appears twenty-seven times, and its interrogatory inversion "am I" appears fifteen times.

In many respects "ARTIS MARTINEAU" reads like a pastiche of Samuel Beckett. No modern writer was as remorselessly unflinching in his meditations on ignorance, impotence, disorientation, disembodiment, and fragmentation. Jeff hears Artis's voice as "a form of chant in a single low tone" (*ZK* 272), the trademark vocal register of almost every Beckett play from the early 1960s onward. The infernal repetitions of "ARTIS MARTINEAU" resonate most closely with Beckett's 1963 play with the self-reflexive title *Play*. This play features three heads (another triad) sticking out of urns (cf. *Urn Burial*) and speaking in rapid monotone. Though they occupy the same stage, each stares unflinchingly forward and betrays no awareness of the others' presence. The urns clearly imply that M (Man), W1 (1st Woman, M's wife), and W2 (2nd Woman, M's mistress) are all dead. Beyond these basic facts, the characters are as clueless as the audience about what is happening. Like Dante's damned, these figures are apparently doomed to replay their tawdry lives over and over again. Like Artis, each figure struggles to figure out precisely what he or she must do to alter this condition. Twice Artis asks, "Why can't I know more. Why just this and nothing else. Or do I need to wait" (ZK 158, 160). M wonders, "Am I hiding something?" (315); "Have I lost. . . the thing you want?" (315); and finally "Am I as much as . . . being seen?" (317) W1 asks, "Is it that I do not tell the truth, is that it, that some day somehow I may tell the truth at last and then no more light at last, for the truth?" (313). W2 frets, "Are you listening to me? Is anyone listening to me? Is anyone looking at me? Is anyone bothering about me at all?" (314). Artis echoes these pleas to be done with it all:

> What I need to do is stop this voice.
>   But then what happens. And how long am I here. And is this all the time or only the least time there is.
>   Is all the time still to come.
>   Can't I stop being who I am and become no one. (*ZK* 160)

Neither Artis nor the doomed figures in *Play* see any signs that their grueling predicaments will ease or cease any time soon. After the last spoken line in *Play*, Beckett deviously interjects the stage direction "*Repeat play*" (317). Jeff ends "ARTIS MARTINEAU" on a similarly endless note, with an italicized conclusion that looks exactly like a Beckettian stage direction: "*On and on. Eyes closed. Woman's body in a pod*" (*ZK* 162).

M, W1, and W2 are not only stuck in urns—they are also stuck in *Play*. When the characters appeal to be released from the obligation to repeat the same routine night after night, every time the spotlight shines upon them, they are above all else asking for a reprieve from their imprisonment within *Play*. If the playwright had not written them into this bind, and if the spotlight would switch off and leave them alone, and if the audience would bloody well go home and stop staring at them, then this would all be over. No such luck: the *Play* must go on. Artis likewise intuits that she is trapped not merely in a cryonic pod but in a work of fiction. She begins to wonder, "Am I someone or is it just the words themselves that make me think I'm someone" (*ZK* 158). It doesn't take long for this query to sink its talons: "Are the words themselves all there is. Am I just the words" (*ZK* 158). Finally, her suspicions solidify into conviction: "I only hear what

FIGURE 10.1 *Frantic W2 (played by Juliet Stevenson) trapped in Anthony Minghella's 2001 film adaptation of Samuel Beckett's* Play *for the* Beckett on Film *project (Blue Angel Films).*

is me. I am made of words" (*ZK* 158). Artis ultimately recognizes that she is a fictional character comprised of words. She also correctly surmises, "I know I am inside something. I am somebody inside this thing I am in" (*ZK* 159). Indeed she is. Artis Martineau is a metafictional prisoner of "ARTIS MARTINEAU," an urn buried inside of *Zero K*.

The situation is complicated further by the fact that this incarnation of Artis is a reincarnation invented by still another fictional character, DeLillo's created creator Jeff Lockhart. Jeff peeks through the text of "ARTIS MARTINEAU" by way of periodic intrusions in a separate narrative voice. The first indication that there is a mediating agency controlling this stream of consciousness is an italicized insertion on the first page: "*She knows these words. She is all words but she doesn't know how to get out of words into being someone, being the person who knows the words*" (*ZK* 157, emphasis in original). This observation is accurate insofar as it goes, but it doesn't go far enough. The rub is the unstable distinction between the experience of the other and the experience of the self, a distinction the narrator gestures toward in literary terms as first-person voice versus third-person voice: "*She is first person and third person both*" (*ZK* 158, emphasis in original). This fissure is soon elaborated upon: "*She is first person and third person with no way to join them together*" (*ZK* 160, emphasis in original). By the end of the section the narrator shifts from description to proscription, dispensing with third person and embracing first person: "*Does she need third person. Let her live down in the soundings inside herself. Let her ask her questions to no one but herself*" (*ZK* 162, emphasis in original). Make note of the slippage in that first sentence between character and author, where the narrator adopts the subject's habit of asking a question that ends in a period.

DeLillo has navigated the fault lines between first and third person several times before. David Bell admits in *Americana*, "The only problem I had was that my whole life was a lesson in the effect of echoes, that I was living in the third person" (*A* 58). Nick Shay in *Underworld* sharpens the blade separating the two perspectives: "The third person watches the first person. The 'he' spies on the 'I.' The 'he' knows things the 'I' can't bear to think about" (*U* 119). In the case of "ARTIS MARTINEAU" the "she" who knows things the "I" can't bear is *Artis as camouflage for Jeff*. After all, if Artis is a fictional construction of words contained within a novel, the same applies equally to Jeff. He has Artis endure the hard facts of metafictional ontology which he himself could not dare to confront directly.

Here the model par excellence is another Beckett play, *Not I*. This play consists of a Mouth shrouded in darkness and whirring away in rapid stream-of-consciousness monologue. As with Artis, it gradually dawns on Mouth that she is a construction of words and voice: ". . . realized . . . words were coming . . . imagine! . . . words were coming . . . a voice she did not recognize . . . at first . . . so long since it had sounded . . . then finally had to admit . . . could be none other . . . than her own" (379). Her condition is also thoroughly metatheatrical, rooted in nightly reiterations on stage and cued by the spotlight. Mouth vaguely intuits her condition, but there are strict limits to her self-awareness. The title *Not I* refers to Mouth's insistence on maintaining third-person voice in speaking about her own experiences. Whenever she approaches the taboo revelation that she is talking about herself, she recoils as if stung by a viper. Five times she repeats her frantic Not-I disclaimer: "what? . . . who? . . . no! . . . she!" (377, 379, 381, 382). In his production note to the play Beckett described this disavowal as Mouth's "vehement refusal to relinquish third person" (375).

Jeff comes closer than Mouth does to admitting the first-person presence behind the third-person mask. "*Does she need the third person*" is a question ultimately directed toward himself, and so is the self-admonition which follows: "*Let her live down in the soundings inside herself. Let her ask her questions to no one but herself*" (*ZK* 162, emphasis in original). In this context, the final line spoken—"But am I who I was" (*ZK* 162)—reads less like a repetition of Artis's question than as Jeff's first forthright assertion of the first-person voice. "Am I [Jeff] who I was?" No. He is no longer speaking as Artis but finally as Jeff, the author of "ARTIS MARTINEAU." After years of closing his eyes and searching within, Jeff finds in fiction an ideal tool for dredging the depths of his "naked shitmost self" (*V* 91). He hints as much in the closing image: "*Eyes closed*" (*ZK* 162, emphasis in original). He projects onto Artis his telltale habit of closing his eyes in the dark, effectively penning his signature to her portrait.

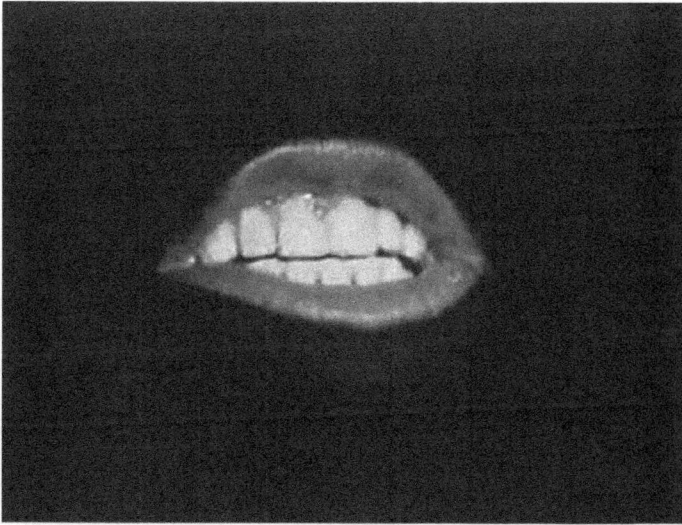

FIGURE 10.2 *Mouth (played by Billie Whitelaw) in the BBC 2 television adaptation of Beckett's* Not I, *directed by Anthony Page. Billie Whitelaw's staggering stage performance premiered in 1973 at the Royal Court Theatre. She reprised the role for film in 1975. This screen adaptation of* Not I *first aired on BBC 2 in 1977 as part of the* Shades *program.*

Such convergence inward runs the risk of solipsistic self-absorption, a trap which ensnares many of DeLillo's contemplative artist-figures. The first of these, David Bell, eventually acknowledges that his film serves as his "ultimate schizogram" for precisely these reasons. He admits, "I wanted to become an artist, as I believed them to be, an individual willing to deal in the complexities of truth. I was most successful. I ended in silence and darkness, sitting still, a maker of objects that imitate my predilection" (*A* 347). Billy Twillig reports a similar experience when in the throes of mathematical meditation. He vividly describes spiraling down into the vortex of solipsism:

There came a time in every prolonged effort when he had a moment of near panic, or "terror in a lonely place," the original semantic content of that word. The lonely place was his own mind. . . . This was the infalling trap, the source of art's private involvement with obsession and despair, neither more nor less than the artist's self-containment, a mental state that led to storms of overwork and extended stretches of depression, that brought on indifference to life and at times the need to regurgitate it, to seek the level of expelled matter. (*RS* 116–18)

Any writer who could compose the passage above knows the temptation of the "infalling trap," the gravitational pull into the black hole of self-obsession and despair. The key difference, however, between Jeff Lockhart, internal author of "ARTIS MARTINEAU," and Don DeLillo, external author of *Zero K*, is that Jeff falls into the solipsistic trap and DeLillo does not.

For all their similarities, DeLillo holds Jeff at arm's length (much as Joyce does with Stephen) so that the reader can view Jeff with greater clarity than the character can see himself. His attraction to solipsism is understandable. He is a byproduct of abandonment and loss who has never found a secure home or position or identity in the real world. He seeks refuge through an internalized fiction that is radically separate from external reality. The fiction he produces is dominated by existential crises he can readily imagine and crippling self-doubt he knows all too well. But his fiction spins its wheels in vicious circles around the braincase. "ARTIS MARTINEAU" is the work of another Narcissus trapped in the gaze of his own reflection. To put it bluntly, Jeff has all the makings of an author—a *failed author*. Fortunately, he and the reader are in the hands of a master. DeLillo offers alternatives to Jeff's dead-end solipsism in *Zero K*. Two key scenes in particular prompt Jeff to open his closed eyes and reach beyond himself toward the ineffable mysteries of life and death.

DeLillo's mysterium

John McClure observes in his essay "DeLillo and Mystery" that "in DeLillo's work it is only by coming to terms with permanent mystery, by accepting finitude and fragility, and by reasoning from this position that humans are able to live less anxiously, act more responsibly, and make contact with the mysterious benignities that circulate in the world" (167). Jeff experiences two such epiphanies in the latter chapters of *Zero K*, moments when he is faced with "mysterious benignities" and challenged to accept "finitude and fragility" rather than dive inward to his narcissistic pool. The first comes in the form of a spectral visit from his dead mother. Sitting in his subterranean room awaiting his father's cryopreservation, Jeff drifts off to sleep.

> I slept for a time in the chair and when I woke up my mother was present in the room. Madeline or her aura. How strange, I thought, that she might find me here, now in particular, in the wake of the woeful choice that Ross has made, her husband for a time. I wanted to sink into the moment. My mother. How ill-suited these two words were to this huge cratered enclosure, where people maintained a studied blankness about their nationality, their past, their families, their names. (*ZK* 247–48)

Jeff joins DeLillo's genealogy of mother-haunted protagonists stretching back to David Bell and tracing their descent through Stephen Dedalus. Call it dream, hallucination, fantasy, or an actual ghost, when Jeff finds himself in times of trouble, Mother Madeline comes to him. However, she doesn't speak words of wisdom. In fact, she is most conspicuous for her silence and stillness.

One customarily expects the dead to return with a specific message, request, or warning. In the second half of the novel Jeff becomes obsessed with silent women he randomly encounters on the streets or in the subway. He feels certain that they have some important message to deliver him. They do not. Failing that, he imaginatively reanimates Artis and imbues her with cryptic dispatches. But his own fiction fails to yield answers. Finally, his dead mother visits, delivering not a message but rather an aura. "Here she is, a breath, an emanation" (ZK 248). Although Madeline solves no riddles per se, her presence does lead Jeff to a quiet epiphany. In one of the most poignant passages of the novel, Jeff reflects on what he learned from his mother's death:

> I'd never felt more human than I did when my mother lay in bed, dying. This was not the frailty of a man who is said to be "only human," subject to a weakness or a vulnerability. This was a wave of sadness and loss that made me understand that I was a man expanded by grief. There were memories, everywhere, unsummoned. There were images, visions, voices and how a woman's last breath gives expression to her son's constrained humanity. (ZK 248)

So much elaborate effort in Zero K is driven by the desire to achieve immortality, as if life's greatest victory would be to defeat death. In this touching late scene, however, Jeff testifies that his single deepest human experience was communion with his dying mother and the devastating grief he felt after she died. Counter to everything the Convergence stands for, Jeff's experience suggests that death confers meaning on life, and that something fundamental to the human experience would be lost or cheapened if death were eliminated. "My mother was ordinary in her own way, free-souled, my place of safe return" (ZK 249). There is a quotidian dignity in Madeline's life and death and the consolation she continues to provide Jeff. Such mysterious benedictions are entirely missing from Jeff's imagined torments for deathless Artis.

DeLillo's final counterweight to "ARTIS MARTINEAU" comes in the radiant final chapter of Zero K. By this point Jeff has returned to New York and to some semblance of normal life. But he is still shaken by the deaths of his father and stepmother, and his scraping thoughts often burrow back to the Convergence. The final scene is set in midtown Manhattan: "This was a crosstown bus, west to east, a man and a woman seated near the driver, a woman and boy at the rear of the bus" (ZK 273). The setup seems simple enough, but I suspect DeLillo's epilogue in *Zero K* is modeled after his prologue in *Players*. He explained his intentions for the opening of *Players* in the LeClair interview:

> All the main characters, seven of them, are introduced in an abstract way. They don't have names. Their connections to each other are not clear in all cases. They're on an airplane, watching a movie, but all the other seats are empty. They're isolated, above the story, waiting to be named. It's a kind of model-building. It's the novel in miniature. We can call it pure fiction in the sense that the characters have been momentarily separated from the storytelling apparatus. They're still ideas, vague shapes. (7)

The mode of transportation may have shifted from a plane to a bus, but the mode of "pure fiction" described above remains the same. It is no accident that the only other passengers on the bus are a man and woman and a mother and child. The man and woman represent the recently deceased Ross and Artis. The mother and child represent the late Madeline and Jeff as lost little boy. Much as the opening plane sequence serves as a vehicle for the characters' arrival/birth into *Players*, the closing bus sequence serves as the characters' departure/death from *Zero K*, their makeshift ride across the River Styx.

An astonishing thing happens during this otherwise mundane bus ride. Jeff notices a sudden glow in the sky. No, it is not a meteor, although it is an astral phenomenon that harks back and bookends that Chelyabinsk emblem. Rather, the tidal flood of light comes from a periodic phenomenon some call "Manhattanhenge." Jeff explains,

> We were in midtown, with a clear view west, and [the boy] was pointing and wailing at the flaring sun, which was balanced with uncanny precision between rows of high-rise buildings. It was a striking thing to see, in our urban huddle, the power of it, the great round ruddy mass, and I knew that there was a natural phenomenon, here in Manhattan, once or twice a year, in which the sun's rays align with the local street grid. (*ZK* 273)

Neil deGrasse Tyson coined the term "Manhattanhenge" to emphasize the uncanny resemblance to Stonehenge.[4] The renowned astrophysicist explicitly poses a question which is implicit in DeLillo's depiction: "What will future civilizations think of Manhattan Island when they dig it up and find a carefully laid out network of streets and avenues?" Tyson answers, "Surely the grid would be presumed to have astronomical significance, just as we have found for the prehistoric circle of large vertical rocks known as Stonehenge, in the Salisbury Plain of England. For Stonehenge, the special day is the summer solstice, when the Sun rises in perfect alignment with several of the stones, signaling the change of the season" (Tyson).

FIGURE 10.3 *The phenomenon known as "Manhattanhenge." © 2015 Mihai Andritoiu, courtesy Adobe Stock.*

For DeLillo, a more apt reference point lies to the west of Stonehenge, in the Boyne Valley of southeastern Ireland, where the ancient passage tomb of Newgrange can be found.[5] Constructed over five thousand years ago, Newgrange is even older than Stonehenge and the Egyptian pyramids. The giant burial mound houses the hallowed dead of the prehistoric tribe which built it. The passage leading to the inner chamber is aligned with the horizon such that the rising sun shines directly into the burial mound on winter solstice, bathing the crypt and its dead ancestors in golden light. Archaeologists who excavated Newgrange speculated that the agrarian people who built it worshipped the sun. The construction exhibits a sophisticated understanding of both astronomy and architecture. Yet its purpose seems rooted in primal fears and fantasies. The winter solstice marks the darkest night of the year, the nadir at which the sun seems to be retreating from the earth, threatening to withdraw its life-giving light and heat forever and to abandon its dependents to a dark and cold death. However, as this primitive people also clearly understood, the winter solstice marks the pivot point at which the days will begin to get longer, the temperatures warmer, and the conditions will return to sow and reap and replenish the earth. Consistent with this pendulum swing from death to life, many speculate that the Newgrange people also believed their dead ancestors were brought back to life on the winter solstice, resurrected from their cold graves by the sunlight streaming into the crypt. They may even have regarded the intercessions of these reanimated ancestors as integral to the process of coaxing the sun into returning for another year to give sustenance to the living.

DeLillo reconstructs these numinous dynamics inside the mobile crypt of the bus in his closing "New(York)grange" scene. Jeff's avatar, the excited boy with his mother, gives pre-verbal voice to the primal ecstasy of the moment: "I didn't know what this event was called but I was seeing it now and so was the boy, whose urgent cries were suited to the occasion, and the boy himself, thick-bodied, an oversized head, swallowed up in the vision" (ZK 273–74). Adult Jeff's response is more subdued, but no less appropriate for the occasion. He suddenly conjures up a memory of Ross, as if the sun inside the bus chamber has temporarily resurrected his dead father: "Then there is Ross, once again, in his office, the lurking image of my father telling me that everybody wants to own the end of the world" (ZK 274). This sudden recollection bends back to the beginning of the book in the cyclical symmetry which has long appealed to DeLillo.[6] In terms of what we might call metafictional ontology, the end of a book always denotes the end of

FIGURE 10.4 *Newgrange in County Meath, Ireland. IrishCentral.com.* © *Brian Morrison, courtesy Tourism Ireland.*

the world for its characters. However, it is equally true that the reader can always return to the beginning, as Jeff does here in his thoughts, and relive the still extant experience all over again.

The "New(York)grange" scene marks a return in several other ways as well. By converting a contemporary Manhattan bus into a prehistoric burial chamber, DeLillo posits a direct and enduring link between our postmodern age and the values and practices of primitive societies. "The boy bounced slightly in accord with the cries and they were unceasing and also exhilarating, they were prelinguistic grunts. I hated to think that he was impaired in some way, macrocephalic, mentally deficient, but these howls of awe were far more suitable than words" (ZK 274). Jeff is at pains to emphasize that the boy's response is not "mentally deficient" but is in fact perfectly appropriate, more attuned to the mystery and majesty of the moment than the jaded response of an urbane New Yorker. Likewise, DeLillo suggests that the primal anxieties and desires which motivated the Newgrange people are just as relevant and operative for us today. We may at first consider it ridiculously irrational to fear that the sun will abandon us. Of course the sun will rise tomorrow, just like it did yesterday. Well, right up until the point it doesn't. As a Convergence official rightly observes, "We are at the mercy of our star" (ZK 65). As a star, the sun is an evolving astral body. At some point it will cease to burn at an intensity compatible with sustaining human life. And before that day comes, the planet may have already been rendered uninhabitable for any number of reasons considered throughout Zero K. So in that sense, the primitive fear of the end of life on Earth is a dress rehearsal for a day that will inevitably come sooner or later. Furthermore, one need not be present for the "end of the world" in the global sense to experience it on a personal level. Every human being will eventually encounter the end of his or her world through death. Each of us will experience our final day of life, after which the sun will never shine for us again. So DeLillo need not take fantastic liberties to connect contemporary humans with our ancient primitive ancestors. In so many fundamental ways, we are still stuck with the same dilemmas, confronting the same fears and groping for ways to cope. The Convergence cognoscenti aren't so different than the shamans at Newgrange when it comes right down to it.

The conclusion of Zero K also offers unmistakable echoes of the conclusion of Ratner's Star. DeLillo employs one more transubstantial literary conversion, morphing Billy Twillig into the boy on the bus, who himself is a reincarnation of young Jeff Lockhart. Recall that the culminating event of Ratner's Star is an unexpected solar eclipse, a "noncognate celestial anomaly" (RS 434) comparable in effect to the solar phenomenon in Zero K. The eclipse exposes the limitations of science and reason, and it prompts the scientists at Field Experiment Number One to revert to primal fears. Billy's mentor Robert Hopper Softly, for instance, is so alarmed that he retreats to the desert and tunnels into a hole. The most remarkable response comes from Billy himself on the final page of the novel. The young genius hops on a tricycle and races madly in an effort to outrun the spreading shadow of the eclipse. Like the boy on the bus, Billy's mood is an exhilarated mixture of terror and ecstatic joy. The boy on the bus also echoes Billy's prelinguistic babble. The final lines of *Ratner's Star* describe Billy making "this noise resembling laughter, expressing vocally what appeared to be a compelling emotion, crying out as he was, gasping into the stillness, emitting as he was this series of involuntary shrieks, particles bouncing in the air around him, the reproductive dust of existence" (*RS* 438). Star dust thou art, and unto star dust shalt thou return. Both *Ratner's Star* and *Zero K* end at the mercy of our star. When interviewer Karen Badt pointed out, "You realize you have a thing for sunsets in your work," DeLillo explained the sun's awe-inspiring effect: "A sunset can remind us of the fact we are on a planet, and it can remind us of the fragility of life, in such a circumstance, one planet in the solar system, a system that contains human consciousness. I think this is something one might automatically interpret from certain sunsets. There is a star 93 million miles away" (Badt).

DeLillo's final chapter constitutes a thoroughgoing renunciation of solipsism in favor of far-reaching, all-embracing, intergenerational (even intracanonical) experience beyond the self, what Rudolf Otto termed the numinous, the *mysterium tremendum*.[7] As McClure puts it in his book *Partial Faiths: Postsecular Fiction in the Age of Pynchon and Morrison*, "DeLillo resacralizes the world in the mode of modernism by subtly loosening the fabric of everyday reality so that something else—presence or emptiness—shines through and by introducing, often without any fanfare, a series of mysterious interruptions of quotidian reality" (65). The "New(York) grange" sequence represents a perfect example of quotidian reality suddenly disrupted, illuminated, and resacrilized. The final lines of the novel suggest that Jeff absorbs the mysterious power of this moment:

> The full solar disk, bleeding into the streets, lighting up the towers to either side of us, and I told myself that the boy was not seeing the sky collapse upon us but was finding the purest astonishment in the intimate touch of earth and sun.
>
> I went back to my seat and faced forward. I didn't need heaven's light. I had the boy's cries of wonder. (*ZK* 274)

Jeff's lingering traumas, resentments, fears, and self-doubts served as apprenticeship and raw material for his composition "ARTIS MARTINEAU." But by the conclusion he has evolved. Before he was prone to close his eyes and withdraw from the world into his solitary and obsessive inner sanctum. In the closing scene, however, he shares not only a chamber but also a moving cosmic experience with man and woman, mother and child. He listens to a boy's cries of wonder in their proper frequency, and he basks in the setting sun's mysterious life-giving glow. By the end of *Zero K* Jeff Lockhart, the embedded author of "ARTIS MARTINEAU," comes into possession of his birthright as a fully realized and self-aware character in a Don DeLillo novel. He becomes another miniature star in DeLillo's fictional cosmos.

Coda

Last Call

A mirror-resembling dream

6 a.m., July 26, 2018, just after waking from a dream about Don DeLillo.

I spent all day yesterday traveling back from Ireland, where I was teaching for two weeks in Xavier University's study abroad program. I had hoped to sleep in late this morning, but I can't stop thinking about the dream and want to get it down before it evaporates. The dream bears all the hallmarks of a scholar's fantasy at the end of a long and absorbing project. It also strikes me as an oddly appropriate place to conclude this study of the self-reflexive art of Don DeLillo, exposing how thoroughly I have assimilated his narcissistic narratives, metafictional labyrinths, secret codes, and literary games of hide-and-seek. Call it my own mise en abyme.

In the dream I meet Don DeLillo at the Rock of Cashel in Ireland. I have been here many times before. I'm not sure how this meeting was arranged or how either of us got here, but I know that the choice of locations was mine. (Before I went to bed last night I was watching Jerry Seinfeld's series Comedians in Cars Getting Coffee. *I suppose this dream was sort of* Critic Meeting Author Visiting Castles. *That would make me Jerry in the dream, though I have neither car nor coffee.)*

I'm not nearly as intimidated or awestruck as I would have expected. DeLillo sets me at ease with his soft manner. He is even thoughtful enough to wear the same clothes from his Wikipedia page (the grey sweater from his 2011 PEN reading), as if concerned that I might not recognize him otherwise.

He must know that I'm writing about him—why else would he agree to meet?—but the subject of my book never comes up in conversation.

My dream DeLillo has never visited the Rock of Cashel before so I proudly show him around. I have chosen this spot not because of its historical significance but because it's a place I know well and DeLillo doesn't. I'm trying to give myself a home-field advantage. I'm also trying to disguise my nervousness and make myself look smart. It seems to be working.

The Rock of Cashel in my dream is a composite of several different places in Ireland. As we walk through the front entrance, we find ourselves in the courtyard at Cahir Castle. I point out various architectural features and defensive measures used to protect the castle from attack. I have innumerable facts at my command. "Here we have a fine example of an overhanging machicolation." "See there where a cannonball is lodged in the wall of the keep? It has been there since the Earl of Essex fired it in the siege of 1599." I salt my comments with dry wit and pepper them with clever anecdotes. DeLillo seems impressed. This is going well.

At some point I get lost down passageways which don't lead where I remembered. I have to hurry ahead to ask a guide for instructions about where I'm going without letting DeLillo see my confusion. He has been politely following my lead, but I detect that his attention is starting to wane. Still, he's too decent to make an open display of his boredom.

DeLillo begins to express interest in the surrounding trees and plants, so we leave the castle to wander down a woodland path. We're now on the grounds of Ballynahinch Castle in distant Connemara. He comments admiringly on the blue hydrangea. I agree that the flowers are beautiful, but I'm hard-pressed to say anything intelligent on the subject. Botany? We're drifting out of my element here. I need to reel him back in.

I ask DeLillo if he has ever been to Thoor Ballylee, the tower house of William Butler Yeats. No, he has not. "Well then we simply must go!" Send me turning and turning up the winding stair over traipsing through a garden any day. Enlisting Irish bards to enchant DeLillo—"Seamus Heaney called Thoor Ballylee the most important building in Ireland!"—I lure my prey away from the waters and the wild and back toward my syllabus.

As we leave the woods and return to the pavements grey outside the Rock of Cashel, a horrifying thought occurs to me. We're back in Tipperary. Thoor Ballylee is all the way out in Galway. How are we going to get there?

(If you recall the Grandmother's sudden realization in Flannery O'Connor's "A Good Man Is Hard to Find" that the old plantation she wants her family to visit is not in Georgia but in Tennessee, then you have some inkling of my dreamt self's mortification.) *What the hell am I going to do?*

Thankfully DeLillo buys me some time by announcing he needs to visit the loo. He heads in that direction but then stops, pivots, and turns back toward me. With a touch of shyness he says, "Before we visit Xavier I wanted to give you this. Only Miko has a copy." He hands me a book. Where could he have been hiding that this whole time?

The book is a new novel by Don DeLillo.

The cover is light blue. It is embossed with faintly visible scrawling, suggesting a palimpsest. I feel almost able to recover some of these buried words, but they elude me and melt back into oblivion. DeLillo refers to his novel by a name, but I don't quite catch it—The [Something] Quartet? It contained a reference to music, I think. Unless it was a chess gambit. Or maybe a mathematical concept. In any case, an entirely different name is printed on the cover, and this title clearly reads Last Call. *I stand dumbstruck as DeLillo disappears into the bathroom.*

A torrent of thoughts rushes in by the jakes as I consider my prize. Oh my God, DeLillo's new novel! I didn't even know he was working on this. And no one else has a copy but Miko (probably my dream's sloppy shorthand for Michiko Kakutani; unless I have mystically intuited DeLillo's secret pet name for the long-time NYT book review editor). *What a boon!*

Also, secondarily, I realize that DeLillo has solved my logistical dilemma. Instead of visiting Thoor Ballylee we can go straight to Xavier, my real home turf, where I can give DeLillo a campus tour. The Fordham grad should feel right at home. (Trust dream logic to dismiss a trip from Tipperary to Galway as impossible, but a jaunt to Cincinnati as well within reason and range.)

The truth is, though, I can't wait to be rid of DeLillo now. Who has time to be leading him around? All I want to do is read the book.

I'll surely have material for a new final chapter, a groundbreaking and definitive interpretation, the first and last word on Last Call. *This Irish rendezvous was a pleasant diversion for a while, but now there is work to be done, with Bloomsbury's deadline looming ever closer.*

How long is he going to be in there? Is DeLillo walking into eternity in the Rock of Cashel toilets?

As the sun dips on the horizon, I wait among the deepening shades for him to return. Should I sneak a peek inside Last Call? *Could the author have included a personal inscription? I gaze in amazement for an exquisite moment at the mysterious gift in my hand. Then I take a deep breath of anticipation, and I open the book. . . .*

NOTES

Chapter 1

1 Instructing the Players on how to play (and not play) their parts, Hamlet implores, "For anything so o'erdone is from the purpose of playing, whose end, both at the first and now, was and is to hold as 'twere the mirror up to nature, to show virtue her feature, scorn her own image, and the very age and body of the time his form and pressure" (Shakespeare III.ii.19–24).

2 In Kenner's initial diagram he leaves the space beneath "Mirror" blank. He goes on to assert that the center of the novel, and the center of its mirror symmetry, occurs in the middle of the third section when Father Arnall pauses during his sermon to check his watch. In other words, Kenner locates a moment of silence at the literal center of Joyce's novel. Kenner then instructs the reader: "So go back to [the diagram] and write 'Silence' in the middle of the bottom line, under 'Mirror'" (Kenner 13).

3 See Tom LeClair, *In the Loop: Don DeLillo and the Systems Novel* (Urbana: U of Illinois P, 1987), 125. *Ratner's Star* is not the only example of a DeLillo work structured according to the principles of chiasmus. For another instance, see Karim Daanoune, "'The Rough Shape of a Cross': Chiastic Events in Don DeLillo's 'Baader-Meinhof'" in *Don DeLillo after the Millennium*, ed. Jacqueline A. Zubeck (Lanham, MD: Lexington Books, 2017), 211–30.

4 Jesse Kavadlo shows how closely Richard Elster's views mirror those of the Bush administration. He cites Ron Suskind's article in the *New York Times Magazine* (October 17, 2004), as evidence that at least one top administration official (probably Karl Rove) saw his job as creating new realities: "The aidse said that guys like me were 'in what we call the reality-based community,' which he defined as people who 'believe that solutions emerge from your judicious study of discernible reality.' I nodded and murmured something about enlightenment principles and empiricism. He cut me off. 'That's not the way the world really works anymore,' he continued. 'We're an empire now, and when we act, we create our own reality'" (qtd Kavadlo 75).

5 For an excellent review of the history of critical debates over *Pale Fire*, as well as the most creative and compelling arguments ever advanced about the novel, see Brian Boyd, *Nabokov's Pale Fire: The Magic of Artistic Discovery* (Princeton, NJ: Princeton UP, 1999).

6 The relevant passage from Hamlet's soliloquy reads:

> For who would bear the whips and scorns of time,
> Th'oppressor's wrong, the proud man's contumely,
> The pangs of disprized love, the law's delay,
> The insolence of office, and the spurns
> That patient merit of th'unworthy takes,
> When he himself might his quietus make
> With a *bare bodkin*? (Shakespeare III.i.71–77, emphasis added)

Chapter 2

1 For an effective synopsis of the "mother-haunted" nature of *Persona*, see Terence Diggory, "The Mother's Role in Bergman's *Persona*," *Film International* (January 20, 2014): http://filmint.nu/?p=10631.

2 For the fullest consideration to date of Baudrillardian applications to DeLillo's work, see Marc Schuster, *Don DeLillo, Jean Baudrillard, and the Consumer Conundrum* (Youngstown, NY: Cambria Press, 2008).

3 Joshua Ferris's contemporary workplace novel *Then We Came to the End* (2006) takes its title from the opening line of *Americana*, and Ferris's entire premise of explicating the corporate office as a microcosm for contemporary America is modeled after DeLillo's debut novel.

4 David Cowart hears the same echo of *The Graduate*, and he also finds traces of James Joyce's "The Dead," in the Old Holly cocktail party (139).

5 Susan Sontag's 1967 review of *Persona* in *Sight & Sound* remains one of the most sensitive, nuanced, and provocative interpretations of the film. Sontag offers a particularly compelling examination of the impossibility of distinguishing between reality and fantasy/hallucination during several sequences like the bedroom scene between Elisabeth and Alma. See Susan Sontag, "Bergman's *Persona*," reprinted in *Ingmar Bergman's* Persona, ed. Lloyd Michaels (New York: Cambridge UP, 2000), 62–85.

Chapter 3

1 For other critical applications of this approach, see Peter Boxall, Chapter 2, *The Possibility of Fiction* (Routledge, 2006); Russell Scott Valentino, "From Virtue to Virtual: DeLillo's *Cosmopolis* and the Corruption of the Absent Body," *Modern Fiction Studies* 53.1 (2007): 140–62; Brian Chappell, "Death and Metafiction: On the 'Ingenious Architecture' of *Point Omega*," *Orbit: Writing Around Pynchon* 4.2 (2016); and Josh Privett, "'I think of Artis': Jeffrey Lockhart as Embedded Author within *Zero K*," *The Don DeLillo Society Newsletter* 11.1 (2018).

2 For select interviews where DeLillo cites Joyce as an influence, see LeClair (4, 10); Begley (88); and Remnick (138).

3 The "Author's Note" at the end of *Libra* is conventionally read as DeLillo's legal disclaimer: "This is a work of imagination. While drawing from the historical record, I've made no attempt to furnish factual answers to any questions raised by the assassination" (*L* 457). Alternatively, one could read the "Author's Note" as a self-reflexive commentary penned by Nicholas Branch, as opposed to Don DeLillo. Having projected his dilemmas onto his characters and inserted third-person vignettes of his former self along the way, Branch finally drops the façade and acknowledges in first person what he has been up to all along. Tim Engles lays the foundation for this metafictional interpretation of the "Author's Note":

> Whether or not this note is part of the text is an open question; that it does not have a page number suggests an exterior status; yet given that it does appear between the covers of the book itself, and given the confidence it expresses in having provided "a way of thinking about the assassination without being constrained by half-facts or overwhelmed by possibilities," we can surmise that in it the storyteller invites us to consider the speculative nature of his story—or any constructor's account of the Kennedy assassination—and to take into account a writer's presence as the evidence-shifter who, like Nicholas Branch, has attempted to put it all together. (256)

If one reads the "Author's Note" as Branch's final signature at the end of his autological narrative, then it bears kinship to the final lines of *A Portrait*, ("Dublin 1904/Trieste 1914") metafictionally attributed to Stephen Dedalus (as distinct from James Joyce) as proof of Stephen's authorship of the narrative the reader has just completed.

4 Although it falls outside the scope of the present chapter and book, another paradigmatic reference point for *Libra* is Gnosticism. For my examination of the Gnostic influences in the novel, see Graley Herren, "Cosmological Metafictions: Gnosticism in Don DeLillo's *Libra*," *Religion & Literature* 47.2 (2016): 87–116.

5 For the best known version of the Daedalus myth, see Book VIII of Ovid's *Metamorphoses*. For a fuller collation of variants on the myth, see Graves (184–89).

6 The equation between book and labyrinth was reinforced by the first English language collection of Borges's stories, *Labyrinths* (New Directions, 1962), which included "The Garden of Forking Paths."

7 It is worth noting that the ecstasy of freedom which Stephen Dedalus enjoys at the conclusion is only temporary if one reads *A Portrait* as the first installment of a serial work continued in *Ulysses*, rather than as a completed work in its own right. In *Ulysses* Stephen returns to the labyrinth of Dublin and the nightmare of Irish history. For the purposes of the present chapter, however, I focus upon *A Portrait* as a single source text with a self-contained and completed character arc. *A Portrait* concludes with the flight of Icarus; *Ulysses* later traces his fall. But by then Joyce's own classical paradigm shifted from Ovid's *Metamorphoses* to Homer's *The Odyssey*. For examples of DeLillo's intertextual dialectic with *Ulysses*, see the next chapter on *Underworld*.

Chapter 4

1 In his book *Miracle Ball: My Hunt for the Shot Heard 'Round the World*, Brian Biegel chronicles his search for "the Holy Grail of sports" (xii), the Bobby Thomson home run ball. Using forensic photographic analysis by multiple experts, supplemented by eyewitness accounts, archival research, and firsthand interviews, and propelled forward through a serendipitous string of coincidences, rumors, and luck, Biegel builds an intriguing case for the person he believes walked away that day with the ball: Sister Helen Rita (née Helen Hojnacki), a rebellious Felician nun and avid baseball fan. He further speculates, in a turn of events which sounds straight out of *Underworld*, that the ball remained in Sister Helen's possession until her death in 1990, when it was thrown out with her few remaining possessions into a California landfill.

2 When Scribner reissued *Pafko at the Wall* as a single volume, the publisher incorporated all of DeLillo's revisions from the Prologue of *Underworld*. The passage I cite here is from the original "Pafko at the Wall" printed in *Harper's*. The careful reader will note a couple of alternate phrasings in this earlier version: the figure listens in the "gloom" instead of the later "gloaming" (*U* 32; *PWS* 44), and "he is filled with total fear" in "Pafko," whereas "he gets the cold creeps" (*U* 32; *PWS* 44) in *Underworld* and the 2001 *Pafko at the Wall*.

3 The fabulist John Barth also invoked this Homeric/Joycean formulation in his metafictional classic *Lost in the Funhouse*. Barth focuses on Menelaus in his penultimate story "Menelaiad" and on Anonymous in the final story "Anonymiad."

4 For a wide-ranging analysis of Rodia, the Watts Towers, and their relation to immigrant experience, see Luisa Del Giudice (ed.), *Sabato Rodia's Tower in Watts: Art, Migrations, Development* (New York: Fordham UP, 2014).

5 For information on the critically endangered status of Manx Gaelic, see UNESCO's Atlas of the World's Endangered Languages at http://www.unesco.org/culture/languages-atlas/en/atlasmap.html.

Chapter 5

1 For an early critical examination of DeLillo's treatment of the Cold War, see John N. Duvall, "Baseball as Aesthetic Ideology: Cold War History, Race, and DeLillo's 'Pafko at the Wall,'" *Modern Fiction Studies* 41.2 (1995): 285–313; as well as Duvall's *Don DeLillo's* Underworld: *A Reader's Guide* (New York: Continuum, 2002). For representative critiques of nostalgia in the novel (to name only a few), see Damjana Mraović-O'Hare, "The Beautiful, Horrifying Past: Nostalgia and Apocalypse in Don DeLillo's *Underworld*," *Criticism* 53.2 (2011): 213–39; Thomas Hill Schaub, "*Underworld*, Memory, and the Recycling of Cold War Narrative," *Don DeLillo*: Mao II, Underworld, Falling Man, ed. Stacey Olster (New York: Continuum, 2011), 69–82; and Tim Engles, "White Male Nostalgia in Don DeLillo's *Underworld*," *Postmodern Literature and Race*, eds. Len Platt and Sara Upstone (New York: Cambridge UP, 2015), 195–210.

2   Nevelson's friend Edward Albee regarded her resurrections of found objects as constructions of alternate reality, the creation of new worlds. In his introductory essay for the catalog to her 1980 retrospective at the Whitney Museum of American Art, Albee put it this way: "Nevelson feels that she began making her 'worlds' as an alternative space, so to speak—to create for herself a fathomable reality in the midst of the outside chaos. What has happened, of course, is that the private has become public, the refuge accessible to all, and, to those who know what a Nevelson looks like, the world is beginning to resemble her art." He concluded, "I hope she's pleased" (30).

3   For a cogent synopsis of the patriarchal biases and institutional obstacles faced by women artists through the early 1970s, see Linda Nochlin's groundbreaking essay "Why Have There Been No Great Women Artists?" first published in the January 1971 issue of *ARTnews*: http://www.artnews.com/2015/05/30/why-have-there-been-no-great-women-artists/.

4   Unlike the clear link between Louise Nevelson and Klara Sax, there is no obvious single model for Acey Greene. She is probably drawn in part from prominent African American women artists like Faith Ringgold and Emma Amos. See, in particular, Ringgold's *American People* series (1963–1967).

5   A theme of racial tension runs throughout *Underworld* and is manifest in multiple black-white relations like Cotter Martin and Bill Waterson or Big Sims and Nick Shay. DeLillo may suggest critique of Klara's relationship with Acey, as if the older white artist is subtly exploiting the younger black artist for her own regenerative purposes. For a specific example from the New York art scene of this brand of cultural appropriation and racial misrepresentation, see bell hooks's chapter "Altars of Sacrifice: Re-membering Basquiat" in *Art on My Mind: Visual Politics* (New York: New Press, 1995), 35–48.

6   The custom among graffiti writers was to adopt an alias (Moonman) followed by the street number (157) where the writer lived and/or focused activities. Ismael Muñoz's moniker places him on 157th Street in Washington Heights, the heart of early New York graffiti scene. In *Graffiti Kings: New York City Mass Transit Art of the 1970s*, Jack Stewart notes, "During the summer of 1969, youths in Washington Heights began to write their names on the walls. The number increased the following summer, as tags spread from the northern tip of Manhattan along the mass transit routes to the Bronx and Brooklyn. The subsequent generation enshrined these first-generation writers in a kind of graffiti hall of fame" (26).

7   See https://graphics8.nytimes.com/packages/pdf/arts/taki183.pdf.

Chapter 6

1   For the first book-length study of DeLillo's plays, see Rebecca Rey, *Staging Don DeLillo* (London: Routledge, 2016).

2   DeLillo equips Nick Shay with this same photo in *Underworld*. Nick tells Big Sims, "I'll show you this picture I've got at home. Great photograph, circa

I don't know, nineteen-fifties. Charlie Parker in a white suit in some club somewhere. Great, great, great picture" (*U* 326).

3 Glenn Gould explicitly interrogated associations with the North in his experimental radio documentary *The Idea of North* (1967), part of a trilogy of documentaries for the Canadian Broadcasting Corporation collectively titled *Solitude Trilogy*. DeLillo explicitly references "the idea of north" in his short play *The Word for Snow* (2014) (Rey 122).

4 The concept for *The Artist Is Present* consciously harks back to Abramović and Ulay's *Nightsea Crossing* series. Between 1981 and 1987 the two performed *Nightsea Crossing* twenty-two different times in a wide variety of venues across the globe. The piece requires ninety days of fasting and silence, and seven hours of performance in which they sit across a table from one another without moving or speaking. MoMA curator Klaus Biesenbach had this work in mind when he came up with the idea for *The Artist Is Present*. As Abramović reports in *Walk Through Walls*, Biesenbach provocatively challenged her: "Marina, why don't you face the reality of who you are now? . . . Your love life is gone. But you have a relationship with your audience, with your work. Your work is the most important thing in your life. Why don't you just do in the MoMA atrium what you did . . . with Ulay—except that instead of Ulay sitting across the table from you, it is the public? Now you're alone: the public completes the work" (300).

5 Scott Dill argues that DeLillo deliberately stretches out the experience of time for the reader in late novels like *The Body Artist*: "Of all of the novelist's available tools for representing temporality, DeLillo has turned toward writing shorter sentences, shorter paragraphs, even shorter novels, that seem to elongate the reading experience rather than compress it" (172).

6 DeLillo has also written four shorter plays: *The Engineer of Moonlight* (1979), *The Rapture of the Athlete Assumed into Heaven* (1990), *The Mystery at the Middle of Ordinary Life* (2000), and *The Word for Snow* (2014).

7 See Bert O. States, *Great Reckonings in Little Rooms: On the Phenomenology of Theater* (Berkeley: U of California P, 1987).

Chapter 7

1 "Baader-Meinhof" was originally published in the April 1, 2002, issue of the *New Yorker*. "The Starveling" was originally published in the autumn 2011 issue of *Granta*. Both stories are included in DeLillo's short story collection *The Angel Esmeralda: Nine Stories* (New York: Scribner, 2011), and those are the versions cited throughout the present study.

2 Karim Daanoune recognizes the back-and-forth structure of "Baader-Meinhof" as well, but he examines this movement in terms of chiasmus. See Karim Daanoune, "'The Rough Shape of a Cross': Chiastic Events in Don DeLillo's 'Baader-Meinhof,'" *Don DeLillo after the Millennium*, ed. Jacqueline A. Zubeck (Lanham, MD: Lexington Books, 2017), 211–30.

3 Stefan Aust, who knew some of the members of the RAF, has written the
   definitive account of the movement. His book *Der Baader Meinhof Komplex*,
   first published in German in 1985, was an avowed influence on Richter's
   October 18, 1977. Most of my own information on the group is drawn from
   the English translation, *Baader-Meinhof: The Inside Story of the RAF*, trans.
   Anthea Bell (Oxford: Oxford UP, 2008).

4 The original leaders had been arrested in 1972 and held in Stammheim Prison in
   Stuttgart. Ulrike Meinhof was found dead by hanging in her cell on May 9,
   1976, prompting an escalation of efforts to free the remaining leaders. The
   RAF kidnapped Hanns-Martin Schleyer in September 1977 and threatened to
   kill him if the remaining RAF prisoners were not released. This agenda was
   supported by militants from the Popular Front for the Liberation of Palestine,
   who hijacked a plane filled with passengers and likewise demanded the
   prisoners' release. German counterterrorism forces staged a successful operation
   to free the passengers and kill the hijackers on October 18, 1977. After learning
   about the siege, three of the RAF prisoners—Andreas Baader, Gudrun Ensslin,
   and Jan-Carl Raspe—apparently followed through on a suicide pact, although
   some supporters maintain that they were murdered. Surviving RAF members
   reacted by killing the hostage Schleyer that same day.

5 There is some question as to which exhibition serves as the setting for DeLillo's
   story. Critics have assumed that he refers to the *October 18, 1977*, MoMA
   exhibition just before 9/11 (November 2000–January 2001); but Richter's series
   was again on display just after 9/11 (February–May 2002, as part of a career
   retrospective), and DeLillo's manuscript of "Baader-Meinhof" bears the date
   February 2002. (I thank Emily Roehl, a research assistant at the Harry Ransom
   Center, for retrieving information on the manuscript's date from the DeLillo
   papers [Box 85, Folders 2–3].) Since the latter show ran contemporaneously
   with the original publication of story, readers of "Baader-Meinhof" could still
   go to MoMA and view the series for themselves, apprehensively looking over
   their shoulders the entire time.

6 For a comparative analysis of *Falling Man* in relation to the notorious "Falling
   Man" photo by Richard Drew, the 1974 high-wire walk between the Twin
   Towers by Philippe Petit, the 2008 documentary *Man on Wire* directed by James
   Marsh based on Petit's *cause célèbre*, and Colum McCann's iconic use of Petit
   in his 2009 novel *Let the Great World Spin*, see my chapter, "Flying Man and
   Falling Man: Remembering and Forgetting 9/11" in *Transatlantic Literature and
   Culture: The Wrong Side of Paradise*, ed. Kristine A. Miller (New York: Palgrave
   Macmillan, 2014), 159–76.

7 DeLillo apparently refers to the small Giorgio Morandi show at the Lucas
   Schoormans Gallery in Chelsea from September 23–December 4, 2004.
   See the exhibition catalog by Laura Mattioli, *Giorgio Morandi: Late Paintings
   1950-1964* (New York: Lucas Schoormans Gallery, 2004).

8 Gudrun Ensslin dabbled with a movie career before becoming radicalized,
   starring in the experimental film *Das Abonnement*, which features her nude in a
   number of sexually explicit scenes. Ensslin was often portrayed in the press as a
   femme fatale, while Ulrike Meinhof, who had twin daughters, was depicted as

a monstrous mother. For a particularly incisive critique of the negative gender stereotypes that distorted media coverage of the RAF women, see Clare Bielby, *Violent Women in Print: Representations in the West German Print Media of the 1960s and 1970s* (Rochester, NY: Camden House, 2012).

9 Brian Chappell ingeniously argues that, in an attempt to fill in the lacuna about Jessie's disappearance and hypothesize the mindset of the perpetrator, Jim Finley authors the "Anonymous" sections. I find this interpretation compelling and perfectly consistent with DeLillo's recurring motif of embedded authors explored in the present book. See Brian Chappell, "Death and Metafiction: On the 'Ingenious Architecture' of *Point Omega*," *Orbit: Writing Around Pynchon* 4.2 (2016).

10 I am indebted to Patrice Kane, the Head of Archives and Special Collections at Fordham University, for kindly providing me with copies of the core curriculum requirements and course catalog descriptions for Fordham University during the period when DeLillo attended as a Communication Arts major (1954–58).

Chapter 8

1 DeLillo has frequently credited international films for exerting a major influence during his formative years as an artist. For instance, he told interviewer Kevin Connolly: "I was a very avid filmgoer through the sixties. That was my personal golden age of movies: Bergman, Antonioni, Godard, and several other people" (39).

2 The Wittgenstein allusions in "Midnight in Dostoevsky" may help locate the unspecified "upstate" college which Robby and Todd attend. Wittgenstein spent July–October 1949 at Cornell University. He stayed with philosophy professor Norman Malcolm, and the two regularly took long walks off campus. These details recommend Wittgenstein as an inspiration for both the philosophy professor Ilgauskas and for the mysterious Hooded Man who wanders the town, which seems modeled after Ithaca, home of Cornell in upstate New York. For more information on Wittgenstein's time at Cornell, see Norman Malcolm, *Ludwig Wittgenstein: A Memoir* (Oxford: Clarendon Press, 1958); and Trevor Pinch and Richard Swedberg, "Wittgenstein's Visit to Ithaca in 1949: On the Importance of Details," *Distinktion: Scandinavian Journal of Social Theory* 14.1 (2013): 1–28.

3 In a story like "Midnight in Dostoevsky" devoted to near-encounters and crossed paths, one wonders whether Don DeLillo and Frank O'Hara ever bumped into each other at MoMA. DeLillo has frequently cited MoMA as one of his major artistic influences. The same was true of Frank O'Hara, who actually worked at the museum from 1951 to 1953, and again from 1955 until his untimely death in 1966. The latter period coincides with DeLillo's formative years as a writer in New York. There can be little doubt, therefore, that the two men must have been in the building at the same time, but to my knowledge there is no evidence of them actually meeting.

4 Excerpts from *Meditations in an Emergency* (1957) © Frank O'Hara, used by permission of Grove/Atlantic, Inc. Any third-party use of this material, outside of this publication, is prohibited.

5 O'Hara died from injuries sustained at Fire Island in the summer of 1966. After a late night out at a dance club, he and some friends hailed a taxi home. The taxi blew out a tire, and while the passengers were standing outside waiting for a repair, O'Hara was struck by a dune buggy. He was rushed to a hospital in Long Island and suffered terribly for many hours before dying of a ruptured liver on July 25, 1966. See the final chapter of Gooch's biography for a detailed account. It may be no coincidence that DeLillo saddles Todd with a congenital liver condition, or that Robby attempts to punch Todd in his vulnerable liver during their climactic fight.

6 The exhibition was a joint venture between The Metropolitan Museum of Art and Galeries Nationales du Grand Palais. The New York show ran September 22–December 13, 1987, before moving on to Paris January 14– April 11, 1988. Jeannine Baticle compiled the catalogue, *Zurbarán*, translated from the French and published by The Met. For contemporary reviews, see John Russell and Michael Brenson.

7 Norma Jeane Mortenson was born in 1926, the same year as Frank O'Hara. Her mother's married name was Baker, and she often went by Norma Jeane (or Jean) Baker. She assumed the name Marilyn Monroe for most of her professional career, but she did not legally change her name until February 1956, the month before "Three Girls" takes place. In an interview with her biographer Greg Johnson, Oates reflected on the inspiration and agenda for her *Blonde*, her 2000 novel about Marilyn Monroe. Her reflections are equally relevant to her 2004 short story:

> I believe I was trying to give life to Norma Jeane Baker, and to keep her living, in a very obsessive way, because she came to represent certain 'life-elements' in my own experience and, I hope, in the life of America. A young girl, born into poverty, cast off by her father and eventually by her mother, who, as in a fairy tale, becomes an iconic 'Fairy Princess' and is posthumously celebrated as 'The Sex Symbol of the 20th Century,' making millions of dollars for other people—it's just too sad, too ironic. (17)

8 Vladimir Nabokov makes a curious allusion to a lost glove in *Pale Fire*. When a publisher casually mentions that Charles Kinbote will be "happy" that a rival scholar has stepped forward to help edit John Shade's manuscript of the poem "Pale Fire," Kinbote reflects, "Now 'happy' is something extremely subjective. One of our sillier Zemblan proverbs says: *the lost glove is happy*. Promptly I refastened the catch of my briefcase and betook myself to another publisher" (17, emphasis in original). The implication is that each glove is sick of being forever paired with the other and is relieved when their bond is severed. The possible nod toward *Pale Fire* invites speculation that Nabokov may exert other influences in "Midnight in Dostoevsky." After all, *Pale Fire* is set at Wordsmith College in New Wye, thinly veiled disguises for Cornell in Ithaca, where Nabokov taught from 1948 to 1959. Both *Pale Fire* and "Midnight in Dostoevsky" present tales of literary obsession combined with

unrequited homoerotic love. DeLillo's story may even draw inspiration from
a fantasized encounter between Nabokov and Wittgenstein. Nabokov was on
the Cornell staff during Wittgenstein's visit, but biographer Brian Boyd reports
that Nabokov was away butterfly-hunting for most of the 1949 summer (Boyd
140–42). Nabokov and Wittgenstein would have been in Ithaca at the same
time from September to October 1949, yet there is no evidence they ever met.
Nevertheless, the temptation of imagining these two eccentric geniuses crossing
paths may have led DeLillo down the path toward "Midnight in Dostoevsky."

Chapter 9

1 Aldous Huxley's dystopian novel *Brave New World* was inspired in part by
   his brother Julian Huxley's work in evolutionary biology and eugenics. Julian
   Huxley was a friend and colleague of Teilhard, and he wrote the introduction to
   The Phenomenon of Man.

2 I refer of course to the opening sentence of DeLillo's first novel *Americana*:
   "Then we came to the end of another dull and lurid year" (*A* 3).

3 Ecological crisis is also a central concern in *The Word for Snow*, the short
   play DeLillo completed while working on *Zero K*. Although his focus on
   environmental catastrophe has sharpened in recent years, the theme has a long
   history in his work. For an extended study of the subject, see Elise A. Martucci,
   The Environmental Unconscious in the Fiction of Don DeLillo (New York:
   Routledge, 2007).

4 For a disturbing compilation of videotaped views of the Chelyabinsk meteor, see
   this YouTube clip: https://www.youtube.com/watch?v=VPFSyokDrec.

5 The narrator retreats from the world, both real and imagined, to lose himself
   instead in devotional study: "Through my quiet days in this hotel in Adrogué,
   I go on revising (though I never intend to publish) an indecisive translation in
   the style of Quevedo of Sir Thomas Browne's *Urne Buriall*" (Borges 81).

6 For a comparative study of metempsychosis in the works of Browne and
   Borges, see Cynthia Stephens, "Borges, Sir Thomas Browne, and the Theme of
   Metempsychosis," *Forum for Modern Language Studies* 28.3 (1992): 268–79.

Chapter 10

1 Josh Privett draws the same conclusion in a piece for *The Don DeLillo Society
   Newsletter*. He applies my "embedded author" theory about Nick Shay to
   identify Jeff Lockhart as the agency behind the "ARTIS MARTINEAU" section
   of *Zero K*. See Josh Privett, "'I think of Artis': Jeffrey Lockhart as Embedded
   Author within *Zero K*," *The Don DeLillo Society Newsletter* 11.1 (2018).

2 See Don DeLillo, "Sine Cosine Tangent," *The New Yorker* (22 February 2016):
   https://www.newyorker.com/magazine/2016/02/22/sine-cosine-tangent.

3 DeLillo cites this passage in his 1997 interview with David Remnick: "As DeLillo thinks about the era we're living in, and writing about it, he also has been thinking about a passage in Hermann Broch's novel *The Death of Virgil*. 'He uses the term "no longer and not yet,"' DeLillo said. 'I think he's referring to the fact that his poet, Virgil, is in a state of delirium, no longer quite alive, and not yet dead'" (144). DeLillo also incorporates the quotation into his play *Love-Lies-Bleeding*. Referring to his catatonic father, the character Sean advocates for euthanasia: "Not that he's alive. Not that he's dead. No longer and not yet. This is where he is. Try to understand. It's not only us. He needs to be released" (*LLB* 48).

4 See Tyson's scientific explanation for this phenomenon at the American Museum of Natural History's website: http://www.amnh.org/our-research/hayden-planetarium/resources/manhattanhenge/.

5 The definitive account of the Newgrange passage tomb was written by Michael J. O'Kelly, the archaeologist who led its reconstruction. See O'Kelly's *Newgrange: Archaeology, Art and Legend* (London: Thames & Hudson, 1982).

6 In the LeClair interview DeLillo remarked, "Somebody ought to make a list of books that seem to bend back on themselves. I think Malcolm Lowry saw *Under the Volcano* as a wheel-like structure. And in *Finnegans Wake* we're meant to go from the last page to the first. In different ways I've done this myself" (12). Yes, and he has continued doing it throughout his career.

7 See Peter Schneck, "'The Great Secular Transcendence': Don DeLillo and the Desire for Numinous Experience," *Terrorism, Media, and the Ethics of Fiction: Transatlantic Perspectives on Don DeLillo*, eds. Peter Schneck and Philipp Schweighauser (New York: Continuum, 2010), 204–20.

BIBLIOGRAPHY

Primary sources by Don DeLillo

(Chronological order)

Americana. New York: Penguin, 1971.

End Zone. New York: Penguin, 1972.

"Notes Toward a Definitive Meditation (By Someone Else) on the Novel 'Americana.'" *Epoch* 21.3 (1972): 327–29.

Great Jones Street. New York: Vintage, 1973.

Ratner's Star. New York: Vintage, 1976.

Players. New York: Vintage, 1977.

Running Dog. New York: Knopf, 1978.

The Engineer of Moonlight: A Play in Two Acts. Cornell Review 5 (1979): 21–47.

The Names. New York: Knopf, 1982.

"American Blood: A Journey through the Labyrinth of Dallas and JFK." *Rolling Stone* (8 December 1983): 21–22, 24, 27–28, 74.

White Noise. New York: Penguin, 1985.

The Day Room. New York: Penguin, 1986.

Libra. New York: Penguin, 1988.

The Rapture of the Athlete Assumed into Heaven. The Quarterly 15 (1990).

Mao II. New York: Penguin, 1991.

"Pafko at the Wall: A Novella, wherein the Giants Clinch the Pennant, Bruegel Descends, a Bomb Explodes, Sinatra Sulks, and a Harlem Boy Plays His Own Game." *Harper's* (October 1992): 35–50, 55–70.

"The Power of History." *New York Times Magazine* (September 7, 1997). Web. https://archive.nytimes.com/www.nytimes.com/library/books/090797article3.html. Accessed May 22, 2017.

Underworld. New York: Scribner, 1997.

Valparaiso. New York: Scribner, 1999.

The Mystery at the Middle of Ordinary Life. Zoetrope: All Story 4.4 (2000): 75–76.

The Body Artist. New York: Simon & Schuster, 2001.

Pafko at the Wall: A Novella. New York: Scribner, 2001.

"In the Ruins of the Future: Reflections on Terror and Loss in the Shadow of September." *Harper's* (December 2001): 33–40.

"Baader-Meinhof." 2002. *The Angel Esmeralda: Nine Stories*. New York: Scribner, 2011. 105–18.

Cosmopolis. New York: Scribner, 2003.

"Counterpoint: Three Movies, a Book, and an Old Photograph." *Grand Street* 73 (2004): 37–53.

Love-Lies-Bleeding. New York: Scribner, 2005.

Falling Man. New York: Scribner, 2007.

"Midnight in Dostoevsky." 2009. *The Angel Esmeralda: Nine Stories.* New York: Scribner, 2011. 119–45.

Point Omega. New York: Simon & Schuster, 2010.

The Angel Esmeralda: Nine Stories. New York: Scribner, 2011.

"The Starveling." *The Angel Esmeralda: Nine Stories.* New York: Scribner, 2011. 183–211.

The Word for Snow. New York: Karma, 2014.

"Sine Cosine Tangent." *The New Yorker* (February 22, 2016). Web. http://www. newyorker.com/magazine/2016/02/22/sine-cosine-tangent. Accessed February 25, 2016.

Zero K. New York: Scribner, 2016.

Secondary sources

Abramović, Marina. *The Artist Is Present.* 736-hour live performance. New York: Museum of Modern Art, 2010.

Abramović, Marina. *Cleaning the Mirror I, II, III.* Video performance. Oxford: Museum of Modern Art, 1995.

Abramović, Marina. *Rhythm 0.* 6-hour live performance. Naples: Studio Morra, 1974.

Abramović, Marina, with James Kaplan. *Walk Through Walls: A Memoir.* New York: Crown Archetype, 2016.

Abramović, Marina and Ulay. *Relation in Time.* 17-hour live performance. Bologna: Studio G7, 1977.

Adler, Tony. "DeLillo Off the Page." *Chicago Reader* (May 11, 2006). Web. https:// www.chicagoreader.com/chicago/delillo-off-the-page/Content?oid=922071. Accessed June 16, 2014.

Adorno, Theodor W. "Valéry Proust Museum." *Prisms.* Trans. Samuel and Shierry Weber. Cambridge, MA: MIT Press, 1967. 173–85.

Albee, Edward. "Louise Nevelson: The Sum and the Parts." *Louise Nevelson: Atmospheres and Environments.* New York: Whitney Museum of American Art, 1980. 12–30.

Apitzsch, Julia. "The Art of Terror—The Terror of Art: DeLillo's Still Life of 9/11, Giorgio Morandi, Gerhard Richter, and Performance Art." *Terrorism, Media, and the Ethics of Fiction: Transatlantic Perspectives on Don DeLillo.* Eds. Peter Schneck and Philipp Schweighauser. New York: Continuum, 2011. 93–108.

Aust, Stefan. *Baader-Meinhof: The Inside Story of the RAF.* Trans. Anthea Bell. Oxford: Oxford UP, 2008.

Badt, Karen. "A Rare Encounter with Don DeLillo in Lisbon." *The Huffington Post* (November 14, 2015). Web. https://www.huffingtonpost.com/karin-badt/a-rare-encounter-with-don_b_8563154.html. Accessed June 16, 2016.

Barth, John. "How To Make a Universe." 1960. *The Friday Book: Essays and Other Nonfiction*. New York: G. P. Putnam's Sons, 1984. 13–25.

Barth, John. "Lost in the Funhouse." *Lost in the Funhouse: Fiction for Print, Tape, Live Voice*. Garden City, NY: Doubleday, 1968. 72–97.

Baticle, Jeannine. *Zurbarán*. Exhibition Catalogue for Metropolitan Museum of Art, New York. 22 September–13 December 1987.

Baudry, Jean-Louis. "Ideological Effects of the Basic Cinematographic Apparatus." Trans. Alan Williams. *Film Quarterly* 28.2 (1974–75): 39–47.

Beckett, Samuel. *Endgame*. 1957. *The Complete Dramatic Works*. London: Faber and Faber, 1986. 89–134.

Beckett, Samuel. *Not I*. 1972. *The Complete Dramatic Works*. London: Faber and Faber, 1986. 373–84.

Beckett, Samuel. *A Piece of Monologue*. 1980. *The Complete Dramatic Works*. London: Faber and Faber, 1986. 423–29.

Beckett, Samuel. *Play*. 1963. *The Complete Dramatic Works*. London: Faber and Faber, 1986. 305–20.

Beckett, Samuel. *Proust*. 1930. *The Selected Works of Samuel Beckett, Volume IV: Poems, Short Fiction, Criticism*. Ed. Paul Auster. New York: Grove Press, 2010. 511–54.

Beckett, Samuel. *Waiting for Godot*. 1953. *The Complete Dramatic Works*. London: Faber, 1986. 7–88.

Begley, Adam. "The Art of Fiction CXXXV: Don DeLillo." 1993. *Conversations with Don DeLillo*. Ed. Thomas DePietro. Jackson: U of Mississippi P, 2005. 86–108.

Benjamin, Walter. "Theses on the Philosophy of History." 1940. *Illuminations*. Ed. Hannah Arendt. Trans. Harry Zohn. New York: Schocken, 1968.

Berkeley, George. *The Principles of Human Knowledge. The Works of George Berkeley, Bishop of Cloyne*. 1710. Volume 2. Eds. A. A. Luce and T. E. Jessop. London: Thomas Nelson and Sons, 1948–57.

Biegel, Brian, with Peter Thomas Fornatale. *Miracle Ball: My Hunt for the Shot Heard 'Round the World*. New York: Crown Publishers, 2009.

Bielby, Clare. *Violent Women in Print: Representations in the West German Print Media of the 1960s and 1970s*. Rochester, NY: Camden House, 2012.

Borges, Jorge Luis. "The Garden of Forking Paths." 1941. *Collected Fictions*. Trans. Andrew Hurley. New York: Penguin, 1998. 119–28.

Borges, Jorge Luis. "Pierre Menard, Author of the *Quixote*." 1941. *Collected Fictions*. Trans. Andrew Hurley. New York: Penguin, 1998. 88–95.

Borges, Jorge Luis. "Tlön, Uqbar, Orbis Tertius." 1940. *Collected Fictions*. Trans. and Ed. Andrew Hurley. New York: Penguin, 1998. 68–81.

Boxall, Peter. *Don DeLillo: The Possibility of Fiction*. London: Routledge, 2006.

Boyd, Brian. *Nabokov's Pale Fire: The Magic of Artistic Discovery*. Princeton, NJ: Princeton UP, 1999.

Boyd, Brian. *Vladimir Nabokov: The American Years*. Princeton, NJ: Princeton UP, 1991.

Brenson, Michael. "Monastic Masterpieces from Zurbaran at Met." *New York Times* (September 25, 1987). Web. https://www.nytimes.com/1987/09/25/arts/monastic-masterpieces-from-zurbaran-at-met.html. Accessed May 31, 2017.

Brooks, Xan. "Don DeLillo: 'I think of myself as the kid from the Bronx.'" *The Guardian* (May 6, 2016). Web. https://www.theguardian.com/books/2016/may/06/don-delillo-kid-from-the-bronx-interview-xan-brooks. Accessed June 16, 2016.

Browne, Thomas. *Hydriotaphia: Urne-Burial. Or, A Brief Discourse of the Sepulchrall Urnes Lately Found in Norfolk.* 1658. *The Works of Sir Thomas Browne.* Volume 1. Ed. Geoffrey Keynes. Chicago: U of Chicago P, 1964. 129–77.

Browne, Thomas. *Religio Medici.* 1636. *The Works of Sir Thomas Browne.* Volume 1. Ed. Geoffrey Keynes. Chicago: U of Chicago P, 1964. 1–93.

Bruegel, Pieter the Elder. *Children's Games.* 1560. Oil on panel. Vienna: Kunsthistorisches Museum.

Bruegel, Pieter the Elder. *The Triumph of Death.* c. 1562. Oil on panel. Madrid: Museo del Prado.

Caravaggio (Michelangelo Merisi). *Narcissus.* 1597–1599. Oil on canvas. Rome: Galleria Nazionale d'Arte Antica.

Chamberlain, Fred, and Linda Chamberlain. "The Question Column." *Cryonics* (August 1984): 8–9.

Chappell, Brian. "Death and Metafiction: On the 'Ingenious Architecture' of *Point Omega," Orbit: Writing Around Pynchon* 4.2 (2016). Web. https://orbit.openlibhums.org/article/doi/10.16995/orbit.133/. Accessed May 20, 2017.

Chénetier, Marc, and François Happe. "An Interview with Don DeLillo." 1999. *Revue française d'études amérilacaines* 87 (2001): 102–11. Web. https://www.cairn.info/revue-francaise-d-etudes-americaines-2001-1-page-102.htm. Accessed February 2, 2013.

Citizen Kane. Directed by and featuring Orson Welles. RKO, 1941.

Coale, Samuel Chase. *Quirks of the Quantum: Postmodern and Contemporary American Fiction.* Charlottesville: U of Virginia P, 2012.

Connolly, Kevin. "An Interview with Don DeLillo." 1988. *Conversations with Don DeLillo.* Ed. Thomas DePietro. U of Mississippi P, 2005. 25–39.

Cowart, David. *Don DeLillo: The Physics of Language.* Revised Edition. Athens: U of Georgia P, 2002.

Cowart, David. "The Lady Vanishes: Don DeLillo's *Point Omega." Contemporary Literature* 53.1 (2012): 31–50.

Crawford, Karin L. "Gender and Terror in Gerhard Richter's *October 18, 1977* and Don DeLillo's 'Baader-Meinhof'." *New German Critique* 36.2 (2009): 207–30. Web. 30 December 2012.

Daanoune, Karim. "'The Rough Shape of a Cross': Chiastic Events in Don DeLillo's 'Baader-Meinhof.'" *Don DeLillo after the Millennium.* Ed. Jacqueline A. Zubeck. Lanham, MD: Lexington Books, 2017. 211–30.

Dällenbach, Lucien. *The Mirror in the Text.* 1977. Trans. Jeremy Whiteley with Emma Hughes. Chicago: U of Chicago P, 1989.

de Botton, Alain. "The Pleasures of Sadness." *Tate Etc.* 1 (May 1, 2004). Web. https://www.tate.org.uk/context-comment/articles/pleasures-sadness. Accessed June 22, 2017.

de Chardin, Pierre Teilhard. *The Phenomenon of Man*. New York: Harper, 1959.

Del Giudice, Luisa, ed. *Sabato Rodia's Tower in Watts: Art, Migrations, Development*. New York: Fordham UP, 2014.

Dewey, Joseph. *Beyond Grief and Nothing: A Reading of Don DeLillo*. Columbia: U of South Carolina P, 2006.

de Zurbarán, Francisco. *Saint Francis in Meditation*. c. 1635–40. Oil on canvas. London: National Gallery of Art.

de Zurbarán, Francisco. *Saint Serapion*. 1628. Oil on canvas. Hartford, CT: Wadsworth Atheneum.

Diggory, Terence. "The Mother's Role in Bergman's *Persona*." *Film International* (January 20, 2014). Web. http://filmint.nu/?p=10631. Accessed June 25, 2018.

Dill, Scott. "Don DeLillo, the Contemporary Novel, and the End of Secular Time." *Don DeLillo after the Millennium*. Ed. Jacqueline A. Zubeck. Lanham, MD: Lexington Books, 2017. 171–89.

Duchamp, Marcel. "The Creative Act." *Marcel Duchamp*. Ed. Robert Lebel. New York: Paragraphic Books, 1959.

Duvall, John N. "Baseball as Aesthetic Ideology: Cold War History, Race, and DeLillo's 'Pafko at the Wall.'" *Modern Fiction Studies* 41.2 (1995): 285–313.

Duvall, John N. *Don DeLillo's* Underworld: *A Reader's Guide*. New York: Continuum, 2002.

Echlin, Kim. "Baseball and the Cold War." 1997. *Conversations with Don DeLillo*. Ed. Thomas DePietro. Jackson: U of Mississippi P, 2005. 145–51.

Eliot, Thomas Stearns "The Love Song of J. Alfred Prufrock." 1915. *Collected Poems, 1909–1962*. London: Faber and Faber, 1974. 13–17.

Engles, Tim. "'Proof of the Loop': Patterns of Habitual Denial in Tim O'Brien's *In the Lake of the Woods* and Don DeLillo's *Libra*." *Tim O'Brien*. Ed. Robert C. Evans. Ipswich, MA: Salem Press, 2015. 254–73.

Engles, Tim. "White Male Nostalgia in Don DeLillo's *Underworld*." *Postmodern Literature and Race*. Eds. Len Platt and Sara Upstone. New York: Cambridge UP, 2015. 195–210.

Ferris, Joshua. *Then We Came to the End*. New York: Little, Brown, 2007.

Fordham University Course Catalog. New York: Fordham University, 1956–58.

Freud, Sigmund. *Beyond the Pleasure Principle*. 1920. *The Standard Edition of the Complete Psychological Works of Sigmund Freud*. Volume 18. Trans. and Ed. James Strachey. London: Hogarth Press, 1975. 7–64.

Freud, Sigmund. "On Narcissism: An Introduction." 1914. *The Standard Edition of the Complete Psychological Works of Sigmund Freud*. Volume 14. Ed. and Trans. James Strachey. London: Hogarth Press, 1925. 66–102.

Friedan, Betty. *The Feminine Mystique*. New York: W. W. Norton, 1963.

Frost, Robert. "Fire and Ice." 1920. *Complete Poems of Robert Frost*. New York: Holt, Rinehart and Winston, 1962. 268.

Gaddis, William. *The Recognitions*. 1952. Champaign, IL: Dalkey Archive Press, 2012.

Gastman, Roger, and Caleb Neelon, eds. *The History of American Graffiti*. New York: Harper Design, 2010.

Gilbert, Stuart. *James Joyce's Ulysses: A Study*. Second Edition. New York: Vintage, 1955.

Gooch, Brad. *City Poet: The Life and Times of Frank O'Hara*. New York: Knopf, 1993.

Gould, Glenn. Liner Notes to Bach: *The Goldberg Variations*. Columbia Masterworks ML 5060 (1956). Web. http://www.rjgeib.com/music/Top-Ten/gould.html. Accessed July 1, 2016.

Gowy, Jacob Peter. *Icarus*. 1635–37. Oil on canvas. Madrid: Museo del Prado.

Graves, Robert. *The Greek Myths*. 1955. Web. http://www.24grammata.com/wp-content/uploads/2011/12/Robert-Graves-The-Greek-Myths-24grammata.com_.pdf. Accessed May 18, 2017.

Heath, Christian, and Dirk vom Lehn. "Configuring Reception: (Dis-)Regarding the 'Spectator' in Museums and Galleries." *Theory, Culture & Society* 21.6 (2004): 43–65. Web. 25 February 2013.

Herren, Graley. "Cosmological Metafictions: Gnosticism in Don DeLillo's *Libra*." *Religion & Literature* 47.2 (2016): 87–116.

Herren, Graley. "Flying Man and Falling Man: Remembering and Forgetting 9/11." *Transatlantic Literature and Culture: The Wrong Side of Paradise*. Ed. Kristine A. Miller. New York: Palgrave Macmillan, 2014. 159–76.

The Holy Bible. King James Version.

hooks, bell. *Art on My Mind: Visual Politics*. New York: New Press, 1995.

Hopper, Edward. *Automat*. 1927. Oil on canvas. Des Moines, IA: Des Moines Art Center.

Hutcheon, Linda. *Narcissistic Narrative: The Metafictional Paradox*. Waterloo, Ontario: Wilfrid Laurier UP, 1980.

Hutcheon, Linda. *A Poetics of Postmodernism: History, Theory, Fiction*. New York: Routledge, 1988.

Johnson, Greg. "Blonde Ambition: An Interview with Joyce Carol Oates." *Prairie Schooner* 75.3 (2001): 15–19.

Johnson, Ken. "At MoMA, Douglas Gordon: The Hourglass Contortionist." *New York Times* (June 9, 2006). Web. https://www.nytimes.com/2006/06/09/arts/design/09gord.html. Accessed March 8, 2013.

Johnson, Samuel. *Lives of the Poets*. 1779. Ed. Roger Lonsdale. Oxford: Oxford UP, 2006.

Joyce, James. *A Portrait of the Artist as a Young Man*. 1916. Norton Critical Edition. Ed. John Paul Riquelme. New York: W. W. Norton, 2007.

Joyce, James. *Ulysses*. 1922. Ed. Hans Walter Gabler. New York: Vintage, 1986.

Kauffman, Linda S. "The Wake of Terror: Don DeLillo's 'In the Ruins of the Future,' 'Baader-Meinhof,' and *Falling Man*." *Modern Fiction Studies* 54.2 (2008): 353–77.

Kavadlo, Jesse. *Don DeLillo: Balance at the Edge of Belief*. New York: Peter Lang, 2004.

Kavadlo, Jesse. "'Here and Gone': *Point Omega*'s Extraordinary Rendition." *Don DeLillo after the Millennium*. Ed. Jacqueline A. Zubeck. Lanham, MD: Lexington Books, 2017. 67–81.

Kellman, Steven G. *The Self-Begetting Novel*. New York: Columbia UP, 1980.

Kellogg, Carolyn. "A Rare Interview with Don DeLillo, One of the Titans of American Fiction." *Los Angeles Times* (April 29, 2016). Web. http://www.latimes.com/books/jacketcopy/la-et-jc-don-delillo-q-a-20160426-story.html. Accessed June 16, 2016.

Kenner, Hugh. "Introduction." *A Portrait of the Artist as a Young Man*. New York: Penguin, 1991. 7–18.

Krasny, Michael. Interview with Don DeLillo. "Forum with Michael Krasny." San Francisco: KQED. Radio broadcast 4 July 2003. Web. https://www.youtube.com/watch?v=uEXGqGkMQTE. Accessed February 13, 2014.

Lacan, Jacques. "The Direction of the Treatment and the Principles of Its Power." 1958. *Écrits: A Selection*. Trans. Alan Sheridan. New York: W. W. Norton, 1977. 226–80.

Lacan, Jacques. *Family Complexes in the Formation of the Individual*. 1938. Trans. Cormac Gallagher. "Jacques Lacan in Ireland." Web. http://www.lacaninireland.com/web/wp-content/uploads/2010/06/FAMILY-COMPLEXES-IN-THE-FORMATION-OF-THE-INDIVIDUAL2.pdf. Accessed May 5, 2015.

Lacan, Jacques. *The Four Fundamental Concepts of Psycho-Analysis*. 1964. Ed. Jacques-Alain Miller. Trans. Alan Sheridan. New York: W. W. Norton, 1977.

Lacan, Jacques. "Function and Field of Speech and Language." 1953. *Écrits: A Selection*. Trans. Alan Sheridan. New York: W. W. Norton, 1977. 30–113.

Lacan, Jacques. "The Mirror Stage as Formative of the Function of the I." 1949. *Écrits: A Selection*. Trans. Alan Sheridan. New York: W. W. Norton, 1977. 1–7.

Lacan, Jacques. "The Signification of the Phallus." 1958. *Écrits: A Selection*. Trans. Alan Sheridan. New York: W. W. Norton, 1977. 281–91.

Laist, Randy. *Technology and Postmodern Subjectivity in Don DeLillo's Novels*. New York: Peter Lang, 2010.

LeClair, Thomas. *In the Loop: Don DeLillo and the Systems Novel*. Urbana: U of Illinois P, 1987.

LeClair, Thomas. "An Interview with Don DeLillo." 1982. *Conversations with Don DeLillo*. Ed. Thomas DePietro. Jackson: U of Mississippi P, 2005. 3–15.

Lentricchia, Frank, and Jody McAuliffe. *Crimes of Art + Terror*. Chicago: U of Chicago P, 2003.

Lessing, Gotthold Ephraim. *Laocoön: An Essay on the Limits of Painting and Poetry*. 1766. Baltimore: Johns Hopkins UP, 1984.

LIMA. "*Cleaning the Mirror 1*, Marina Abramović (1995)." Web. http://www.li-ma.nl/site/catalogue/art/marina-abramovic/cleaning-the-mirror-i/7819#. Accessed September 23, 2018.

Mailer, Norman. "The Faith of Graffiti." *The Faith of Graffiti*. Eds. Mervyn Kurlansky and Jon Naar. New York: Praeger, 1974.

Malcolm, Norman. *Ludwig Wittgenstein: A Memoir*. Oxford: Clarendon Press, 1958.

Marina Abramović: The Artist Is Present. Directed by Matthew Akers and Jeff Dupre. Featuring Marina Abramović and Ulay. Show of Force, 2012.

Martucci, Elise A. *The Environmental Unconscious in the Fiction of Don DeLillo*. New York: Routledge, 2007.

Mattioli, Laura. *Giorgio Morandi: Late Paintings 1950–1964*. New York: Lucas Schoormans Gallery, 2004.

McBride, Margaret. *Ulysses and the Metamorphosis of Stephen Dedalus*. Lewisburg, PA: Bucknell UP, 2001.

McCarthy, Mary. "Bolt from the Blue." *The New Republic* (June 4, 1962). Web. https://newrepublic.com/article/63440/bolt-the-blue. Accessed July 7, 2018.

McClure, John A. "DeLillo and Mystery." *The Cambridge Companion to Don DeLillo*. Ed. John N. Duvall. Cambridge: Cambridge UP, 2008. 166–78.

McClure, John A. *Partial Faiths: Postsecular Fiction in the Age of Pynchon and Morrison*. Athens: U of Georgia P, 2007.

Medley, Mark. "In Zero K, Don DeLillo's Voice is Strong as Ever." *The Globe and Mail* (June 10, 2016). Web. https://www.theglobeandmail.com/arts/books-and-media/in-his-new-novel-zero-k-don-delillos-voice-is-strong-as-ever/article30392724/. Accessed June 12, 2016.

"Meteor Hits Russia Feb 15, 2013—Event Archive." YouTube. https://www.youtube.com/watch?v=dpmXyJrs7iU. Posted by Tuvix72 on 18 February 2013. Accessed June 25, 2016.

Metz, Christian. *The Imaginary Signifier: Psychoanalysis and the Cinema*. Trans. Ben Brewster. Bloomington: Indiana UP, 1977.

Morandi, Giorgio. *Still Life (Natura morta)*. 1956. Oil on canvas. Private collection.

Morley, Catherine. "Excavating *Underworld*, Disinterring *Ulysses*: Don DeLillo's Dialogue with James Joyce." *Comparative American Literature* 4.2 (2006): 175–96.

Moss, Maria. "'Writing as a Deeper Form of Concentration': An Interview with Don DeLillo." 1999. *Conversations with Don DeLillo*. Ed. Thomas DePietro. Jackson: U of Mississippi P, 2005. 155–68.

Mraović-O'Hare, Damjana. "The Beautiful, Horrifying Past: Nostalgia and Apocalypse in Don DeLillo's *Underworld*." *Criticism* 53.2 (2011): 213–39.

Mulvey, Laura. "Visual Pleasure and Narrative Cinema." 1975. *Feminism and Film Theory*. London: British Film Institute, 1988. 57–68.

Nabokov, Vladimir. *Lectures on Literature*. Ed. Fredson Bowers. New York: Harcourt Brace Jovanovich, 1980.

Nabokov, Vladimir. "Nabokov on Dostoyevsky." *New York Times* (August 23, 1981). Web. https://www.nytimes.com/1981/08/23/magazine/nabokov-on-dostoyevsky.html. Accessed June 30, 2018.

Nabokov, Vladimir. *Pale Fire*. New York: Vintage International, 1962.

Nabokov, Vladimir. *Speak, Memory: An Autobiography Revisited*. New York: G. P. Putnam's Sons, 1966.

Nabokov, Vladimir. *Strong Opinions*. New York: McGraw-Hill, 1973.

Naughton, Jim. "Don Delillo, Caught in History's Trap." *Washington Post* (August 24, 1988). Web. https://www.washingtonpost.com/archive/lifestyle/1988/08/24/don-delillo-caught-in-historys-trap/48a5b0b1-8bd9-412f-8426-843a405896fe/?utm_term=.092f7f8bfe0f. Accessed May 20, 2017.

Nevelson, Louise. *Dawns + Dusks: Taped Conversations with Diana MacKown*. New York: Scribner, 1976.

Nevelson, Louise. *Sky Cathedral*. 1958. Painted wood. New York: Museum of Modern Art.

Nevelson, Louise. *Sky Tree*. 1977. Black Cor-Ten Steel. San Francisco: Embarcadero Center.

Nochlin, Linda. "Why Have There Been No Great Women Artists?" *ARTnews* (January 1971). Web. http://www.artnews.com/2015/05/30/why-have-there-been-no-great-women-artists/. Accessed June 29, 2018.

Not I. Directed by Anthony Page. Featuring Billie Whitelaw. BBC 2, 1973.

Oates, Joyce Carol. "Don DeLillo's Americana (1971) Revisited." *Uncensored: Views & (Re)views*. New York: Ecco, 2005. 339–40.

Oates, Joyce Carol. "Three Girls." *I Am No One You Know: Stories*. New York: Ecco, 2004. 271–80.

O'Hara, Frank. "Meditations in an Emergency." *Meditations in an Emergency*. New York: Grove, 1957. 38–40.

O'Kelly, Michael J. *Newgrange: Archaeology, Art and Legend*. London: Thames & Hudson, 1982.

Osteen, Mark. *American Magic and Dread: Don DeLillo's Dialogue with Culture*. Philadelphia: U of Penn P, 2000.

Osteen, Mark. "DeLillo's Dedalian Artists." *The Cambridge Companion to Don DeLillo*. Ed. John N. Duvall. New York: Cambridge UP, 2008. 137–50.

Osteen, Mark. "Echo Chamber: Undertaking *The Body Artist*." *Studies in the Novel* 37.1 (2005): 64–81.

Ovid. *Metamorphoses*. Book III. Trans. Brookes Moore. 1922. Web. http://www.theoi.com/Text/OvidMetamorphoses3.html. Accessed May 9, 2015.

Ovid. *Metamorphoses*. Book VIII. Trans. Brookes Moore. 1922. Web. http://www.theoi.com/Text/OvidMetamorphoses8.html. Accessed May 18, 2017.

Perry, R. Michael. "A Brief History of Alcor Research." *Cryonics* 15.4 (1994): 5–9.

Persona. Directed by Ingmar Bergman. Featuring Liv Ullmann and Bibi Andersson. AB Svensk Filmindustri, 1966.

Pinch, Trevor, and Richard Swedberg. "Wittgenstein's Visit to Ithaca in 1949: On the Importance of Details." *Distinktion: Scandinavian Journal of Social Theory* 14.1 (2013): 1–28.

Play. Beckett on Film. Directed by Anthony Minghella. Featuring Alan Rickman, Kristin Scott Thomas, and Juliet Stevenson. Blue Angel Films, 2001.

Porphyry. *The Life of Pythagoras*. Trans. Kenneth Sylvan Guthrie. Web. http://www.tertullian.org/fathers/porphyry_life_of_pythagoras_02_text.htm. Accessed July 1, 2016.

Privett, Josh. "'I Think of Artis': Jeffrey Lockhart as Embedded Author within *Zero K*." *The Don DeLillo Society Newsletter* 11.1 (2018). Web. https://delillosociety.com/archive/newsletter-11-1/. Accessed September 3, 2018.

Psycho. Directed by Alfred Hitchcock. Featuring Anthony Perkins and Janet Leigh. Paramount Pictures, 1960.

Rapaport, Brooke Kamin. "Louise Nevelson: A Story in Sculpture." *The Sculpture of Louise Nevelson: Constructing a Legend*. Ed. Brooke Kamin Rapaport. New York: The Jewish Museum, 2007. 3–25.

Remnick, David. "Exile on Main Street: Don DeLillo's Undisclosed Underworld." 1997. *Conversations with Don DeLillo*. Ed. Thomas DePietro. Jackson: U of Mississippi P, 2005. 131–44.

Rey, Rebecca. *Staging Don DeLillo*. London: Routledge, 2016.

Richter, Gerhard. *Confrontation 1*. 1988. Oil on canvas. Cologne: Atelier Richter.

Richter, Gerhard. *Dead*. 1988. Oil on canvas. Cologne: Atelier Richter.

Richter, Gerhard. *Funeral*. 1988. Oil on canvas. Cologne: Atelier Richter.

Riquelme, John Paul. *Teller and Tale in Joyce's Fiction: Oscillating Perspectives*. Baltimore, MD: Johns Hopkins UP, 1983.

Rothstein, Mervyn. "A Novelist Faces His Themes on New Ground." 1987. *Conversations with Don DeLillo*. Ed. Thomas DePietro. Jackson: U of Mississippi P, 2005. 20–24.

Rubin, Louis D., Jr. *The Teller in the Tale*. Seattle: U of Washington P, 1967.

Russell, John. "Art View: The Holy Landscape of Spain's Zurbaran." *New York Times* (September 20, 1987). Web. https://www.nytimes.com/1987/09/20/arts/art-view-the-holy-landscape-of-spain-s-zurbaran-by-john-russell.html. Accessed May 31, 2017.

Schaub, Thomas Hill. "*Underworld*, Memory, and the Recycling of Cold War Narrative." *Don DeLillo: Mao II, Underworld, Falling Man*. Ed. Stacey Olster. New York: Continuum, 2011. 69–82.

Schneck, Peter. "'The Great Secular Transcendence': Don DeLillo and the Desire for Numinous Experience." *Terrorism, Media, and the Ethics of Fiction: Transatlantic Perspectives on Don DeLillo*. Eds. Peter Schneck and Philipp Schweighauser. New York: Continuum, 2010. 204–20.

Schuster, Marc. *Don DeLillo, Jean Baudrillard, and the Consumer Conundrum*. Youngstown, NY: Cambria Press, 2008.

The Seven Year Itch. Directed by Billy Wilder. Featuring Marilyn Monroe and Tom Ewell. 20th Century Fox, 1955.

The Seventh Seal. Directed by Ingmar Bergman. Featuring Max von Sydow. AB Svensk Filmindustri, 1957.

Shakespeare, William. *Hamlet, Prince of Denmark*. c. 1602. *The Complete Works of Shakespeare*. Sixth Edition. Ed. David Bevington. Pearson-Longman, 2009. 1097–149.

Sontag, Susan. "Bergman's *Persona*." 1967. Ingmar Bergman's Persona. Ed. Lloyd Michaels. New York: Cambridge UP, 2000. 62–85.

States, Bert O. *Great Reckonings in Little Rooms: On the Phenomenology of Theater*. Berkeley: U of California P, 1987.

Stephens, Cynthia. "Borges, Sir Thomas Browne, and the Theme of Metempsychosis." *Forum for Modern Language Studies* 28.3 (1992): 268–79.

Stewart, Jack. *Graffiti Kings: New York City Mass Transit Art of the 1970s*. Abrams, NY: Melcher Media, 2009.

Stewart, Susan. *On Longing: Narratives of the Miniature, the Gigantic, the Souvenir, the Collection*. Durham, NC: Duke UP, 1993.

Storr, Robert. *Gerhard Richter: Forty Years of Painting*. New York: Museum of Modern Art, 2002.

Storr, Robert. *Gerhard Richter: October 18, 1977*. New York: Museum of Modern Art, 2000.

Suskind, Ron. "Faith, Certainty and the Presidency of George W. Bush." *New York Times Magazine* (October 17, 2004). Web. https://www.nytimes.com/2004/10/17/magazine/faith-certainty-and-the-presidency-of-george-w-bush.html. Accessed July 9, 2018.

"'Taki 183' Spawns Pen Pals." *New York Times* (July 21, 1971). Web. https://graphics8.nytimes.com/packages/pdf/arts/taki183.pdf. Accessed June 29, 2018.

Tempest, Kate. "Don DeLillo and Kate Tempest in Conversation." *Picador* (June 10, 2016). Web. https://www.panmacmillan.com/blogs/literary/don-delillo-and-kate-tempest-in-conversation. Accessed June 21, 2016.

Tyson, Neil deGrasse. "Manhattanhenge." American Museum of Natural History. Web. https://www.amnh.org/our-research/hayden-planetarium/resources/manhattanhenge/. Accessed June 16, 2016.

Valentino, Russell Scott. "From Virtue to Virtual: DeLillo's *Cosmopolis* and the Corruption of the Absent Body." *Modern Fiction Studies* 53.1 (2007): 140–62.

Whistler, James Abbott McNeill. *Arrangement in Grey and Black No. 1.* 1871. Oil on canvas. Paris: Musée d'Orsay.

Wilson, Laurie. *Louise Nevelson: Light and Shadow.* New York: Thames & Hudson, 2016.

Wittgenstein, Ludwig. *Tractatus Logico-Philosophicus.* 1921. Trans. D. F. Pears and B. F. McGuinness. London: Routledge and Kegan Paul, 1961.

Woolf, Virginia. *A Room of One's Own.* 1929. San Diego: Harcourt Brace, 1981.

INDEX

Page numbers in bold indicate entire chapters or extensive sections devoted to the index term.

Abraham, Karl 23
Abramović, Marina **119–23**, 242 n.6.4
   The Artist Is Present 121–3, 242 n.6.4
   Cleaning the Mirror 120–1
   Nightsea Crossing (with Ulay) 242 n.6.4
   Relation in Time (with Ulay) 122
   Rhythm 0 119–20
   Self Portrait with Skeleton 120
   Walk Through Walls 120–3, 242 n.6.4
Adam 52
Adler, Tony 128–9
Adorno, Theodor 149
Akers, Matthew 123
Albee, Edward 128–30, 241 n.5.2
Alberts, Crystal xiv
Alcor Life Extension Foundation (Scottsdale) 208–9
Alighieri, Dante 163, 220
Allison, Lynn 132
Amos, Emma 241 n.5.4
anagram 7, 19, **206–10**, 211
Anderson, Laurie 119
Andersson, Bibi 25, 28, 37
Anelli, Sergio 147
Antonioni, Michelangelo 244 n.8.1
Apitzsch, Julia 147
archives
   Atelier Richter (Cologne) 141, 144, 162
   Fordham University Archives and Special Collections (New York) 244 n.7.10

Harry Ransom Center (Austin) 125, 243 n.7.5
   LIMA (Amsterdam) 121
   Marina Abramović Archives (Bonn) 120, 122
   National Archives and Records Administration (College Park) 95
   Saving and Preserving Arts and Cultural Environments (SPACES) (Aptos) 98
Athena 51
Aust, Stefan 243 n.7.3

B-52 Boneyard (Tucson) 85
Baader, Andreas 141, 149, 243 n.7.4
Baader-Meinhof Group. *See* Red Army Faction
Bach, Johann Sebastian 113–14, 137
Badt, Karen 203
Ballynahinch Castle (Ireland) 234
Barrow, Clyde 149
Barth, John 1–2, 10, 14, 206, 240 n.4.3
Basquiat, Jean-Michel 241 n.5.5
Baticle, Jeannine 173, 175–6, 245 n.8.6
Baudrillard, Jean 26, 30, 238 n.2.2
Baudry, Jean-Louis 24–6
Bay of Pigs Invasion (Cuba) 52
Beckett, Samuel 108, 118, 132, 134–6, 169, 185, 216, **219–23**
   Endgame 118
   Footfalls 132
   Not I 222–3
   A Piece of Monologue 185

Play 134–6, 220–1
Proust 108
Rockaby 132
Waiting for Godot 185
Begley, Adam 10, 20, 127, 196, 239
  n.3.2
Benjamin, Walter 47
Bergman, Ingmar 25–6, 28, 37,
  167–8, 187, 238 nn.2.1, 2.5,
  244 n.8.1
  Persona 25, 28, 37, 238 nn.2.1,
  2.5
  The Seventh Seal 167–8
Berkeley, George 161
Bernhard, Thomas 113–14, 116–18
Biegel, Brian 240 n.4.1
Bielby, Clare 243–4 n.7.8
Biesenbach, Klaus 242 n.6.4
Blake, William 194
Bohr, Niels 125
Borges, Jorge Luis **10–14**, 20, 55,
  194, 239 n.3.6, 246 n.9.5–6
  "The Garden of Forking Paths" 55,
  203, 205, 239 n.3.6
  "Pierre Menard, Author of the
  Quixote" 194, 203
  "Tlön, Uqbar, Orbis Tertius"
  10–11, 13–14, 205, 246 n.9.5
Borromeo, Charles 176
Boxall, Peter viii–ix, 36, 44–5, 55, 77,
  108, 110, 169, 238 n.3.1
Boyd, Brian 19, 237 n.1.5, 246 n.8.8
Branca, Ralph 59, 70–1
Brando, Marlon 186
Brenson, Michael 245 n.8.6
Broch, Hermann 82, 134, 219, 247
  n.10.3
Brooks, Xan 207, 209
Browne, Thomas 204–5, 207, 246
  nn.9.5–6
Bruegel, Pieter the Elder 81–2, 105,
  191
  Children's Games 105
  The Triumph of Death 81–2
Bush, George W. 13, 237 n.1.4

Cahir Castle (Ireland) 234
Caravaggio (Michelangelo Merisi) 40

Narcissus 40
Carroll, Lewis 196–7
Casares, Adolfo Bioy 10
Castro, Fidel 52
Catholicism 36, 53, 65, 171. *See also*
  Jesuits
Central Intelligence Agency (CIA) 42,
  48–50, 52
Chamberlain, Fred and Linda 208
Chappell, Brian 238 n.3.1, 244 n.7.9
Chekhov, Anton 194
Chelyabinsk meteor 197–201, 226,
  246 n.9.4
Chénetier, Marc 62
chiasmus 6–8, 237 n.1.3, 242 n.7.2
Chopin, Kate 104
Clark, Matthew Cameron 129
Coale, Samuel Chase 125
Cold War 59, 67, 82, 84–6, 200, 240
  n.5.1
Connolly, Kevin 55, 211, 244 n.8.1
Conrad, Joseph 43
conspiracy 11, 42, 44, 46, 48, 50,
  56, 58
Costales, Bryan 89
Cowart, David viii–ix, 9–10, 21–2,
  27, 36, 39, 64, 124, 127, 154,
  165–6, 173–4, 238 n.2.4
Crawford, Karin 157
cryonics 12, 189–91, 196, 198, 202,
  207–8, 213–14, 217–20
Cummings, E. E. 181

Daanoune, Karim 237 n.1.3, 242
  n.7.2
Da Cunha Lewin, Katie xiv
Daedalus 41–3, 47, 50–3, 65, 239
  n.3.5
Dällenbach, Lucien 63–4
de Botton, Alain 187
de Cervantes, Miguel 5, 194
de Chardin, Pierre Teilhard 154, 190,
  200, 246 n.9.1
deflection 14, 30, 73, 118, 159, 165,
  168, 212
déjà vu 125–6, 131, 194, 200
Del Giudice, Luisa 240 n.4.4
DeLillo, Don

Americana   2, 7, 9–10, 12–13, 20,
    21–40, 43, 86, 113, 155, 179,
    190, 194, 206, 217, 222, 238
    n.2.3, 246 n.9.2
"American Blood: A Journey
    through the Labyrinth of
    Dallas and JFK"   43–4, 49
*The Angel Esmeralda: Nine
    Stories*   142, 157, 165, 242
    n.7.1
"Baader-Meinhof"   **140–52, 155–7,
    159–63**, 165, 237 n.1.3, 242
    nn.7.1–2, 243 n.5
The Body Artist   3, 42, 114,
    118–28, 137, 242 n.6.5
Cosmopolis   3, 42, 195, 238 n.3.1
"Counterpoint: Three Movies,
    a Book, and an Old
    Photograph"   **113–18**, 137
The Day Room   128, 130–1, 136,
    139
End Zone   14–15, 113,
    168–9, 191
*The Engineer of Moonlight: A Play
    in Two Acts*   242 n.6.6
Falling Man   140, **145–9**, 162, 240
    n.5.1, 243 n.7.6
Great Jones Street   2, 42, 87, 113
"In the Ruins of the Future:
    Reflections on Terror and
    Loss in the Shadow of
    September"   146–7
Libra   3, 11–12, 14, 16, **41–58**, 59,
    64, 86, 113, 239 n.3.3–4
Love-Lies-Bleeding   16, 87, 114,
    118, **128–37**, 247 n.10.3
Mao II   3, 42, 87, 113, 142, 192,
    214–15, 240 n.5.1
"Midnight in Dostoevsky"   **165–87**,
    244 nn.8.2–3, 245–6 n.8
*The Mystery at the Middle of
    Ordinary Life*   242 n.6.6
The Names   13, 61, 63, 113, 139,
    192–4, 206–8
"Notes Toward a Definitive
    Meditation (By Someone
    Else) on the Novel
    'Americana'"   22, 32

"Pafko at the Wall: A Novella,
    wherein the Giant Clinch the
    Pennant, Bruegel Descends,
    a Bomb Explodes, Sinatra
    Sulks, and a Harlem Boy
    Plays His Own Game"
    [*Harper's*]   61–2, 67, 72,
    240 nn.4.2, 5.1
Pafko at the Wall [Scribner's]   240
    n.4.2
Players   2, 113, 195, 226
Point Omega   13, 42, 117, 140,
    151–4, 162, 165, 190, 207,
    238 n.3.1, 244 n.7.9
"The Power of History"   47–8, 55
*The Rapture of the Athlete Assumed
    into Heaven*   242 n.6.6
Ratner's Star   2, 6–7, 14, 42, 87,
    113, 125, 133, 169, 190,
    196–209, 211, 229–30, 237
    n.1.3
Running Dog   72, 113
"Sine Cosine Tangent"   213, 246
    n.10.2
"The Starveling"   3, 119, 140,
    157–63, 165, 242 n.7.1
Underworld   3, 4, 12, 16, 42,
    59–79, 81–112, 113, 123,
    185, 212, 217, 222, 239
    n.3.7, 240 nn.4.1–2, 5.1, 241
    n.5.5, 241–2 n.6.2
Valparaiso   3, 117, 128
White Noise   3, 113, 125, 131, 207
The Word for Snow   242 nn.6.3,
    6.6, 246 n.9.3
Zero K   4, 12, 16, 42, 130,
    189–209, 211–31, 238 n.3.1,
    246 nn.9.3, 10.1
DeLillo Archives. *See* Harry Ransom
    Center
De Palma, Brian   186
de Quevedo, Francisco   246 n.9.5
Descartes, René   134
Devereux, Robert (2nd Earl of
    Essex)   234
Dewey, Joseph   36
de Zurbarán, Francisco   166, **173–7**,
    187, 245 n.8.6

Saint Francis in Meditation   175–7
Saint Serapion   173–5
Dickinson, Angie   186
Diggory, Terence   238 n.2.1
Dill, Scott   242 n.6.5
DiMaggio, Joe   182
Diogenes   205
Dostoevsky, Fyodor   16, 170, 172–4,
        177, 181–2
dreams   9, 15, 20–2, 26–7, 29, 32–3,
        37–8, 40, 42–3, 46–9, 52, 57,
        87, 100–1, 117–18, 122, 133,
        158, 214, 225, **233–6**
Drew, Richard   146, 243 n.7.6
Duchamp, Marcel   142–3
Dupre, Jeff   123
Duvall, John   xiv, 72, 240 n.5.1

Echlin, Kim   7, 62, 71
Einstein, Albert   125, 201
Eisenhower, Dwight D.   181
Ekerot, Bengt   168
ekphrasis   142, 148, 157
Eliot, T. S.   159
embedded author. *See under*
        metafiction
Engles, Tim   46, 239 n.3.3, 240 n.5.1
Ensslin, Gudrun   141, 149, 162, 243
        n.7.4, 243–4 n.7.8
Eurydice   172, 186
Eve   52

fabulism   1, 10–13, 65, 178,
        240 n.4.3
Faulkner, William   5, 82
Ferris, Joshua   238 n.2.3
film and television studios
    20th Century Fox
        (Hollywood)   183
    AB Svensk Filmindustri
        (Stockholm)   25, 28, 37, 168
    Blue Angel Films (Dublin)   135,
        221
    British Broadcasting Corporation
        (BBC) (London)   223
    Canadian Broadcasting
        Corporation (Ottawa)   242
        n.6.3

Odeon Films (Toronto)   116
    Paramount Pictures
        (Hollywood)   153
    RKO Pictures (Hollywood)   63
    Show of Force (New York)   123
Finley, Karen   119
Forman, Miloš   218
Freud, Sigmund   5, 21–3, 28–9, 31–2,
        154
Friedan, Betty   103–4
Frost, Robert   199

Gaddis, William   **7–10**, 20
    The Recognitions   **7–10**
galleries
    Galeries Nationales du Grand Palais
        (Paris)   245 8.6
    Galleria Nazionale d'Arte Antica
        (Rome)   40
    Lucas Schoormans Gallery
        (New York)   147, 243 n.7.7
    The National Gallery
        (London)   175–6
    Pace Gallery (New York)   92
    Sean Kelly Gallery (New
        York)   120, 122
Garbo, Greta   169
Gastman, Roger   94–6
Gide, André   63
Gilbert, Lynn   92
Gilbert, Stuart   197
Gleason, Jackie   74
Gnosticism   8, 239 n.3.4
God   x, 8, 13, 16, 23, 52–3, 65, 155,
        167, 190, 205, 235
Godard, Jean-Luc   25, 244 n.8.1
Gooch, Brad   170–1, 245 n.8.5
Gordon, Douglas   151–4
    24 Hour Psycho   151–4
Gould, Glenn   **113–18**, 137, 242 n.6.3
Gowy, Jacob Peter   51
    Icarus   51
graffiti writers. *See also* New York
        City, Subway
    CRASH   96
    DINO NOD   95
    JUNIOR-161   95
    LSD OM   95

PHASE-2   95
PHIL T GREEK   95
SNAKE   95
STAY HIGH-149   95
SUPER KOOL-223   95
TAKI-183   95–6, 241 n.5.7
Graves, Robert   239 n.3.5

Happe, François   80
Haynes, Roy   114–15
Heaney, Seamus   234
Heath, Christian   144
Heisenberg, Werner   125
Hemingway, Ernest   5
Hitchcock, Alfred   9, 26, 33,
   151–5
   Psycho   151–5
Hodges, Russ   72
Homer   64–5, 239 n.3.7,
   240 n.4.3
hooks, bell   241 n.5.5
Hoover, J. Edgar   82, 85–6
Hopper, Edward   106, 186–7
   Automat   186–7
Hutcheon, Linda   5, 11–12
Huxley, Aldous   246 n.9.1
Huxley, Julian   246 n.9.1

Icarus   18, 51–2, 239 n.3.7
imago   23–4, 26, 28, 33–6, 38, 152
incest   21–2, 30–3, 35–9

Jernigan, Daniel   xiv
Jesuits   60, 65, 68, 154–5, 200, 205.
   See also Catholicism
Jesus Christ   8–9, 23, 27, 46, 52, 69,
   155, 173
John, Elton   182
Johnson, Greg   245
Johnson, Ken   151
Johnson, Lyndon B.   13
Johnson, Samuel   219
Joyce, James   5–8, 20, **41–6**, 64–5,
   74, 192–3, 197, 217, 224,
   237 n.1.2, 238 n.2.4, 239
   nn.3.2–3, 3.7, 240 n.4.3
   "The Dead"   238 n.2.4
   Finnegans Wake   193

*A Portrait of the Artist as a Young
   Man*   **5–8, 41–6**, 48, 65, 171,
   217, 237 n.1.2, 239 nn.3.3, 3.7
Stephen Hero   45
Ulysses   5, 43, 45, 64, 74, 82, 192,
   197, 217, 225, 239 n.3.7
Jung, Carl   23

Kabbalah   203, 205–7
Kafka, Franz   119, 158, 169, 181, 216
Kakutani, Michiko   235
Kauffman, Linda   145, 156–7, 161
Kavadlo, Jesse   viii, 44, 78, 237 n.1.4
Kazan, Elia   186
Kellman, Steven   64
Kellogg, Carolyn   6–7, 207
Kennedy, John F.   12, 42–3, 46, 48,
   52, 56, 59, 182, 239 n.3.3
Kenner, Hugh   5–6, 8, 237 n.1.2
Kerr, Deborah   24
Klee, Paul   108
Krasny, Michael   125–6
Künstlerroman   5, 42, 44, 46, 64, 68,
   86
Kunuk, Zacharias   114, 116
   Atanarjuat: The Fast Runner   114,
   116
Kurosawa, Akira   25

labyrinths   **10–14, 41–4**, 48, 50–2,
   55–8, 86, 203, 233, 239
   n.3.6, 240 n.3.7
Lacan, Jacques   **21–35**, 39–40, 152
   "The Direction of the Treatment
   and the Principles of Its
   Power"   32
   *Family Complexes in the Formation
   of the Individual*   23, 40
   *The Four Fundamental Concepts of
   Psycho-Analysis*   29, 35
   "Function and Field of Speech and
   Language"   29
   "The Mirror Stage as Formative of
   the Function of the I"   **22–5**,
   29, 33–4, 152
   "The Signification of the
   Phallus"   32
Laist, Randy   viii, 21, 34, 36–7, 103

Lancaster, Burt 24, 26, 38
LeClair, Tom viii, ix, 6, 14, 16, 41,
	54, 82, 115–16, 150, 168,
	178, 196–7, 211–12, 226,
	237 n.1.3, 239 n.3.2, 247
	n.10.6
Lentricchia, Frank 140
Lessing, Doris 103
Lessing, Gotthold 125
Lévi-Strauss, Claude 194
Lindsay, John 96
Lowrie, John Patrick 132
Lowry, Malcolm 82, 247 n.10.6
Lucifer 8, 52–4

MacAuliffe, Jody 140
McBride, Margaret 45, 217
McCann, Colum 243 n.7.6
McCarthy, Mary 17
McClure, John viii, 224, 230
MacLean, Alex S. 85
Mailer, Norman 96–7
Malcolm, Norman 244 n.8.2
Malcolm X 74
Mansfield, Jayne 93
Maranzano, Attilio 120
Marker, Stitch 129
Marsh, James 243 n.7.6
Martinez, Hugo 96
Martucci, Elise 246 n.9.3
Marx, Karl 26, 48
Massys, Quentin 63
Mattioli, Laura 243 n.7.7
Medley, Mark 191
Meinhof, Ulrike 141–3, 159, 243
	n.7.4, 243–4 n.7.8
Mekas, Jonas 9, 27
Melville, Herman 5
Memling, Hans 63
Menelaus 240 n.4.3
metafiction 1–20, 189–91, 193, 203,
	208, 238 n.3.1, 239 nn.3.3–4,
	240 n.4.3, 244 n.7.9
	autology 45–6, 189, 217, 239
		n.3.3
	embedded author
		in Cosmopolis 42, 238 n.3.1
		in Libra 12, 16, 41–58

	in Love-Lies-Bleeding 16,
		131–7
	in Point Omega 42, 238 n.3.1,
		244 n.7.9
	in Ratner's Star ix, 14, 42, 238
		n.3.1
	in Underworld 12, 16, 42,
		59–79
	in Zero K 12, 16, 42, 211–31,
		238 n.3.1, 246 n.10.1
	genealogy for DeLillo's work 1–20
	historiographic metafiction 10–13
	narcissistic narrative 5
metamorphosis 41, 48, 64, 67, 89,
		90–102, 108, 112, 143
metatheater 130–7
metempsychosis 74, 127, 189–97,
		201, 204–5, 212, 246 n.9.6
Metz, Christian 25–6
Michelangelo 38
Miller, Arthur 182
Miller, Kristine xiv, 243 n.7.6
Milton, John 219
Minghella, Anthony 135, 221
Mingus, Charles 114–15
Minos 51
mirrors 1–20, 23–8, 30–1, 37–9, 44,
		57, 63, 86, 93, 98–9, 119–22,
		140, 146, 148, 152, 155–9,
		189, 196–7, 205, 207, 233,
		237 nn.1.1–2, 1.4
Mirror Stage. See Lacan, Jacques
mise en abyme 2, 7–10, 19, 61–5, 93,
		208–9, 233
Monk, Thelonious 113–17
Monroe, Marilyn (Norma Jean
		Baker) 180–4, 245 n.8.7
Moon, Sun Myung 215
Morandi, Giorgio 147–8, 158, 243
		n.7.7
	Still Life (Natura Morta) 147–8
Morley, Catherine 64
Morrison, Toni 230
Moss, Maria 7, 60
Mraović-O'Hare,
		Damjana 240 n.5.1
Mulvey, Laura 26, 34–5
museums

American Museum of Natural
    History (New York)   247
    n.10.4
Des Moines Art Center
    (Des Moines)   186
Kunsthistorisches Museum
    (Vienna)   106
Los Angeles County Museum of Art
    (Los Angeles)   66
Metropolitan Museum of Art (The
    Met) (New York)   96, 175,
    186, 245 n.8.6
Musée d'Orsay (Paris)   107
Museo del Prado (Madrid)   51, 81
Museum of Modern Art (MoMA)
    (New York)   96, 120–1, 141,
    149, 151, 153–4, 156, 170,
    242 n.6.4, 243 n.7.5, 244 n.8.3
Wadsworth Atheneum Museum of
    Art (Hartford)   173–4
Whitney Museum of American Art
    (New York)   241 n.5.2

Nabokov, Vladimir   **14–20**, 82, 237
    n.1.5, 245–6 n.8.8
    Lectures on Literature   17
    "Nabokov on Dostoevsky"   16
    Pale Fire   **17–20**, 82,
        237 n.1.5, 245–6 n.8.8
    Speak, Memory   16–17
    Strong Opinions   17
Narcissus   18, 21–4, 27, 29–30, 35,
    39–40, 106, 224
Naughton, Jim   57
Neelon, Caleb   94–6
Nevelson, Louise   **87–92**, 99, 103,
    241 nn.5.2, 5.4
    Dawns + Dusks   87, 89–91
    Moon Garden + One   87–8
    Sky Cathedral   88
    Sky Gate   88–9
    Sky Tree   88–9
    Winged City   89
Newgrange (Ireland)   227–9, 247
    n.10.5
New York City   64, 87, 90, 93, 114–15,
    120, 122, 147, 170–2, 179,
    225, 228–30, 241 n.5.5

American Museum of Natural
    History   247 n.10.4
The Bronx   5, 20, 60–2, 73, 78, 83,
    94, 96, 101, 103–4, 106, 109,
    158, 241 n.5.6
Brooklyn Dodgers   59, 62, 82
Fordham University   155, 171,
    235, 244 n.7.10
Lucas Schoormans Gallery   147,
    243 n.7.7
Manhattan   96, 118, 170, 195,
    216–17, 225–6, 229
Manhattanhenge   226–7, 241
    n.5.6, 247 n.10.4
Metropolitan Museum of Art (The
    Met)   96, 175, 186,
    245 n.8.6
Museum of Modern Art
    (MoMA)   96, 120–1, 141,
    149, 151, 153–4, 156, 170,
    242 n.6.4, 243 n.7.5, 244
    n.8.3
The New Yorker   145, 165, 213,
    242 n.7.1, 246 n.10.2
New York Giants   59, 74, 82
The New York Times   95–6, 151,
    175, 235, 237 n.1.4
New York University   180
New York Yankees   61
Ogilvy, Benson & Mather   19
Pace Gallery   92
Polo Grounds   73, 82
Sean Kelly Gallery   120, 122
Strand Book Store   180–4
Subway   56, 94–7, 131, 134, 172,
    183, 225, 241 n.5.6
Whitney Museum of American
    Art   241 n.5.2
World Trade Center   88, 146, 148,
    243 n.7.6
Yankee Stadium   75
Nichols, Mike   30
Nixon, Richard M.   13
Nochlin, Linda   241 n.5.3

Oates, Joyce Carol   165–6, **179–87**,
    245 n.8.7
    I Am No One You Know   179

"Three Girls" 166, **179–87**, 245
        n.8.7
Uncensored 179
"Where Are You Going, Where
        Have You Been?" 180
O'Connor Flannery 235
Odysseus 77, 192
Oedipus 22, 29
Oedipus Complex. *See* Freud, Sigmund
O'Hara, Frank 165–6, **170–7**,
        182, 186–7, 244 n.8.3, 245
        nn.8.4–5
    "Meditations in an
        Emergency" 165–6, **170–7**,
        245 n.8.4
O'Kelly, Michael 247 n.10.5
Oldenburg, Claes 97
Olson, Charles 194
Olympia typewriter 60, 119, 191,
        193
Omega Point. *See* de Chardin, Pierre
        Teilhard
Oppenheimer, J. Robert 200
Orpheus 172, 186
Osteen, Mark viii–ix, xiv, 33, 41–2,
        66, 119, 127, 197
Oswald, Lee Harvey 42–4, 46,
        48–50, 54–7
Otto, Rudolf 230
Ovid 39, 41–2, 51, 239 nn.3.5, 3.7

Pafko, Andy 59
Page, Anthony 223
Parent, Bob 115
Parker, Bonnie 149
Parker, Charlie 114–15, 242 n.6.2
Parnell, Charles Stewart 46
Pasiphaë 51
Penelope 192
Perdix (Talos) 51–2
Perkins, Anthony 153
Perón, Juan 13
Persephone 69
Perry, R. Michael 208
Petit, Philippe 243 n.7.6
Pickerell, Jim 95
Pinch, Trevor 244 n.8.2
Plato 24, 205

Poe, Edgar Allan 63
Pollock, Jackson 93
Porphyry 196–7
Poseidon 51
postmodernism 5, 11–12, 21–2, 39,
        117, 229, 240 n.5.1
Pound, Ezra 181
Powers, Francis Gary 54
Privett, Josh 238 n.3.1, 246 n.10.1
projection 14, 19, 24–5, 38, 42, 73,
        108, 118, 124, 143, 146, 149,
        155, 158, 195, 202, 212, 222,
        239 n.3.3. *See also* screens
Proust, Marcel 38, 108, 117, 212
Pynchon, Thomas 230, 238 n.3.1,
        244 n.7.9
Pythagoras 196–7, 213

Rapaport, Brooke Kamin 99
Raspe, Jan-Carl 243 n.7.4
Red Army Faction (RAF) 141–3,
        145–6, 149, 156, 243
        nn.7.3–4, 243–4 n.7.8
Remnick, David 61, 239 n.3.2, 247
        n.10.3
Rey, Rebecca 241 n.6.1
Richter, Gerhard 141–6, 149–51,
        156–7, 162, 243 nn.7.3, 7.5
    Confrontation I 162
    Dead 141
    Funeral 143–4, 156–7
    October 18, 1977 141–3, 151,
        156–7, 243 nn.7.3, 7.5
Rilke, Rainer Maria 194
Ringgold, Faith 241 n.5.4
Riquelme, John Paul 45
Rivers, Larry 171–2
Rock of Cashel (Ireland) 233–4, 236
Rodia, Sabato (Simon) 65–6, 77,
        97–8, 240 n.4.4
Roehl, Emily 243 n.7.5
The Rolling Stones 90
Rosen, Seymour 98
Roth, Sanford 66
Rothstein, Mervyn 130–1, 136
Rove, Karl 237 n.1.4
Rubin, Louis 45
Ruby, Jack 54

Russell, John   245 n.8.6

Saint, Eva Marie   186
Saint Augustine   193–4, 206
Saint Francis   175–7
Saint Ignatius of Loyola   65,
    155, 176
Saint Serapion   172–5, 182
Saint Stephen   46
Sartre, Jean-Paul   181
Satanta   194
Schaub, Thomas Hill   240 n.5.1
Schleyer, Hanns-Martin   243 n.7.4
Schneck, Peter   247 n.10.7
Schneemann, Carolee   119
Schrödinger, Erwin   125
Schuster, Marc   238 n.2.2
Schweighauser, Philipp   247 n.10.7
screens   19, 24–6, 34, 38, 78, 108,
    143, 146, 151–2, 155, 157,
    159, 163, 195–6, 223. See
    also projection
Seinfeld, Jerry   233
self-reflexivity. See metafiction;
    metatheater
September 11th Attacks (9/11)   88,
    145–8, 156, 195, 243
    nn.7.5–6
Shakespeare, William   2, 19, 39, 63,
    237 n.1.1, 238 n.1.6
"Shot Heard 'Round
    the World"   59, 62, 82, 240
    n.4.1
solipsism   112, 130–3, 158, 223–4,
    230
Sontag, Susan   238 n.2.5
States, Bert O.   133, 242 n.6.7
Stephens, Cynthia   246 n.9.6
Sterne, Laurence   5
Stevenson, Juliet   221
Stewart, Jack   241 n.5.6
Stewart, Susan   70
Stonehenge (England)   226–7
Storr, Robert   143, 145–6
sublimation   73, 165, 175
Sunderland, Tracy   128–9, 132
Suskind, Ron   237 n.1.4
Swedberg, Richard   244 n.8.2

Taupin, Bernie   182
Telemachus   71, 192
Tempest, Kate   191–2, 195, 212,
    216–17
theaters
    Apple Tree Theatre (Chicago)   128
    Boise Contemporary Theater
        (Boise)   128–9, 132
    Royal Court Theatre (London)   223
    Steppenwolf Theatre (Chicago)   128
Thích Quảng Đức   195
Thomson, Bobby   12, 59–61, 70, 74,
    77, 240 n.4.1
Thoor Ballylee (Ireland)   234
Tillich, Paul   194
Timon of Phlius   205
triangulation   14, 165–6, 171, 173,
    177, 179–80, 187, 212–13
Trotsky, Leon   48, 194
Trump, Donald J.   14
Tyson, Neil deGrasse   226, 247 n.10.4

Ulay (Uwe Laysiepen)   121–3, 242 n.6.4
Ullmann, Liv   25, 28, 37
United Graffiti Artists   96
United Nations Educational, Scientific
    and Cultural Organization
    (UNESCO)   73, 240 n.4.5
universities
    Cornell University (Ithaca)   244
        n.8.2, 245–6 n.8.8
    Harvard University
        (Cambridge)   170
    New York University (New York)
        180
    University of Michigan
        (Ann Arbor)   170
    Xavier University (Cincinnati)
        xiv–xv, 233, 235
Ungaretti, Giuseppe   133–4

Valentino, Russell Scott   238 n.3.1
Velázquez, Diego   63
Vietnam War   13, 15, 93, 141, 195
Virgil   82, 134, 247 n.10.3
Virgin Mary   46
vom Lehn, Dirk   144
von Goethe, Johann Wolfgang   63

Vonnegut, Kurt   126, 202
von Sydow, Max   168

Wachowski, Lana and Lilly   218
Wallon, Henri   23
Ward, Kiron   xiv
Warhol, Andy   182
War on Terror   13
Watts Towers (Los Angeles)   65–6, 77,
        97–9, 240 n.4.4
Welles, Orson   63
    Citizen Kane   63
Whistler, James Abbott McNeill
        106–8, 110–11
    *Arrangement in Grey and Black
        No. 1* (*Whistler's Mother*)
        106–8, 110–11
Whitelaw, Billie   223

Wilde, Oscar   172
Wilder, Billy   183
    Seven-Year Itch   183
Wilson, Laurie   87, 89, 103
Winchester, Jeremy   129, 132
Wittgenstein, Ludwig   15, 168–70,
        187, 244 n.8.2, 246 n.8.8
Woolf, Virginia   99, 103
Wordsworth, William   172
World War II   170

Yeats, William Butler   73, 181, 193,
        234

Žižek, Slavoj   26
Zubeck, Jacqueline   xiv, 237 n.1.3,
        242 n.7.2
Zwingli, Ulrich   194